AF754032

The Endogenous Formation of Economic Coalitions

THE FONDAZIONE ENI ENRICO MATTEI (FEEM) SERIES ON ECONOMICS AND THE ENVIRONMENT

Series Editor: Carlo Carraro, *University of Venice, Venice and Research Director, Fondazione Eni Enrico Mattei (FEEM), Milan, Italy*

Editorial Board

Kenneth J. Arrow, *Department of Economics, Stanford University, Stanford, California, USA*

William J. Baumol, *CV Starr center for Applied Economics, New York University, New York City, USA*

Partha Dasgupta, *Cambridge University, Cambridge, UK*

Karl-Göran Mäler, *The Beijer International Institute of Ecological Economics, The Royal Swedish Academy of Sciences, Stockholm, Sweden*

Ignazio Musu, *University of Venice, Venice, Italy*

Henry Tulkens, *Center for Operations Research and Econometrics (CORE), Université Catholique de Louvain, Louvain-la-Neuve, Belgium*

The Fondazione Eni Enrico Mattei (FEEM) was established in 1989 as a non-profit, non-partisan research institution. It carries out high-profile research in the fields of economic development, energy and the environment, thanks to an international network of researchers who contribute to disseminate knowledge through seminars, congresses and publications. The main objective of the Fondazione is to foster interactions among academic, industrial and public policy spheres in an effort to find solutions to environmental problems. Over the years it has thus become a major European institution for research on sustainable development and the privileged interlocutor of a number of leading national and international policy institutions.

The Fondazione Eni Enrico Mattei (FEEM) Series on Economics and the Environment publishes leading-edge research findings providing an authoritative and up-to-date source of information in all aspects of sustainable development. FEEM research outputs are the results of a sound and acknowledged cooperation between its internal staff and a worldwide network of outstanding researchers and practitioners. A Scientific Advisory Board of distinguished academics ensures the quality of the publications.

This series serves as an outlet for the main results of FEEM's research programmes in the areas of economics, energy and the environment.

The Endogenous Formation of Economic Coalitions

Edited by

Carlo Carraro

Professor of Econometrics and Environmental Economics, University of Venice, Italy, Research Director, Fondazione Eni Enrico Mattei (FEEM), Milan, Italy and Associate Fellow, Centre for European Policy Studies (CEPS), Brussels, Belgium

THE FONDAZIONE ENI ENRICO MATTEI (FEEM) SERIES ON ECONOMICS AND THE ENVIRONMENT

Edward Elgar

Cheltenham, UK • Northampton, MA, USA

© Fondazione Eni Enrico Mattei 2003

All rights reserved. No part of this publication may be reproduced, stored in a retrieval system or transmitted in any form or by any means, electronic, mechanical or photocopying, recording, or otherwise without the prior permission of the publisher.

Published by
Edward Elgar Publishing Limited
Glensanda House
Montpellier Parade
Cheltenham
Glos GL50 1UA
UK

Edward Elgar Publishing, Inc.
136 West Street
Suite 202
Northampton
Massachusetts 01060
USA

A catalogue record for this book
is available from the British Library

Library of Congress Cataloguing in Publication Data

The endogenous formation of economic coalitions / edited by Carlo Carraro.
p. cm. – (The Fondazione Eni Enrico Mattei (FEEM) series on economics and the environment)
Includes index.
1. Cooperation. 2. Trade blocs. 3. Coalition (Social sciences) 4. Commerce. I. Carraro, Carlo. II. Series

HD2961.E63 2003
330′.01′5193–dc21 2003044897

ISBN 1 84376 265 X

Printed and bound in Great Britain by MPG Books Ltd, Bodmin, Cornwall

Contents

Figures

Tables

Contributors

Myrna Wooders
University of Warwick, Economic Department, England

Francis Bloch
GREQAM – Université de la Méditerranée, France

Licun Xue
University of Aarhus, Department of Economics, Denmark

Sang-Seung Yi
Seoul National University, School of Economics, Korea

Michael Finus
University of Hagen, Institute of Economic Theory, Germany

Marco Mariotti
University of Exeter, Department of Economics, England

Carlo Carraro
University of Venice, Fondazione Eni Enrico Mattei, Italy

Carmen Marchiori
Fondazione Eni Enrico Mattei, Italy

Alexander Kovalenkov
University of North Carolina, Department of Economics, USA

Bianca Rundshagen
University of Hagen, Institute of Economic Theory, Germany

Acknowledgements

The Editor of this book is grateful to the authors of the six chapters for their patience and motivation in writing excellent and clear overviews of a recent, important, economic and game-theoretic literature. He is also grateful to all those who have cooperated in the development of new ideas in the field of coalition formation, especially to Domenico Siniscalco with whom several papers have been written and who helped in promoting research and disseminating knowledge in this field. In this respect, the logistic and financial support of the Fondazione Eni E. Mattei (FEEM) must be acknowledged. In the last ten years, most of the new results on the endogenous formation of economic coalitions have been developed either within the research activities of FEEM or within those of the Coalition Theory Network, promoted and coordinated by FEEM in cooperation with CORE (Louvain), GREQAM (Marseille) and CODE (Barcelona). Finally, the Editor is grateful to Monica Eberle, Carmen Marchiori and Marni Wood for their valuable help and assistance.

Introduction

Carlo Carraro

The formation of coalitions is a widespread phenomenon in old and contemporary economies. A coalition emerges when a group of citizens form a club, when firms set up a cartel, when countries agree on free trade. A firm can be seen as a coalition, the outcome of international negotiations on environmental matters or on other economic issues are coalitions (for example, a monetary union is a coalition), a family can also be classed as a coalition. Research joint ventures and federal states are also coalitions. Relevant economic coalitions are numerous and cover the most important aspects of economic life.

Economists and game-theorists have been working on coalition theory for many years. Most recently, their main goal was not to understand how a group of economic agents share the benefit of forming a coalition (as in Nash's seminal work and subsequently in Rubinstein's important characterization). On the contrary, the main goal was to understand whether economic agents have an incentive to form a coalition, that is, whether they actually decide to form a coalition. Therefore, the issue is not whether the coalition is profitable and how this profit can be shared among coalition members, but whether the coalition is stable or self-enforcing, that is, which economic agents join the coalition and why.[1] Most importantly, the reformulation of the problem of coalition formation in non-cooperative terms can handle the issue of competition between coalitions which in traditional cooperative theory was largely ignored (see the introduction to Kovalenkov and Wooders in this volume).

The non-cooperative approach to coalition formation can be loosely described as follows (see the chapters by Bloch and Yi in this book for a detailed presentation). The decision of whether or not to join the coalition is a 'meta-decision' that precedes the cooperative strategy characterising the behaviour of coalition members once the coalition is formed. This meta-decision is taken non-cooperatively. Thus, the outcome of the meta-game in which agents decide whether or not to join a coalition – and which coalition – is identified via a non-cooperative equilibrium concept. In addition, the partition function approach (surveyed by Yi in this volume) can be applied and interactions between coalitions are taken into account. The main objective of this book is to provide an overview of these recent advances in the non-cooperative game-theoretic approach to coalition formation.

In recent years, there have indeed been several attempts to provide a comprehensive theory of coalition formation using a non-cooperative approach. Many equilibrium concepts have been proposed and their implications on the coalition structure have been derived. The emergence of coalition structures with multiple coalitions has been stressed /highlighted. The size of these coalitions and their sensitivity to changes in the economic environment have been analysed. Applications of these new theories to industrial organizations (extending traditional cartel theory and RJVs theory), environmental economics (mainly focusing on international environmental treaties), trade theory (free trade areas, custom unions), public finance (public and club good provisions) and so on have been proposed.

This book is the first attempt to provide an overview of the main theoretical results and of their applications. Chapters 2–6 survey the different approaches to endogenous (that is, non-cooperative) coalition formation, discuss and compare the diversity of equilibrium concepts, and analyse the main features of the emerging coalition structures. Each chapter discusses different applications of the theory proposed and how these applications improve our understanding of relevant economic problems.

Most applications discussed in this book deal with global and local public goods and with club goods. The focus on public and club goods is related to the well-known difficulty of achieving efficient outcomes in the presence of free-riding incentives. The chapters of this book address this difficulty by using the non-cooperative approach to coalition formation – where a coalition can be seen as a group of agents who cooperate to provide a club or public good – and show that in general cooperation emerges at the equilibrium as a result of independent and voluntary decisions taken by each agent.

Before presenting the non-cooperative approach to coalition formation and its applications, this book highlights some important advances achieved by using the cooperative approach to coalition formation. Therefore, the first chapter of this book, written by Alexander Kovalenkov and Myrna Holtz Wooders, is a bridge between the cooperative and non-cooperative approach. Its starting point is the relationship between the core and competitive economies, two concepts apparently antithetic. The authors note that in the analysis of models of private goods exchange economies, price-taking competitive equilibrium outcomes and cooperative outcomes – particularly the core – have played a central role. However, in cases like network economies, clubs, coalition production, matching models, and local public goods, the analogue of price-taking equilibrium is not clear. Moreover, price-taking equilibrium depends on the details of the economic model. This and the close relationship between the core and price-taking equilibrium in a variety of contexts and their equivalence in large economies, motivates the study of the core as an analogue of the competitive equilibrium, especially in the context of games with many players. The concept of the core encounters difficulty, however, because apart from idealised situations it may well be empty. This has given rise to a literature demonstrating that cooperative games with many players have nonempty approximate cores and the approximation can become very close as the games become large. Moreover, there are outcomes in approximate cores that treat most or all similar players nearly identically, a property of price-taking equilibrium outcomes.

The chapter by Kovalenkov and Wooders explores all the aforementioned outcomes and results and also provides interesting examples and applications. In particular, Kovalenkov and Wooders treat games with side payments and present some recent results for this specific case. Their analysis can be used, for example, to deal with economies with local public goods – public goods subject to exclusion and congestion. Their results can also be applied to the case of multijurisdictional economies, where it is natural to allow an individual to belong to several jurisdictions and where jurisdictions may overlap. For example, an individual could be a member of a marriage, an employee of a University, a citizen of a country and a member of a large international environmental organization. Through application of their results, Kovalenkov and Wooders demonstrate that, when individuals belong to multiple clubs and when small groups are effective, then large club economies have nonempty approximate cores.

As said, the theoretical framework adopted by Kovalenkov and Wooders is still a cooperative one. Therefore, the main problem with Kovalenkov and Wooders' framework is that it allows the payoffs to a coalition to be affected by the actions of the coalition, but the choices of a coalition are assumed to have no effect on the payoffs of the complementary coalitions. Suppose, for example, coalitions form to produce pure public goods so that the goods produced by one coalition can be consumed by the entire player set. Each coalition is then affected by the actions chosen by members of the complementary coalitions. This situation cannot be dealt with using Kovalenkov and Wooders' results. Therefore, the cooperative game framework is most applicable to situations where what a coalition can achieve is independent of the actions of the complementary coalitions.

Extensions of the theory of coalition formation to situations in which the opportunities available to a group of players depend on the activities of the non-members of the group have been recently proposed in several papers (see, for example, Ray and Vohra, 1997, 1999; Yi, 1997; Bloch,

1996). The remaining chapters of this book present the main results achieved within the non-cooperative approach to coalition formation.

Chapter 2, Non-cooperative models of coalition formation in games with spillovers by Francis Bloch, is a comprehensive survey of the non-cooperative approach to coalition formation. In the first part of his survey, Bloch analyses in particular the role of spillovers between coalitions and the different representations of games with externalities. He emphasizes the limits of the classical cooperative approach based on the characteristic function and shows how various partition function games can be derived. As said, this approach has the advantage of capturing the possibility of *externalities across coalitions*, because it allows the change in the coalition structure to affect the values of *all* coalitions, whereas the characteristic function approach cannot incorporate such externalities across coalitions.

Bloch then discusses a first class of non-cooperative games where all agents simultaneously announce their decision to cooperate. The various outcome rules for the simultaneous announcement game, and the related different solution concepts, are analysed and discussed. In the second part of his chapter, Bloch analyses a second class of games where agents announce sequentially their decision to participate in the coalition. He compares different specifications of the extensive form games reflect differences in the procedures of coalition formation.

Bloch also studies some cooperative solution concepts that were proposed to analyse the stability of coalition structures in games with spillovers. While those stability concepts are not based on non-cooperative processes, they provide interesting benchmarks and give new insights to the study of coalition formation with spillovers.

The third part of the survey is devoted to economic applications. Bloch distinguishes between games with positive and negative spillovers. Games with positive spillovers are games where the formation of a coalition increases the payoff of external members. The formation or cartels and the provision of public goods are examples of games with positive spillovers. Games with negative spillovers are games where the formation of a coalition is harmful to external members. For example, the formation of trade unions or associations of firms are games with negative spillovers. The final part of the survey discusses the most recent contributions to the study of coalition formation with spillovers, and outlines some open questions to be addressed in future research.

Chapter 3, Endogenous formation of economic coalitions: a survey of the partition function approach by Sang-Seung Yi, also emphasizes how coalition formation among autonomous agents is an integral part of economic activity. Examples are taken from industrial organization, international trade and environmental economics. In industrial organizations,

Japanese firms have established R&D alliances such as the Very Large Scale Integration (VLSI) consortium and the Fifth Generation Computer Project with the purpose of gaining an edge on international competition. In international trade, there has been a resurgence of regionalism. Casual observation suggests that the world is moving towards the formation of three major trading blocs consisting of the European Union (EU), the North American Free Trade Agreements (NAFTA) zone, and a potential Asian bloc. In environmental economics, policy coordination on greenhouse gas emissions through the 1995 Rio Convention and the 1997 Kyoto Protocol has heightened both economists' and policy makers' interest in the stability of global environmental agreements. Economic coalitions such as research joint ventures and free-trade areas have two distinguishing characteristics. First, several coalitions coexist and compete with each other. Second, the formation, expansion and merger of economic coalitions typically create *externalities* on non-members.

Yi surveys recent developments in the non-cooperative theory of coalition formation that emphasize these two characteristics of economic alliances: the formation of *multiple, competing* coalitions that create *externalities* on nonmembers. His work is also based on the partition function approach to coalition formation. This approach is presented at the beginning of his survey. Yi then reviews several rules of coalition formation that have been proposed in the literature and discusses the equilibrium outcomes of specific coalition games.

In the fourth chapter, Farsightedness in coalition formation by Marco Mariotti and Licun Xue, an extension of the partition function approach is proposed. In particular, new equilibrium concepts, based on the assumed enhanced farsightedness of coalition members, are discussed. Loosely speaking, a coalition is farsighted when it looks ahead at the ultimate consequences of its actions. For example, if a sub-coalition breaks up from a larger coalition, will this cause further break-ups? And how will the members who are excluded from the deviating coalition react? To deal with these questions, Mariotti and Xue start from von Neumann and Morgenstern's stable set for cooperative games and from Greenberg's (1990) generalization of this stability notion.[2] One of the situations studied by Greenberg is the 'coalitional contingent threat situation' associated with a strategic game, a negotiation process in which coalitions make open threats contingent on the strategy profile under consideration. This situation is subsequently studied in Chwe (1994) and others (for example, Mariotti, 1997; Xue, 1998, 2000). The results obtained by these authors are surveyed in this chapter. In addition, this chapter analyses several applications of the above literature, including bargaining theory, repeated games, theory of unemployment and environmental negotiations.

Chapter 5 focuses on the stability of coalitions that have already formed. This chapter, entitled Stable coalitions and written by Carlo Carraro and Carmen Marchiori, examines recent theoretical developments of the theory of coalition stability. It focuses on the relationship between the incentives to defect from a coalition, the size of the resulting equilibrium coalition structure, and the different assumptions on membership rules, coalition behaviour, players' conjectures and so on. The paper considers several cases: simultaneous vs. sequential moves, linear vs. circular order of moves, Nash vs. rational conjectures, open vs. exclusive membership, monotonic vs. non monotonic payoff functions, and orthogonal vs. non-orthogonal reaction functions. The profitable and stable coalitions are derived for each possible configuration of the rules of the game, the payoff functions and the membership rules. The results show that the size of the profitable and stable coalition highly depends on the chosen configuration and that the equilibrium outcome ranges from a small coalition with a few signatories to full cooperation. This chapter explores under which conditions a large stable coalition is likely to emerge, and identifies the institutional setting that favours the emergence of such coalition.

The final chapter, Endogenous coalition formation in global pollution control: a partition function approach by Michael Finus and Bianca Rundshagen, expands on the work by Carraro and Marchiori by allowing for multiple coalitions. Again equilibrium coalitions are derived under different 'rules of the game' and compared with each other. Finus and Rundshagen consider internal and external stability and equilibrium binding agreements in the cartel formation game, coalition-proof and strong Nash equilibria in the open-membership game and in the exclusive membership α- and γ-games, subgame-perfect equilibria in the sequential move unanimity game and in the equilibrium binding agreement game. They show that farsightedness and exclusive membership leads to a more concentrated coalition structure, implying lower global emissions and higher global welfare. Moreover, they evaluate the different coalition formation games with respect to their ability to explain existing international environmental agreements and with respect to their theoretical consistency.

The six chapters of this book provide a substantial overview of recent advances in coalition theory. They are written by some of the most important authors in the field and enable the reader to compare different approaches and results. In addition, they show the many applications of coalition theory and its ability to address difficult economic problems (for example, the provision of global public goods). Therefore, this book provides a new set of tools that can be applied to several economic issues (a phenomenon which is already taking place and which confirms the timing of this book).

NOTES

1. Of course, the study of this latter issue also depends on the way in which the coalition benefit is shared among coalition members, but the two are different and are analysed with different economic tools.
2. Greenberg's contribution spawned literature which aimed to extend, modify and apply the original theory. For example, Chwe (1994) considers a social environment which, although less general than a situation, is sufficiently flexible to integrate the presentation of some negotiation processes associated with cooperative, strategic and extensive games. Chwe's main objective is to offer a notion that captures foresight and is likely to be non-empty. Xue (1998) shows that Chwe's notion captures only partial foresight and offers a solution concept that captures perfect foresight using Greenberg's framework.

REFERENCES

Bloch, F. (1996), 'Sequential formation of coalition in games with externalities and fixed payoff division', *Games and Economic Behaviour*, **14**, 90–123.

Chwe, M.S.Y. (1994), 'Farsighted coalition stability', *Journal of Economic Theory*, **54**, 299–325.

Greenberg, J. (1990), *The Theory of Social Situations*, Cambridge: Cambridge University Press.

Mariotti, M. (1997), 'A model of agreements in strategic form games', *Journal of Economic Theory*, **73**, 196–217.

Ray, D. and R. Vohra (1997), 'Equilibrium binding agreements', *Journal of Economic Theory*, **73**, 30–78.

Ray, D. and R. Vohra (1999), 'A theory of endogenous coalition structure', *Games and Economic Behaviour*, **26**, 286–336.

Xue, L. (1998), 'Coalitional stability under perfect foresight', *Economic Theory*, **1**, 603–27.

Xue, L. (2000), 'Negotiation proof nash equilibrium', *International Journal of Game Theory*, **29**, 339–57.

Yi, S. (1997), 'Stable coalition structures with externalities', *Games and Economic Behaviour*, **20**, 201–23.

1. Advances in the theory of large cooperative games and applications to club theory; the side payments case

Alexander Kovalenkov and Myrna Wooders

1. INTRODUCTION

While the notion that individuals will act in their own self interests is fundamental to game theory and also to economics, the notion that if there are potential gains to be realized from cooperation then individuals will attempt to capture these gains is also fundamental. Indeed, the economic notion of the *contract curve* – the set of outcomes of trade for a two-person, two-commodity private goods exchange economy with the properties that each person's trade is individually rational and the outcome cannot be improved upon by both traders acting together – already appears in Edgeworth (1881). In his seminal work, Edgeworth showed that the contract curve converges to the set of allocations arising from price-taking economic equilibrium.

The game-theoretic notion of the *core* as the set of payoffs of a game that cannot be improved upon by any coalition, as a solution concept for cooperative games, was developed by Shapley (1952) and Gillies (1953). Since Shubik's (1959) seminal paper highlighting the relationship between the core and the contract curve, the study of the core has generated numerous papers in both economics and in game theory. The most celebrated of these works are Debreu and Scarf (1963), showing that the core of an exchange economy, represented by allocations of commodities to individual traders, converges to the set of outcomes of price-taking economic equilibrium, a formalization and extension of Edgeworth's result, and Aumann (1964), further extending Edgeworth's insight in the context of a game with a continuum of players. Numerous subsequent papers further investigated the issue of convergence of the core of an economy with private goods to the set of price-taking equilibrium outcomes; an entire chapter of the *Handbook of Game Theory*, Volume 1 (Anderson, 1992) is devoted to a survey of these papers.

The idea of convergence of cores to equilibrium outcomes is intriguing. The competitive equilibrium requires that individuals take prices as given (by some unknown source) and individually optimize, while the core is based on the idea that if a group of individuals could be better off by forming a coalition and reallocating resources and activities within that coalition, then the group will do so. While the notions themselves of core and of competitive equilibrium are appealing, they are totally different in spirit, in fact, almost opposing. One notion is based on self-interested individualistic behaviour, while the other notion takes as given that individuals will cooperate to achieve the benefits of cooperation whenever such a possibility exists. The convergence of outcomes based on these two quite dissimilar notions is truly remarkable.

Outside of the highly stylized framework of an exchange economy with infinitely divisible commodities and with quasi-concave preferences, both the notions of the core and of competitive equilibrium are problematic. The core may be empty and competitive equilibrium may not exist. A condition for nonemptiness of cores was demonstrated in Bondareva (1962) and Shapley (1967). Intuitively, the condition, called *balancedness*, dictates that if coalitions were able to operate part-time, total feasible payoff could not be improved.[1] The balancedness condition was extended to games without side payments (*NTU games*), and nonemptiness of cores of balanced NTU games was demonstrated by Scarf (1967). Balancedness, however, rules out many interesting classes of cooperative games, including games derived from economies with indivisible commodities, with nonmonotonicities, with coalition production and economies with other deviations from classic models of exchange economies.

Except for special classes of situations, balancedness assumptions rule out economies where participants are required to arrange themselves into groups for the attainment of benefits of cooperation within groups.[2] This is problematic since, as is being increasingly recognized in economic research and indeed, as recognized in this volume, our social and economic life is carried out within groups – firms, families, nations, market places and political jurisdictions, for example, in addition to social and professional networks. In such situations, individuals may cooperate within groups to benefit from increasing returns to group size and coordination of activities. Individuals may compete within groups for shares of the surplus generated by the activities of the group. There may be competition between groups for scarce resources and for group members. In these sorts of situations, the core may well be empty.

To treat the problem of the emptiness of the core of a large game, a continuing line of research has investigated conditions for nonemptiness of approximate cores of large games and economies. Shapley and Shubik (1966) showed that large replica exchange economies – exchange economies with a fixed distribution of a finite number of types of players – with quasi-linear preferences have nonempty approximate cores. Under the assumptions of *superadditivity* and *per capita boundedness* Wooders (1980, 1983) demonstrated nonemptiness of approximate cores of large replica games with and without side payments.[3] *Superadditivity* dictates that a coalition is at least as profitable as any partition of the coalition into smaller coalitions – there are no diseconomies of scale. *Per capita boundedness* is simply the condition that the supremum of average payoff over all games in the collection is finite. Since these early results, there have been a number of further contributions to this literature, including Shubik and Wooders (1983), Kaneko and Wooders (1982, 1986, 1996) and Wooders and Zame (1984).[4]

More recent literature demonstrating that large games/economies with small effective groups are like competitive exchange economies has relied on the condition of *small group effectiveness* (SGE), dictating that all or *almost all* gains to collective activities can be realized by cooperation only within relatively small groups of participants (Wooders, 1992,1994a,b). This condition is less restrictive than it may seem since, when there are many players of each type that appears in the games, small group effectiveness is equivalent to the condition of per capita boundedness (Wooders, 1994a, Theorem 4).

The literature noted above on approximate cores of large games uses the framework of a *pregame*. A pregame consists of a compact metric space of player types, possibly finite, and a worth function ascribing a payoff possibilities set to each conceivable group of players. The worth function depends continuously on the types of players in a coalition. Note that the pregame framework treats collections of games that can all be described by a *single* worth function. This has hidden consequences; for example, as we will illustrate, the equivalence between small group effectiveness and per capita boundedness demonstrated in Wooders (1994a) is not necessarily true outside the pregame context.

We note here two particular further results for games derived from pregames that provide further motivation for the study of large games. The first is that large games with side payments are equivalent to market games, games generated by economies with side payments or, in standard terminology from economics, quasi-linear utilities (Wooders 1994a, b).[5] This means that for *any* economy with quasi-linear utilities, whether one with local public goods, clubs, indivisible commodities and so on, there is a set of commodities (which may be the types of players) so that, relative to that set of commodities, in an approximate sense the economy has a competitive equilibrium and the competitive outcomes are equivalent to the core. Another important result is that approximate cores converge to outcomes with the *equal treatment property*, that is, similar individuals are assigned similar payoffs (Wooders 1979, 1980, 1994b).[6] Since competitive payoffs have the equal-treatment property, this result indicates another way in which economies with small effective groups resemble markets.[7]

The pregame framework is especially useful for examining limiting properties of large games, as demonstrated by research on equivalence of large games and markets for example. Relative to a specific game with a finite number of players, a pregame requires substantial information and does not lead to statements about individual games, separate from the pregame structure.[8] In examining any particular game derived from a pregame, however, only a small part of the pregame structure is relevant. Moreover, results concerning one pregame do not provide information about 'similar' pregames or, in fact, about how one might even describe pregames or games as 'similar'.

To study properties of individual games, Kovalenkov and Wooders, in a series of papers (*Games and Economic Behavior*, 2001a; *Mathematics of Operations Research*, 2001b; and *Journal of Economic Theory*, 2003, to appear), introduced the framework of the parameterized collections of games. This framework describes collections of games in terms of a set of parameters. The parameters bound (a) the number of approximate types of players and the size of the approximation and (b) the size of nearly effective groups of players and their distance from exact effectiveness. For some results, including those of this chapter, an additional parameter is required on per capita payoffs. In this chapter, we treat games with side payments and present versions of some of our recent results for this special case. A game with side payments summarizes the worth of a coalition by one real number, the total 'payoff' achievable by the coalition. In contrast, a game without side payments describes the possibilities open to a coalition by a set of outcomes, where each outcome states a payoff for each player in the coalition. The concepts of games with and without side payments are not disjoint; a game with side payments can be described as a game without side payments. Because of the simplicity of a game with side payments, cooperative game theory has been more extensively developed for games with side payments than for games without side payments. The results to be presented in this paper are in the literature for games without side payments.[9] Our presentation here makes these results more accessible for the case of games with side payments.

Turning to the motivation for our research on economies with clubs and local public goods, one of the many interesting economic situations for which small group effectiveness may hold is that of an economy with local public goods – public goods subject to exclusion and congestion. Inspired by the insightful Tiebout Hypothesis (Tiebout, 1956) that large economies with local public goods are 'market-like', a number of papers have shown that in the context of economies where it is optimal or near-optimal to have many jurisdictions or clubs producing local public goods, approximate cores are nonempty and converge to price-taking equilibrium outcomes. Wooders (1999) provides a short, concise survey.

In the context of multijurisdictional economies, it is natural to allow an individual to belong to several jurisdictions and jurisdictions may overlap. For example, an individual could be a member of a marriage, an employee of a University, a citizen of a country and a member of a large, international environmental organization. Such a model was introduced in Shubik and Wooders (1982), where it is shown that with a fixed distribution of player types, under the apparently mild condition of boundedness of per capita payoffs and superadditivity, approximate cores are nonempty and treat most identical players similarly.[10] Through application of their game-theoretic results, Kovalenkov and Wooders (2003) demonstrated that when individuals may belong to multiple clubs and when small groups are effective, then large club economies have nonempty approximate cores. In this chapter we present a version of this result for economies with side payments.[11]

The pregame framework and the framework of parameterized collections of games both have application to situations with environmental externalities, where the payoff to a coalition depends on the actions of the complementary coalition. Concepts and ideas arising out of research on games derived from pregames have facilitated some studies of economic situations with widespread externalities. We have in mind research by Kaneko and Wooders (1986), Hammond, Kaneko and Wooders (1989), Kaneko and Wooders (1989) and Hammond (1999), studying economies where coalitions are constrained to be relatively small, due to coalition formation costs, for example, and where externalities are widespread. Since externalities are widespread, the activities of members of a coalition affect the payoffs of members of the complementary coalition. A question that immediately arises in this sort of situation is what a coalition assumes about the behaviour of the complementary coalition. In their papers treating situations with widespread externalities, Hammond, Kaneko and Wooders make a 'Nash' sort of assumption that a permissible coalition takes as given the actions of the complementary coalition. This assumption is most appropriate in economies with many participants and where the effect of any permissible coalition on aggregate outcomes is small. These papers demonstrate that when coalitions are constrained to be small relative to the total player set while externalities are widespread, so that they cannot be 'internalized' within coalitions, then the core is equivalent to the set of competitive equilibrium outcomes but the competitive equilibrium outcome is not optimal. These sorts of results could also be obtained using the framework of parameterized collections of games.

The framework of parameterized collections of games can also treat collections of games where the payoff to a group of players depends on the economy in which it is embedded. For example, in the classic paper by Shapley and Shubik (1969b) on cores of economies with externalities, the authors describe a situation of factories located around a lake. Each factory contributes to pollution of the lake and thus raises the costs of all factories around the lake. The payoff to every factory already established decreases with the entry of an additional factory. Such a collection of games, with varying numbers of factories (the players) can be accommodated within the framework of parameterized collections of games. Further examples of situations with widespread externalities are developed in the body of this chapter.[12]

While our framework of parameterized collections of games allows the payoffs to a coalition to be affected by the actions of all members of the coalition, the choice of activity of a coalition is assumed to have no effect on the payoffs of the complementary coalition. When coalitions are not constrained to be negligible or near negligible relative to the total player set and externalities are widespread, then the problem that the choice of actions of a coalition affects the payoffs to the members of the complementary set of players cannot be reasonably ignored. Suppose, for example, coalitions form to produce pure public goods so that the public good produced by one coalition can be consumed by the entire player set. The public good may be a radio programme, for example. Then each coalition is affected by the actions chosen by members of the complimentary coalition. Typically, it is assumed that the complementary coalition does its *worst*; for our example, this means that for any coalition S in defining the payoff possibilities for the members of S it would be assumed that members of the complementary set of players produce zero public goods. Indeed, the cooperative game framework may be most applicable to situations where what a coalition can achieve is independent of the actions of the complementary coalition. Thus, our game-theoretic results are most applicable to situations where the question of the appropriate definition of payoff sets of coalitions is not an issue. We note that an important line of research, which takes into account that the opportunities available to a group of players may depend on the activities of the non-members of the group (see, for example, Yi, 1997; Bloch, 1996; Ray and Vohra, 1999) and thus may be better suited to treat widespread externalities, is further discussed in other chapters in this volume.

This chapter is organized as follows. The next section introduces the basic definitions and states two results on the nonemptiness of approximate cores of large games, one using the framework of a pregame and the other using the framework of parameterized collections of games. Section 3 includes examples illustrating the advantages of the latter result. Section 4 presents an application to a very general model of economies with clubs. Section 5 concludes the body of the paper.

2. NONEMPTINESS OF ε-CORES OF LARGE GAMES: TWO FRAMEWORKS

A *game with side payments* is a pair (N, v) where $N=\{1, ..., n\}$ is a finite set and v is a function from the subsets of N to the nonnegative real numbers with the property that $v(\emptyset)=0$. A game (N, v) is *superadditive* if $v(S)\geq\Sigma_k v(S^k)$ for all groups $S\subset N$ and for all partitions $\{S^k\}$ of S. We will restrict our attention to superadditive games; this is appropriate whenever the union of coalitions can obtain at least as much total payoff as could be realized by the coalitions acting separately. Let $|S|$ denote the number of players in a group S.

Let (N, v) be a game with side payments and let $x\in \mathbb{R}^N$ be called a *payoff vector*. Given $\varepsilon\geq 0$, the payoff vector x is in the *ε-core* of the game if:

$$v(S)-\varepsilon|S|\leq x(S) \text{ for all groups } S\subset N \text{ and}$$
$$x(N)\leq v(N),$$

where $x(S):=\Sigma_{i\in S} x_i$. When $\varepsilon=0$, the 0-core is called simply the *core*.

Nonemptiness of ε-cores of large games is the first question to be addressed. Prior to the research of Kovalenkov and Wooders (2001a, b, 2003) this question, as well as the further questions on the properties of the ε-cores of large games, was addressed primarily within the framework of pregames.

2.1 Pregames

For simplicity, we treat here only pregames with a finite number of types of players. The more general setting of pregames with a compact metric space of player attributes and small group effectiveness, SGE, appears in Wooders (1992, 1994a, b, 2002).[13]

Let T be a positive integer, let $\mathbb{Z}^T_+$ denote the T-fold Cartesian product of the nonnegative integers and let Ψ be a function from $\mathbb{Z}^T_+$ to $\mathbb{R}_+$. Then the pair (N,Ψ) is a *pregame* (with T types of players).

Let (T,Ψ) be a pregame with T types and let $n=(n_1, ..., n_T)\in\mathbb{Z}^T_+$. Define

$N = \{(t,q): t = 1, \ldots, T$ and $q = 1, \ldots, n_t\}$ and, for each coalition $S \subset N$, define the vector *profile* $(S) \in Z_+^T$ by its components:

$$profile_t(S) = |\{(t, q) : q = 1, \ldots, n_t\} \cap S|,$$

$t = 1, \ldots, T$. Then *the game induced by* Ψ *and* n is denoted by (N, v), where v maps subsets of N into the nonnegative real numbers:

$$v(S) = \Psi\,(profile\,(S)),$$

for each nonempty subset S of N and:

$$v(\varnothing) = 0.$$

Given a profile f let us define $\|f\| = \Sigma_{t=1}^{T} f_t$. A *partition* of a profile f is a collection of profiles $\{f^k\}$ satisfying the property that $\Sigma_k f^k = f$. A pregame (T,Ψ) satisfies *superadditivity* if for every profile f and every partition $\{f^k\}$ of f it holds that $\Psi(f) - \Sigma_k \Psi(f^k) \geq 0$.[14] A pregame (T,Ψ) satisfies *small group effectiveness* (SGE) if, for each $\varepsilon > 0$, there is an integer $\eta_0(\varepsilon)$ such that for every profile f there is a partition $\{f^k\}$ of f satisfying:

$$\|f^k\| \leq \eta_0(\varepsilon) \text{ for each profile } f^k, \text{ and}$$
$$\Psi(f) - \Sigma_k \Psi(f^k) \leq \varepsilon\, \|f\|.$$

Informally, as stated in the Introduction, SGE dictates that all or almost all gains to collective activities are realizable by groups of players bounded in size.[15] For the following discussion, think of a profile as a description of a player set or simply as a player set. In the definition of SGE the parameter ε provides a measure of the distance, in per capita terms, between total payoff realizable by a total player set and payoff realizable by a partition of that set into smaller groups. Given $\varepsilon > 0$, there is a bound on group size, $\eta_0(\varepsilon)$, such that, no matter how large the total player set there is a partition of that player set into groups, all bounded in size by $\eta_0(\varepsilon)$, with the property that the total payoff achievable by cooperation only within these groups is within ε of the total payoff to the entire player set. Note that as $\| f \|$ becomes large, $(\eta_0(\varepsilon)/\| f \|)$ tends to zero – near-effective groups become negligible.

For completeness, we include the definition of per capita boundedness. A pregame (T,Ψ) satisfies *per capita boundedness* (PCB) if there is a constant C such that for every profile f it holds that:

$$\frac{\Psi(f)}{\|f\|} \leq C.$$

The next result summarizes nonemptiness of the ε-cores of large games derived from pregames satisfying SGE. Notice that this result holds also in the more general setting of pregames with a compact metric space of player attributes.[16]

Theorem 1: *Nonemptiness of the ε-cores of large games satisfying small group effectiveness* (Wooders 1992, 1994b). Let (T, Ψ) be a pregame satisfying small group effectiveness and let $\varepsilon > 0$ be given. Then there is an integer $\eta_1(\varepsilon)$ such that all games (N, v) induced by pregame with $|N| > \eta_1(\varepsilon)$ have nonempty ε-cores.

From Wooders (1994a, Theorem 4), it follows that if there are sufficiently many players of each type that appears in the games, then the above result continues to hold when SGE is replaced by PCB. The following result also appears as Corollary 3.2 in Wooders (1994b).

Theorem 1′: *Nonemptiness of the ε-cores of large games satisfying per capita boundedness* (Corollary to Wooders 1994a, Theorem 4). Let (T, Ψ) be a pregame satisfying per capita boundedness. Let ρ be a positive real number and let $\varepsilon > 0$ be given. Then there is an integer $\eta_2(\varepsilon,\rho)$ such that all games (N, v) induced by pregame and satisfying for every $t = 1, \ldots, T$ either $profile_t(N) = 0$ or $profile_t(N) > \rho|N|$ and $|N| > \eta_2(\varepsilon,\rho)$ have nonempty ε-cores.[17]

The pregame framework appears to be especially well suited to the study of limiting properties of large games. For example, in Wooders (1994a, b) it is shown that 'in the limit', the per capita payoff function to large games derived from a pregame is concave and can be interpreted as the utility function used in describing the canonical representation of a game as a market (see also Shapley and Shubik, 1969a).[18] From the viewpoint of the analysis of large finite games, a substantial drawback of the pregame framework is that it permits results only for a fixed pregame. Moreover, the bounds obtained, such as $\eta_1(\varepsilon)$ in the above result, depend on the entire pregame. The pregame approach does not permit *uniform* treatment of large games that are not necessarily derived from the *same pregame*. For example, marriage or matching games and games where any two players are effective both have two-person effective coalitions but they cannot be modelled in one pregame. The pregame framework cannot encompass even situations with small *externalities* (when the payoff to a coalition depends on the game where it is embodied). These considerations motivate the approach introduced in Kovalenkov and Wooders (2001a, b, 2003).

2.2. Parameterized collections of games

Recall that given a game (N, v), players i and j are *substitutes* if, for all coalitions S with $i, j \notin S$, it holds that $v(S \cup \{i\}) = v(S \cup \{j\})$. A fundamental property of games derived from pregames with a compact space of player types, and indeed of replicated player sets, is that in derived games with many players, most players have many close substitutes. There are counterexamples showing the necessity of this condition for the result that games with many players have nonempty approximate cores. Our notion of parameterized collections of games does not require any topological structure on the space of player types, but does rely on the notion of approximate substitutes.

Let (N, v) be a game and let δ be a non-negative real number. A δ-*substitute partition* of N is a partition $\{N[t]: t = 1, \ldots, T\}$ of N with the property that, for any type-consistent permutation τ and any coalition S,

$$|v(S) - v(\tau(S))| \leq \delta |S|.$$

Note that when $\delta = 0$, two players who are 0-substitutes are substitutes in the usual sense of the term. The notion of δ-substitutes extends the notion of a compact metric space of player types. Note that given any game (N, v) and any $\delta \geq 0$ it is possible to determine the minimum number T so that the player set can be partitioned into a T-member δ-substitute partition.

Let β be a given non-negative real number, and let B be a given integer. A game (N, v) has β-*effective B-bounded groups* if for every group $S \subset N$ there is a partition $\{S^k\}$ of S into subgroups with $|S^k| \leq B$ for each k and:

$$v(S) - \Sigma_k v(S^k) \leq \beta |S|.$$

The notion of β-effective B-bounded groups extends the notion of small group effectiveness (SGE) from Wooders (1992, 1994a, b) and the earlier notion of strict SGE. The condition SGE, defined for pregames, dictates that all or almost all gains to collective activities can be realized by coalitions bounded in size or by relatively small coalitions, where the bound or the size of the required coalitions depends on the distance allowed from achievement of *all* gains to collective activities. The notion of β-effective B-bounded groups makes explicit how close coalitions bounded in size by B are to being able to realize all gains to collective activities for a given game. Then $\beta = 0$, 0-effective B-bounded groups are called *strictly effective B-bounded groups.*

Let C be a positive real number. A game (N, v) has a *per capita bound* of C if:

$$\frac{v(S)}{|S|} \leq C,$$

for all coalitions $S \subset N$. Within the pregame framework, small group effectiveness implies per capita boundedness and, if the numbers of players of each type (or approximate type) is sufficiently large, then per capita boundedness implies small group effectiveness (Wooders 1994a, Theorem 4). This is no longer true in the context of parameterized collections of games, as we will illustrate in the next section by examples.

Given nonnegative real numbers δ and β and positive integers T, C and B, a *parameterized collection of games with side payments*, denoted by $\Gamma((\delta, T), C, (\beta, B))$, is a collection of games with the properties that for each game (N, v) in the collection:

1. There is a δ-substitute partition of N into no more than T subsets $\{N[t] : t=1, ..., T', T' \leq T\}$.
2. The game has a *per capita bound* of C.
3. The game has β-effective B-bounded groups.

Note that given any game (N, v) it is possible to determine δ, T, β, B and C so that (N, v) belongs to the collection $\Gamma((\delta, T), C, (\beta, B))$. Given δ and β one can determine the minimum required values of T and B, although if δ and β are both 'small' and there are increasing returns to coalition size, it may be that $T = B = |N|$, the worst case.

Given non-negative real numbers δ and β and positive integers T, C and B, let $(N, v) \in \Gamma((\delta, T), C, (\beta, B))$, let $\{N[t]\}$ be a partition of N into δ-substitutes, and let x be a payoff vector for (N, v). We say that x is an *equal-treatment payoff vector* if, for each $N[t]$ and for all i and j in $N[t]$, it holds that $x_i = x_j$. Note that we could use a weaker definition of an equal treatment payoff; in particular, we could require, for example, only that similar players are treated similarly.

Theorem 2: *(Nonemptiness of the equal-treatment ε-core from Kovalenkov and Wooders, 2001b.)* Let $(N, v) \in \Gamma((\delta, T), C, (\beta, B))$ and let ε be a positive real number. If:

$$\varepsilon \geq \frac{TC(B-1)}{|N|} + \delta + \beta,$$

then the equal treatment ε-core of (N, v) is nonempty.[19]

The bound presented in the above theorem is the exact bound in some cases. First, it is interesting to observe that for inessential games, which always have nonempty cores, Theorem 2 gives a bound on ε of zero. Let

(N,v) be a game where all coalitions are inessential (that is, only singleton coalitions matter). Such a game has a nonempty core. Thus, the ε-core is nonempty for any $\varepsilon \geq 0$. To apply Theorem 2 notice that $(N,v) \in \Gamma((0,|N|), C, (0,1))$ for some per capita bound C. The lower bound given by the expression above, $(TC(B-1)/|N|)+\delta+\beta$ is zero since $\delta=0$, $\beta=0$ and $(B-1)=0$. Even in this extreme case, the bound works well.

Now let us consider games where, given some positive real number K, within each game: all players are identical, only two-player coalitions are effective, and any two-player coalition can earn a payoff of less than or equal to $2K$. Obviously all these games belong to the class $\Gamma((0, 1), K, (0, 2))$. In this case, $(TC(B-1)/|N|)+\delta+\beta=(K/|N|)$. The core is empty if the number of players is odd. Let $|N|=2m+1$ for some positive integer m. But we can easily determine the least lower bound on ε so that the ε-core is nonempty for any game (N,v) in the collection with $|N|=2m+1$. In particular, suppose we assign each of the first $2m$ players the payoff $K-\varepsilon$ and the remaining player the payoff $2m\varepsilon$. Suppose ε^* solves $K-\varepsilon^*=2m\varepsilon^*$. Then the ε-core is nonempty for any game in the collection for any $\varepsilon \geq \varepsilon^*$, but may be empty otherwise. (Take, for example, $K=1$ and $m=1$. Then $\varepsilon^*=1/3$ and the ε-core is empty for any $\varepsilon<1/3$). Solving for ε^*, we obtain:

$$\varepsilon^* = \frac{K}{(2m+1)} = \frac{K}{|N|}.$$

This bound coincides with the bound given by the Theorem. Thus the bound given in the Theorem is the best possible bound for this collection.

In the following section we present further examples illustrating the theorem.

3. EXAMPLES AND COMPARISONS

We begin with a very simple and straightforward example of matching models.

Example 1: *Exact types and strictly effective small groups.*
Let us consider a game (N,v) with two types of players. Assume that any player alone can get only 0 units or less, that is $v(\{i\})=0$ for all $i \in N$. Suppose that any coalition of the two players of types i and j can get up to γ_{ij} units of payoff to divide. Let γ_{11}, $\gamma_{12}=\gamma_{21}$, and γ_{22} be some numbers from the interval $[0,1]$. An arbitrary coalition can gain only what it can obtain in partitions where no member of the partition contains more than two players. We leave it to the reader to check that $(N,v) \in \Gamma((0,2), 1/2, (0,2))$. Thus, we have from Theorem 2 that for $\varepsilon \geq (1/|N|)$ the equal-treatment

ε-core of (N, v) is nonempty. Notice that this result holds uniformly for all possible numbers γ_{11}, $\gamma_{12} = \gamma_{21}$, and γ_{22}.

The following example illustrates how our result can apply to games derived from pregames with a compact metric space of player types. For brevity, our example is somewhat informal. While the example is worded in terms of firms and workers, as in Crawford and Knoer (1981), for example, it could easily be modified to treat the hospital and intern matching problem as in Roth (1984) or any such assignment problem.

Example 2: *Approximate player types.*
Consider a pregame with two sorts of players, firms and workers. The set of possible types of workers is given by the points in the interval [0,1] and the set of possible types of firms is given by the points in the interval [1, 2]. Formally, let N be a finite player set and let ξ be an *attribute function*, that is, a function from N into [0, 2]. If $\xi(i) \in [0, 1]$ then i is a worker and if $\xi(i) \in [1, 2]$ then i is a firm. Firms can profitably hire up to three workers and the payoff to a firm i and a set of workers $W(i) \subset N$, containing no more than 3 members, is given by $v(\{i\} \cup W(i)) = \xi(i) + \Sigma_{j \in W(i)} \xi(j)$. Workers and firms can earn positive payoff only by cooperating so $v(\{i\}) = 0$ for all $i \in N$. For any coalition $S \subset N$ define $v(S)$ as the maximum payoff the group S could realize by splitting into coalitions containing either workers only, or 1 firm and no more than 3 workers. This completes the specification of the game. We leave it to the reader to verify that for any positive integer m every game (N, v) derived from the pregame is a member of the class $\Gamma((1/m, 2m), 2, (0,4))$. Then Theorem 2 implies that for any $\varepsilon \geqslant (12m/|N|) + (1/m)$ the equal-treatment ε-core of (N, v) is nonempty.

This implies that for any $\varepsilon^0 > 0$ there exists a positive integer $N(\varepsilon^0)$ such that for any $|N| \geq N(\varepsilon^0)$ the game (N, v) has a nonempty equal-treatment ε^0-core. (For an explicit bound take an integer $m^0 \geqslant (2/\varepsilon^0)$ and define $N(\varepsilon^0) \geqslant (24m^0/\varepsilon^0)$.)

For completeness, we present a simple but formal example with nearly effective groups. It also presents a collection of games that cannot be described by a single pregame thus demonstrating a broader applicability of our Theorem.

Example 3: *Nearly effective groups.*
Call a game (N, v) a k-quota game if any coalition $S \subset N$ of size less than k can realize only 0 units (that is, $v(S) = 0$ if $|S| < k$), any coalition of size k can realize 1 unit (that is, $v(S) = 1$ if $|S| = k$), and an arbitrary coalition can gain only what it can obtain in partitions where no member of the partition contains more than k players. Let Q be a collection, across all k, of all k-quota games with player set N. We leave it to the reader to verify that for

any positive integer $m>1$, the class Q is contained in the class $\Gamma((0,1), 1, (1/m, m-1))$. Hence Theorem 2 implies that for any $\varepsilon \geq ((m-2)/|N|) + (1/m)$ and for any $(N,v) \in Q$ the equal-treatment ε-core of (N,v) is nonempty. This implies that for any $\varepsilon^0 > 0$ there is a positive integer $N(\varepsilon^0)$ such that for any $|N| \geq N(\varepsilon^0)$ any game $(N,v) \in Q$ has a nonempty equal-treatment ε^0-core. (For an explicit bound take an integer $m^0 \geq (2/\varepsilon^0)$ and define $N(\varepsilon^0) \geqslant (2(m^0-2)/\varepsilon^0)$.)

This example also illustrates some differences between parameterized collections of games and games derived from pregames. A pregame takes as given a topological space of player types and a *single* worth function determining payoff sets for groups of players described by their types. It is immediate that the payoff structure of a pregame is invariant in the sense that only the size and composition of player sets can vary, not the payoff to a given set of players described by their types. Given the player set N, the class Q consists of games generated by varying the payoff structure of the games. Thus, the collection Q cannot be described as a collection of games generated by a pregame.

Theorem 2 requires both per capita boundedness and small group effectiveness. As noted previously, in the context of pregames with side payments, when arbitrarily small percentages of players of any particular type is ruled out, then these two conditions are equivalent. But in important economic contexts, neither condition implies the other. The next example illustrates voting games satisfying per capita boundedness. There is only one player type in each game so the 'thickness' condition of the equivalence result of Wooders (1994a) is satisfied. But small group effectiveness does not hold and Theorem 2 does not apply.

Example 4: *Voting games.*
Consider a sequence of games $(N^m, v^m)_{m=1}^{\infty}$ where the mth game has $3m$ players. Suppose that there are widespread positive externalities so that in the mth game, any group S consisting of at least $2m$ players can get up to $2m$ units of payoff to divide among its members, that is, $v^m(S)=2m$. Assume that if $|S|<2m$, then $v^m(S)=0$. We can think of the games as a sequence of voting games where a winning group must contain two-thirds of the population, for example, impeachment of a President of the United States or ratification of a treaty in some parliaments.

Observe that each game in the sequence has one exact player type and a per capita bound of 1. That is, $T=1$, $C=1$, and $\delta=0$. However, the 1/7-core of the game is empty for arbitrarily large values of m.

To see that the 1/7-core is empty, observe that for any feasible payoff vector there are m players that are assigned, in total, no more than

$(2m/3m)m = (2/3)m$. There are another m players that get in total no more than $(2m/2m)m = m$. These $2m$ players can form a group and receive $2m$ in total. This group can improve upon the given payoff vector for each of its members by 1/6, since $((2m-(5/3)m)/(2m) = 1/6$.

The following example, of matching games with widespread positive externalities, illustrates economic situations where per capita boundedness does not hold and Theorem 2 does not apply.

Example 5: *A matching game with widespread positive externalities.* The economic situation we have in mind is one where any two players can carry out some job but their reward from the job depends on the size of the economy in which they live. (It would be easy to modify the example to become a two- or many-sided matching game.) Consider a sequence of games $(N^m, v^m)_{m=1}^{\infty}$ where the mth game has $2m+1$ players. Assume that any player alone can get only 0 units or less, that is $v^m(\{i\}) = 0$ for all $i \in N$. Also assume that any two-player group can get up to $2m$ units of payoff to divide; $v^m(S) = 2m$ if $|S| = 2$. An arbitrary group can gain only what it can obtain in partitions where no member of the partition contains more than two players.

The games $(N^m, v^m)_{m=1}^{\infty}$ are members of the collection of games with one exact player type and strictly effective small groups of two. That is, $T=1$, $B=2$, and $\delta = \beta = 0$. However, the 1/7-core of the game is empty for arbitrarily large values of m.

To see that the 1/7-core is empty, observe that for any feasible payoff vector there is a player whose payoff is no more than $(2m^2/2m+1)$. There is another player whose payoff must be no more than $(2m^2/2m) = m$. These two players may form a group and realize $2m$. Thus they gain $m - (2m^2/2m+1) = (m/2m+1) \geqslant (m/3m) = (1/3)$. Obviously, together this two-player group can improve upon the given payoff by 1/6 for each member of the group.

In the next section we present the main example on the broad applicability of Theorem 2 – a very general model on the economies with clubs.

4. ECONOMIES WITH CLUBS AND MULTIPLE MEMBERSHIPS

In Kovalenkov and Wooders (2003), by application of Theorems on nonemptiness of cores and approximate cores, it is shown that a class of economies with apparently mild restrictions on club formation has nonempty approximate cores. In particular, following Shubik and Wooders (1982), individuals may belong to multiple clubs – that is, multiple memberships are permitted.

Here, we illustrate the Kovalenkov and Wooders model of club economies for situations with side payments. This highlights the fact that our results for large games and economies apply even with multiple memberships.

We define admissible club structures in terms of natural properties and take as given the set of all admissible club structures for each group of players. We remark that it would be possible to separate crowding types of players (those observable characteristics that affect the utilities of others, or, in other words, their external characteristics) from taste types, as in Conley and Wooders (1996, 1997, 2001), and have players' roles as club members depend on their crowding types. Moreover, following Conley and Wooders (1996, 2001), it is possible to endogenize choice of crowding type (skills, education and so on). In those papers, however, the separation of crowding type and taste type has an important role; the authors show that prices for public goods – or club membership prices – need only depend on observable characteristics of players and not on their preferences. The current paper treats only the core; at this point separation of taste and crowding type would have no essential role.

Agents: There are T 'types' of agents. Let $\rho=(\rho_1,\ldots,\rho_T)$ be a given profile, called the *population profile*. The set of agents is given by:

$$N_\rho=\{(t,q):q=1,\ldots,\rho_t \text{ and } t=1,\ldots,T\},$$

and (t, q) is called the qth *agent of type t*. It will later be required that all agents of the same type may play similar role in club structures. For example, in a traditional marriage model, all females could have the role of 'wife'. Define $N_\rho[t] := \{(t, q): q=1,\ldots,\rho_t\}$. For our Proposition members of $N_\rho[t]$ will be approximate substitutes for each other.

Commodities: The economy has L private goods. A vector of private goods is denoted by $y=(y_1,\ldots, y_l,\ldots, y_L)\in\mathbf{R}^L_+$.

Clubs: A *club* is a nonempty subset of players. For each club $S\subset N_\rho$, a *club structure of* S, denoted by $\boldsymbol{S}$, is a set of clubs whose union coincides with S. The set of *admissible club structures for* S, denoted by $C(S)$, is assumed to be nonempty for any $S\neq\emptyset$. This assumption ensures that a club consisting of only one player has a unique admissible club structure – a singleton set. The sets $C(S)$ are also required to satisfy the following two properties:

1. If S and S' are nonempty disjoint subsets of players and $\boldsymbol{S}$ and $\boldsymbol{S'}$ are admissible club structures of S and S' respectively, then $\{C : C\in \boldsymbol{S}\cup\boldsymbol{S'}\}$ is an admissible club structure of $S\cup S'$ (unions of admissible

club structures of disjoint groups are admissible club structures of the unions of the groups).

2. Let S and S' be subsets of players with the same profiles, let $\boldsymbol{S}$ be an admissible club structure of S and let φ be a type-preserving 1-1 mapping from S onto S' (that is, if $(t, q) \in S$ then $\varphi((t, q)) = (t, q')$ for some $q' = 1,\ldots,\rho_t$). Then:

$$\boldsymbol{S}' = \{C \subset S' : \varphi^{-1}(C) \in \boldsymbol{S}\}$$

is an admissible club structure of S' (admissible club structures depend only on profiles, that is, all players of the same type have the same roles in clubs).

The first property is necessary to ensure that the game derived from the economy is superadditive. It corresponds to economic situations where one option open to a group is to form smaller groups. Since the singletons are always admissible club structures for clubs of one player, this property implies that the partition of any set $S \subset N_\rho$, $S \neq \varnothing$, into singletons is an admissible club structure for S. The second property corresponds to the idea that the opportunities open to a group depend on the profile of the group.

Club activities: For each club C there is a given set of *club activities* $\boldsymbol{A}(C)$. These club activities could include provision of morning coffee for the club members, or a swimming pool, or a purely social club. An element α of $A(C)$ requires input $x(C, \alpha) \in \mathbf{R}^L$ of private goods. For any two clubs C and C' with the same profile we require that if $\alpha \in A(C)$, then $\alpha \in A(C')$ and $x(C, \alpha) = x(C', \alpha)$. In other words, the club activities feasible for a set of players depend only on the profile of the club membership. For 1-player clubs $\{(t,q)\}$, we assume that there is an activity α_0 with $x(\{(t, q)\}, \alpha_0) = 0$, that is, there is an activity requiring no use of inputs.

Preferences and endowments: Only private goods and money are endowed. Let $\omega^{tq} \in \mathbf{R}^L_+$ be the *endowment of the* $(t, q)^{th}$ *participant of private goods* and let ξ^{tq} be his endowment of money.

Given $S \subset N_\rho$, $(t, q) \in S$, and a club structure $\boldsymbol{S} \in C(S)$, *the consumption set of the* $(t, q)^{th}$ player (relative to $\boldsymbol{S}$) is given by:

$$\Phi^{tq}(\boldsymbol{S}) := X^{tq}(\boldsymbol{S}) \times \mathsf{R} \times \Pi_{C \in \boldsymbol{S}} A(C),$$

where $X^{tq}(\boldsymbol{S}) \subset \mathbf{R}^L$ is the *private goods consumption set relative to* $\boldsymbol{S}$, assumed to be closed and $\mathbf{R}$ is the real line. Note that the private goods part of the consumption set of a player, $X^{tq}(\boldsymbol{S})$, may depend on the club structure. To illustrate the motivation for this feature, notice that some clubs may provide food for their members. Whether an individual belonged to such a club would affect the private goods required for subsistence. The entire consumption set of the $(t,q)^{th}$ player is given by:

$$\Phi^{tq} := \bigcup_{S \subset N_\rho:\,(t,q)\in S} \bigcup_{\boldsymbol{S}\in C(S)} \Phi^{tq}(\boldsymbol{S}).$$

We assume that the $(t,q)^{th}$ player can subsist in isolation. That is:

$$(\omega^{tq}, \bar{\xi}^{tq}, \alpha_0) \in \Phi^{tq}(\{(t, q)\}).$$

It is also assumed that for each (t, q), each $S \subset N_\rho$, $(t, q) \in S$, and each club structure $\boldsymbol{S}$ of S, the preferences of the $(t, q)^{th}$ agent are represented by a continuous utility function $u^{tq}(\bullet\,;\boldsymbol{S})$ defined on $\Phi^{tq}(\boldsymbol{S})$.

States of the economy: Let S be a nonempty subset of N_ρ and let $\boldsymbol{S} \in C(S)$. A *feasible state of the economy S relative to* $\boldsymbol{S}$, or simply *a state for* $\boldsymbol{S}$, is a triple (y^S, ξ^S, α^S) where:

a) $y^S = \{y^{tq}\}_{(t,q)\in S}$ with $y^{tq} \in X^{tq}(\boldsymbol{S})$ for $(t, q) \in S$;
b) $\xi^S = \{\xi^{tq}\}_{(t,q)\in S}$ with $\xi^{tq} \in \mathsf{R}$ for $(t, q) \in S$;
c) $\alpha^S = \{\alpha^C\}_{C\in \boldsymbol{S}}$ with $\alpha^C \in A(C)$ for $C \in \boldsymbol{S}$; and
d) the allocations of private goods and money are feasible, that is:

$$\Sigma_{C\in \boldsymbol{S}}\, x(C, \alpha^C) + \Sigma_{(t,q)\in S}\, y^{tq} = \Sigma_{(t,q)\in S}\, \omega^{tq} \text{ and}$$
$$\Sigma_{C\in \boldsymbol{S}}\, \xi^{tq} = \Sigma_{C\in \boldsymbol{S}}\, \bar{\xi}^{tq}.$$

Feasible payoffs vectors: A payoff vector $(\bar{u}^{tq})_{(t,q)\in S}$ is *feasible for a group S* if there is club structure $\boldsymbol{S} \in C(S)$ and a feasible state of the economy for S relative to $\boldsymbol{S}$, (y^S, ξ^S, α^S), such that $\bar{u}^{tq} = u^{tq}(y^{tq}, \xi^{tq}, \alpha^S; \boldsymbol{S})$ for each $(t, q) \in S$.

The game induced by the economy: For each group $S \subset N_\rho$, define:

$$v(S) = \max\{\Sigma_{(t,q)\in S}\, \bar{u}^{tq}: \text{a payoff vector } (\bar{u}^{tq})_{(t,q)\in S} \text{ is feasible for } S\}.$$

It is immediate that the player set N_ρ and function v determine a game with side payments (N_ρ, v).

ε-domination: Let N be a club structure of the total player set N_ρ and let (y^N, ξ^N, α^N) be a feasible state of the economy N_ρ relative to N. A group S can *ε-dominate* the state (y^N, ξ^N, α^N) if there is a club structure $\boldsymbol{S} = \{S_1, ..., S_K\} \in C(S)$ and a feasible state $(y'^S, \xi'^S, \alpha'^S)$ for the economy S such that for all consumers $(t,q) \in S$ it holds that:

$$u^{tq}(y'^{tq}, \xi'^{tq}, \alpha'^S; \boldsymbol{S}) > (y^{tq}, \xi^{tq}, \alpha^N; N) + \varepsilon.$$

The core of the economy and ε-cores: A state (y^N, ξ^N, α^N) of the economy N_ρ relative to N is in the *core of the economy* if it cannot be 0-dominated by any group S. Notice that the core of the economy may include states of the economy relative to different club structures of the set N_ρ. It is clear, that if (y^N, ξ^N, α^N) is a state in the core of the economy then the utility vector induced by that state is in the core of the induced game. Similarly, if $(\bar{u}^{tq})_{(t,q)\in N_\rho}$ is in the core of the game induced by an economy then there exist a club structure N of the total player set N_ρ and a state in the core of the economy (y^N, ξ^N, α^N) such that the utility vector induced by that state is $(\bar{u}^{tq})_{(t,q)\in N_\rho}$. Notion of the ε-core of the economy is defined in the obvious way.

To obtain our results we require few restrictions on the economy:

(A.0) For some $\delta \geq 0$ the players in the set $N_\rho[t] = \{(t,q): q = 1, ..., \rho_t\}$ are δ-substitutes for each other in the game induced by the economy.
(A.1) There are $\beta \geq 0$ and an integer B so that the game derived from the economy has β-effective B-bounded groups.
(A.2) There is a constant C such that the condition of per capita boundedness of C is satisfied by the game derived from the economy.

Then the next result follows from Theorem 2.

Proposition 1: *Nonemptiness of the equal-treatment ε-core.* Let T and B be positive integers. Let δ, β and C be nonnegative real numbers. Assume that (A.0), (A.1) and (A.2) hold and let ε be a positive real number. Then if:

$$\varepsilon \geq \frac{TC(B-1)}{|N|} + \delta + \beta,$$

the equal-treatment ε-core of the economy is nonempty.

In subsequent research, Allouch and Wooders (2002 and research in progress) demonstrate existence of approximate competitive equilibrium and convergence result for economies with networks, including club economies with overlapping memberships.[20] Their condition of *desirability of wealth* on primitives ensures that per capita boundedness (and, indeed, small group effectiveness) is satisfied. Informally, desirability of wealth is simply that, for each player, enough wealth, in terms of private goods, and a few friends can dominate any feasible equal treatment state of the economy, no matter how large the total player set. Note that this condition allows ever-increasing returns to club sizes and memberships since no feasible equal treatment state of the economy may permit anyone to be so wealthy.

5. FINAL REMARKS

Remark 1: *Absolute or relative sizes?*
It is possible to obtain similar results with bounds on *relative* sizes of effective groups. In a finite game with a given number of players, assumptions on absolute sizes and on relative sizes of effective groups are equivalent. We have chosen to develop our results using bounds on absolute sizes of near-effective groups since this seems to reflect typical economic and social situations. Examples include: marriage and matching models (see Kelso and Crawford, 1982; Roth and Sotomayor, 1990); models of economies with shared goods and crowding (see Conley and Wooders, 1998, for a survey); and private goods exchange economies (see, for example, Mas-Colell, 1979; Hammond, Kaneko and Wooders, 1989; Kaneko and Wooders, 1989). In fact, assumptions on proportions of economic agents typically occur only when there is a continuum of players, cf. Ostroy (1984).

Remark 2: *Further properties of ε-cores.*
In the subsequent research of the authors, additional interesting properties of the ε-cores of games without side payments have been studied using the framework of the parameterized collection of games. However, some of these papers are incomplete and none is published. Thus we decided to concentrate in this review on the nonemptiness issue.

Remark 3: *Immediate applications.*
The class of economies defined above is very broad. The Proposition can be applied to extend results already in the literature on economies with group structures, such as those with local public goods (called club economies by some authors), cf. Shubik and Wooders (1982). For example, there are a number of papers showing core-equilibrium equivalence in finite economies with local public goods and one private good and satisfying strict effectiveness of small groups, cf. Conley and Wooders (2001) and references therein. In these economies, from the results of Wooders (1983) and Shubik and Wooders (1983), existence of approximate equilibrium where

an exceptional set of agents is ignored is immediate. (Just take the largest subgame having a nonempty core and consider the equilibria for that subeconomy; ignore the remainder of the consumers.) Our results in case of the private good being a money allow the immediate extension of these results to results for all sufficiently large economies – no restriction to replication sequences is required.

Remark 4: *Other applications.*
In principle, it appears that our results on nonemptiness of approximate cores of large games may have other applications. As suggested already by the title of Allouch and Wooders (2002), they can be applied to an interesting class of socially networked economies. They may also have application to economies with asymmetric information, as in Forges, Heifetz and Minelli (2001) for example.

NOTES

1. For games with side payments, a game is balanced if and only if it has a nonempty core. See Hildenbrand and Kirman (1976) or Kannai (1992), for example, for very clear expositions of balancedness.
2. Some of these special situations are matching models and assignment games (Gale and Shapley, 1962), certain classes of partitioning games (Kaneko and Wooders, 1982), games with a 'tree structure' on the set of admissible coalitions (Demange, 1982; Greenberg and Weber, 1986; Le Breton, Owen and Weber, 1992; Demange, 1994; for example), and games with lotteries (Garratt and Qin, 1996), among others.
3. See also Shubik and Wooders (1982). Wooders (1983) treats NTU games.
4. Unlike the prior literature using only per capita boundedness, Wooders and Zame (1984) require that individual marginal contributions to coalitions be bounded, an assumption that turns out to be unnecessarily restrictive, since it implies small group effectiveness, as demonstrated by Wooders (1994b), Proposition 3.9. Example 3.1 of the same paper shows that small group effectiveness does not imply boundedness of marginal contributions.
5. Shapley and Shubik (1969a) showed that 'totally balanced' games with side payments are equivalent to games generated by private goods exchange economies with quasi-linear and concave utilities; thus, totally balanced games are frequently called *market games*. A game is totally balanced if the game and all its subgames have nonempty cores. Based on the results of Wooders (1980), Shubik and Wooders (1982) noted that large games satisfying per capita boundedness and superadditivity are approximately totally balanced – all sufficiently large subgames are approximately balanced – and thus are approximately market games. The required concavity of the limiting per capita payoff function was noted by Aumann (1987)
6. See also Shubik and Wooders (1982) and Bennett and Wooders (1979).
7. The prior game theoretic results are applied to models of large economies in Wooders (2002). See references there for further discussions of related models.
8. For example, statements are typically of the form 'For all games with sufficiently many players derived from the pregame ...'.
9. We refer the reader to Kaneko and Wooders (1994b) for a more in-depth discussion of the concepts of games with and without side payments.
10. These results are in an approximate or asymptotic sense. More precisely, given $\varepsilon > 0$ there

is some replication number r_0 so that all larger replica economies (with the same distribution of player types but with possibly improved payoff opportunities due to gains to scale), ε-cores are nonempty and most players of the same type are treated nearly equally.

11. Actually, we apply a strong result for games with side payments from Kovalenkov and Wooders (2001b) to the side-payments variation of the model of economies with clubs from Kovalenkov and Wooders (2003).
12. Kaneko and Wooders (1994a) also contains a number of examples with widespread externalities.
13. The side payments pregame framework first appeared in Wooders (1979) and was extended to a compact metric space of player types in Wooders and Zame (1984), which used a more restrictive condition than SGE. The case of games without side payments was addressed in Wooders (1983).
14. The assumption of superadditivity is slightly stronger than required. It would suffice to define feasible payoffs for a coalition of players as any payoffs that could be achieved by some partition of the coalition. See Wooders (2002) for further discussion.
15. *Strict* small group effectiveness, the property that *all* gains to collective activities can be realized by groups of players bounded in size (albeit with a different name) was introduced in Wooders (1979) and has appeared in a number of subsequent papers including Bennett and Wooders (1979) and most recently, for some of the results in Wooders (1994b).
16. For the finite type case the following Theorem is also immediate from Wooders (1994a), since large games are uniformly approximated by market games and market games are totally balanced.
17. This result extends the nonemptiness of approximate cores of Wooders (1980) and Shubik and Wooders (1982) for games with side payments to hold uniformly for games derived from a pregame with sufficiently many players of each type. Recall that these papers require the same conditions of superadditivity and per capita boundedness. Since the games considered have a fixed distribution of player types, the 'thickness' condition is automatically satisfied.
18. In fact, in the literature of private goods exchange economies since Kannai (1970), an analogous construct has been used to treat limiting properties of large economies. In particular, a pair consisting of a space of endowments and a space of preferences is taken as given; this pair could be described as a pre-economy. Then an economy is determined by a set of agents and a function assigning each agent a preference relation and an endowment. Our approach here, like Anderson (1978) and Manelli (1991), treats individual games.
19. A form of this Theorem, with a larger bound, appeared in Wooders (1994c). We note β-effective *B*-bounded groups permit all coalitions containing no more than *B* members. Were we to restrict the set of permissible coalitions further, a better bound may be obtained.
20. The first decentralization results for situations where individuals may belong to multiple clubs appear in Ellickson et al. (1999). Their model requires that club sizes be bounded. Thus, clubs must become infinitesimal in large economies. In contrast, the Kovalenkov and Wooders (2001a,b, 2003) and Allouch and Wooders (2002) formulations, as that of Shubik and Wooders (1982), allow clubs as large as the entire player set.

REFERENCES

Allouch, N. and M. Wooders (2002), 'Competitive pricing in socially networked economies', University of Warwick Discussion Paper No. 639.

Anderson, R.M. (1978), 'An elementary core equivalence theorem', *Econometrica,* **46** (6), 1438–87.

Anderson, R.M. (1992), 'The core in perfectly competitive economies', in R.J. Aumann and S. Hart (eds), *Handbook of Game Theory*, vol. 1, Amsterdam: Elsevier Science, 413–57.
Aumann, R.J. (1964), 'Markets with a continuum of traders,' *Econometrica*, **32** (1–2), 39–50.
Aumann, R.J. (1987), 'Game theory', in J. Eatwell, M. Milgate and P. Newmann (eds), *The New Palgrave: A Dictionary of Economics*, The Macmillan Press.
Bennett, E. and M. Wooders (1979), 'Income distribution and firm formation', *Journal of Comparative Economics*, **3**, 304–17.
Bloch, B. (1996), 'Sequential formation of coalitions with fixed payoff division', *Games and Economic Behavior*, **14** (1), 90–123.
Bondareva, O. (1962), 'Theory of the core in an *n*-person game', *Vestnik of Leningrad State University*, **13**, 141–2 (in Russian).
Conley, J. and M. Wooders (1996), 'Taste homogeneity of optimal jurisdictions in a Tiebout economy with crowding types and endogenous educational investment choices', *Richerche Economiche*, **50** (4), 367–87.
Conley, J. and M. Wooders (1997), 'Equivalence of the core and competitive equilibrium in a Tiebout economy with crowding types', *Journal of Urban Economics*, **41** (3), 421–40.
Conley, J. and M. Wooders (1998), 'Anonymous pricing in Tiebout economies and economies with clubs', in D. Pines, E. Sadka and I. Zilcha (eds), *Topics in Public Finance*, Cambridge: Cambridge University Press.
Conley, J. and M. Wooders (2001), 'Tiebout economies with differential genetic types and endogenously chosen crowding characteristics', *Journal of Economic Theory*, **98** (2), 261–94.
Crawford, V. and E. Knoer (1981), 'Job matchings with heterogeneous firms and workers', *Econometrica*, **49** (2), 437–50.
Debreu, G. and H. Scarf (1963), 'A limit theorem on the core of an economy', *International Economic Review*, **4** (3), 235–46.
Demange, G. (1982), 'Single peaked orders on a tree', *Mathematical Social Sciences*, **3** (4), 389–96.
Demange, G. (1994), 'Intermediate preferences and stable coalition structures', *Journal of Mathematical Economics*, **23** (1), 45–58.
Edgeworth, F.Y. (1881), *Mathematical Psychics*, London: Kegan Paul.
Ellickson, B., B. Grodal, S. Scotchmer and W.R. Zame (1999), 'Clubs and the Market', *Econometrica*, **67** (5), 1185–218.
Forges, F., A. Heifetz and E. Minelli (2001), 'Incentive compatible core and competitive equilibria in differential information economies', *Economic Theory*, **18** (2), 349–65.
Gale, D. and L.S. Shapley (1962), 'College admissions and the stability of marriage', *American Mathematical Monthly*, **69** (1), 9–15.
Garratt, R. and C.-Z. Qin (1996), 'Cores and competitive equilibria with indivisibilities and lotteries', *Journal of Economic Theory*, **68** (2), 531–43.
Gilles, D.B. (1953), *Some Theorems on* n*-person Games*, Ph.D. Dissertation, Department of Mathematics, Princeton: Princeton University.
Greenberg, J. and S. Weber (1986), 'Strong Tiebout equilibrium with restricted preference domain', *Journal of Economic Theory*, **38** (1), 101–17.
Hammond, P.J. (1999), 'On *f*-core equivalence with general widespread externalities', *Journal of Mathematical Economics*, **32** (2), 177–84.
Hammond, P.J., M. Kaneko and M. Wooders (1989), 'Continuum economies with

finite coalitions; Core, equilibrium and widespread externalities', *Journal of Economic Theory*, **49** (1), 113–34.

Hildenbrand, W. and A.P. Kirman (1976), *Introduction to Equilibrium Analysis*, Amsterdam: Elsevier Science.

Kaneko, M. and M. Wooders (1982), 'Cores of partitioning games', *Mathematical Social Sciences*, **3** (4), 313–27.

Kaneko, M. and M. Wooders (1986), 'The core of a game with a continuum of players and finite coalitions: The model and some results', *Mathematical Social Sciences*, **12** (2), 105–37.

Kaneko, M. and M. Wooders (1989), 'The core of a continuum economy with widespread externalities and finite coalitions: From finite to continuum economics', *Journal of Economic Theory*, **49** (1), 135–68.

Kaneko, M. and M. Wooders (1994a), 'Widespread externalities and perfectly competitive markets', in R. Gilles, P. Ruys and D. Talman (eds), *Economic Behaviour in an Imperfect Environment*, Boston: North Holland, 71–87.

Kaneko, M. and M.Wooders (1994b), 'Utility theories in cooperative games', University of Tsukuba Discussion Paper, to appear in the *Handbook of Utility Theory*, P. Hammond and C. Seidel (eds), on-line at http://www.warwick.ac.uk/fac/soc/economics/staff/faculty/wooders.

Kaneko, M. and M. Wooders (1996), 'The nonemptiness of the *f*-core of a game without side payments', *International Journal of Game Theory*, **25** (2), 245–58.

Kannai, Y. (1970), 'Continuity properties of the core of a market', *Econometrica*, **38** (1), 791–815.

Kannai, Y. (1992), 'The core and balancedness', in R.J. Aumann and S. Hart (eds), *Handbook of Game Theory*, vol. 1, Amsterdam: Elsevier Science, 355–95.

Kelso, A.S. and V.P. Crawford (1982), 'Job matching, coalition formation, and gross substitutes', *Econometrica*, **50** (6), 1483–504.

Kovalenkov, A. and M. Wooders (2001a), 'Epsilon cores of games with limited side payments; Nonemptiness and equal treatment', *Games and Economic Behavior*, **36** (2), 193–218.

Kovalenkov, A. and M. Wooders (2001b), 'An exact bound on epsilon for nonemptiness of epsilon cores of games', *Mathematics of Operations Research*, **26** (4), 654–78.

Kovalenkov, A. and M. Wooders (2003), 'Approximate cores of games and economies with clubs', University of Warwick Department of Economic Working Paper No. 634, combining Autonomous University of Barcelona WP 390.97 and 391.97 (1997), forthcoming in *Journal of Economic Theory*.

Le Breton, M., G. Owen and S. Weber (1992), 'Strongly balanced cooperative games', *International Journal of Game Theory*, **20** (4), 419–28.

Manelli, A.M. (1991), 'Monotonic preferences and core equivalence', *Econometrica*, **59** (1), 123–38.

Mas-Colell, A. (1979), 'A refinement of the core equivalence theorem', *Economic Letters*, **3**, 307–10.

Ostroy, J. (1984), 'A reformulation of the marginal productivity theory of distribution', *Econometrica*, **52** (3), 599–630.

Ray, D. and R. Vohra (1999), 'A theory of endogenous coalition structures', *Games and Economic Behavior*, **26** (2), 286–336.

Roth, A.E. (1984), 'The evolution of the labor market for medical interns and residents: A case study in game theory', *Journal of Political Economy*, **92** (6), 991–1016.

Roth, A.E. and M. Sotomayor (1990), *Two-sided Matching; A Study in Game-theoretic Modeling and Analysis*, Cambridge: Cambridge University Press.

Scarf, H.E. (1967), 'The core of an *n*-person game', *Econometrica*, **35** (1), 50–67.

Shapley, L.S. (1952), 'Notes on the N-Person game III: Some variants of the von-Neumann-Morgenstern definition of Solution', Rand Corporation research memorandum, RM- 817.

Shapley, L.S. (1967), 'On balanced sets and cores', *Naval Research Logistics Quarterly*, **14**, 453–60.

Shapley, L.S. and M. Shubik (1966), 'Quasi-cores in a monetary economy with non-convex preferences', *Econometrica*, **34** (4), 805–27.

Shapley, L.S. and M. Shubik (1969a), 'On market games', *Journal of Economic Theory*, **1** (1), 9–25.

Shapley, L.S. and M. Shubik (1969b), 'On the core of an economic system with externalities', *American Economic Review*, **59** (4), 678–84.

Shubik, M. (1959), 'Edgeworth Market Games', in F.R. Luce and A.W. Tucker (eds), *Contributions to the Theory of Games IV, Annals of Mathematical Studies, 40*, Princeton: Princeton University Press.

Shubik, M. and M. Wooders (1982), 'Near-markets and market-games', Cowles Foundation Discussion Paper No. 657, published as 'Clubs, near-markets and market-games' in M. Wooders (ed.), *Topics in Mathematical Economics and Game Theory; Essays in Honor of Robert J. Aumann*, Fields Institute Communication Volume, Providence: American Mathematical Society, 1999, on-line at http://www.warwick.ac.uk/fac/soc/economics/staff/faculty/wooders.

Shubik, M. and M. Wooders (1983), 'Approximate cores of replica games and economies: Part I. replica games, externalities, and approximate cores', *Mathematical Social Sciences*, **6** (1), 27–48, on-line at http://www.warwick.ac.uk/ fac/soc/economics/staff/faculty/wooders.

Tiebout, C. (1956), 'A pure theory of local expenditures', *Journal of Political Economy*, **64** (5), 416–24.

Wooders, M. (1978), 'Equilibria, the core, and jurisdiction structures in economies with a local public good', *Journal of Economic Theory*, **18** (2), 328–48.

Wooders, M. (1979), 'A characterization of approximate equilibria and cores in a class of coalition economies', Stony Brook Department of Economics, Working Paper No.184, 1977, Revised 1979, on-line at http://www.warwick.ac.uk/fac/soc/economics/staff/faculty/wooders.

Wooders, M.H. (1980) 'Asymptotic cores and asymptotic balancedness of large replica games', Stony Brook Working Paper No. 215, Revised July 1980, on-line at http://www.warwick.ac.uk/fac/soc/economics/staff/faculty/wooders.

Wooders, M. (1983), 'The epsilon core of a large replica game', *Journal of Mathematical Economics*, **11** (3), 277–300, on-line at http://www.warwick.ac.uk/economics/wooders/.

Wooders, M. (1992), 'Inessentiality of large groups and the approximate core property; An equivalence theorem', *Economic Theory*, **2** (1), 129–47.

Wooders, M. (1994a), 'Equivalence of games and markets', *Econometrica*, **62** (5), 1141–60, on-line at http://www.warwick.ac.uk/fac/soc/economics/staff/faculty/wooders.

Wooders, M. (1994b), 'Large games and economies with effective small groups' J.-F. Mertens and S. Sorin (eds), '*Game Theoretic Methods in General Equilibrium Analysis*', London: Kluwer, on–line at http://www.warwick.ac.uk/fac/soc/economics/staff/faculty/wooders.

Wooders, M. (1994c), 'Approximating games and economies by markets', University of Toronto Working Paper No. 9415.

Wooders, M. (1999), 'Multijurisdictional economies, the Tiebout Hypothesis, and sorting', *Proceedings of the National Academy of Sciences*, **96** (19), 10585–7, on-line at http://www.pnas.org/cgi/content/full/96/19/10585.

Wooders, M.H. (2002) 'The attribute core, core convergence, and small group effectiveness; The effects of property rights assignments on attribute games', University of Toronto Working Paper (1993) revised, to appear in *Essays in Honour of Martin Shubik*, P. Dubey and J. Geanakoplos (eds), to appear on line at http://www.warwick.ac.uk/fac/soc/economics/staff/faculty/wooders.

Wooders, M.H. and W.R. Zame (1984), 'Approximate cores of large games', *Econometrica*, **52** (6), 1327–50, on-line at http://www.warwick.ac.uk//fac/soc/economics/staff/faculty/wooders.

Yi, S.-S. (1997), 'Stable coalition structures with externalities', *Games and Economic Behavior*, **20** (2), 201–27.

2. Non-cooperative models of coalition formation in games with spillovers

Francis Bloch

1. INTRODUCTION

Since the publication of *Theory of Games and Economic Behavior* by von Neumann and Morgenstern (1944), the study of coalition formation has been one of the central questions in game theory. In the words of its founders, one of the purposes of game theory is to 'determine everything that can be said about coalitions between players, compensations between partners in every coalition, mergers or fights between coalitions . . .' (von Neumann and Morgenstern, 1944, p. 240). This quotation clearly poses the three basic questions of endogenous coalition formation: Which coalitions will be formed? How will the coalitional worth be divided among coalition members? How does the presence of other coalitions affect the incentives to cooperate?

As noted by Maschler (1992) in his survey on bargaining sets, cooperative game theory has focused mostly on the second question – the division of the payoff between coalition members. In fact, it is even surprising to note that the first question has been assumed away in most cooperative game theory. Even the Aumann–Maschler (1964) bargaining set, which was specially designed to analyse the formation of coalitions, specifies an exogenous coalition structure and falls short of determining which coalition structure will form.[1] Finally, the third question, dealing with competition between coalitions, is simply ignored in traditional cooperative game theory, since the coalitional function cannot take into account externalities among coalitions.

In recent years, the limitations of cooperative game theoretic solution concepts has led to the emergence of a new strand of the literature describing the formation of coalitions as a non-cooperative process. This reformulation of the old problem of endogenous coalition formation in non-cooperative terms can actually handle the issue of competition between coalitions which was ignored in traditional cooperative game theory. In this survey, my aim is to review those recent contributions and to discuss their applications to various economic problems.

In fact, the study of specific economic models is what prompted the renewed interest in coalition formation. In international trade, the formation of competing customs unions and the question of 'regionalism' in trade is one of the foremost current topics of debate. In environmental economics, international cooperation to control cross-border pollution (and the possibility that cooperation would only take place among a small subset of countries) has recently become an important subject of discussion. In industrial organization, the study of cartels of firms, strategic alliances or standardization committees are also examples of the application of endogenous coalition formation. Finally, in local public finance, the financial difficulties faced by large cities have led to a spur of interest in the study of spillovers between jurisdictions, and the taxation of neighbouring communities for local public goods provided by one jurisdiction.

While the previous examples are taken from various fields of economics and deal with very different problems, they all share a common structure. In all these applications, the coalitions formed are smaller than the grand coalition, and the spillovers between coalitions are important. The presence of spillovers and the lack of superadditivity of the underlying coalitional game require the use of a framework, which is a more general than classical cooperative game theory. The appropriate framework to deal with spillovers are *games in partition function form* where the worth of a coalition depends on the entire coalition structure.

In the next section of this survey, I analyse precisely the role of spillovers and the different representations of games with externalities. I first emphasize the limits of the classical approach and show how various partition function games can be defined. This leads me to define a general structure of payoffs for games with spillovers.

In section 3, I discuss a first class of non-cooperative games of coalition formation, where all agents announce *simultaneously* their decision to cooperate. I analyse various outcome rules for the simultaneous announcement games, and discuss different solution concepts. In particular, I show that, in order to select among the Nash equilibria of these games, more restrictive solution concepts must be used, such as coalition-proof Nash equilibria (CPNE) or strong Nash equilibria (SNE).

Section 4 is devoted to a second class of games, where agents announce *sequentially* their decision to participate in the coalition. These extensive-form games are meant to capture the 'forward looking' aspects of coalition formation: each agent is aware that her decision to form a coalition might affect the behaviour of other agents, and takes into account the final consequences of her decision. I analyse different specifications of the extensive-form games that reflect differences in the procedures of coalition formation.

In section 5, I study some *cooperative* solution concepts that were proposed to analyse the stability of coalition structures in games with spillovers. While those stability concepts are not based on non-cooperative processes, they often provide interesting benchmarks and give some new insights into the study of coalition formation with spillovers.

In the last sections of the survey, I discuss applications of the different models of coalition formation to economic problems. It turns out that most economic situations can be classified into two categories: games with *positive spillovers* where the formation of a coalition by other players increases the payoff of an agent, and games with *negative spillovers* where the formation of a coalition decreases the payoff of agents who are not members of the coalition. In section 6, I discuss games with positive spillovers, and compare the outcomes of the different models of coalition formation in that setting. In section 7, I perform the same analysis for games with negative spillovers.

In the last section, I conclude by mentioning the problems attached to the various games of coalition formation, and by providing some directions for future research.

While most of this survey is devoted to theoretical models of coalition formation, I believe that the results obtained should be viewed as *operational tools* that can be used in the study of coalition formation in various economic settings. Hence, rather than emphasizing the theoretical aspects of the research, I have tried to give examples in order to show how the theory can be applied to specific economic models.

Finally, it is important to mention the exact range of questions covered by this survey. I have chosen to focus on models of coalition formation *in games with spillovers*, thereby excluding the large literature on games without spillovers. For cooperative solution concepts on games without spillovers, the reader is referred to the excellent survey on coalition structures by Joseph Greenberg in the *Handbook of Game Theory* (Greenberg, 1994). Simultaneous games of coalition formation in games without spillovers have recently been surveyed by Konishi, Le Breton and Weber (1997). Yi's (2000) survey, also contained in this volume, complements this chapter by focussing on specific economic applications and giving a different view on the formation of coalitions in partition function games. The large (and growing) literature on sequential games of coalition formation in cooperative situations has not been surveyed yet. The reader is encouraged to go back to the original articles by Chatterjee et al. (1993) and Perry and Reny (1994) for a rapid introduction to this literature.

2. GAMES WITH SPILLOVERS AND THE PARTITION FUNCTION FORM

2.1 The Classical Approach

The classical representation of gains from cooperation does not allow for spillovers between coalitions. A *game in coalitional function form* is characterized by a coalitional function $v(\cdot)$, assigning to each coalition C a real number $v(C)$ representing the worth of the coalition.[2] The absence of spillovers is implicit in the derivation of the coalitional function: the set $v(C)$ represents whatever the coalition can get irrespective of the behaviour of other players.

Clearly, depending on the meaning assigned to 'irrespective of the behaviour of other players', various definitions of coalitional function games can be obtained. Following von Neumann and Morgenstern (1944), the primitive description of a game is a *strategic form* $\Gamma = \{N, \{S_i\}_{i \in N}, \{u_i\}_{i \in N}\}$ where N is the set of players, S_i the strategy space of player i and u_i the payoff function of player i, assigning to each profile of strategies s a real number. We let σ_i denote mixed strategies. The different coalitional functions $v(C)$ are then derived by different *conversions* of the non-cooperative game into a game in coalitional function form.

In von Neumann and Morgenstern's (1944) analysis of n-person, zero-sum games, the coalitional value $v(C)$ is obtained as follows. Consider the two 'composite' players C and $N\backslash C$. (The 'composite' player C is defined to have a strategy set given by $S_C = X_{i \in C} S_C$ and a payoff function $u_c = \Sigma_{i \in C} u_i$) The two-person zero-sum game Γ' with players C and $N\backslash C$ possesses a value defined by:

$$v = \max_{s_C} \min_{s_{N/C}} u_C(\sigma_C, \sigma_{N/C}) = \min_{s_{N/C}} \max_{s_C} u_C(\sigma_C, \sigma_{N/C}),$$

and the coalition worth $v(C)$ is simply the value v of the game Γ'.

In non-zero-sum games, the minimax is not necessarily equal to the maximin, and hence two different conversions are possible. These conversions have been labelled by Aumann (1967) the α and β conversions, and are defined as follows:

$$v^{\alpha}(C) = \min_{S_{N/C}} \max_{S_C} u_C(\sigma_C, \sigma_{N/C}),$$

$$v^{\beta}(C) = \max_{S_C} \min_{S_{N/C}} u_C(\sigma_C, \sigma_{N/C}).$$

In the α framework, a coalition C obtains the worth it can guarantee itself, irrespective of the strategy choice of the other players; in the β conversion, the coalition C obtains the worth it cannot be prevented from getting by players in $N \backslash C$. Clearly, both conversions embody a very pessimistic conjecture on the part of the members of coalition C on the behaviour of the complementary coalition. Hence, although this formulation might be adequate for very competitive situations, such as two-person zero-sum games, it is less convincing for general games, where players' interests may coincide. Why should the players in $N \backslash C$ behave in such an aggressive way if it is against their interest?

In order to mitigate this aggressivity, Harsanyi (1959) has proposed a different conversion of non-cooperative games, based on Nash's (1950) bargaining solution. In this formulation, we will let $A = \max_{S_N} u_N(s_N)$ denote the total gains from cooperation of the grand coalition. Define then $v(C)$ to be the maximiser of the Nash product:

$$\Pi = (x - \min_{S_{N/C}} \max_{S_C} u_C(S_C, S_{N/C}))(A - x - \min_{S_C} \max_{S_{N/C}} u_{N/C}(S_C, S_{N/C})).$$

Clearly, Harsanyi's (1959) conversion supposes a less extreme behaviour on the part of players outside the coalition. However, it still rests on two very specific assumptions: (i) players outside the coalition behave as a single complementary coalition, and (ii) the two coalitions C and $N \backslash C$ bargain over the total gains from cooperation and obtain shares corresponding to Nash's (1950) bargaining solution.

In essence, all the conversions described above assume away externalities among coalitions and are ill-suited to handle situations where the actions of other players may affect the worth of the coalition. In Shubik's (1982) terminology, the coalitional function seems well suited to handle 'competitive games' (or c-games) where coalitions have antagonistic interests, or 'orthogonal' games where each coalition's worth is genuinely independent of the actions of the other players.[3] In any other situation, the description of the economic situation requires a more complete specification of the interactions between coalitions.

2.2 Partition Function Games

The earliest attempt to generalize coalitional functions to the case of externalities among coalitions is the introduction of *partition function games* by Thrall and Lucas (1963). In their original definition, Thrall and Lucas (1963) only considered TU games and simply proposed to extend coalitional functions by making the worth of a coalition a function of *all* the coalitions formed in the game. Before stating the formal definition recall that a *coalition structure* π is a partition of the set N of players, $\pi = \{C_1, C_2, \ldots, C_m\}$, representing all the coalitions formed in the game.

Definition 2.1: *A partition function v is a mapping which associates to each coalition structure π a vector in $\Re^{|\pi|}$, representing the worth of all the coalitions in π.*

It is easy to see that partition function games are a generalization of coalitional function games. If the worth of a coalition C is independent of the coalitions formed by the other players, the two definitions coincide. If, on the other hand, the formation of coalitions affects all the players in the game, there is no univocal relationship between partition functions and coalitional functions, and a game in partition function form carries more information about the underlying situation than a game in coalitional function form.

While partition function games may appear to be a natural extension of coalitional games, their interest is undermined by some conceptual difficulties in the definition and use of partition functions. First of all, partition functions have proved difficult to handle, and the extensions of cooperative solution concepts to partition functions due to Thrall and Lucas (1963) and Lucas and Maceli (1978) have yielded mixed results.

Second, and more importantly, the derivation of partition functions from games in strategic form poses some difficulties. To understand these problems, consider a game in strategic form and a coalition structure π. The given coalition structure imposes a fixed pattern of coalitions of players and, in particular, may include more than two coalitions. With more than two coalitions being formed, the minimax conversion of Aumann (1967) and the bargaining conversion of Harsanyi (1959) are not valid any longer. Rather, one needs to specify exactly how the various coalitions compete with one another.

Perhaps the most natural conversion is to suppose that, inside each coalition, players act cooperatively in order to maximize the coalitional surplus, but that coalitions compete in a non-cooperative way. This formalization was originally proposed by Ichiishi (1983), and later used by Ray and Vohra (1997). The partition function is then obtained as a Nash equilibrium payoff of the game played by the coalitions.

Formally, for a fixed coalition structure $\pi = \{C_1, C_2, \ldots, C_m\}$, let s^* be a vector of strategies such that:

$$\forall C_i \in \pi^i, \sum_{j \in C_i} u_j(s^*_{C_i}, s^*_{N/C_i}) \geq \sum_{j \in C_i} u_j(s_{C_i}, s^*_{N/C_i}),\ \forall s_{C_i} \in X_{j \in C_i} S_j.$$

Then define $v(C_i, \pi) = \sum_{j \in C_i} u_j(s^*)$.

This approach is clearly more satisfactory than the classical conversions based on *ad hoc* assumptions on the behaviour of the complementary coalition, but it also raises new difficulties. First, this approach cannot easily be extended to NTU games since, in that case, 'cooperative' behaviour inside each coalition is not well defined.[4] Second, even in the case of TU games, if the Nash equilibrium of the game played by coalitions is not unique, the partition function is not well defined.[5]

A third difficulty is linked to the interpretation of transferable utility in partition function games. The definition implicitly supposes that utility is transferable inside each coalition, but not across coalitions. The lack of transferability of utility across coalitions is in fact the defining feature of the partition function approach. In order to model cooperative situations with spillovers by partition function, one thus needs to justify this lack of transferability on either institutional or conceptual grounds.

Finally, it is useful to study how the classical properties of coalitional functions can be extended to partition functions. First of all, partition functions should satisfy *superadditivity* since, as in the case of coalitional functions, whatever strategies chosen by two coalitions A and B can be replicated by the coalition $A \cup B$. However, in partition function games, the definition of superadditivity needs to be qualified: for superadditivity to hold, it must be that the coalition structure formed by players in $N \backslash (A \cup B)$ remains constant.

Definition 2.2: *A partition function v is* superadditive *if and only if, for any coalition structure* π *and any two coalitions* A *and* B *in* π, $v(A \cup B, \pi \backslash \{A,B\} \cup \{A \cup B\}) \geq v(A,\pi) + v(B,\pi)$.

By a similar extension, one can define *monotonicity* of a partition function as follows.

Definition 2.3: *A partition function v is* monotonic *if for any two coalitions A and* $B \subset A$, for any partition π *containing A and any partition* π' *containing B such that* π *and* π' *coincide on* $N \backslash A$, $v(A,\pi) \geq v(B,\pi')$.

The following lemma is easily established:

Lemma 2.4: *If a partition function v is superadditive, then it is monotonic.*
Proof: Consider two sets A, $B \subset A$ and two partitions π and π' coinciding on $N \backslash A$ such that $A \in \pi$ and $B \in \pi'$. Since π and π coincide on $N \backslash A$, there must exist a collection $\{C_1, C_2, \ldots, C_m\}$ in π' such that $B \cup C_1 \cup C_2 \cup \ldots \cup C_m = A$. By superadditivity:

$$v(B \cup C_1, \pi' \backslash \{B, C_1\} \cup \{B \cup C_1\}) \geq v(B, \pi'),$$

and by a repeated application of this inequality, $v(A,\pi) \geq v(B,\pi')$.

Note that the monotonicity of partition functions implies that the grand coalition is always an efficient coalition structure. Hence in any game of coalition formation, the formation of a fragmented coalition structure is an inefficient outcome.

The additional information contained in the partition function allows us to describe new properties which cannot be defined in games in coalitional function form. In particular, the effect of the formation of a coalition on external players can be precisely described. Depending on whether the formation of a coalition is beneficial or harmful to external players, the two concepts of positive and negative spillovers can be defined.

Definition 2.5: *A partition function v exhibits* positive spillovers *if, for any partition* π, *and any two coalitions A and B in* $\pi, v(C, \pi \backslash \{A,B\} \cup \{A \cup B\}) \geq v(C,\pi)$, *for all coalitions* $C \neq A,B$ in π.

Definition 2.6: *A partition function v exhibits* negative spillovers *if, for any partition* π, *and any two coalitions A and B in* $\pi, v(C,\pi \backslash \{A,B\} \cup \{A \cup B\}) \leq v(C,\pi)$, *for all coalitions* $C \neq A,B$ in π.

2.3 Valuations

While the partition function represents the natural extension of coalitional functions to games with externalities, most economic applications yield a specific representation of gains from cooperation, called a *valuation*. As opposed to a partition function, a valuation assigns to each coalition structure, not a vector of coalitional worths but a vector of individual payoffs.[6] The term 'valuation' indicates that each agent is able to evaluate directly the payoff she obtains in different coalition structures.

Valuations thus emerge when the rule of division of the payoffs between coalition members is fixed. Arguably, this assumption is a severe restriction on the cooperative situations which can be represented by valuations. However, fixed rules of division appear naturally in many economic applications and in theoretical studies of coalition formation based on a two-stage structure.

Many studies of coalition formation distinguish between two stages: a first stage of coalition formation and a second stage in which payoffs are distributed among coalition members. Hence, at the time the coalition is formed, players evaluate the payoff they obtain in different coalition structures according to a fixed sharing rule. This is the structure adopted by Shenoy (1979) and Hart and Kurz (1983) in their study of endogenous coalition formation, by Myerson (1978) in his 'threats and settlement game' and by Aumann and Myerson (1988) in their analysis of the endogenous formation of links between players. The valuations used by these authors differ. Shenoy (1979) adopts Aumann and Drèze's (1974) extension of the

Shapley value to games with fixed coalition structures, Hart and Kurz (1983) consider Owen's (1977) extension of the Shapley value to games with groups of players and Aumann and Myerson (1988) use Myerson's (1977) value for games with graphs of players.

In economic applications, valuations emerge as the outcome of a two-stage process where coalitions are formed in the first stage and agents make decisions, given a fixed coalition structure, in the second stage. For example, firms form cartels or associations in the first stage of the game and then compete on the market in the second stage. Similarly, countries form customs unions in the first stage of the game, abolishing tariffs among themselves and selecting jointly an external tariff, thereby affecting the environment in which firms compete in the second stage of the game. In these economic applications, if individual decisions in the second stage of the game give rise to a unique payoff to all agents, the cooperative situation can be represented by a valuation mapping coalition structures into vectors of individual payoffs.[7]

Definition 2.7: *A valuation v is a mapping which associates to each coalition structure* π *a vector of individual payoffs in* $\Re^n$.

The description of gains from cooperation by a valuation thus assumes away one of the original problems of endogenous coalition formation: the distribution of the coalitional surplus among coalition members. On the other hand, this formulation allows us to analyse more precisely the role of spillovers between coalitions, and in most of this survey I will be working with valuations.

Importantly, it should be noted that *valuations are not necessarily super-additive nor monotonic*. Since the rule of payoff division is fixed, the usual reasoning showing that, in the coalition $A \cup B$, agents necessarily obtain higher payoffs than in the separate coalitions A and B, does not hold. As a consequence, an agent might receive a lower payoff in the coalition A than in a subset B of that coalition. Hence, in games described by a valuation, *the grand coalition is not necessarily efficient* and games of endogenous coalition formation might yield fragmented coalition structures.[8]

Finally, I just mention that positive and negative spillovers can easily be defined in the context of valuations, and the formal definitions are given below.

Definition 2.8: *A valuation v exhibits* positive (resp. negative) spillovers *if, for any partition* π, *and any two coalitions A and B in* π, $v_i(\pi \backslash \{A,B\} \cup \{A \cup B\}) \geq (\text{resp.} \leq) v_i(\pi)$, *for all players* $i \notin A \cup B$.

3. SIMULTANEOUS GAMES OF COALITION FORMATION

The first class of simultaneous games I consider are *simultaneous games* where all players announce at the same time their decision to form coalitions. In such games, it appears that the set of Nash equilibria is often quite large – forcing the analyst to use some refinements in order to make interesting predictions. These refinements, in turn, are usually of a cooperative nature, involving joint moves on the part of players. Hence the study of simultaneous games of coalition formation is at the frontier between cooperative and non-cooperative game theory, borrowing ideas and results from the two fields. Following Yi and Shin (1995), I separate simultaneous games of coalition formation into two types: (i) open membership games and (ii) exclusive membership games. Open membership games are games where players are free to join or leave any coalition. Exclusive membership games are games where outsiders are not free to join a coalition. In both cases, I start the analysis with the simplest games, the open membership game proposed by d'Aspremont et al. (1983) and the exclusive membership game due to von Neumann and Morgenstern (1944). The study is then extended to more complex processes of coalition formation, and various refinements of Nash equilibrium are introduced.

3.1 Open Membership Games

In open membership games, any player is free to join or leave a coalition. Accordingly, players cannot specify in advance the coalition they wish to form. Rather, players announce a message (for instance, their willingness to participate in a coalition), and coalitions are formed by all players who make the same announcement. We will discuss two such games: the cartel formation game of d'Aspremont et al. (1983) and the open membership game proposed by Yi and Shin (1995).

3.1.1 The cartel formation game

The cartel formation game of d'Aspremont et al. (1983) is the simplest example of an open membership game. All players in N simultaneouly announce a choice in the set $\{Y, N\}$. Let C be the set of all players who announce Y. This set is the coalition formed in the game, the coalition structure formed is $\pi = C \cup \{j\}_{j \notin C}$ and each player receives a payoff given by $v_i(C \cup \{j\}_{j \notin C})$.

This simple participation game has been used by d'Aspremont et al. (1983) to analyse the formation of a 'dominant' cartel on a market. They analyse the *Nash equilibria* of the game and show that the Nash equilibrium outcomes correspond to the two intuitive concepts of *internal stability* (no player who announces Y has an incentive to announce N) and *external stability* (no player who announces N has an incentive to announce Y). It is important to note that, in this game, membership to the cartel is open, but individual players cannot be forced to accept the formation of a cartel, that is, by announcing N, individual players commit to remain independent in the game.

It is easy to see that the cartel formation game always has a Nash equilibrium where no coalition is formed. In fact, if all $n-1$ other players announce N, announcing N is obviously a best response. Whether or not this game possesses a non-trivial equilibrium is a more difficult question.[9] In general, there is no guarantee that a non-trivial equilibrium exists, and if it exists, that it is unique.[10] This, of course, may force us to consider refinements of the set of Nash equilibria.

Another obvious defect of the cartel formation game is that it only allows for the formation of *one* coalition on the market. The next game I present retains the features of open membership while allowing for an arbitrary coalition structure to form.

3.1.2 The open membership game

The general open membership game I discuss below was suggested by Yi and Shin (1995). In this game, the strategy space of the players is a message space M with $|M| \geq n$. (There are at least as many different messages as players.) All players simultaneously announce a message in M. Coalitions are then formed by all players who have announced the same message, $C(m) = \{i \in N, m_i = m\}$ for all $m \in M$. The coalition structure formed is then given by $\pi = \{C(m)\}$, $\forall m, C(m) \neq \emptyset$, and each player obtains a payoff $v_i(\{C(m)\})$.

It turns out that this game is not a direct generalization of the cartel formation game of d'Aspremont et al. (1983) because individual players cannot commit to remain independent in the game. In fact, in the general open membership game, any player can form a coalition with another player simply by announcing the same message.[11] Since players can thus 'force' the formation of coalitions with other players, it is not necessarily true that the trivial coalition structure consisting of singletons is a Nash equilibrium of the game.[12] On the other hand, since entry into a coalition is free, it is easy to obtain a condition under which the only Nash equilibrium outcome of the game is the grand coalition.

Proposition 3.1 (Yi, 1997): *Suppose that, for any two coalitions A and B with* $|A| \geq |B|$, *any player i in B and any partition* π *containing A and B,* $v_i(\pi \backslash \{A,B\} \cup \{A \cup \{i\}, B \backslash \{i\}\}) > v_i(\pi)$, *then the only Nash equilibrium outcome of the open membership game is the grand coalition.*

Proof: First note that, if all other players announce a message m, by the hypothesis, player i obtains a higher payoff in the grand coalition than in the coalition structure $\pi = \{N \backslash \{i\}, \{i\}\}$ so that it is a best response to announce the same message m. On the other hand, for any other coalition structure, it is possible to find a player who belongs to a small coalition and who would benefit from joining a larger coalition.

Proposition 3.1 shows that under a rather mild monotonicity requirement the only Nash equilibrium outcome of the open membership game is the grand coalition.[13] In fact, since coalition members cannot prevent the entry of outsiders into the coalition, the coalition structures formed under open membership can be expected to be larger than under exclusive membership.

3.2 Exclusive Membership Games

In exclusive membership games, players are not free to join an existing coalition. The composition of coalitions is announced in advance and only those coalitions which are announced can be formed. Two situations may arise: either coalitions are formed as soon as some of their members agree to join (this is the case in the game Δ), or the formation of a coalition requires the unanimous agreement of its members (this is the case in the game Γ). In both cases, Nash equilibria are usually not unique, and refinements need to be imposed in order to obtain a sharp prediction on the equilibrium coalition structures.

3.2.1 The game Γ

The first example of a simultaneous game of coalition formation is the game originally proposed by von Neumann and Morgenstern (1944, pp. 243–4). This game was later reintroduced by Hart and Kurz (1983) as the game Γ. In this game, the strategy (or message) space of any player i is the set of all coalitions to which she belongs:

$$S_i = \{C \subset N, i \in C\}.$$

A coalition C is formed if and only if all members i of C have chosen $s_i = C$. Hence, in the game Γ, a coalition can only be formed if all its members unanimously agree to participate.

Intuitively, in the game Γ, membership is exclusive because all members announce beforehand the list of potential coalition members. Furthermore, for a coalition to form, unanimous agreement of all potential members is required. This definition implies that whenever a member deviates and leaves a coalition, the coalition breaks apart and all former coalition members form singletons.

3.2.2 The game Δ

Hart and Kurz (1983) propose an alternative exclusive membership game, called the game Δ. In this game, the strategy space of agent i is the same as in game $\Gamma(S_i = \{C \subset N, i \in C\})$, but the outcome function is different. In the game Δ, coalitions are formed by all players who have announced the same coalition, whether or not the formation of the coalition has been approved unanimously by all its members. Formally, for any possible message (for example, coalition) m, let $C(m) = \{i, s_i = m\}$ denote the coalition formed by all players who have announced m. Notice that, as in the case of open membership games, messages in the game Δ are used as coordination devices. However, as opposed to the case of open membership, messages also carry an important restriction on the coalitions that can be formed. Only those coalitions that are announced by the players are feasible in the game.

Intuitively, in the game Δ, membership is exclusive because players announce beforehand the list of coalition members. However, for a coalition to form, the participation of all listed members is not needed: all those agents who agree to participate form a coalition. This definition implies that, whenever a member leaves a coalition, she assumes that all other coalition members remain together as in the open membership games. In an interesting extension to the two games studied in Hart and Kurz (1983), Thoron (2000) proposes the following set up: after some players have chosen to deviate, the members of the coalitions they left can choose whether to disintegrate or stick together. In this extension of the model, external players thus react strategically (though in a limited sense) to the deviation of a group of players.

3.2.3 Cooperative refinements of Nash equilibrium

In both the game Γ and the game Δ, as in the case of cartel formation, the trivial coalition structure with singletons is a Nash equilibrium outcome: if all other players announce singletons, it is a best response for a player to announce a singleton as well. It thus appears that the set of Nash equilibria is too large to allow for sharp predictions.

In order to refine the set of equilibria, Yi and Shin (1995) and Hart and Kurz (1983) propose to consider cooperative refinements: coalition-proof Nash equilibria in the case of Yi and Shin (1995), and strong Nash equilibria in Hart and Kurz (1983). I recall here the definitions of these two solution concepts due to Bernheim, Peleg and Whinston (1987) and Aumann (1959) respectively.

In order to define coalition-proof Nash equilibria some preliminary notation is needed. For any strategic game $G = \{N, \{S_i\}_{i \in N}, \{u_i\}_{i \in N}\}$, and any fixed strategy profile σ define the reduced game for coalition C given σ as follows:

$$G_\sigma^C = \{C, \{S_i\}_{i \in C}, \{\tilde{u}_i\}_{i \in C}\},$$

where $\tilde{u}_i(s) = u_i(s_C, \sigma_{N/C})$. In words, the reduced game is obtained by fixing the strategies of all the players outside C and defining the utility of every player given this fixed strategy choices. Coalition-proof Nash equilibria are then defined recursively.

Definition 3.2 (Bernheim, Peleg and Whinston, 1987): *For $n = 1$, σ_i is a coalition-proof Nash equilibrium (CPNE) if and only if σ_i is a maximiser of u_i over S_i. Let $n > 1$ and assume that CPNE have been defined for all $m < n$. Then:*

- σ is self-enforcing for G if and only if, for all $C \subset N$, $C \neq N$, σ_C is a CPNE of G_s^C.
- *σ is a CPNE if and only if it is self-enforcing and there does not exist another self-enforcing strategy σ' such that $u_i(\sigma') > u_i(\sigma)$ for all $i \in N$.*

Definition 3.3 (Aumann, 1959): *A* strong Nash equilibrium (SNE) *is a strategy profile σ for which there does not exist a coalition $C \subset N$ and a strategy profile σ'_C for players in C such that $u_i(\sigma'_C, \sigma_{N \setminus C}) > u_i(\sigma) \forall i \in c$.*

Very briefly, these two solution concepts introduce a cooperative element in the analysis of the game. An SNE is not only immune to unilateral deviations, but also to deviations by coalitions. In a CPNE, the only coalitional deviations which are considered are those which satisfy a 'consistency' requirement – coalitional deviations must themselves be immune to further deviations by subcoalitions.

In their study of the SNE of the games Γ and Δ, Hart and Kurz (1983) only prove, by a counter-example, that SNE may fail to exist.

Proposition 3.4: *The games Γ and Δ may not admit SNE.*
Proof: See the counter-example in Hart and Kurz (1984).

For CPNE, Yi and Shin (1995) do not prove any general result. They characterise the CPNE of the games Δ and Γ for the specific case of cartel formation in Cournot oligopolies.[14] The existence of CPNE of the games Γ and Δ in general settings is still an open question.

As a final remark, the non-existence of SNE and CPNE may be due to the fact that *any coalition* is allowed to propose a deviation. In many applications, such as local public finance, the creation of new coalitions may be prohibitively costly. In that case, the right equilibrium concept should only involve individual moves. However, since individual players move from one coalition to another, the approval of the coalitions which are left or joined may be required. This in turn induces a restriction on the set of coalitions who may propose a deviation which might lead to an existence result.[15]

4. SEQUENTIAL GAMES OF COALITION FORMATION

The study of simultaneous games of coalition formation raises three important difficulties: (i) the set of Nash equilibria is usually very large, (ii) this multiplicity of equilibria imposes the use of a selection mechanism which might be too stringent (as in the case of SNE studied by Hart and Kurz (1983)), and (iii) in simultaneous games, players cannot be 'far-sighted' in the sense that individual deviations cannot be countered by subsequent moves. I view this last difficulty as the most disturbing feature of simultaneous coalition formation games. For example, consider the departure of a player from a coalition. In the simultaneous games of coalition formation, either the other coalition members remain together (in the open membership games and in the game Δ) or the coalition breaks apart (in the game Γ). But in both these formulations, members of the coalition that was left by the deviator respond in an *ad hoc* fashion; they are not allowed to react to the move of the deviator.

The problems of simultaneous games of coalition formation have led to the formulation of *sequential games of coalition formation* where the process is described by an explicit extensive form non-cooperative game. The earliest extensive form game was proposed by Aumann and Myerson (1988) in a setting slightly different from the classical coalition formation problem.[16] Aumann and Myerson (1988) explicitly emphasize that they want to study farsighted players, who take their actions envisioning the final consequences of their decisions.

In the context of games without spillovers, sequential processes have been proposed by Selten (1981), Chatterjee et al. (1993), Moldovanu (1992) and Perry and Reny (1994) among others. In most of these games, the basic structure is an extension to n players of Rubinstein's (1982) alternative-offers bargaining model. This structure was extended to games with spillovers by Bloch (1996) and Ray and Vohra (1999). These are the two models that will be presented here.

4.1 Sequential Coalition Formation with Fixed Payoff Division

In the first paper, Bloch (1996) studies a sequential game of coalition formation when the rule of payoff division is fixed, so that the underlying cooperation structure is represented by a valuation. The exact specification of the extensive form borrows from Rubinstein's (1982) bargaining game and its extension by Chatterjee et al. (1993).

The game proceeds as follows. Players are ordered according to a fixed rule. The first player starts the game by proposing the formation of a coalition C to which she belongs. Each prospective member responds to the proposal in the order determined by the fixed rule. If one of the players rejects the proposal, she must make a counteroffer and propose a coalition C' to which she belongs. If all members accept, the coalition is formed. All members of C then withdraw from the game, and the first player in $N \backslash C$ starts making a proposal.

This game describes in the simplest way a procedure where coalitions are formed *in sequence*. The main characteristic of the game is that, once a coalition has been formed, the game is only played among the remaining players. The extensive form thus embodies a high degree of commitment by the players. When players agree to join a coalition, they are bound to remain in that coalition. They can neither leave the coalition nor propose to change the coalition at later stages of the game.

It is assumed that players do not discount the future. Rather, in the case of an infinite play, the players who are still in the game receive a payoff of zero. Otherwise, if the game finishes in finite time, a coalition structure is formed and players receive their payoff according to the underlying valuation.

As is well known, infinite-horizon games based on an alternating-offers scheme may have a multiplicity of subgame perfect equilibria. It is therefore important to restrict the set of subgame perfect equilibria by considering *stationary* strategies, which only depend on the current state of the game. The first result in Bloch (1996) shows that a stationary perfect equilibrium may fail to exist. This result is based on the following example:

Example 4.1: $N=\{a,b,c\}$, and ρ defines $a<b<c$

π	$v_a(\pi)$	$v_b(\pi)$	$v_c(\pi)$
$a\|b\|c$	1	1	1
$ab\|c$	3	2	1
$ac\|b$	2	1	3
$a\|bc$	1	3	2
abc	1	1	1

In this example, player a wants to form a coalition with player b, player b with player c, and player c with player a.

To show that the game does not admit any stationary equilibrium coalition structure, observe first that the three coalition structures $\{\{a,b,c\}\}$, $\{\{a\},\{b\},\{c\}\}$ and $\{\{a\},\{b,c\}\}$ cannot be supported by any equilibrium since player a would benefit from deviating and offering the formation of the coalition $\{a,c\}$ which player c would accept. The two other coalition structures $\{\{a,b\},\{c\}\}$ and $\{\{a,c\},\{b\}\}$ can be supported by equilibria in non-stationary strategies but not by a stationary perfect equilibrium.

For $\{\{a,b\},\{c\}\}$ to be supported by a stationary perfect equilibrium, it must be that player c rejects the offer $\{b,c\}$. But, in equilibrium, player c will only reject the offer $\{b,c\}$ if player a accepts the offer $\{a,c\}$. By stationarity, player b accepts the offer $\{a,b\}$ irrespective of the history of rejections which have preceded it. Hence, since player b always accepts the offer $\{a,b\}$, player a cannot accept the offer $\{a,c\}$.

Similarly, the coalition structure $\{\{a,c\},\{b\}\}$ is only supported by a strategy prescribing that player b rejects the offer $\{a,b\}$, implying that player c accepts the offer $\{b,c\}$. Since by stationarity, player a always accepts the offer $\{a,c\}$, player c should reject the offer $\{a,c\}$. Hence the game does not admit any stationary perfect equilibrium.

Even when they exist, stationary perfect equilibria of the sequential game differ in general from the SNE of the simultaneous games, as the following proposition shows:

Proposition 4.2 (Bloch, 1996): *The coalition structures generated by the stationary perfect equilibria of the sequential game may differ from the coalition structures generated by SNE of the games* Γ *and* Δ.
Proof: See the example in Bloch (1996).

However, Bloch (1996) shows that there exists a specific class of valuations for which stationary perfect equilibria exist and are easily characterized. These are *symmetric* valuations where the value of a coalition structure only depends on the size of coalitions and not on the identity of coalition members.[17] For symmetric valuations, a simple finite procedure is defined to characterize the symmetric stationary perfect equilibria of the game.

The finite procedure runs as follows. Player 1 starts the game and chooses an integer k_1 in the interval $[1, n]$. Player k_1+1 then moves and chooses an integer k_2 in the set $[1, n-k]$. Player k_1+k_2+1 chooses at the next stage an integer k_3 in the set $[1, n-k_1-k_2]$. The game continues until the sequence of integers $(k_1,k_2,\ldots,k_j,\ldots,k_J)$ satisfies $\Sigma k_j=n$.

The exact equivalence between symmetric stationary perfect equilibria of the sequential game and the coalition structures obtained as outcome of the finite procedure is described in the following two propositions:

Proposition 4.3 (Bloch, 1996): *For any coalition structure generated by a symmetric stationary perfect equilibrium of the sequential game, there exists an equivalent coalition structure which is obtained as a subgame perfect equilibrium of the finite procedure.*

Proposition 4.4 (Bloch, 1996; Ray and Vohra, 1999): *Consider a coalition structure π obtained as a subgame perfect equilibrium of the finite procedure with the property that payoffs are decreasing in the order in which coalitions are formed. Then there exists a symmetric stationary perfect equilibrium of the sequential game generating a coalition structure equivalent to π.*
Proof: See Bloch (1996).

Since the finite procedure described above always yields a subgame perfect equilibrium, and this equilibrium is generically unique, the equivalence result of propositions 4.3 and 4.4 imply the following corollary:

Corollary 4.5: *For symmetric valuations, when the finite procedure yields a coalition structure with the property that payoffs are decreasing in the order in which coalitions are formed, there exists a symmetric stationary perfect equilibrium of the sequential game. Furthermore, this equilibrium is generically unique.*

To conclude, for a specific class of valuations (symmetric valuations with the additional property that payoffs are decreasing in the order in which coalitions are formed), the sequential game proposed by Bloch (1996) yields a particularly sharp prediction. A symmetric stationary equilibrium always exists and is (generically) unique. This result should be contrasted to the multiplicity of Nash equilibria (and the possible non-existence of SNE) in the simultaneous case.[18] In applications, the sequential game might thus prove to be more useful than the simultaneous games.

4.2 Sequential Coalition Formation and Bargaining

In a recent paper, Ray and Vohra (1999) have generalized the game proposed by Bloch (1996) by allowing for an *endogenous distribution of coalitional gains*. This paper represents a very important step in the study of endogenous coalition formation, since it is the first paper to tackle simultaneously the three questions posed in the Introduction to this book.

In Ray and Vohra (1999), the underlying cooperative situation is represented by a *TU partition function game* rather than a valuation. The main difference between the game proposed by Bloch (1996) and the game studied by Ray and Vohra (1999) stems from the strategy spaces of the players. In Bloch (1996), players simply announce the coalition they want to form; in Ray and Vohra (1999), players simultaneously announce a coalition and the division of the coalitional worth.[19]

Ray and Vohra's (1999) first result shows the existence of a stationary perfect equilibrium of the bargaining game (in mixed strategies). An important feature of their existence result is that players only need to use a mixed strategy in their choice of coalitions (and not in their offer of division of the coalitional worth).

In symmetric games, where the partition function only depends on the size composition of the coalition structures, Ray and Vohra (1999) analyse in depth the stationary perfect equilibria of the bargaining game. They introduce the notion of *proposer-symmetric* equilibria, where at any stage of the game the payoff of player i as a proposer is identical to the payoff of player j as a proposer.

Ray and Vohra (1999) introduce a finite algorithm to compute coalition structures, which is almost equivalent to that proposed in Bloch (1996). (The only difference is that, in case of indifference between two strategies, Ray and Vohra (1999) assume that a player selects the *largest* coalition size.) They show that the coalition structure generated by proposer-symmetric equilibria must be equivalent to those obtained in the finite algorithm. Ray and Vohra (1999) also study no-delay equilibria and prove that if an equilibrium does not involve delay it must be proposer-symmetric.

The results in Ray and Vohra (1999) can be summarized by the following list of inclusions:

Proposition 4.6: *Let E_1 be the set of stationary perfect equilibria (SPE) of the bargaining game, E_2 the set of SPE yielding the coalition structure obtained by the finite algorithm, E_3 the set of proposer-symmetric SPE and E_4 the set of no-delay SPE. Then:*

$$E_1 \supset E_2 \supset E_3 \supset E_4.$$

Proof: See Ray and Vohra (1999).

In their paper, Ray and Vohra (1999) present examples to show that these inclusions may be strict. Furthermore, it is important to observe that the existence of SPE (nonemptiness of the set E_1) does not guarantee that a SPE yielding the same coalition structure as the finite algorithm always exists (that is, that the set E_2 is nonempty.) In the paper, Ray and Vohra

(1999) propose a stronger requirement in order to show that the set E_4 is nonempty. The sufficient condition they define can be interpreted intuitively as the fact that, in a constrained version of the finite algorithm, the payoffs obtained by coalition members are always decreasing in the order in which coalitions are formed.

In the second part of their paper, Ray and Vohra (1999) generalize their results to all TU partition function games and provide a general algorithm for computing the no-delay SPE of the bargaining game. I would like to emphasize what I believe are the two most important contributions of Ray and Vohra (1999): (i) they show that, in symmetric games, the assumption of equal division can be supported in a bargaining game and that the coalition structures formed can be obtained by the same finite algorithm as in the fixed payoff division case, and (ii) they provide a generalization of the finite algorithm to the non-symmetric case.

4.3 Recent Contributions to Sequential Coalition Formation

In recent years, two important contributions to the theory of sequential formation of coalitions in partition function games have been made.

Montero (1999) extends Okada (1996)'s model of sequential formation of coalitions to games with externalities. This extensive form differs from the extensive form studied in Bloch (1996) and Ray and Vohra (1999) in that players are randomly chosen to make an offer after the rejection of any proposal. In a sense, Montero's (1999) extensive form gives less incentives for a player to reject a proposal, since she is not chosen with probability 1 to make a counter offer next period. In turn, this affects the strategies of a player when it is her turn to propose the formation of a coalition.

On balance, it is difficult to point out precisely how differences in the extensive form affect the equilibrium coalition structure. Montero (1999) provides examples to compare her analysis with that of Ray and Vohra (1999). She shows that efficiency can sometimes be achieved through random choice of proposers when it is not obtained with a fixed rule of order, and that the game with random proposers does not necessarily lead to the formation of coalitions maximizing average per capita payoffs. In Montero's (1999) paper, the emphasis is put on the efficiency of the subgame perfect equilibrium outcome of the game. Two sources of inefficiency can arise: delay in reaching the agreement, and the formation of an inefficient coalition structure. Focussing on the case where the grand coalition is the efficient coalition structure, Montero (1999) provides some (surprisingly) stringent sufficient conditions for efficiency of the subgame perfect equilibrium outcome.

Gomes (1999) directly tackles the issue of the inefficiency of the coalition structures obtained in Bloch (1996) and Ray and Vohra (1999) by allowing players to renegotiate the formation of an efficient structure after the coalitions have been formed. More precisely, Gomes (1999) considers an extensive form similar to Gul's (1989) non-cooperative game implementing the Shapley value. At any period in time, two players are matched and bargain over the acquisition of the assets of the other player. Flow payoffs accrue according to an underlying game in partition function form. In three-player games, Gomes (1999) shows that there exists a unique expected stationary perfect equilibrium payoff, termed the 'negotiation value'. The negotiation value is shown to be efficient, to coincide with the Nash bargaining solution in bargaining problems, and with the Shapley value in zero-sum and majority voting games.

5. STABLE COALITION STRUCTURES

In this section, I turn my attention to *cooperative* concepts of stability which have been proposed for games with spillovers. Unfortunately, most of these stability concepts lack clear non-cooperative foundations. Nevertheless, they provide useful benchmarks and have been used extensively in economic applications. I first describe the most elementary stability concepts, which are based on two extreme notions of core stability. I then describe various restrictions on the set of deviations and deviating coalitions which have been proposed in the literature.

5.1 Core Stable Coalition Structures

As noted by Greenberg (1994), in games without spillovers the most natural concept of stability is directly derived from the core: a coalition structure is said to be *core stable* if there does not exist a group of agents who would obtain a higher payoff by forming another coalition. Unfortunately, this simple definition does not easily generalize to games with spillovers. In a game represented by a valuation, or a partition function, the payoff obtained by a deviating coalition is not well defined. This payoff depends on the *reaction of external players* to the deviation.

Two extreme solution concepts have been proposed to deal with this issue. The first solution concept, initially proposed by Shenoy (1979) and termed 'core stability', supposes that, following a deviation, external players react as if they were *maximizing* the payoff of the deviating coalition. This is clearly a very optimistic conjecture on the part of members of the deviating coalition. On the other hand, Hart and Kurz (1983) suggest looking at α and β stability concepts where members of the deviating coalition expect the worst from external players. As in the definitions of the α and β core, in an α stable coalition structure it is assumed that there does not exist a group of players who could obtain a higher payoff irrespective of the behaviour of the external players; in a β stable structure, there is no group of players who are guaranteed to obtain a higher payoff whatever the behaviour of the external players.

Formally, we define core stable, α stable and β stable coalition structures below. We assume that the underlying cooperative situation is represented by a valuation, but similar definitions could be given for partition function games.

Definition 5.1: *A coalition structure π is* core stable *if there does not exist a group C of players and a coalition structure $\pi' \supset C$ such that $\forall i \in C$, $v_i(\pi') > v_i(\pi)$.*

Definition 5.2: *A coalition structure π is* α-stable *if there does not exist a group C of players and a partition π'_C such that, for all partitions $\pi_{N\backslash C}$ formed by external players, $\forall i \in C$, $v_i(\pi'_c \cup \pi_{N\backslash C}) > v_i(\pi)$.*

Definition 5.3: *A coalition structure π is* β-stable *if there does not exist a group C of players such that, for all partitions $\pi_{N\backslash C}$ of external players, there exists a partition π_C of C such that $\forall i \in C$, $v_i(\pi_C \cup \pi_{N\backslash C}) > v_i(\pi)$.*

From the definitions, it is easy to see that deviations occur more frequently under core stability than under β stability, and under β stability than under α-stability. Hence, letting C_c, C_β and C_α denote the set of core stable, β-stable and α-stable coalition structures, one easily obtains the following inclusions: $C_c \subset C_\beta \subset C_\alpha$. Furthermore, as we have noted, the SNE of the games Γ and Δ can also be analysed as cooperative concepts of stability, where the external players behave according to an *ad hoc* rule. In the game Δ, members of a coalition left by some players stick together, whereas in the game Γ, coalitions left by some players dissolve. Since these *ad hoc* rules of behaviour can be viewed as intermediate assumptions on the behaviour of an external player, we obtain the following list of inclusions:

Proposition 5.4: (Hart and Kurz, 1983; Kurz, 1988) *Let C_c, C_γ, C_δ, C_β and C_α denote the stable coalition structures under core stability, the Γ game, the Δ game, β-stability and α-stability respectively. Then:*

$$C_c \subset (C_\gamma \cup C_\delta) \subset C_\beta \subset C_\alpha.$$

Proof: Immediate from the definitions.

It thus appears that all concepts of stability proposed in Hart and Kurz (1983) can be ranked by inclusion. Unfortunately, even the largest solution concept C_α may be empty, as Hart and Kurz (1984) show in an example of a ten-player symmetric majority game:

Proposition 5.5 (Hart and Kurz, 1984): *There exist valuations v for which the set C_α is empty.*

5.2 Equilibrium Binding Agreements

The possible emptiness of the set of α stable coalition structures may indeed be due to the fact that *all* coalitional deviations are allowed. Ray and Vohra (1997) propose a new solution concept which, as the CPNE of Bernheim, Peleg and Whinston (1987) for non-cooperative games, rules out coalitional deviations which are not themselves immune to further deviations by subcoalitions. This solution concept – termed 'Equilibrium Binding Agreements' (EBA) – can be viewed as the most sophisticated notion of stability for games with spillovers. It is defined for games in strategic form, and EBA are strategy profiles. A coalition structure will be termed 'stable' if it can be supported by an EBA.

Intuitively, in their analysis of stable coalition structures, Ray and Vohra (1997) restrict the set of possible deviations by imposing a consistency requirement on the deviation. Furthermore, rather than postulating a fixed rule of behaviour on the part of external players. Ray and Vohra (1997) propose an ingenious definition of the reaction of external players to a deviation.

The formal definition of Equilibrium Binding Agreements is recursive and goes as follows. For the finest partition, consisting only of singletons, the set of EBA is simply the set of Nash equilibria of the game. Suppose now that EBAs have been defined for all partitions finer than a fixed partition π. Take a strategy profile x for the coalition structure π which is obtained as a Nash equilibrium of the game between coalitions, and cooperative play inside each coalition.

We say that (π,x) is *blocked* by (π',x') if π' is a refinement of π and there exists a collection of agents in the move from π to π' such that:

- x' is an EBA for π'.
- There exists a group of agents C such that $\forall i \in C, u_i(x') > u_i(x)$.
- Any remerging of other agents is also blocked by (π',x').
- Now x is an EBA for π if there does not exist any (π',x') which blocks (π,x).

In words, for a strategy profile to be an EBA, it must be immune to a coalitional deviation which (i) is consistent in the sense that no further deviations will occur inside the coalition, and (ii) can be supported by external players in the sense that if some external players were to remerge, this remerging would again be blocked by the same deviation.

In spite of its apparent complexity, the definition of EBA thus corresponds to natural consistency requirements on coalitional deviations. Clearly, as in other cooperative notions of stability, the process analysed by Ray and Vohra (1997) does not generally yield a unique stable coalition structure. Rather, the focus of the analysis in Ray and Vohra (1997) is on *efficiency* of the coalition structures supported by EBAs.

5.3 Membership Rights

The last class of cooperative stability concepts is closer in spirit to traditional solution concepts. In this class, it is the set of *deviating coalitions* which is restricted rather than the set of *coalitional deviations*. In particular, it is assumed that only individual players can deviate and that the only coalitions that may have a say are the coalitions left and joined by the player.

The motivation for restricting attention to individual moves comes from some economic applications, where the creation of new coalitions is prohibitively costly and movements of players only take place across existing coalitions. For example, in the studies inspired by Tiebout (1956) on the provision of local public goods, jurisdictions are usually assumed to be fixed, and economic agents can only move from one jurisdiction to another.

Formally, there exists a variety of solution concepts based on individual moves depending on which coalitions can object to the move of the player. In Greenberg's (1977) original concept of *individually stable coalition structures*, agreement was required from the coalition joined by the individual player. The concept of *individually stable contractual coalition structures* later proposed by Drèze and Greenberg (1980) requires agreement both from the coalition left and the coalition joined by the player. Recently, Sertel (1993) and Eren (1993) have generalized these solution concepts by defining *property rights* for coalitions. These property rights are money transfers which need to be paid for participation in a coalition or departure from a coalition.

It should be noted that, in the context of games without spillovers, the existence of individually stable coalition structures has been proved for a large class of models (see Greenberg, 1994). In fact, it turns out that by only allowing deviations by a group formed by an individual and a coalition, this solution concept is much less demanding than concepts based on core stability. It thus seems that the existence of individually stable coalition structures in games with spillovers could be obtained for some classes of games. But the study of existence of stable coalition structures with property rights in games with spillovers still remains to be done.

6. GAMES WITH POSITIVE SPILLOVERS

In this section, I present and discuss the outcome of several models of coalition formation in situations where the underlying cooperative game exhibits positive spillovers. Positive spillovers arise in a number of economic models, where outsiders benefit from the formation of a coalition. In these models, coalition members provide some type of public good which benefits all the players, and external members enjoy the public good without supporting its cost. The two most studied examples of coalition formation with positive spillovers are the formation of cartels on oligopolistic markets and of coalitions providing pure public goods. I will study both of these models in turn. However, before entering into the details of the models, I first present some general results on games with positive spillovers due to Yi (1997).

6.1 Games with Positive Spillovers: General Results

In his study of games with positive spillovers, Yi (1997) compares the outcomes of different games of coalition formation for a class of symmetric valuation satisfying three properties: (i) positive spillovers, (ii) negative association between coalition size and payoff, and (iii) inverse monotonicity for small coalitions. Before I can formally list these three axioms, I need to define Yi and Shin's (1995) concept of *concentration*, which is not to be confused with the more classical notion of coarsening.

Definition 6.1: *A coalition structure* $\pi=\{n_1,n_2,\ldots,n_m\}$ *is a* concentration *of a coalition structure* $\pi'=\{n'_1,n'_2,\ldots,n'_{m'}\}$ *if there exist two subcoalition structures, D and D′ of* π *and* π', $D=\{k_1,k_2,\ldots,k_s\}$ *with* $k_1 \geq k_2 \geq \ldots \geq k_s$ *and* $D'=\{k'_1,k'_2,\ldots,k'_{s+t}\}$ *with* $k'_1 \geq k'_2 \geq \ldots \geq k'_{s+t}$ *such that (i)* $\pi \backslash D=\pi' \backslash D'$ *and (ii)* $\Sigma_{i=1}^{j} k_i > \Sigma_{i=1}^{j} k'_j$ *for all* $j=1,2\ldots,s$.

In words, a coalition structure π is a concentration of π' if it can be obtained by picking members of some coalitions in π' and adding those members to larger or equal sized coalitions in π'. Not that this definition *is not* equivalent to the more classical definition of a coarsening. It is easy to see that any coarsening is a concentration, but the following example shows that the reverse implication is not necessarily true. The coalition structure

$\pi = \{3,3\}$ is a concentration of the coalition structure $\pi' = \{2,2,2\}$ but it is not a coarsening. The three axioms can then be expressed as follows:

Axiom 6.2 (Positive spillovers): *Consider two coalition structures π and π' such that $C \in \pi'$ and $\pi \backslash C$ is a concentration of $\pi' \backslash C$ then $v_i(\pi) > v_i(\pi')$ for all $i \in C$.*

Axiom 6.3 (Negative association): *For any coalition structure π and any two coalitions C and D in π, for all $i \in C, j \in D$, $v_i(\pi) < v_j(\pi)$ if and only if $|C| > |D|$.*

Axiom 6.4 (Inverse montonicity): *Consider two coalitions C and D in π with $|C| > |D|$. Then $\forall i \in D$, $v_i(\pi) > v_i(\pi \backslash \{C,D\} \cup \{C \backslash \{j\}, D \cup \{j\}\})$.*

Under these three axioms, Yi and Shin (1995) and Yi (1997) study the outcomes of the open membership game, the games Γ and Δ, the sequential game of coalition formation and Ray and Vohra's (1997) equilibrium binding agreements. The results are as follows:

Proposition 6.5 (Yi and Shin, 1995; Yi, 1997): *Suppose that the three axioms of positive spillovers, negative association and inverse monotonicity hold. The coalition structures obtained as a CPNE of the open membership game are always less concentrated than any CPNE of the game Δ. All SNE of the game Γ give rise to coalition structures which are more concentrated than in the CPNE of the game Δ. The unique SPE of the sequential game gives rise to a coalition structure which is more concentrated than the coalition structures obtained as CPNE of the game Δ. Finally, the EBA can support coalition structures which are more concentrated than those obtained as CPNE of the game Δ.*

Proof: See Yi and Shin (1995) and Yi (1997).

The studies by Yi (1997) and Yi and Shin (1995) thus provide a general ordering on the coalition structures obtained under various games of coalition formation. In order to obtain a complete characterization of the coalition structures, one needs to go back to specific economic models.

6.2 Cartel Formation in a Homogeneous Cournot Oligopoly

The most famous economic model in which the issue of coalition formation with positive spillover arises is the model of cartels on oligopolistic markets. I consider here the simplest version of the model, where firms compete in quantities, produce a homogeneous good and face a linear demand schedule. Formally, let the inverse demand be given by:

$$P = 1 - \Sigma q_i.$$

I assume that all firms are identical, and may produce the homogeneous good at a constant marginal cost equal to zero. In this framework, fix a cartel structure $\pi = \{C_1, C_2, \ldots, C_k\}$ consisting of k different cartels. Given the assumption made on cost and demand structures, it is easy to see that competition between cartels gives rise to the same output as competition between k independent firms. Hence, each cartel will produce a quantity $q = (1/k+1)$ and obtain a profit $Pr = (1/(k+1)^2)$. The valuation (which gives the profit a firm obtains in any cartel structure) can thus be defined for any firm i in cartel C_j as:

$$v_i(\pi) = \frac{1}{(k+1)^2 \, |C_j|}.$$

It appears that the profit obtained by a firm only depends on (i) the size of the cartel to which it belongs, and (ii) the total number of cartels formed on the market. Furthermore, it is easy to check that the valuation satisfies the three axioms defined above. In fact, when the other players form a more concentrated coalition structure, the total number of cartels k goes down, thus increasing the payoff of an outside firm. It is also clear that, for a fixed coalition structure, members of smaller cartels obtain a higher payoff. Finally, it is easy to check that if one firm leaves a cartel C to join a cartel D, all members of the cartel D are worse off. Using the valuation defined above, I can now characterize the outcome of various games of coalition formation.

First, I need to define, following Salant, Switzer and Reynolds (1983), the *minimal profitable coalition size*. This is the smallest coalition size for which a coalition member obtains a higher payoff than if all firms are independent, that is:

$$k^* = \min\left\{k, \frac{1}{k(n-k+1)^2} \geq \frac{1}{(n+1)^2}\right\}.$$

It is easy to see that:

$$k^* = \frac{2n+3-\sqrt{4n+5}}{2},$$

a value which is never smaller than $0.8n$, namely 80 per cent of the firms on the market. Table 2.1 summarizes the outcomes of the games of coalition formation.

Table 2.1 Cartels

Open membership	$\{1,1,\ldots,1\}$
Game Γ	$\{k,1,\ldots,1\}$ for any $k \geq k^*$
Game Δ	$\{1,1,\ldots,1\}$
Sequential game	$\{k^*,1,\ldots,1\}$
α stability	$\{k,1,\ldots,1\}$ for any $k \geq k^*$
β stability	$\{k,1,\ldots,1\}$ for any $k \geq k^*$
Equilibrium binding agreements	Cyclical pattern for n to be stable

The precise proofs of these statements can be found in the papers by Yi and Shin (1995), Bloch (1996), and Ray and Vohra (1997). The intuition underlying the results is easy to grasp. In the game Δ and the open membership game, following the departure of one firm, members of a cartel remain together. This assumption makes it easy for a firm to leave the cartel and free-ride on the output reduction of other cartel members. Hence, in the only Nash equilibrium (and CPNE) of the game, firms remain independent and no cartel is formed.[20] In the game Δ and under the α and β stability concepts, following the departure of a firm, the cartel breaks down. This assumption clearly makes deviations more difficult and in fact any cartel of size greater than k^* can be supported as an SNE. In the sequential game, firms commit to stay out of the cartel until the number of remaining firms equals the minimal profitable cartel size. At that point, the remaining firms form a cartel. Finally, EBAs exhibit an interesting cyclical pattern, whereby the grand coalition $\pi = \{n\}$ is sometimes supported as a stable coalition structure, sometimes not, depending on the number of firms on the market.[21]

Important new contributions to the study of cartel formation in oligopolies have been made in recent years. Adopting a purely cooperative framework, Espinosa and Inarra (1995) and Horn and Persson (1996) characterize stable cartel structures in linear oligopolies. Espinosa and Inarra (1995) consider an oligopoly model with fixed costs, and show that, according to the values of the fixed costs, in the von Neumann and Morgenstern stable sets, one, two, three or n firms may be active on the market. Horn and Persson (1996) define a specific dominance relation for games in partition function form, and provide conditions under which the stable coalition structure comprises two firms and is efficient. Espinosa and Macho Stadler (2000) study the difficult problem of cartel formation when the members of the cartel provide an unobservable effort to reduce their costs. In this model of team production with moral hazard, they obtain a partial characterization of the equilibrium coalition structures in the sequential game of coalition formation introduced by Bloch (1996) and Ray and Vohra (1999). Finally, in a very original contribution, Cho, Jewell and Vohra (1999) analyse the formation of cartels of bidders in an auction with liquidity constrained bidders. Using the sequential model of coalition formation of Bloch (1996) and Ray and Vohra (1999), they show that in the equilibrium coalition structure either all bidders form a single cartel (when the bidders as a whole are not constrained) or form two coalitions of unequal size (when the bidders as a whole are liquidity constrained).

6.3 Pure Public Goods

The second application of games with positive spillovers are economies with pure public goods. In these economies, agents have an incentive to form coalitions in order to benefit from increasing returns to size in the production of public goods, but also have an incentive to leave the coalition and free-ride on the provision of public goods by coalition members. Recently, models inspired by pure public goods economies have been proposed to study the formation of International Environmental Agreements (IEA). Carraro and Siniscalco (1993), Carraro and Moriconi (1998), Barrett (1994) and Chander and Tulkens (1992) study the participation of countries to IEAs by which they commit to reduce (or abate) the pollution they emit. In that case, pollution abatement is viewed as a pure public good provided by the signatories of the IEA. I analyse here a simple public good model inspired by Barrett's (1994) study of IEAs. (See also Ray and Vohra (2001) for a complete analysis of a similar model.)

I consider an economy with n identical agents. Each agent benefits from the public good and obtains a utility which is assumed to be linear in the total amount of public good provided:

$$U_i(x) = x.$$

I also assume that each agent owns a technology to produce the public good, and that the cost of producing the amount x_i of the public good is given by:

$$C_i(x_i) = \frac{1}{2} x_i^2.$$

Note that, since individual cost functions are convex and exhibit decreasing returns to scale, it is cheaper to produce an amount x of public goods using all n technologies than using a single technology. Hence, coalitions benefit from increasing returns to size in the production of the public good.

Next, I suppose that, once the coalition structure $\pi = \{C_1, C_2, \ldots, C_m\}$ is formed, each coalition of agents acts non-cooperatively, and chooses a level of public good in response to the contributions of the other coalitions. However, inside every coalition, agents act cooperatively and the level of public good is chosen to maximize the sum of utilities of the coalition members.

Hence, for any coalition structure π, the level of public good x_i chosen by the coalition C_i solves:

$$\max |C_i| \left(x_i + \Sigma_{j \neq i} x_j - \frac{1}{2} \left(\frac{x_i^2}{|C_i|} \right) \right),$$

yielding a total level of public good provision for the coalition $x_i = |C_i|^2$.

In equilibrium, any member of the coalition C_i thus provides an amount $|C_i|$of the public good, and receives a utility:

$$V_i(\pi) = \Sigma_{j=1}^{m} |C_j|^2 - \frac{1}{2} |C_i|^2.$$

Again, it is easy to see that whenever the coalition structure formed by other agents is more concentrated, the payoff $v_i(\pi)$ increases. It is also immediate to note that larger coalitions receive lower payoffs and that the arrival of a new member decreases the payoff of members of smaller cartels. Hence, the three axioms defined by Yi (1997) are satisfied.

In order to characterize the outcomes of the various games of coalition formation, it appears to be useful to recall the definition of the sequence of *Fibonacci numbers*, $f_0 = 1, f_1 = 2$ and $f_n = f_{n-1} + f_{n-2}$. Next consider, for any integer n, the following partition. In the first step, select the largest Fibonnaci number f^1 smaller than n. At any step k, select the largest Fibonacci number f^k smaller than $n - \Sigma_{i=1}^{k-1} f^1$. This is a finite procedure, and it yields a unique result that we call the *Fibonacci decomposition of n*, denoted $\Phi(n)$.

The computations underlying the construction of Table 2.2 can be found in the Appendix. It appears that, as opposed to the case of cartel formation, in a public good economy, agents have an incentive to form coalitions of at least two players. Hence, even in the open membership game and in the game Δ, there exist non-trivial coalition structures emerging as Nash equilibrium outcomes. (Note, however, that there does not exist any SNE for these games, since in any coalition structure obtained in equilibrium, members of two coalitions have an incentive to merge.) It is also worthwhile to note that the sizes of the coalitions formed is rather small (2 or 3).

This result is reminiscent of Barrett's (1994) observation that International Environmental Agreements typically have only a small number of signatories. The game Γ admits a large number of SNE, all char-

Table 2.2 Coalitions providing public goods

Open membership	$\{c_1,c_2,\ldots,c_m\}$ with $c_i \leq 3$ for all i and $c_j = 1 \Rightarrow c_i \neq 1$ for all $i \neq j$
Game Γ	$\{c_1,c_2,\ldots,c_m\}$ with $c_1 < c_2 < \ldots < c_m$ and $c_i \leq (c_i + 1)/2$ for all i
Game Δ	$\{c_1,c_2,\ldots,c_m\}$ with $c_i \leq 3$ for all i and $c_j = 1 \Rightarrow c_i \neq 1$ for all $i \neq j$
Sequential game	$\Phi(n)$
α stability	$\{c_1,c_2,\ldots,c_m\}$ with $c_1 < c_2 < \ldots < c_m$ and $c_i \leq (c_i + 1)/2$ for all i
β stability	$\{c_1,c_2,\ldots,c_m\}$ with $c_1 < c_2 < \ldots < c_m$ and $c_i \leq (c_i + 1)/2$ for all i
Equilibrium binding agreements	Cyclical pattern for n to be stable

acterized by a wide variation in the sizes of the coalitions formed. For a coalition structure to emerge as a SNE of the game Γ, it must contain coalitions such that, for any two consecutive coalitions, the smaller contains fewer than half the number of players of the larger. Now it is clear that in games with positive spillovers, the three concepts of α, β and γ stability coincide, so that there also exist a large number of α and β stable coalitions.

The most intriguing result is obtained for the sequential game. Following Ray and Vohra (1999), I assume that whenever an agent is indifferent between forming two coalitions of different sizes, she chooses the larger coalition size. It then appears that the coalitions formed in equilibrium follow a simple recursive structure (given by Fibonacci numbers), and can be viewed as the 'most concentrated' coalitions satisfying the property that, for any two consecutive coalitions, the size of the smaller is less than half that of the larger. Finally, for EBAs, Ray and Vohra (1997) prove, in a different public good economy, that a cyclical pattern emerges, in which the grand coalition is sometimes, but not always, supported by an EBA.

7. GAMES WITH NEGATIVE SPILLOVERS

In games with negative spillovers, the formation of a coalition by external players has an adverse effect on the profit of a player. Negative spillovers arise naturally in many oligopolistic games where the formation of a coalition leads to a decrease in the production cost of member firms. For example, the formation by firms of associations or of Research Joint Ventures (RJVs) leads to a decrease in production costs, which makes coalition members behave more aggressively on the market. Similarly, the formation of customs unions enables firms of member states to benefit from increasing returns to scale and to exploit that cost advantage on the world market. More generally, these examples suggest that negative spillovers emerge in two-stage games where cooperation improves the position of players who compete against each other in the second stage of the game. I first present some general results on games with negative spillovers due to Yi (1997) before analysing in detail models of associations of firms and of customs unions.

7.1 Games with Negative Spillovers: General Results

As in his study of games with positive spillovers, Yi (1997) first introduces three general axioms that can be shown to be satisfied by most economic examples of games with negative spillovers.

Axiom 7.1 (Negative spillovers): *Let* π *and* π' *be two coalition structures such that* $C \in \pi$, $C \in \pi'$ *and* $\pi' = \pi \backslash \{D_1, D_2\} \cup \{(D_1 \cup D_2)\}$ *for some coalitions* D_1 *and* D_2, *then, for all* $i \in C$, $v_i(\pi) > v_i(\pi')$.

Axiom 7.2 (Monotonicity for small coalitions): *Let* π *and* π' *be two coalition structures such that* $\pi' = \pi \backslash \{C_1, C_2, \ldots, C_k\} \cup \{C_1 \cup C_2 \cup \ldots \cup C_k\}$ *where* $c_1 \geq c_2 \geq \ldots \geq c_k$ *then for all* $i \in C_k$, $v_i(\pi') > v_i(\pi)$.

Axiom 7.3 (Individual monotonicity): *Let* π *and* π' *be two coalition structures such that* $\pi' = \pi \backslash \{C, D\} \cup \{C \cup \{i\}, D \backslash \{i\}\}$ *for some* $i \in D$ *and* $c \geq d$, *then* $v_i(\pi') > v_i(\pi)$.

The three axioms can easily be interpreted. The first axiom states that whenever two coalitions of external players merge, the payoff of a player decreases: this is the negative spillovers axiom. The second and third axioms introduce a monotonicity requirement on the valuation v. The axiom of monotonicity of small coalitions states that whenever a group of coalitions merge, members of the smaller coalition benefit from the merger. The axiom of individual monotonicity indicates that an individual player always has an incentive to leave a coalition in order to join a coalition of equal or larger size.

It is easy to see that, under the individual monotonicity axiom, the only Nash equilibrium of the open membership game is the grand coalition. Yi (1997) states and proves a more general proposition, comparing the outcomes of the open membership game, the sequential game of coalition formation and EBAs.

Proposition 7.4 (Yi, 1997): *In games satisfying individual monotonicity, the NE outcome of the open membership game is more concentrated than the SPE outcomes of the sequential game or any of the EBAs. Under some additional conditions, the SPE outcome of the sequential game is more concentrated than any of the EBAs.*

Proof: See Yi (1997).

7.2 Associations of Firms

Cooperation among competing firms is increasingly common on oligopolistic markets. More and more often, competing firms agree to share information, build common facilities or launch common research programmes in order to decrease their production costs. Bloch (1995) studies the formation of these associations of firms in a very simple model where the benefits from cooperation increase linearly in the size of the association (see also Yi, 1998).

I assume that demand is linear and given by $P=\alpha-\Sigma_{i=1}^{n}q_i$. Firms have a constant marginal cost of production, which is decreasing in the size of the association they belong to. The cost of a firm i in an association A of size a is thus given by: $c_i=\lambda-\mu\, a$. Finally, I suppose that the parameter values α, λ and μ are chosen in such a way that for any coalition structure, all firms are active in a Cournot equilibrium.

Once associations are formed on the market, firms select non-cooperatively the quantities they offer on the market. For a coalition structure $\pi=\{A_1,A_2,\ldots,A_k\}$, it is easy to see that there exists a unique Cournot equilibrium on the market, and that each firm's profit is a monotonically increasing function of the following valuation:

$$v_i(\pi)=\frac{\alpha-\lambda}{n+1}+\mu a(i)-\mu\frac{\Sigma_{j=1}^{k}a_j^2}{n+1},$$

where $a(i)$ denotes the size of the association firm i belongs to. It is easy to check that this valuation satisfies the three axioms in Yi (1997). Negative spillovers arise because the merger of two outside associations leads to a decrease in the valuation. The two monotonicity axioms can also easily be shown to hold for the valuation v defined above. I describe the outcomes of the various games of coalition formation for associations of firms in Table 2.3.

It turns out that, with the exception of the open membership game and the game Γ, all models of coalition formation give the same solution: a

Table 2.3 Associations of firms

Open membership	$\{n\}$
Game Γ	No SNE. All π are NE.
Game Δ	$\{k^*, n-k^*\}$ where $k^*=(3n+1)/4$
Sequential game	$\{k^*, n-k^*\}$ where $k^*=(3n+1)/4$
α stability	$\{k^*, n-k^*\}$ where $k^*=(3n+1)/4$
β stability	$\{k^*, n-k^*\}$ where $k^*=(3n+1)/4$

dominant association grouping around three quarters of the industry forms, and the remaining firms form a smaller association. This result can be understood by recalling the following two observations, which are proved in Bloch (1995): (i) an association has an incentive to accept new members until its size reaches $n/2$, and (ii) when two associations form, the size $k^* = (3n+1)/4$ is the optimal size from the viewpoint of the first association.

From these two observations it is easy to check that the only α and β stable coalition structure is $\pi = \{k^*, n-k^*\}$, which is also immune to deviations by coalitions in the game Δ. Bloch (1995) shows that this coalition structure is also the unique SPE outcome of the sequential game. Note, however, that this structure is not a SNE in the game Γ: firms obtain a higher payoff in the structure $\pi' = \{(n/2), 1, \ldots\ldots, 1\}$ and hence the coalition structure $\pi = \{k^*, n-k^*\}$is not immune to a coalitional deviation in the game Γ. Since, in the game Γ, individual players never have an incentive to leave any coalition and are not free to join the coalition they want, any coalition structure is a NE outcome of the game.

7.3 Customs Unions

The second example I present is the formation of customs unions in international trade. The emergence of three regional trading blocks in North America, Europe and Asia has prompted considerable interest in the study of the formation of customs unions. Recent contributions to the study of trading blocs have focused on cooperative solution concepts (Riezman, 1995; Macho-Stadler et al., 1994) on symmetric trading blocs (Krugman, 1991; Bond and Syropoulos, 1993) or on very specific coalition structures (Baldwin, 1993; Haveman, 1996).[22] I consider here a simplified version of Yi's (1996) model of customs unions formation, which does not impose any restriction on the coalition structure formed.[23]

Following Krugman (1991), a customs union is modelled as a coalition of countries which eliminate tariffs among themselves and impose a common external tariff. In a model of imperfect competition with increasing returns to scale, it turns out that firms in larger trading blocs have a lower production cost and behave more aggressively on the world market. Hence the game exhibits negative spillovers and the formation of customs unions can be viewed as a special case of games with negative spillovers.

More precisely, let there be n countries. The utility function of a representative consumer in country i is quasi-linear and quadratic in the consumption of the good:

$$u_i = aq_i - \frac{1}{2}q_i^2 + M_i,$$

where q_i is the consumption of the good and M_i the numeraire good consumption.

In each country, the good is produced by a monopolistic firm at a constant marginal cost (measured in the numeraire good) equal to c. Letting τ_{ij} denote the tariff imposed by country i on goods from j, firm j's effective cost of production in country j is $c + \tau_{ij}$. Hence the firm of country j chooses a production q_{ij} in order to maximize its profit:

$$P_{ij} = (a - \Sigma_{k=1}^{n} q_{ik} - c - \tau_{ij})\, q_{ij}.$$

In a Nash equilibrium of the model, the quantity offered by firm j on market i is thus given by:

$$q_{ij}^* = \frac{1 + \Sigma_{k=1}^{n} \tau_{ik} - (n+1)\tau_{ij}}{n+1}.$$

Next, suppose that a customs unions structure $\pi = \{C_1, C_2, \ldots, C_m\}$ forms. Each customs union abolishes tariffs inside the union and selects a common external tariff in order to maximize the sum of welfare of its members. Simple computations show that the optimal tariff only depends on the size c_i of the customs union, and is given by:

$$\tau = \frac{2c_i + 1}{n + 1 + (c_i + 1)(2c_i + 1)}.$$

One can then compute the total welfare of country i in customs union C_i as:

$$W_i = u_i + \Sigma_{j=1}^{n} P_{ji},$$

and replacing by the equilibrium values of τ and q_{ij}^*, we obtain the valuation:

$$v_i(\pi) = \frac{1}{2} - \frac{1}{n + 1 + (c_i + 1)(2c_i + 1)} + \Sigma_{j=1, j \neq i}^{m} \frac{c_j}{((n+1) + (c_j + 1)(2c_j + 1))^2}.$$

Table 2.4 Customs unions

Open membership	$\{n\}$
Sequential game	$\{k^*, n-k^*\}$ where k^* maximizes $v_i(\{k, n-k\})$
α stability	$\{k^*, n-k^*\}$ where k^* maximizes $v_i(\{k, n-k\})$
β stability	$\{k^*, n-k^*\}$ where k^* maximizes $v_i(\{k, n-k\})$

This valuation has been studied by Yi (1996), who shows in particular that it satisfies the three axioms of games with negative spillovers. Table 2.4 reproduces some of Yi's (1996) results for 'reasonable values' of the number n of countries.[24]

The complexity of the valuation does not permit a full characterization of the coalition structures emerging as the outcomes of the various games of coalition formation. In particular, nothing is known about the outcomes of the games Δ and Γ in that model. For the open membership game and the sequential game of coalition formation, Yi (1996) only obtains the partial characterization given above (see Table 2.4).

8. CONCLUSIONS AND OPEN QUESTIONS

In this survey, I have described some recent contributions to the theory of endogenous coalition formation. I have discussed various representations of games with externalities among coalitions and presented some noncooperative procedures which were recently proposed to analyse cooperation situations with spillovers. I have also shown how these models can be applied to address various economic problems, taken from public economics, industrial organizations and industrial economics. As I conclude this survey, I would like to mention what I view as important open problems in the area.

Cooperative study of partition function games: The study of partition function games is still very rudimentary. The following questions should be addressed: (i) conversion of strategic form games into partition function games, (ii) extension of classical cooperative concepts to partition function games, (iii) nonemptiness of the core in partition function games, and (iv) relation between the core and the various Shapley values for games with fixed coalition structures. Some properties of partition function games also need to be studied (for example, convexity, negative and positive spillovers) and used to prove results on cooperative solution concepts.

Efficiency and transfers across coalitions: All the solution concepts studied in this survey prohibit transfers across coalitions. Since transfers across coalitions are not allowed, the coalition structures obtained might be inefficient. Games with transfers among coalitions could be defined both in the simultaneous and sequential cases. Simultaneous games with transfers should be developed along the lines of Kamien and Zang's (1990) acquisition game. (See also Carraro and Siniscalco (1993) for a discussion of the role of transfers in the formation of coalitions.) Alternatively, one could analyse games with additional players acting as 'developers' of coalitions, as in Perez-Castrillo (1994). The issue of competition to attract members inside a coalition, and of the existence of a 'market' for coalitions, is still understudied and should be investigated further. In the sequential setting, the extensive form could embody different rounds of negotiations, as in Gul (1989). It would then be interesting to study how players form temporary coalition structures in order to increase their bargaining power in future negotiations. (Gomes (1999) provides a first step in this direction.)

Applications: While some economic applications have been discussed in the survey, there is still need for further studies of economic models of coalition formation. The inherent difficulty of computing stable coalition structures may prevent a general characterization of coalitions in economic models, but some simple illustrative examples could provide additional insights into many areas. For instance, in public economics the study of the provision of local public goods with spillovers is still very rudimentary. Another important area of application is the formation of coalitions of countries (for instance, customs unions or signatories of different treaties) and the interrelation between the various issues over which those countries (or coalitions of countries) bargain. (A preliminary analysis of the endogenous formation of coalitions when issues are linked can be found in Conconi and Perroni (2000).) Finally, in political science the models described above could be used and tested against data on the formation of coalitional governments in democratic countries.

NOTES

This paper is a revised and updated version of the paper published in Carlo Carraro and Domenico Siniscalco (eds) *New Directions in the Economic Theory of the Environment*, Cambridge University Press, 1997 and reprinted in C. Carraro (ed.) *Governing the Global Commons*, Edward Elgar, 2002. I owe a great debt to Debraj Ray, Rajiv Vohra and Sang-Seung Yi for the ideas contained in this book. My thoughts on coalition formation have been shaped by the numerous discussions I had with them over time. Part of this survey is based on work I did during my Ph.D. dissertation at the University of Pennsylvania and later as a post-doctoral fellow at CORE. I have greatly benefitted from discussions with Beth Allen, George Mailath, Andrew Postlewaite and Yves Younès at Penn and with Claude d'Aspremont, Jean Gabszewicz, Heracles Polemarchakis and Jacques Thisse at CORE. Finally, I gratefully acknowledge the financial support of the Fondazione ENI Enrico Mattei in the preparation of this survey.

1. More recent definitions of the bargaining set due to Mas-Colell (1989) and Zhou (1994) allow for the possibility that the coalition structure be endogenously formed. However, these bargaining sets were never used to build a general theory of endogenous coalition formation.
2. This definition corresponds to games with transferable utilities (TU games). In the case of NTU games, $v(C)$ is a subset of the Euclidean space $\mathbb{R}^{|C|}$. For most of the discussion, I will focus on TU games.
3. As an example of a situation where the worth of a coalition is independent of the action of other players, consider an exchange economy. The worth of a coalition C of agents who form an exclusive trading group is independent of the actions of the other traders.
4. In order to deal with that problem, Zhao (1992) suggests to use the α core allocations inside each coalition.
5. In that case, Ray and Vohra (1997) suggest taking the best Nash equilibrium payoff from the coalition's point of view. But this might be unfeasible, since the best equilibrium might be different for different coalitions. Other selection devices could be used as well.
6. In that sense, a valuation can be viewed as a specific example of an NTU partition function, where each player gets a rectangular utility set.
7. The differences between these different values will not be discussed here. Kurz (1988) contains an excellent survey of the various extensions of the Shapley value to games with coalition structures.
8. The lack of superadditivity of valuations is of course linked to the existence of a fixed division rule. In the literature the possible lack of superadditivity of cooperative games has always been problematic. Aumann and Drèze (1974) discuss at length the reasons for which a cooperative game may not be superadditive. (See also Greenberg, 1994, pp. 1308–9.) Guesnerie and Oddou (1981) give a public goods example of a game with a fixed division rule, which is not superadditive.
9. In their model of a 'dominant' cartel, d'Aspremont et al. (1983) show that the answer is always affirmative. However, in the traditional model of Cournot oligopoly with homogeneous goods studied by Salant, Switzer and Reynolds (1983), and more recently by Thoron (1998), the answer is negative: there is no stable cartel of firms on the market.
10. See Donsimoni, Economides and Polemarchakis (1986) for examples where there exist multiple equilibria in the cartel formation game.
11. A generalization of the cartel formation game would be obtained if individual players had the opportunity to announce a message by which they commit to remain independent.
12. In fact, the existence of a Nash equilibrium in pure strategies is not guaranteed in this open membership game.
13. It will be seen in section 7 that this monotonicity requirement is satisfied in many economic games with negative spillovers.
14. These results will be discussed in section 6.
15. These ideas are pursued in more detail in section 5 on stable coalition structures.
16. Aumann and Myerson (1988) study the formation of *bilateral links* between players yielding a *cooperation graph* rather than a coalition structure. For recent studies of link formation games see Qin (1996) and Dutta, Tijs and van Nouweland (1995).

17. Symmetric valuations are obtained when all players are *ex ante* identical.
18. In fact, the example used by Hart and Kurz (1984) to show inexistence of an SNE for the two games Γ and Δ involves precisely a symmetric valuation where the payoffs are decreasing in the order in which coalitions are formed. See Bloch (1996) for details.
19. There is another difference in the way the future is discounted. In Ray and Vohra (1999), as opposed to Bloch (1996), players discount the future at a constant rate δ. The game proposed by Ray and Vohra (1999) is thus a direct generalization of the game in Chatterjee et al. (1993) to the case of games with spillovers.
20. It is worthwhile to note that this Nash equilibrium is not an SNE. All firms obtain a higher profit under the grand coalition $\pi = \{n\}$.
21. See Ray and Vohra (1997) for details.
22. The literature on customs unions formation is already very large – and growing rapidly. I have only mentioned here those papers that deal explicitly with the theoretical issue of coalition formation.
23. The formulation I use is identical to that proposed by Krishna (1998).
24. Yi (1996) shows that the results are true for $n \leq 2^{18} = 262144$! Beyond that limit, the characterization of the SPE of the sequential game does not hold any longer.

REFERENCES

Aumann, R. (1959), 'Acceptable points and general n-person cooperative games', *Annals of Mathematical Studies*, **40**, 287–324.

Aumann, R. (1967), 'A survey of games without side payments', in M. Shubik (ed.), *Essays in Mathematical Economics*, Princeton: Princeton University Press, pp. 3–27.

Aumann, R. and J. Drèze (1974), 'Cooperative games with coalition structures', *International Journal of Game Theory*, **3**, 217–37.

Aumann, R. and M. Maschler (1964), 'The bargaining set for cooperative games', in M. Dresher, L. Shapley and A. Tucker (eds), *Advances in Game Theory*, Princeton: Princeton University Press, pp. 443–70.

Aumann, R. and R. Myerson (1988), 'Endogenous formation of links between players and of coalitions: an application of the Shapley value', in A. Roth (ed.), *The Shapley Value: Essays in Honor of Lloyd Shapley*, Cambridge: Cambridge University Press, pp. 175–91.

Baldwin, R. (1993), 'A domino theory of regionalism', NBER Working Paper 4465.

Barrett, S. (1994), 'Self-enforcing international environmental agreements', *Oxford Economic Papers*, **46**, 878–94.

Bernheim, D., B. Peleg and M. Whinston (1987), 'Coalition-proof Nash equilibria. I. Concepts', *Journal of Economic Theory*, **42**, 1–12.

Bloch, F. (1995), 'Endogenous structures of association in oligopolies', *Rand Journal of Economics*, **26**, 537–56.

Bloch, F. (1996), 'Sequential formation of coalitions in games with externalities and fixed payoff division', *Games and Economic Behaviour*, **14**, 90–123.

Bond, E. and C. Syropoulos (1993), 'Optimality and stability of regional trading blocs', *mimeo*, Department of Economics, Pennsylvania State University.

Carraro, C. and F. Moriconi (1998), 'Endogenous formation of environmental coalitions', *mimeo*, FEEM and University of Venice.

Carraro, C. and D. Siniscalco (1993), 'Strategies for the international protection of the environment', *Journal of Public Economics*, **52**, 309–28.

Chander, P. and H. Tulkens (1992), 'Theoretical foundations of negotiations and cost sharing in transfrontier pollution problems', *European Economic Review*, **36**, 388–98.

Chatterjee, K., B. Dutta, D. Ray and K. Sengupta (1993), 'A noncooperative theory of coalitional bargaining', *Review of Economic Studies*, **60**, 463–77.

Cho, I.K., K. Jewell and R. Vohra (1999), 'A simple model of coalitional competition', *mimeo*, Department of Economics, Brown University.

Conconi, P. and C. Perroni (2000), 'Issue linkage and issue tie-in in international negotiations', *mimeo*, Department of Economics, Warwick University.

d'Aspremont, C., A. Jacquemin, J.J. Gabszewicz and J. Weymark (1983), 'On the stability of collusive price leadership', *Canadian Journal of Economics*, **16**, 17–25.

Donsimoni, M.P., N. Economides and H. Polemarchakis (1986), 'Stable cartels', *International Economic Review*, **27**, 317–27.

Drèze, J. and J. Greenberg (1980), 'Hedonic coalitions: optimality and stability', *Econometrica*, **48**, 987–1003.

Dutta, B., S. Tijs and A. van Nouweland (1995), 'Link formation in cooperative situations', *International Journal of Game Theory*, **27**, 245–56.

Eren, N. (1993), 'Coalitional structural form games and stability under property rights', *mimeo*, Bogazici University.

Espinosa, M.P. and E. Inarra (1995), 'Von Neumann and Morgenstern stable sets in a merger game', *mimeo*, Department of Economics, Universidad del Pais Vasco.

Espinosa, M.P. and I. Macho Stadler (2000), 'Endogenous formation of partnerships with moral hazard', *mimeo*, Department of Economics, Universitat Autonoma de Barcelona and Universidad del Pais Vasco, forthcoming, *Games and Economic Behaviour*.

Gomes, A. (1999), 'A theory of negotiations and formation of coalitions', CARESS WP 99-11, Department of Economics, University of Pennsylvania.

Greenberg, J. (1977), 'Pure and local public goods', in A. Sandmo (ed.), *Public Finance*, Lexington, MA: Heath and Co.

Greenberg, J. (1994), 'Coalition structures', in R. Aumann and S. Hart (eds), *Handbook of Game Theory with Applications,* vol. II, Amsterdam: North-Holland, pp. 1305–37.

Guesnerie, R. and C. Oddou (1981), 'Second best taxation as a game', *Journal of Economic Theory*, **25**, 67–91.

Gul, F. (1989), 'Bargaining foundations of the Shapley value', *Econometrica,* **57**, 81–95.

Harsanyi, J. (1959), 'A bargaining model for the cooperative n-person game', in A. Tucker and D. Luce (eds), *Contributions to the Theory of Games*, Princeton: Princeton University Press, pp. 324–56.

Hart, S. and M. Kurz (1983), 'Endogenous formation of coalitions', *Econometrica*, **51**, 1047–64.

Hart, S. and M. Kurz (1984), 'Stable coalition structures', in M. Holler (ed.), *Coalitions and Collective Action*, Vienna: Physica Verlag, pp. 236–58.

Haveman, J. (1996), 'Some welfare effects of sequential customs union formation', *Canadian Journal of Economics*, **29**, 941–58.

Horn, H. and L. Persson (1996), 'Endogenous mergers in concentrated markets', *mimeo*, Institute for International Economics, Stockholm University.

Ichiishi, T. (1983), 'A social coalitional equilibrium existence lemma', *Econometrica*, **49**, 369–77.

Kamien, M. and I. Zang (1990), 'The limits of monopolization through acquisition', *Quarterly Journal of Economics*, **105**, 465–99.
Konishi, H., M. Le Breton and S. Weber (1997), 'Group formation in games without spillovers: a noncooperative approach', in C. Carraro and D. Sinsicalco (eds) *New Directions in the Economic Theory of the Environment*, Cambridge: Cambridge University Press, pp. 281–310.
Krishna, P. (1998), 'Regionalism and multilaterialism: a political economy approach', *Quarterly Journal of Economics*, **113**, 227–51.
Krugman, P. (1991), 'Is bilateralism bad?', in E. Helpman and A. Razin (eds), *International Trade and Trade Policy*, Cambridge, MA: MIT Press, pp. 9–24.
Kurz, M. (1988), 'Coalitional value', in A. Roth (ed.), *The Shapley Value: Essays in Honor of Lloyd Shapley*, Cambridge University Press, pp. 155–73.
Lucas, W. and J. Maceli (1978), 'Discrete partition function games', in P. Ordeshook (ed.), *Game Theory and Political Science*, New York: Academic Press, pp. 191–213.
Macho-Stadler, I., D. Perez-Castrillo and C. Ponsati (1994), 'Stable multilateral trade agreements', *mimeo*, Department of Economics, University Autonoma Barcelona.
Mas-Colell, A. (1989), 'An equivalence theorem for a bargaining set', *Journal of Mathematical Economics*, **18**, 129–39.
Maschler, M. (1992), 'The bargaining set, Kernel and Nucleolus', in R. Aumann and S. Hart (eds), *Handbook of Game Theory with Applications*, Volume I, Amsterdam: North-Holland, pp. 591–667.
Moldovanu, B. (1992), 'Coalition-proof Nash equilibria and the core in three-player games', *Games and Economic Behaviour*, **4**, 565–81.
Montero, M. (1999), 'Coalition formation in games with externalities', *mimeo*, Center, Tilburg University.
Myerson, R. (1977), 'Graphs and cooperation in games', *Mathematics of Operations Research*, **2**, 225–9.
Myerson, R. (1978), 'Threat equilibria and fair settlements in cooperative games', *Mathematics of Operations Research,* **3**, 265–74.
Nash, J. (1950), 'The bargaining problem', *Econometrica*, **28**, 155–62.
Okada, A. (1996), 'A noncooperative coalitional bargaining game with random proposers', *Games and Economic Behaviour*, **16**, 97–108.
Owen, G. (1977), 'Value of games with a prori unions', in R. Hein, and O. Moeschlin (eds), *Essays in Mathematical Economics and Game Theory*, New York: Springer-Verlag, pp. 76–88.
Perez-Castrillo, D. (1994), 'Cooperative outcomes through noncooperative games', *Games and Economic Behaviour*, **7**, 428–40.
Perry, M. and P. Reny (1994), 'A noncooperative view of coalition formation and the core', *Econometrica*, **62**, 795–817.
Qin, C.Z. (1996), 'Endogenous formation of cooperation structures', *Journal of Economic Theory*, **69**, 218–26.
Ray, D. and R. Vohra (1997), 'Equilibrium binding agreements', *Journal of Economic Theory*, **73**, 30–78.
Ray, D. and R. Vohra (2001), 'Coalitional power and public goods', *Journal of Political Economy*, **109**, 1355–1384.
Ray, D. and R. Vohra (1999), 'A theory of endogenous coalition structures', *Games and Economic Behaviour*, **26**, 286–336.

Riezman, R. (1995), 'Customs unions and the core', *Journal of International Economics*, **19**, 355–66.

Rubinstein, A. (1982), 'Perfect equilibrium in a bargaining model', *Econometrica*, **50**, 97–109.

Salant, S., S. Switzer and R. Reynolds (1983), 'Losses from horizontal mergers: the effects of an exogenous change in industry structure on Cournot-Nash equilibrium', *Quarterly Journal of Economics*, **98**, 185–99.

Selten, R. (1981), 'A noncooperative model of characteristic function bargaining', in V. Bohm and H. Nachtkamp (eds), *Essays in Game Theory and Mathematical Economics in Honor of Oskar Morgenstern*, Mannheim: Bibliographisches Institut Mannheim, pp. 131–51.

Sertel, M. (1993), 'Membership property rights, efficiency and stability', *mimeo*, Bogazici University.

Shenoy, P. (1979), 'On coalition formation: a game theoretical approach', *International Journal of Game Theory*, **8**, 133–64.

Shubik, M. (1982), *Game Theory in the Social Sciences*, Cambridge, MA: MIT Press.

Thoron, S. (1998), 'Formation of a coalition-proof stable cartel', *Canadian Journal of Economics*, **31**, 63–76.

Thoron, S. (2000), 'Strategic reactions of a frustrated coalition', *mimeo*, GREQAM, Marseille.

Thrall, R. and W. Lucas (1963), 'N-person games in partition function form', *Naval Research Logistics Quarterly*, **10**, 281–98.

Tiebout, C. (1956), 'A pure theory of local expenditures', *Journal of Political Economy*, **64**, 416–24.

von Neumann, J. and O. Morgenstern (1944), *Theory of Games and Economic Behavior*, Princeton: Princeton University Press.

Yi, S.S. (1996), 'Endogenous formation of customs unions under imperfect competition: open regionalism is good', *Journal of International Economics*, **41**, 153–77.

Yi, S.S. (1997), 'Stable coalition structures with externalities', *Games and Economic Behaviour*, **20**, 201–37.

Yi, S.S. (1998), 'Endogenous formation of joint ventures with efficiency gains', *Rand Journal of Economics*, **29**, 610–31.

Yi, S.S. (2000), 'Endogenous formation of economic coalitions: a survey of the partition function approach', in this volume.

Yi, S.S. and H. Shin (1995), 'Endogenous formation of coalitions in oligopoly', *mimeo*, Department of Economics, Dartmouth College.

Zhao, J. (1992), 'The hybrid solutions of an n-person game', *Games and Economic Behaviour*, **4**, 145–60.

Zhou L. (1994), 'A new bargaining set of an n-person game and endogenous coalition formation', *Games and Economic Behaviour*, **6**, 512–26.

APPENDIX

Equilibrium Coalition Structures for Public Goods

I start by establishing three simple facts, which will be used repeatedly in the computations. Note that whenever we compare the payoffs in two different coalition structures, it is enough to consider those coalitions that have changed from one structure to the other, since the payoff is an additive function of the sizes of external coalitions.

Fact 1: If $c \geq 4$ and members of coalition C remain together after the departure of an agent, then it pays to leave the coalition.

To establish this fact, notice that the inequality $1+(k-1)^2-(1/2) \geq (1/2)k^2$ is true for all $k \geq 4$. Hence, it always pays to leave a coalition of more than four members, if the remaining coalition members remain together.

Fact 2: For any two coalitions C and D with $c \geq d$, members of D have an incentive to merge if and only if $d \geq (c/2)$.

Note that the payoff to a member of D before the merger is $c^2+(1/2)d^2$, to be compared with the payoff after the merger of $(1/2)(c+d)^2$.

The latter is larger than the former if, and only if, $d \geq (c/2)$.

Fact 3: Suppose that, following the departure of some member, the coalition C breaks off, then it never pays any subcoalition D of C to deviate.

In coalition C, the payoff is given by $(1/2)c^2$. After the deviation of the subcoalition D, its members receive $(1/2)d^2+(c-d)$. Since $c \geq d$ and $c \geq 2$, the latter payoff is higher than the former, and the deviation does not benefit members of D.

Using facts 1 and 2, the Nash equilibrium outcomes of the open membership game and the game Δ can easily be derived. By fact 1, coalitions cannot contain more than three members, and by fact 2, there cannot exist two coalitions of size 1. Note, however, that the coalition structures found as NE outcomes cannot be strong Nash equilibria: as soon as it contains more than one coalition of size 2 or 3, members of these coalitions have an incentive to merge by fact 2.

To compute the SNE of the game Γ, first note that, when coalitions left by some member dissolves, it never pays for a player to leave a coalition, because $c-(1/2) \leq (1/2)c^2$ for all coalition sizes c. Furthermore, by fact 2, two coalitions C and D in an SNE coalition structure must satisfy the following condition: if $d \leq c$, then $d \leq (c/2)$.

It remains to show that any such coalition forms a SNE. Consider then a deviation by a coalition D. By fact 3, it never pays for a subcoalition to deviate. Hence the only candidates for deviations are supercoalitions, consisting of members of k different coalitions $C_1, C_2, \ldots, C_k$. However, by a repeated application of fact 2, it appears that members of the smaller coalition never gain by merging successively with members of larger coalitions.

Finally, I establish that the coalition structure Φ is the unique subgame perfect equilibrium of the sequential game, when ties are broken by making players choose the largest coalition when they are indifferent between two coalitions. The proof is by induction on the number n of players. First, it is easy to see that, for $n=1$, the characterisation of equilibrium is correct.

Now pick $n>1$ and consider the Fibonacci decomposition of $n=f_1+f_2+\ldots+f_k$ with $f_k > f_{k-1}$ for all k. The induction hypothesis is written as follows: for any $m<n$, in the unique SPE, the first player chooses f_K, the smallest coalition size in the Fibonacci decomposition.

I now prove that the induction hypothesis is true for n. Consider first a choice of coalition size $c>f_K$. Let the Fibonacci decompositions of $n-c$ and $n-f_K$ be denoted by F and F' respectively. Since $c>f_K$, $v_i(\mathsf{F})<v_i(\mathsf{F}')$, $\forall i \in C$ and $v_i(\mathsf{F}')<v_j(\mathsf{F}')$ for all $i \in C, j \in F_K$. Hence, choosing a coalition of size $c>f_K$ cannot be a profitable deviation.

Suppose now that there exists a profitable deviation, by choosing a coalition size $c<f_K$. By fact 2, it must have $c<(f_k/2)$. But then, by the definition of Fibonacci numbers, and calling f^1 the number preceding $f_K=f^0$ in the Fibonacci sequence, I must have:

$$f^0 - c > f^1,$$

so that, following the departure of c members, the coalition structure formed is of the form $\pi = \{f_1, \ldots, f_{K-1}, f^1, \ldots, f^L\}$. Now, I claim that c must be less than $(1/2)f^1$. If not, by fact 2, members of C have an incentive to merge with the coalition of size f^1, thus forming a coalition of size greater than $(1/2)f^0$. But then, by fact 2, members of C obtain a higher profit in the coalition of size f_K than in C and the deviation cannot be profitable. Repeating the argument, it turns out that, for a deviation to be profitable, the deviating coalition C must have a size satisfying: $c<(f/2)$ for all Fibonacci numbers f. In particular, $c<(1/2)$, a contradiction.

To conclude, I have shown that in a game with n players, the first player's optimal strategy is to choose a coalition size f_K. Now it is clear that, in a game with $n-f_K$ players, the last term of the Fibonacci decomposition is f_{K-1}, so that the next coalition formed is the size of coalition f_{K-1}. A repeated application of this argument gives the desired result.

3. Endogenous formation of economic coalitions: a survey of the partition function approach

Sang-Seung Yi

1. INTRODUCTION

Coalition formation among autonomous agents is an integral part of economic activity. Examples abound from industrial organization to international trade to environment. In industrial organization, Japanese firms have established R&D alliances such as the Very Large Scale Integration (VLSI) consortium (1976–79) and the Fifth Generation Computer Project (1981–90) with the purpose of gaining an edge on international competition. Due largely to the perceived success of such Japanese cooperative projects, American firms founded the Microelectronics and Computer Technology Corporation (MCC) in 1982 and the Semiconductor Manufacturing Technology Corporation (Sematech) in 1987. In the nascent High Definition Television (HDTV) industry in the US, three research coalitions, the Zenith-AT&T coalition, the NBC-Phillips-Thompson-Sarnoff coalition, and the General Instruments-MIT coalition, had been competing for adoption of their own technology by the Federal Communications Commission before they formed a 'Grand Alliance' in 1993 at the strong urging of the Commission.

In international trade, there has been a resurgence of regionalism. Casual observation suggests that the world is moving towards the formation of three major trading blocs consisting of the European Union (EU), the North American Free Trade Agreements (NAFTA) zone, and a potential Asian bloc. This new development has raised concerns that the formation of these regional trading blocs may undermine the spirit of global free trade that has been promoted in the multilateral setting of the General Agreement of Tariffs and Trade (GATT) (now the World Trade Organization (WTO)).

In environment, international policy coordination on greenhouse gas emissions through the 1995 Rio Convention and the 1997 Kyoto Protocol has heightened both economists' and policy makers' interest in the stability of global environmental agreements. In particular, each country has the option of joining or not joining the international coalition, and thus the size of the signatories will be endogenously determined.[1]

These economic coalitions raise several important issues for economists and policy makers. First, what are the private and social benefits of the formation, expansion, and the merger of economic coalitions? (For example, in the case of trading blocs, how does the formation of a customs union or a free-trade area affect the volume and terms of trade and welfare of member and nonmember countries?) Second, if economic agents can form coalitions freely so that the number and sizes of coalitions are endogenously determined, does a stable coalition structure exist? What coalition structure is stable? Is the grand coalition, which maximizes total social surplus under some regularity conditions, a stable outcome? (For example, what is the stable structure of trading blocs? Is global free trade a stable outcome? Are regional trading blocs stepping stones or stumbling blocks toward global free trade? Can one design a rule for trading bloc formation that will sustain global free trade as the equilibrium outcome?)

The aforementioned economic coalitions such as research joint ventures and free-trade areas have two distinguishing characteristics. First, several coalitions coexist and compete with each other, as in the case of the HDTV industry. Second, the formation, expansion, and merger of economic coalitions typically create *externalities* on nonmembers. For example, in the classical example of output cartels in oligopoly, output reduction by cartel members raises output price, which benefits nonmember firms. In the case of coalitions that form to provide public goods (such as pollution control), nonmembers free-ride on the provision of public goods by the members. These two cases are examples of what I call *coalitions with positive externalities.*

On the other hand, an important motivation for oligopolistic firms to form joint ventures with competitors is to exploit complementarities of both tangible and intangible assets of venture partners. If members of a joint venture realize efficiency gains by pooling their complementary assets, nonmember firms may suffer a competitive disadvantage against member firms. In the case of regional customs unions, the abolition of tariffs on trade among member countries and the readjustment of external tariffs may worsen nonmember countries' terms of trade with member countries. These are examples of *coalitions with negative externalities.*

This chapter surveys recent developments in the noncooperative theory of coalition formation that emphasizes these two characteristics of economic alliances: the formation of *multiple, competing* coalitions that create *externalities* on nonmembers. Indeed, ever since the publication of von

Neumann and Morgenstern's (1944) pioneering work, *Theory of Games Economic Behavior,* the endogenous formation of coalitions with economic applications has been an important topic of research for game theorists and economists. Von Neumann and Morgenstern themselves recognized the importance of coalitions in game theory and economic activity. For example, on p. 15 of their magnum opus, they say, 'Our subsequent discussion of "games of strategy" will show that the role and size of "coalitions" is decisive throughout the entire subject.' Various extensions of von Neumann and Morgenstern's original work produced elaborate solution concepts such as the core, bargaining set, Shapley value, which have been proven to be fruitful for examining many economic issues.

However, the vast majority of the models before the 1990s are based on the *characteristic function approach*, which assigns a coalition S its value $v(S)$. While appealing in situations such as a pure exchange economy, where a coalition of economic agents can guarantee an aggregate sum of (transferable) utilities, this approach is unsatisfactory in many strategic form games, that is, settings involve strategic play among economic agents. A typical procedure for obtaining $v(S)$ in a strategic form game assumes that the complementary coalition of S minmaxes the members of S, as in the α-core. But, as Ray and Vohra (1997) argue, why should the complementary coalition of S behave in such a 'bloodthirsty' fashion? If the underlying situation involves strategic play among economic agents, shouldn't strategic play govern the behavior of coalitions as well? Then the value of a coalition should depend on the entire *coalition structure*, not just on the coalition in question.

Hence I, along with Bloch, Ray and Vohra, advocate using the *partition function approach*, which maps the coalition structure into a vector of values for each coalition in the coalition structure.[2] Beginning in the early 1990s, these authors (and others) independently and simultaneously revived the partition function approach.[3] This approach has the advantage of capturing the important possibility of *externalities across coalitions*, because it allows the change in the coalition structure to affect the values of *all* coalitions. The characteristic function approach cannot incorporate such externalities across coalitions.[4]

The current chapter conducts a survey on the recent models of coalition formation that rely on the partition function approach. Like many surveys, this chapter is selective, because only a part of the fast growing literature on economic coalitions with externalities is reviewed.[5] Furthermore, this survey draws heavily from my earlier work on coalition formation. In particular, I follow closely Yi (1997), who provides a unified framework of a two-stage coalition formation for the recent models of coalition formation among symmetric players, such as Bloch (1995, 1996), Ray and Vohra

(1997, 1999), Yi (1996a, 1998, 2000) and Yi and Shin (2000) and many others. First, a partition function approach to coalition formation is introduced (section 2). Second, I review several rules of coalition formation that have been proposed in the literature (section 3). Third, various economic coalitions are classified as either 'coalitions with positive externalities' or 'coalitions with negative externalities,' depending on the effects the formation of a coalition has on nonmembers (sections 4 and 5). I extend Yi (1997) by adding several more coalition formation games (such as the Single Coalition Formation Game, the Exclusive Membership game and the simultaneous-move version of the Coalition Unanimity game) and more examples of economic coalitions (such as free trade areas and R&D coalitions with spillovers). Finally, some concluding remarks, including some future research topics, are offered in section 6.

2. THE PARTITION FUNCTION APPROACH TO COALITION FORMATION AMONG SYMMETRIC PLAYERS WITH EQUAL SHARING OF COALITION PAYOFF

Webster's Dictionary defines a coalition as 'a temporary alliance of distinct persons, parties, or states for joint action or to achieve a common purpose.' Economic coalitions can take many forms with diverse purposes. For coalitions among firms, the common purpose can be output reduction (cartels) or avoiding duplication of research efforts, achieving scale economies in research, or exploiting complementarities in research assets (research joint ventures). For coalitions among countries, the common aim can be free trade among member countries (trading blocs) or coordination of environmental policies (environmental treaties).

The current survey focuses on the case of *symmetric* players, that is, the case in which (1) all players have the same strategy sets and payoff functions; and (2) the identities of the players do not matter so that the interchange of players *i*'s and *j*'s strategies results in the interchange of player *i*'s and *j*'s payoffs but does not affect other players' payoffs. Obviously, the assumption of symmetric players is restrictive. However, as a first step towards building a more comprehensive theory of coalition formation in a general setting, the case of symmetric players is reviewed. (See the concluding remarks for more discussion on this point.)

Definition 2.1: A coalition structure $C=\{B_1, B_2, ..., B_m\}$ is a partition of the player set $P=\{P_1, P_2, ..., P_N\}$. $B_i \cap B_j = \emptyset$ for $i \neq j$ and $\cup_{i=1}^{m} B_i = P$.[6]

Consider the following two-stage game of coalition formation. In the first stage, players form coalitions according to the given rule of coalition formation. (Section 3 introduces some representative rules that have been proposed in the literature.) In the second stage, players engage in a non-cooperative game given the coalition structure that is determined in the first stage.

In order to simplify the analysis, I assume that the second-stage game has a unique Nash equilibrium outcome for *any* coalition structure.[7] Under this assumption, the second-stage game can be reduced to the payoff functions that map a coalition structure into payoffs for each player: π^i: $\mathbf{C} \rightarrow R$, where $\mathbf{C}$ is the set of all feasible coalition structures and R is the set of real numbers. The symmetry and the uniqueness assumptions imply that, in a given coalition structure, a coalition's second-stage equilibrium payoff (that is, the sum of payoffs to its members) depends only on the *number* and the *sizes* of coalitions in the coalition structure. However, the second-stage equilibrium payoffs do not depend on which player belongs to which coalition. Thus, with a slight abuse of notation, I identify a coalition by its size. Specifically, I will write $C = \{n_1, n_2, ..., n_m\}$, where n_i is the size of the i-th coalition B_i in $C = \{B_1, B_2, ..., B_m\}$.[8] We necessarily have $\Sigma_{i=1}^{m} n_i = N$.

In the main part of the current paper, I assume *equal sharing* of the coalition payoff among coalition members: each player in a given coalition receives the same payoff as the other members. That is, I rule out any *side-payments* with respect to membership decisions. I rely upon the assumption of ex-ante identical players in order to justify the equal division of the coalition payoff. Indeed, Ray and Vohra (1999) provide a justification for this assumption of equal division of coalition payoff. In an infinite-horizon model of coalition formation among symmetric players with endogenous sharing rules, they show that the equal sharing of coalition payoff emerges as the equilibrium sharing rule in any equilibrium without delay. (See Section 5.3 on more discussion of side-payments.)

Under the equal sharing assumption, we can denote by $\pi(n_i;C)$ the *per-member* payoff of a member of the size-n_i coalition in the coalition structure $C = \{n_1, n_2, ..., n_m\}$. Thus, $\pi(n_i;C)$ is a *per-member partition function*. For example, $\pi(1;\{3,1\})$ is the payoff of a member of the size-1 coalition in a coalition structure $\{3,1\}$. (If the payoff of a coalition does not depend on the actions of the rest of players, then $\pi(n_i;C)$ depends only on n_i. Then, the per-member partition function can be written as $\pi(n_i)$, and $\Pi(n_i) \equiv n_i \times \pi(n_i)$ is the familiar characteristic function, under the added assumption that the identities of coalition members are payoff-irrelevant.)

The following definition, which Yi and Shin (2000) introduce, proves useful in comparing the equilibrium coalition structures under different rules of coalition formation.

Definition 2.2: $C = \{n_1, n_2, ..., n_m\}$ is a *concentration* of $C' = \{n'_1, n'_2, ..., n'_{m'},\}$, $m' \geq m$, if and only if there exists a sequence of coalition structures $C^1 = \{n^1_1, n^1_2, n^1_{m(1)}\}$, $C^2 = \{n^2_1, n^2_2, \ldots, n^2_{m(2)}\}, \ldots, C^R = \{n^R_1, n^R_2, ..., n^R_{m(R)}\}$, such that:

1. $C = C^1$ and $C' = C^R$; and
2. $C^{r-1} = C^r \backslash \{n^r_{i(r)}, n^r_{j(r)}\} \cup \{n^r_{i(r)} + 1, n^r_{j(r)} - 1\}$, $n^r_{i(r)} \geq n^r_{j(r)}$, for some $i(r)$, $j(r) = 1, \ldots, m(r)$ and for all $r = 2, \ldots, R$.

$C = \{n_1, n_2, \ldots, n_m\}$ is a concentration of $C' = \{n'_1, n'_2, ..., n'_{m'},\}$ if one can obtain C from C' by a finite sequence of moving one member at a time from a coalition in C' to another coalition of *equal or larger size*. (In the above formal definition, one player is moved from the size-$n^r_{j(r)}$coalition to the size-$n^r_{i(r)}$ coalition, where $n^r_{i(r)} \geq n^r_{j(r)}$. Notice that $m' - m \geq 0$ coalitions are dissolved in the process.) Concentration, like the usual notion of refinement/coarsening of coalition structures, is a partial ordering on the set of coalition structures. To see why, notice that there are coalition structures, such as {3,3} and {4,1,1}, which cannot be ranked under concentration. (For $N \leq 5$, however, it is easy to see that concentration is a complete ordering on the set of coalition structures.) Yi (1997) shows that if a coalition structure C is coarser than another coalition structure C', then C is more concentrated than C'. However, the reverse is not true: there exist some coalition structures which cannot be ranked under refinement but which can be ranked under concentration. For example, {5,1} is more concentrated than {3,3}, which in turn is more concentrated than {2,2,2}. These three coalition structures cannot be ordered under refinement.

3. GAMES OF COALITION FORMATION

In examining endogenous coalition formation, one encounters several important issues. Is the membership in a coalition open to outsiders? Does the formation, expansion, merger, or break-up of coalitions require the unanimous approval of members? When can one say that a coalition structure is 'stable'? In order to provide some answers to this question, I review several rules of coalition formation that have been proposed in the literature. The Open Membership game is designed to describe an institutional environment in which an outsider can join an existing coalition without the consent of its existing members. For example, memberships in both Sematech and MCC were open to all US firms that were willing to contribute their share of research funds to the consortia.[9] Under the Exclusive Membership game, on the other hand, consent of the existing members is required for an outsider to join a coalition. For example, the research coalitions in the HDTV industry fall into the category of the Exclusive Membership rule. In the Coalition Unanimity game, the formation, expansion or merger of coalitions require the unanimous approval of the prospective members. In the Equilibrium Binding Agreements game, a coalition can only break up into smaller subcoalitions.

3.1 The Simultaneous-Move Single Coalition Formation Game (d'Apresmont et al., 1983)

As a preliminary step towards the analysis of stable coalition structures, I begin with a game in which at most one nondegenerate coalition (a coalition with two or more members) is allowed to form. This game is based on d'Apresmont et al. (1983), who examine the size of the stable cartel. They assume that only one cartel can form and that firms simultaneously decide to join the cartel or not. One can formalize this game by letting each player strategy set be {In, Out}. The players who announce 'In' join the single coalition and those who announce 'Out' stay as independent players (one-player coalitions).

This single coalition formation game has been much in use (especially before the appearance of full partition-function models that allow for multiple coalitions). For example, Katz (1986) and Poyago-Theotoky (1995) use this game for research joint ventures, Carraro and Siniscalco (1993) for environmental coalitions, Baldwin (1995) for regional trading blocs, and Kohler (2002) for monetary unions.

3.2 The Simultaneous-Move Open Membership Game (Yi and Shin, 2000)

In this game, each player simultaneously announces an 'address'. The players that announce the same address belong to the same coalition. Formally, each player chooses one address from the set $A \equiv \{a_1, a_2, \ldots, a_N\}$. (The number of distinct addresses must be greater than or equal to the number of players.) Let α^i be player i's strategy, or announcement. Given the players' announcements $\alpha \equiv (\alpha^1, \alpha^2, \ldots, \alpha^N)$, the resulting coalition structure is $C = \{B_1, B_2, \ldots, B_m\}$, where players i and j belong to the same coalition B_k if, and only if, $\alpha^i = \alpha^j$, that is, they choose the same address. (m is the number of different addresses chosen by the players.) For example, suppose that there are four players and that $\alpha = (a_1, a_1, a_4, a_3)$. Since players 1 and 2 choose the same address, a_1, they belong to the same coalition. Players 3 and 4 each form a one-player coalition, because they announce addresses different from each other and from players 1 and 2. The resulting coalition structure is {2,1,1} and player 1's (and player 2's) payoff is π (2;{2,1,1}), player 3's (and player 4's) payoff is π (1;{2,1,1}). Notice that player 3 (or player 4) can join the coalition of players 1 and 2 by changing its announcement from a_4 (from a_3) to a_1.[10]

3.3 The Simultaneous-Move Exclusive Membership Game (Hart and Kurz, 1983)[11]

Each player simultaneously announces a list of players (including itself) with whom it is *willing* to form a coalition. The players that announce exactly the same list of firms belong to the same coalition. Formally, player *i*'s strategy α^i is to choose a set of players S^i (itself included), a subset of $S \equiv \{P_1, P_2, \ldots, P_N\}$. Given the players' announcements $\alpha \equiv (S^1, S^2, \ldots, S^N)$, the resulting coalition structure is $C = \{B_1, B_2, \ldots, B_m\}$, where players *i* and *j* belong to the same coalition B_k if and only if $S^i = S^j$, that is, they choose exactly the same list of players. (*m* is the number of different lists chosen by the players.) For example, suppose that there are four players and that $\alpha = (\{P_1, P_2\}, \{P_1, P_2\}, \{P_3\}, \{P_3, P_4\})$. Since players 1 and 2 choose exactly the same list of players, they belong to the same coalition. Players 3 and 4 each form a one-player coalition, because they announce lists different from each other and from players 1 and 2. The resulting coalition structure is {2,1,1} and player 1's (and player 2's) payoff is π (2;{2,1,1}), player 3's (and player 4's) payoff is π (1;{2,1,1}). While player 4 cannot join player 3's coalition unless player 3 changes its strategy, player 3 *can* join player 4's coalition by switching its own announcement to $\{P_3, P_4\}$. That is, player 3's announces that it is *not* willing to form a coalition with any other player, but player 4 announces that it is willing to form a coalition with player 3.

Remark: The formulation of the Single Coalition Formation game in Section 3.1 assumes that the membership of the cartel is open to outsiders. Indeed, one can view the Single Coalition Formation game as a special case of the Open Membership game, in which one takes the address quoted most frequently by the players and let the players who announce that address form the big coalition.[12] All other players form singleton coalitions. However, this need not be the case. The membership of the nondegenerate coalition can be exclusive. In this case, the strategies and rule of coalition formation are the same as in the Exclusive Membership game, but all coalitions other than the biggest one are dissolved.

3.4 The Simultaneous-Move Coalition Unanimity Game (von Neumann and Morgenstern, 1944)[13]

In the two games described above, when some members of a coalition leave to join and/or form other coalitions, the remaining members stay on as a smaller coalition. In the Coalition Unanimity game, however, a member's departure results in the dissolution of the coalition. Put differently, a coalition forms if and only if all potential members agree to join it (hence, the term 'Coalition Unanimity'). This game goes back to von Neumann and Morgenstern (1994, section 57.3.1).[14] As in the Exclusive Membership game, each player announces a subset of players (including himself) with which he is willing to form the coalition, but a coalition forms only upon unanimous approval by the prospective members. Formally, for each n-tuple of strategies $\alpha = (S^1, S^2, \ldots, S^N)$, the resulting coalition structure is $C = \{B_1, B_2, \ldots, B_m\}$ where $P_i \in B_k (= S_i)$ if and only if $S^i = S^j$ for *all* $P_j \in S^i$, and $P_i \in \{P_i\}$ otherwise. For example, suppose that there are four players and that $\alpha = (\{P_1, P_2, P_3\}, \{P_1, P_2, P_3\}, \{P_3\}, \{P_3, P_4\})$. In the Exclusive Membership game, P_1 and P_2 form a coalition, because they announce the same list of players. But in Coalition Unanimity game, they stay as singleton coalitions, because P_3 does not participate in their coalition. Hence, the resulting coalition structure is $\{1,1,1,1\}$. In the Exclusive Membership game, P_2's announcement of $\{P_1, P_2, P_3\}$ signals his *willingness* to form a coalition with *any* subset of the players who are on his list. In the Coalition Unanimity game, on the other hand, the same announcement by P_2 means that he will form a coalition with the players on his list if and only if *all* prospective members participate in the coalition. In other words, upon the departure of some members of a coalition, the remaining members stay as a smaller coalition in the Exclusive Membership game (and in the Open Membership game), but they dissolve their coalition and become singleton coalitions in the Coalition Unanimity game. In my opinion, there is no one 'correct' answer to the question of which coalition formation rule is a universally appropriate one.[15] Instead, I shall attempt to uncover the endogenous stability properties of different membership rules by examining stable coalition structures under various membership rules.

Remark: In principle, the above four games can be turned into *finite-horizon* sequential-move games by letting the N players announce their strategies sequentially from P_1 to P_N. I report some results on the sequential-move versions of the above games in Sections 4 and 5.

3.5 The Infinite-Horizon Sequential-Move Coalition Unanimity Game (Bloch, 1996)

Bloch (1996) analyses an infinite-horizon sequential-move version of the above Coalition Unanimity game. First, the first player P_1 makes a proposal for a coalition including himself, for example, $\{P_1, P_3, P_4, P_7\}$. Then, the player on P_1's list with the smallest index (not including P_1) – here, it is P_3 – accepts or rejects the proposal. If P_3 accepts, then it is P_4's turn to accept or reject the proposal, and the process goes on until we reach the last player on P_1's list. If any of the potential members rejects P_1's proposal, then the current proposal is thrown out (there is no coalition formation among the players who agree to the original proposal), and the player who first rejects the proposal starts over by proposing his own coalition. If, instead, all potential members accept P_1's proposal, then they form a coalition. The remaining players continue the coalition formation game, starting with the player with the smallest index making a proposal to the rest of the players. Notice that once a coalition forms, it cannot break apart, admit new members, or merge with other coalitions, regardless of how the rest of the players form coalitions.

Bloch's (1996) main result shows that the infinite-horizon Coalition Unanimity game yields the same stationary subgame perfect equilibrium coalition structure as the following 'Size Announcement' game: P_1 first announces the size of his coalition s_1, and the first s_1 players form a size-s_1 coalition, and then P_{s_1+1} proposes s_2, and the next s_2 players form a size-s_2 coalition, and so on until P_N is reached. (See Ray and Vohra (1999) for an important technical correction on Bloch's initial result.) Intuitively, this equivalence theorem is a result of the symmetry assumption. In an equilibrium with no delay, P_1 makes a proposal which is going to be accepted immediately. Since the *identities* of the members do not matter, P_1 (and all other subsequent proposers) may as well pick the size of his coalition s_1 under the assumption that the next $s_1 - 1$ players will be his coalition partners. It is straightforward to see that this 'Size Announcement' game has a (generically) unique subgame perfect equilibrium coalition structure. That is, unless there are ties in coalition payoffs $\pi(n_i;C)$, the unique subgame perfect equilibrium coalition structure of the Size Announcement game can be derived by induction on the number of players. To see why, suppose that $\pi(n_i;C) \neq \pi(n'_j;C')$, for all n_i, n'_j, C and C', such that $n_i \in C'$, $n'_j \in C'$ and $C \neq C'$. For $N=2$, P_1 will announce 2 if and only if $\pi(2;\{2\}) > \pi(1;\{1,1\})$. Hence, the subgame perfect equilibrium is unique. Now suppose that for $N' < N$, the subgame perfect equilibrium is unique. For N, P_1 has N choices to make. If it announces N, then the grand coalition forms and P_1 will earn $\pi(N;\{N\})$. If it announces $k < N$, then, by assumption, the remaining $N-k$

players will form a unique coalition structure, given P_1's announcement. Let it be $\{B(k)\}$. Then P_1's payoff is $\pi(k;\{k, B(k)\})$. Thus in equilibrium P_1 will make a unique choice over $\pi(N;\{N\})$ and $\pi(k;\{k,B(k)\})$, $k=1, 2, \ldots, N-1$.

3.6 The Equilibrium Binding Agreements Game

Ray and Vohra (1997) introduce the notion of equilibrium binding agreements and the stable coalition structures that form under such agreements. The critical assumption in their analysis is that *coalitions can only break up into smaller subcoalitions*. The main idea of their equilibrium concept is as follows. To begin with, the degenerate coalition structure $\{1,1, \ldots, 1\}$ is *defined* to be stable, because no one-player coalition can break up into a smaller subcoalition. A non-degenerate coalition structure $C=\{n_1,n_2, \ldots, n_m\}$ is stable if and only if there do *not* exist (1) a size-$\hat{n}_i$ subcoalition of a size-n_i coalition in C and (2) a more refined coalition structure C' (a stable outcome itself under the Equilibrium Binding Agreements) which can be 'induced' by a deviation by these $\hat{n}_i$ 'leading perpetrators', such that these $\hat{n}_i$ leading perpetrators are better off under C' than under C. The term 'induced' needs to be more carefully defined. The deviation by $\hat{n}_i$ leading perpetrators may result in the break-up of the other coalitions (including the subcoalition consisting of $n_i-\hat{n}_i$ remaining members of the formerly size-n_i coalition) and/or the further break-up of the size-$\hat{n}_i$ subcoalition consisting of the leading perpetrators. (Remember that Ray and Vohra's rule permits the breakup of coalitions only.) This further refinement in coalition structure will occur unless the coalition structure created by the breakup of the size-n_i coalition into size-$\hat{n}_i$ and size-$(n_i-\hat{n}_i)$ subcoalitions is stable. The leading perpetrators look ahead at the end outcome of their deviation and decide to carry out the deviation if they are better off in the final coalition structure induced by their deviation than in the *status quo* coalition structure.

More formally, a non-degenerate coalition structure $C=\{n_1,n_2, \ldots, n_m\}$ is stable under the Equilibrium Binding Agreements rule if and only if there do not exist $C^1=\{n_1^1, n_2^1, n_{m(1)}^1\}$, $C^2=\{n_1^2, n_2^2, \ldots, n_{m(2)}^2\}, \ldots, C^R=\{n_1^R, n_2^R, \ldots, n_{m(R)}^R\}$, such that

1. $C^1=C$ and $C^{r+1}=C^r\backslash\{n_{i(r)}^r\}\cup\{\hat{n}_{i(r)}^r, \{n_{i(r)}^r-\hat{n}_{i(r)}^r\}$, for some $i(r)=1, \ldots, m(r)$ and for all $r=1, \ldots, R-1$;
2. C^R is stable but $C^2, C^3, \ldots, C^{R-1}$ are not; and
3. $n_{i(1)}^1$ leading perpetrators are better off under the final coalition structure C^R than under the original coalition structure $C=C^1$.

Notice that C^{r++} is a coarsening, and thus a concentration, of C^{r+1} in the above definition.

4. ECONOMIC COALITIONS WITH POSITIVE EXTERNALITIES

In this section, I examine the case of positive externalities, that is, the case in which the formation, expansion or merger of coalitions creates positive external effects on nonmembers. I first introduce a set of conditions on the per-member partition function $\pi(n_i;C)$. I then examine several simple models of economic coalitions that satisfy these conditions. Finally, an analysis of stable coalition structures follows.

4.1 Conditions on the Per-Member Partition Function: Positive Externalities

$(P.1)$ $\pi(n_k;C)<\pi(n_k;C')$, where C' is more concentrated than C and $n_k \in C$ and C'.

If the coalition structure becomes more concentrated, members of a coalition *not* involved in the change in the coalition structure earn higher payoffs.

Condition $(P.1)$ is the cornerstone condition of coalition formation with positive externalities. The next condition ranks per-member payoffs of coalitions in a given coalition structure.

$(P.2)$ $\pi(n_i;C)<\pi(n_j;C)$ if and only if $n_i>n_j$.

In any coalition structure, small coalitions have higher *per-member* payoffs than big coalitions.

Now suppose that a member of a coalition leaves his coalition to join a larger or equal-sized one. The next two conditions concern the effect on the remaining members of the (now) smaller coalition and the deviator, respectively.

$(P.3)$ $\pi(n_j;C)<\pi(n_j-1;C')$, where $C'=C\setminus\{n_i,n_j\}\cup\{n_i+1,n_j-1\}$, $n_i\geq n_j\geq 2$.

If a member of the size-n_j coalition leaves his coalition to join a larger or equal-sized coalition, then the remaining members of the (formerly) size-n_j coalition become better off.

(P.4) $\pi(n_j;C) > \pi \quad (n_i+1;C')$, where $C' = C\backslash\{n_i,n_j\} \cup \{n_i+1,n_j-1\}$, $n_i \geq n_j \geq 2$.

If a member of the size-n_j coalition leaves his coalition to join a larger or equal-sized coalition, then the deviator becomes worse off.[16]

4.2 Economic Models of Coalition Formation with Positive Externalities

This subsection shows that the above four conditions are satisfied by several interesting economic coalitions, output cartels in oligopoly, public goods coalitions, research coalitions with spillovers. Some other economic coalitions, such as free-trade areas, satisfy (P.1) but may or may not satisfy other conditions.

4.2.1 Output cartels in Cournot oligopoly

Consider a Cournot oligopoly with inverse demand $P(X)$, where X is the industry output, $P'(X)<0$ and $2P'(X)+P''(X)<0$ when $P(X)>0$. (The last condition states that the industry revenue is a concave function of the industry output. This is a common assumption in Cournot oligopoly.) Firm i's cost function is given $c(x_i)=cx_i$, $c>0$, where x_i is firm i's output. Suppose that the cartel structure is $C=\{n_1,n_2, \ldots, n_m\}$ and consider the size-n_i cartel, $i=1, \ldots, m$. Without loss of generality, suppose that the first n_i firms belong to this cartel. The members of this cartel choose their output to maximize their joint profit:

$$\underset{\{x_i\}}{Max}\ \Sigma_{i=1}^{n_i} [P(X)x_i - cx_i]. \tag{4.1}$$

Let $X(n_i;C)$ be the equilibrium output of the size-n_i coalition and let $X(C) \equiv \Sigma_{i=1}^{m} X(n_i, C)$ be the *industry* output under the coalition structure C. The first-order condition for the size-n_i cartel is:

$$P(X(C)) + P'(X(C))X(n_i;C) - c = 0. \tag{4.2}$$

Notice that under constant marginal (and average) cost, a large coalition has no cost advantage over a small coalition, since one plant is as good as several plants. (This is the case that Economides (1986) examines.) As a result, in a given condition structure, regardless of size, all coalitions make the same amounts of profit in the unique Cournot equilibrium. Let $\Pi(m)$ be a coalition's profit under $C=\{n_i, \ldots, n_m\}$. Then:

$$\pi(n_i;\ C) = \Pi(m)/n_i, \quad i=1, \ldots, m. \tag{4.3}$$

A special case is the linear demand function $P(X) = A - X$. A simple derivation shows that:

$$\pi(n_i;C) = \frac{(A-c)^2}{n_i(m+1)^2}, \; i = 1, \ldots, m. \tag{4.4}$$

It is apparent that conditions (P.2), (P.3), and (P.4) hold in equation (4.3): large coalitions have lower per-member profits than small coalitions [(P.2)]; if a member of a large coalition moves to a small coalition, then the existing members of the small coalition earn lower profits [(P.3)], but the deviator earns a higher profit [(P.4)]. Finally, Yi (1999) shows that if coalitions merge, the merging coalitions reduce their total output. As a result, output price increases and outsiders benefit. In summary:

Lemma 4.1 Output cartels in a Cournot oligopoly satisfy (P.1) – (P.4) for the inverse demand function $P(X)$, with $P'(X) < 0$ and $2P'(X) + P''(X) < 0$, and the cost function $c(x) = cx$.

Remark: The above model of coalition formation is restrictive in that the aggregate profit of a large coalition is the same as the profit of a small coalition. When the marginal cost is increasing, a large coalition enjoys a cost advantage against a small coalition, and hence earns a higher profit. Yi (1999) derives a result that parallels Lemma 4.1 under some conditions on the cost function.

4.2.2 Research coalitions with spillovers

Yi and Shin (2000) examine the following model of research joint ventures (RJV) that form to internalize R&D externalities.[17] That is, members of a research coalition set their R&D investments to maximize the aggregate profits of the members of their coalition. Let x_i be firm i's R&D investments, $\mathbf{x} \equiv (x_1, \ldots, x_N)$ be the investment vector, and $X \equiv \Sigma_{i=1}^{N} x_i$ be total R&D investments. Yi and Shin assume that firm i's profit in the second-stage R&D competition, denoted by V^i, depends only on its R&D investments and on industry R&D investments: $V^i(\mathbf{x}) \equiv V(x_i, X)$. Firm i's profit function is assumed to be concave in x_i, holding other firms' investments fixed. Consider a research joint venture (RJV) with k members, which are taken to be firms 1, ..., k. Given other firms' investments, the members of the size-k RJV choose their R&D investments $(x_1, \ldots, x_k)$ in order to maximize their joint profits $\Sigma_{i=1}^{k} V(x_i, X)$. Denote partial derivatives by subscripts: $V_x^i \equiv V_x(x_i, X) \equiv \partial V(x_i, X) / \partial x_i$, for example. Yi and Shin make the following two assumptions:

Assumption 4.1: $V_X(x_i, X) > 0$.

Assumption 4.2:

1. $V_{xx}(x_i, X) + kV_{xX}(x_i, X) < 0$;
2. $V_{xx}(x_i, X) + (k+N)V_{xX}(x_i, X) + kNV_{XX}(x_i, X) < 0$; and
3. $V_X(x_i, X) + kV_{xX}(x_i, X) > 0$ and $V_{xx}(x_i, X) - k[V_{xxx}(x_i, X) + kV_{xxX}(x_i, X)] \leq 0$, $k = 1, \ldots, N$.

Under Assumption 4.1, an increase in a firm's R&D investments raises other firms' profits. That is, R&D investments create positive externalities on other firms and, as a result, in the absence of R&D cooperation firms will *underinvest* in R&D for joint profit maximization. This assumption captures the public-good nature of R&D investments. Assumption 4.2 is a more technical assumption (concavity and stability assumption) that guarantees sensible comparative statics results.

Yi and Shin show that the above two assumptions are satisfied in the following widely-examined linear-quadratic model of cost-reducing R&D investments with spillovers in Cournot oligopoly (Katz, 1986; d'Aspremont and Jacquemin, 1988). Let q_i be firm i's output and let Q be the industry output. Suppose that the inverse demand function is given by $P(Q) = a - bQ$. Let c_i be firm i's marginal cost of production. In an interior equilibrium, firm i's product-market equilibrium profit is equal to

$$[a - (N+1)c_i + \Sigma_{j=1}^{N} c_j]^2 / [b(N+1)^2].$$

Let β be the inter-firm spillover rate in research, $0 \leq \beta \leq 1$. The spillover rate β measures the degree to which one firm's R&D investments benefit competitors without direct compensations through reverse engineering, leaks, and personnel movements. As in d'Aspremont and Jacquemin (1988), Katz (1986) and Spence (1984), firm i's marginal cost is assumed to be a decreasing function of its 'effective' R&D investments, defined by $x_i + \beta\Sigma_{j \neq i} x_j$: the sum of its R&D investments and the spillover rate times the competitors' total investments. Let $\bar{c}$ be the firms' marginal cost of production in the absence of R&D investments. Then firm i's marginal cost of production given the R&D investment vector $\mathbf{x} = (x_1, x_2, \ldots, x_N)$ is $c_i(\mathbf{x};\beta) \equiv \bar{c} - (x_i + \beta\Sigma_{j \neq i} x_j) = \bar{c} - ([1-\beta]x_i + \beta X)$.

Firm i's cost of R&D, denoted by $I^i(x_i)$, is a quadratic function of its own R&D: $I^i(x_i) = [\gamma/2]x_i^2$, $\gamma > 0$. Under these specifications, firm i's reduced-form profit function in the R&D game is given by:

$$V(x_i, X) = \frac{[A + (N+1)(1-\beta)x_i + (2\beta - 1)X]^2}{b(N+1)^2} - \frac{\gamma}{2} x_i^2. \qquad (4.5)$$

where $A \equiv a - \bar{c}$ is assumed to be positive. Yi and Shin show that assumptions 4.1 and 4.2 hold in the linear-quadratic model of cost-reducing R&D in Cournot oligopoly for $\beta > 1/2$ and $b\gamma \geq 2$.

Going back to the general model, let $x(n_i,C)$ be *per-member* equilibrium R&D investments of the size-n_i RJV, $X(n_i,C) \equiv n_i x(n_i,C)$ be *total* equilibrium R&D investments of the size-n_i RJV, and $X(C) \equiv \Sigma_{i=1}^m X(n_i, C) = \Sigma_{i=1}^m n_i x(n_i; C)$ be the *industry* R&D investments under the RJV structure $C = \{n_1, n_2, \ldots, n_m\}$. $x(n_i,C)$ satisfies the first-order condition:

$$V_x(x(n_i, C), X(C)) + n_i V_X(x(n_i, C), X(C)) = 0, \; i = 1, \ldots, m. \qquad (4.6)$$

Yi and Shin (2000, Appendix B) show that solving in the linear quadratic model yields:

$$\pi(n_i; C) = \frac{\gamma A^2[\Gamma - B(n_i)^2]}{2[\Gamma - B(0)B(n_i)]^2 [1 - \Lambda(C)]^2}, \qquad (4.7)$$

where $B(n_i) \equiv (N+1)(1-\beta) + n_i(2\beta - 1)$, $\Gamma \equiv \gamma b(N+1)^2/2$, and $\lambda(n_i) \equiv [(2\beta - 1)\ B(n_i)]/[\Gamma - B(0)\ B(n_i)]$, and $\Lambda(C) \equiv \Sigma_{i=1}^m = n_i \lambda(n_i)$. Yi and Shin show that (4.7) satisfy $(P.1) - (P.4)$.

Lemma 4.2: Research coalitions for internalization of R&D externalities satisfy $(P.1)$ – $(P.3)$ under Assumptions 4.1 and 4.2. They also satisfy $(P.4)$ for the linear-quadratic model of cost-reducing R&D investments with spillovers in Cournot oligopoly.

The intuition behind Lemma 4.2 is simple. A member of a research coalition internalizes the positive externalities its investments generate on member firms. Hence, a member of a large RJV (which has more partner firms than a member of a small RJV does) invests more in R&D than a member of a small RJV does (equation (4.6)). Hence, a member of a small RJV *free-rides* on the higher R&D investments by a member of a large RJV, thus earning a higher profit than a member of a large RJV does [$(P.2)$]. Next, suppose that two RJVs merge so that the coalition structure becomes more concentrated. The members of the merged RJV increase their R&D investments as they internalize positive externalities on new members. More generally, if a firm leaves its RJV to join another RJV of larger or equal size, the aggregate investments by these two coalitions increase. Firms which are not involved in the change in the RJV structure *and* the remaining members of the deviator's RJV benefit by *free-riding* on the increase in industry R&D investments [(P.1) and (P.3)]. Finally, in the linear-quadratic model, when a member of a coalition leaves it to join an equal-sized or larger one, the deviator's significantly increases its contributions to the 'public good' of R&D investments so that its payoff decreases [(P.4)].

4.2.3 Public goods (environmental) coalitions

Consider the following model of public goods coalitions that Yi (1997) considers, which is based on Ray and Vohra (1997). Each player is endowed with 1 unit of a private good. At cost $c(x_i)$, agent P_i can provide x_i units of the public good. Let $X=\Sigma_{i=1}^{N} x_i$ be the total amount of the public good. Each player enjoys the same benefit from consuming the public good, $g(X)$. Assume that $g'(X)>0$, $g''(X)\geq 0$, $c'(x_i)>0$, $c''(x_i)>0$, and $2[c''(x_i)]^2 > c'(x_i)c'''(x_i)$. (The last condition is quite weak. For example, it is satisfied by the constant-elasticity cost functions $c(x)=cx^{\gamma}$, $c>0$ and $\gamma>1$, because $2[c''(x)]^2-c'(x)c'''(x)=c\gamma(\gamma-1)x^{2\gamma-2}>0$ for $\gamma>1$.) Player Pi's net utility is given by $g(X)-c(x_i)$.

One example of a public goods coalition is an environmental coalition that forms to reduce international pollutants such as carbon dioxide. Think of x_i as country i's efforts in reducing its CO_2 at the cost of $c(x_i)$. Since the benefit of pollution control is global but the cost falls on the individual country that reduces pollution, an environmental coalition (such as the Rio Convention or the Kyoto Protocol) can be viewed as a public-goods coalition. It is impossible to list the countless papers written on environment. Some of papers that emphasize coalition formation are Carraro and Siniscalco (1993), Heal (1994), Carraro (1997) and Carraro and Moriconi (1998). In particular, the last two papers examine stable structures of environmental coalitions.

Suppose that the coalition structure is $C=\{n_1,n_2, \ldots, n_m\}$ and consider the size-n_i coalition. Without loss of generality, suppose that the first n_i players belong to this coalition. The members of the size-n_i coalition choose their provision of public goods to maximize their joint utility $\Sigma_{j=1}^{n_i}[g(X)-c(x_j)]=n_i g(X)-\Sigma_{j=1}^{n_i}c(x_j)$. Let $x(n_i;C)$ be the *per-member* provision of the public good by the size-n_i coalition, $X(n_i;C)=n_i x(n_i;C)$ be the total public good provided by the size-n_i coalition, and let $X(C)=\Sigma_{i=1}^{m}X(n_i;C)$ be the aggregate amount of the public good produced under the coalition structure $C=\{n_1,n_2, \ldots, n_m\}$. The first-order condition for an optimal level of public goods provided by a member of the size-n_i coalition is:

$$n_i g'(X(C))-c'(x(n_i;C))=0, \text{ for } i=1, \ldots, m. \quad (4.8)$$

In the case of linear utility function $g(X)=X$ and quadratic cost function $c(x)=dx^2$, $d>0$, equation (4.8) becomes $n_i-2dx(n_i;C)=0$, which leads to:

$$\pi(n_i;C) = (1/4d)\{2\Sigma_{j=1}^{m} n_j^2 - n_i^2\}. \tag{4.9}$$

Yi (1997) shows that this model of public goods coalitions satisfies the four conditions on the partition function with positive externalities:

Lemma 4.3: Public goods coalitions with utility function $g(X)$ and cost function $c(x_i)$ satisfy $(P.1)-(P.3)$ if $g'(X)>0$, $g''(X)\geq 0$, $c'(x_i)>0$, $c''(x_i)>0$, and $2[c''(x_i)]^2 > c'(x_i)c'''(x_i)$. They also satisfy $(P.4)$ for $g(X)=X$ and $c(x) = dx^2$, $d>0$.

The idea behind Lemma 4.3 is simple. Equation (4.8) shows that a member of the size-n_i coalition ($n_i \geq 2$) produces more public good than the amount which maximizes his *individual* utility given other agents' production of the public good. This result follows from the fact that, in determining the optimal amount of the public good to produce, a member of the size-n_i coalition takes into account the positive externality on members of his coalition. An inspection of equation (4.8) further reveals that, in a given coalition structure, a member of a large coalition produces more public good than a member of a small coalition does. Hence, a member of a large coalition enjoys lower net utility than a member of a small coalition does [$(P.2)$]. If a member of a coalition leaves it to join a larger or equal-sized one, these two coalitions increase their total amount of the public good, thus benefiting members of other coalitions [$(P.1)$]. But the remaining members of the deviator's former coalition reduce their production of the public good. As a result, the remaining members of the deviator's former coalition become better off [$(P.3)$]. Finally, the deviator becomes worse off [$(P.4)$], for example, for $g(X)=X$ and $c(x)=dx^2$, $d>0$, because he bears (with the existing members of his new coalition) the burden of increasing the total amount of the public good. These results reflect the fundamental *free-riding* problems associated with the formation of public goods coalitions.

4.2.4 Free-trade areas

Yi (2000) considers a simple model of free-trade areas with N ex-ante symmetric countries.[18] Member countries of a free-trade area abolish tariffs on imports from each other, but each member country sets its external tariffs to maximize its own welfare. Each country transforms the endowment (numeraire good, denoted by M) to a final product (denoted by q_i) using a linear production function. Let c be the constant unit cost of producing q_i. There are no transportation costs. The representative consumer in country i has a utility function of the form $u^i(\mathbf{q}_i;\ M_i)=v(\mathbf{q}_i)+M_i=M_i + aQ_i - Q_i^2/2$, where q_{ij} is country i's consumption of country j's product,

$\mathbf{q}_i = (q_{i1, \ldots, qiN})$ is country i's consumption profile, $Q_i = \Sigma_{j=1}^{N} q_{ij}$, M_i is country i's consumption of the numeraire good.[19] The numeraire good is transferred across countries to settle the balance of trade. The profits of the domestic firm and the tariff revenues are rebated back to the consumers. Thus, country i's welfare (W^i) consists of four components: the domestic consumer surplus (CS^i), the domestic firm's profit in home market (π^{ii}), the tariff revenue (TR^i), and the home firm's export profits (π^{ji}, $j \neq i$): $W^i = CS^i + \pi^{ii} + TR^i + \Sigma_{j \neq i} \pi^{ji}$. Let τ_{ij} be country i's *specific* tariff on imports from country j. Then, country j's *effective* unit cost of exporting to country i is $c_{ij} = c + \tau_{ij}$. Yi assumes that markets are segmented so that firms compete by choosing quantities in each country. Country i's inverse import demand for country j's product is given by $p_{ij}(Q_i) = a - Q_i$. Consider a free trade area of size k. Without loss of generality, suppose that countries 1, 2, ..., k belong to the free-trade area and consider country i, $i = 1, \ldots, k$. It solves:

$$\text{Max } W^i = CS^i + \pi^{ii} + TR^i + \Sigma_{j \neq i} \pi^{ji}, \ \{\tau_{ij}\}_{j=k+1}^{N} \tag{4.10}$$

where $\tau_{ij} = 0$ for $j = 1, \ldots, k$. Yi (2000) shows that the welfare of a member of a free-trade area of size-n_i in a coalition structure $C = \{n_1, n_2, \ldots, n_m\}$ is given by:

$$W^F(n_i;C) = \frac{1}{2} - \frac{2n_i - 1}{[(2n_i - 1)(N+1) + 3(n_i + 1)]} + [n_i - 1]\left\{\frac{2(n_i + 1)}{[(2n_i - 1)(N+1) + 3(n_i + 1)]}\right\}^2 + \Sigma_{j=1, j \neq i}^{m} n_j \left\{\frac{2n_j - 1}{[(2n_j - 1)(N+1) + 3(n_j + 1)]}\right\}^2. \tag{4.11}$$

(I am using the superscript F in order to make a distinction between free-trade areas and customs unions in the next section.) An inspection of $W^F(n_i;C)$ shows that a nonmember country's volume of exports and export profits to a free-trade area are increasing functions of the size of the free-trade area:

Lemma 4.4. Free-trade areas with the utility function $u(Q;\ M) = aQ - [1/2]Q^2 + M$ and the cost function $c(q) = cq$ satisfy ($P.1$).

Intuitively, when a free-trade area forms, member countries abolish tariffs on imports from each other. In the above model, tariffs extract foreign countries' rent in the home country at the expense of domestic consumer surplus. When country A reduces its external tariffs on country B (say due to signing a free-trade agreement), imports from other countries, say country C, decrease. Since tariff revenue is proportional to the volume of imports, country A's welfare-maximizing tariffs on country C decreases. In the above model, it turns out that the reduction in external tariffs is sufficiently large to make nonmember countries better off [(P.1)].

While the above model of free-trade areas satisfies (P.1), it may violate other conditions. For example, (P.2) is violated for $N=3$, because $\pi(2;\{2,1\})=0.4488>\pi(1;\{2,1\})=0.4408$. (A tedious derivation shows that $\pi(1;\{N-1,1\})<\pi(N-1;\{N-1,1\})$ for $N=3$ and 4 but $\pi(1;\{N-1,1\})>\pi(N-1;\{N-1,1\})$ for $N\geq 5$.)

4.2.5 Other economic coalitions with positive externalities

Economic coalitions that confer positive external effects on nonmembers are not limited to the above examples. For example, Kohler (2002) shows that the formation of a monetary union (a set of countries that coordinate monetary policies) creates positive effects for the outside countries by promoting price stability [(P.1)].[20]

4.3 Equilibrium coalition structures with positive externalities

The following definition is useful in characterizing equilibrium coalition structures with positive external effects:

Definition 4.1: $C=\{n_1,n_2, ..., n_m\}$ is *stand-alone stable* if and only if $\pi(n_i;C)\geq\pi(1;C_i)$, $C_i=C\backslash\{n_i\}\cup\{n_i-1,1\}$ for all $i=1, ..., m$.

A coalition structure C is stand-alone stable if and only if no player finds it profitable to leave his coalition to form a singleton coalition, *holding* the rest of coalition structure constant (including his former coalition). Notice that, by definition, the degenerate coalition structure $\{1,1, ..., 1\}$ is stand-alone stable.

In the case of output cartels in the linear Cournot oligopoly model whose per-member partition function is given by equation (4.4), the only stand-alone stable coalition structure is $\{1,1, ..., 1\}$. For the linear-quadratic model of the public-goods coalitions whose per-member partition function is given by (4.9), a coalition structure is stand-alone stable if and only if the size of the largest coalition is less than or equal to 3.

In order to save on notation, let $\{\mathbf{a}_p,\mathbf{b}_q, ..., \mathbf{h}_w\}=\{a, ..., a,b, ..., b, ..., h, ..., h\}$, where there are p entries of a, q entries of b, ..., and w entries of h. Let

$I(N/k)$ denote the next higher integer to N/k, including N/k. (For example, $I(2.5)=I(3)=3$.)

Before presenting general results, let us consider the following example:

Example 4.1: $N=4$. The five coalition structures are as follows (where the small numbers below a coalition are the per-member profits for that coalition in that coalition structure): $\underset{11}{\{4\}}$, $\underset{7\;16}{\{3,1\}}$, $\underset{9\;9}{\{2,2\}}$, $\underset{3\;6\;6}{\{2,1,1\}}$, and $\underset{4\;4\;4\;4}{\{1,1,1,1\}}$. There are two stand-alone stable coalition structures: {2,2} and {1,1,1,1}.

1. The single coalition formation game By the rule of the game, {2,2} is not feasible. The unique Nash equilibrium coalition structure (NE CS) of the simultaneous-move Single Coalition Formation game is {1,1,1,1} supported by a strategy profile in which all four players announce 'Out'. A strong Nash equilibrium coalition structure (SNE CS) does not exist, because all four players can profitably deviate to the grand coalition by announcing 'In'. However, {1,1,1,1} is coalition-proof, because the above deviation is not self-enforceable.[21] To see why, notice that the group deviation does not constitute a Nash equilibrium among the deviators (holding other players' strategies fixed).

In the sequential-move version of this game, {1,1,1,1} is the unique subgame-perfect Nash equilibrium coalition structure (SPE CS), because all four players announce 'Out' in the unique SPE path of the game. To see why, consider P_4 first. Since the only stand-alone stable coalition structure is {1,1,1,1}, P_4's optimal strategy is to announce 'Out' regardless of history (that is, how many previous players have announced 'In'). Now, consider P_3 and let k be the number of previous players who have announced 'In'. (k can be 0, 1, 2.) In each case, regardless of P_3's announcement, P_4 announces 'Out' in the unique equilibrium path of the subgame. Since $\pi(k;\, k,\mathbf{1}_{N-k}\}) < \pi(1;\{k-1,\mathbf{1}_{N-k+1}\})$ for $k=2, 3, 4$, P_3's sequentially rational strategy is to announce 'Out'. Similar arguments establish that all four players announce 'Out' along the unique SPE path.

2. The simultaneous-move open membership game There are two pure-strategy NE coalition structures. {2,2} can be supported by $\alpha=(a_1, a_1, a_2, a_2)$. Each player earns 9. ({2,2} is an NE CS, because if a player, say P_1, deviates and joins the other size-2 coalition by announcing a_2, then the resulting coalition structure is {3,1} and the player will receive 7. If P_1 instead announces a_3 and forms a singleton coalition, then it will earn 6.) The other NE CS is {1,1,1,1}, which can be supported by $\alpha=(a_1, a_1, a_2, a_2)$. Each player earns 4. No other coalition structure can be supported as a pure-strategy NE outcome. Now, the unique CPNE CS is {2,2}. First, notice that the only profitable group deviation from {2,2} is the one to the grand coalition. (Therefore, no SNE CS exists.) The grand coalition can be formed, for example, by P_3 and P_4 agreeing to announce a_1. However, even though the agreement is profitable, it is not self-enforceable, because a deviator (say P_3) will not carry it out given that the other deviator does. Similarly, we can check that there is no other self-enforceable agreement form {2,2} to {4}. On the other hand, from {1,1,1,1}, all four players can make a profitable and self-enforceable agreement to form {2,2} by agreeing to $\alpha = (a_1, a_1, a_2, a_2)$. The agreement is self-enforceable because it constitutes a CPNE.[22]

3. The simultaneous-move exclusive membership game There are three NE coalition structures: {3,1} supported by, say ($\{P_1\}$, $\{P_2, P_3, P_4\}$, $\{P_2, P_3, P_4\}$, $\{P_2, P_3, P_4\}$); {2,2} by, say, ($\{P_1, P_2\}$, $\{P_1, P_2\}$, $\{P_3, P_4\}$, $\{P_3, P_4\}$); and {1,1,1,1} by, say, ($\{P_1\}$, $\{P_2\}$, $\{P_3\}$, $\{P_4\}$). Unlike the Open Membership game, there may be multiple CPNE coalition structures.[23] In this example there are two CPNE CS: {3,1} and {2,2} . In the Open Membership game, {3,1} could not be supported as a NE outcome, because a member of the size-3 coalition can earn a higher profit by announcing the same address as the player who belongs to the singleton coalition. However, in the Exclusive Membership game, given P_1's strategy above, there is no way for other players to form a coalition with P_1 without the consent of P_1. Since P_1 earns the highest payoff possible by remaining as a singleton coalition in {3,1}, there are no profitable group deviations from the above strategy profile.[24] {2,2} is another CPNE CS.[25]

4. The simultaneous-move coalition unanimity game The grand coalition {4} is a SNE CS, supported by a strategy profile in which all four players announce $\{P_1, P_2, P_3, P_4\}$. If a group of players deviate, then the remaining members form singleton coalitions. Hence, at least *some* deviators are worse off. {3,1} and {2,2} are SNE coalition structures as well.

5. The infinite-horizon sequential-move coalition unanimity game In the unique equilibrium path of the Size Announcement game, P_1 announces '1' and P_2 announces '3'. (Given that P_1 has announced '1', {2,2} is not a feasible coalition structure. If P_2 announces '2', {2,1,1} forms and P_2's payoff is 3. If P_2 instead announces '1', P_3 follows by announcing '1', resulting in {1,1,1,1}. P_2's payoff is 4.)

6. The equilibrium binding agreements game {2,1,1} is not stable, because the two players in the size-2 coalition would dissolve their coalition and earn higher payoffs. {2,2} is stable, because the dissolution of a size-2 coalition would result in the break-up of the other size-2 coalition and the resulting coalition structure is {1,1,1,1}. {3,1} is stable, because any deviation by a subset of members of the size-3 coalition result in {1,1,1,1}. {4} is not stable, because one member would deviate to form a singleton coalition. The remaining three members of the (formerly) grand coalition stay as a size-3 coalition, because {3,1} is stable.

The above example illustrates several points. First, if one were to allow for only one non-degenerate coalition (as in the Single Coalition Formation game), one would come to a completely different prediction about the stable coalition structure from the case in which one allows for the formation of multiple coalitions (as in the other five games). In the Single Coalition Formation Game, the unique stable outcome is {1,1,1,1}, whereas coalition structures that are at least as concentrated as {2,2} are stable in the other five games. Hence, if the underlying economic situation allows for multiple coalitions, one might come to a very misleading conclusion about stable coalition structures if one were to allow for only one nondegenerate coalition. Second, except in the Simultaneous-Move Coalition Unanimity game, the grand coalition is not a stable outcome. This result reflects the *free-riding* problems inherent for economic coalitions with positive externalities. Whereas all players would be collectively better off under the grand coalition, free-riding problems lead to more fragmented coalition structures in the stable outcome.

In the remainder of this section, the above results are formally demonstrated.

4.3.1 A single coalition formation game

In this restricted game, the possible coalition structures are $\{N\}$, $\{N-1\}$, $\{N-2\}$, ..., {1,1, ..., 1}. Yi (1999) shows that the most concentrated coalition structure among these N 'single' coalition structures is a stable outcome.

Proposition 4.1: Suppose that $C_s \equiv \{k_s, 1, \ldots, 1\}$ is stand-alone stable, but $\{k, 1, \ldots, 1\}$ is not, for $k_s < k \leq N$. Under (P.1) and (P.2):

1. C_s is the (generically) unique CPNE CS of the simultaneous-move Single Coalition Formation Game. Since {1,1, ..., 1} is stand-alone stable, a CPNE CS exists.[26]
2. C_s is the (generically) unique SPE CS of the sequential-move Single Coalition Formation Game.

The above result shows that the grand coalition is the equilibrium outcome of the Single Coalition Formation game if and only if it is stand-alone stable. However, in coalition formation games with positive externalities and with three or more players, the grand coalition is rarely stand-alone stable. For example, in the linear Cournot cartel model (equation (4.4)), the industry-wide cartel is not stand-alone stable for $N \geq 3$. In the linear-quadratic model public-goods coalitions (equation (4.9), the industry-wide cartel is not stand-alone stable for $N \geq 4$. In the linear-quadratic model of research joint ventures with spillovers (equation (4.7)), Yi and Shin (2000) show that the industry-wide coalition is not stand-alone stable for $N \geq 5$. Finally, in Kohler's (2002) model of monetary unions, the grand union is not stand-alone stable for $N \geq 4$.

4.3.2 The simultaneous-move open membership game

Economic models with positive externalities in Section 4.2 show that (*P*.4) requires more stringent conditions on the underlying model than (*P*.1)–(*P*.3) do. Indeed, it can be shown that (*P*.4) is violated under some parameter values in Deneckere and Davidson's (1985) model of cartel formation in Bertrand oligopoly. Hence, Yi and Shin (2000) begin their analysis with only (*P*.1)–(*P*.3).

Proposition 4.2: For $N \leq 4$, a NE CS exists in the simultaneous-move Open Membership game. Under (*P*.1)–(*P*.3), the most concentrated NE CS is the unique CPNE CS.

For $N \geq 5$, however, a Nash equilibrium coalition structure may fail to exist in the Open Membership game even under (*P*.1)–(*P*.3). Consider the following example that Yi and Shin (2000) consider:

Example 4.2: Nonexistence of an NE CS in the simultaneous-move Open Membership game is illustrated below:

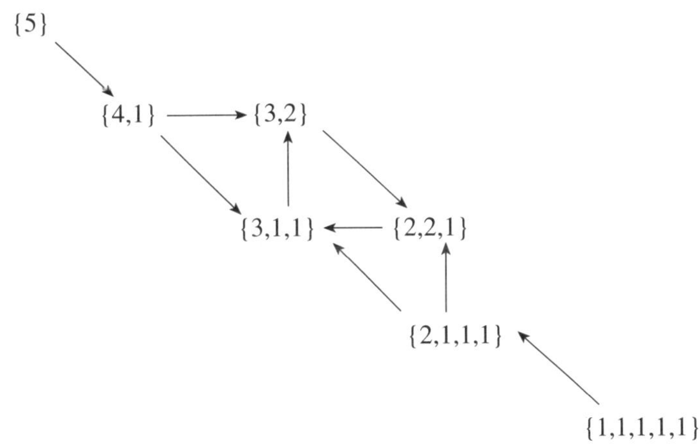

An arrow from a coalition structure C to another coalition structure C' means that there is a member of a coalition in C who becomes better off by changing his membership to some coalition in C'. (C' can be obtained from C by changing one player's coalition affiliation.) For example, $\{4,1\} \rightarrow \{3,2\}$ means that $\pi(4;\{4,1\}) < \pi(2;\{3,2\})$. It is easy to see that *no* coalition structure can be supported as a Nash equilibrium outcome, because in any coalition structure there is at least one player who becomes better off by leaving its coalition either to join another one or to form a one-player coalition. The problem in Example 4.2 is that there is a 'circle' among $\{3,2\}$, $\{3,1,1\}$ and $\{2,2,1\}$. Condition (P.4) prevents such a circle from arising by making all arrows point to the 'right' (to a less concentrated coalition structure) between two coalition structures with the same number of coalitions.

Remark: One may argue that a player should be allowed not to form a coalition with other players even in the Open Membership game. (That is, the membership of any coalition with two or more players is open, but a player should not be forced to form a coalition with other players.) Technically, one can allow for this possibility by expanding the strategy space in the Open Membership game to include an address '0'. Any player who announces '0' forms a one-player coalition which other players cannot join. Then, $\{1,1, ..., 1\}$ can always be supported as a Nash equilibrium outcome of this modified Open Membership game by letting each player choose '0'. We find this 'solution' to the existence problem unsatisfactory. Even in this modified game, a stable coalition structure may not exist if one allows for a 'pairwise' deviation in which any two players can deviate jointly. Since $\pi(2;\{2,\mathbf{1}_3\}) > \pi(1;\{\mathbf{1}_5\})$ in Example 4.2, no 'pairwise' stable coalition structure exists.

Under (P.4), the only coalition structures which can be Nash equilibrium outcomes are $C = \{n_1, n_2, ..., n_m\}$, $n_1 \geq n_2 \geq ... \geq n_m$, with $n_1 \leq n_m + 1$. There are N such coalition structures: ignoring integer constraints, these are $\{N\}$, $\{N/2, N/2\}$, $\{N/3, N/3, N/3\}$, $\{N/4, N/4, N/4\}$, ..., $\{2,2, ..., 2\}$, $\{2,2, ..., 2,1,1\}$, ..., $\{2,1,1, ..., 1\}$, and $\{1,1, ..., 1\}$. (More precisely, Consider $C = \{n_1, n_2, ..., n_m\}$, $n_1 \geq n_2 \geq ... \geq n_m$, with $n_1 \leq n_m + 1$. Let $k = I(N/m)$ and $q = mk - N$ (≥ 0). Then $C = \{\mathbf{k}_{m-q}, \mathbf{k-1}_q\}$. C is a 'symmetric' coalition structure given the integer constraint.) Notice that $\{N\}$ is more concentrated than $\{N/2, N/2\}$, which in turn is more concentrated than $\{N/3, N/3, N/3\}$, and so on.

Yi and Shin (2000) show that, under (P.4), the most concentrated standalone stable coalition structure among these N coalition structures is a Nash equilibrium outcome. When one adds (P.1)–(P.3), it is the unique CPNE CS of the Open Membership game.

Proposition 4.3: Suppose that $C^{**} \equiv \{\mathbf{k}^{**}_{m^{**}-q^{**}}, \mathbf{k}-\mathbf{1}^{**}_{q^{**}}\}$ is stand-alone stable, where $k^{**} = I(N/m^{**})$ and $q^{**} = m^{**}k^{**} - N$ (≥ 0). Further suppose that $\{\mathbf{k}_{m-q}, \mathbf{k}-\mathbf{1}_q\}$ is not stand-alone stable, where $k = I(N/m)$ and $q = mk - N$, for all $m = 1, \ldots, m^{**} - 1$. Then, in the simultaneous-move Open Membership game:

1. Under (P.4), C^{**} is the most concentrated NE CS; and
2. Under (P.1)–(P.4), C^{**} is the unique CPNE CS.

Several remarks are in order. First, C^{**} in the above proposition is well-defined: it is the most concentrated stand-alone stable coalition structure among N 'symmetric' coalition structures $C = \{\mathbf{k}_{m-q}, \mathbf{k}-\mathbf{1}_q\}$. Second, the grand coalition is a Nash equilibrium outcome if and only if it is stand-alone stable (as in the Single Coalition Formation game). Third, roughly speaking, C^{**} is a coalition-proof Nash equilibrium outcome, because (1) any deviation which creates a bigger coalition than k^{**} is not self-enforceable (if it is a 'symmetric' coalition structure, it is not stand-alone stable and the deviator who belongs to the biggest coalition in the new coalition structure is better off by further deviating to form a singleton coalition; otherwise, by (P.4), he is better off by further deviating to join one of the smaller coalitions); and (2) any deviation that breaks up coalitions in C^{**} is not profitable for some deviators by a combination of the standalone stability of C^{*} and (P.1)–(P.3).

4.3.3 The simultaneous-move exclusive membership game

Yi and Shin (2000) establish the following results. Unlike in the Open Membership game, the existence of an NE CS is guaranteed in the simultaneous-move Exclusive Membership game. But there can be many NE coalition structures. The most concentrated NE CS is coalition-proof (as in the Open Membership game), but there can be multiple CPNE coalition structures (as in Example 4.1). The most concentrated CPNE CS of the Exclusive Membership game is at least as concentrated as the unique CPNE CS of the Open Membership game.

Proposition 4.4: A coalition structure is an NE CS of the Exclusive Membership game if and only if it is stand-alone stable. Since $\{1, 1, \ldots, 1\}$ is stand-alone stable, an NE CS exists in the Exclusive Membership game.

Intuitively, stand-alone stability is a *necessary* condition for an NE CS, because if a coalition structure is not stand-alone stable, then there is a coalition whose member is better off by leaving it to form a singleton coalition, *provided* that the remaining members stay as a smaller coalition. In the

Exclusive Membership game (as well as in the Single Coalition game and in the Open Membership game), the remaining members do stay as a smaller coalition. Stand-alone stability is also a *sufficient* condition for a NE CS of the Exclusive Membership game, because one can support a stand-alone stable coalition structure as a NE outcome by a strategy profile in which every player announces the list of his coalition members only. Then, no player can join other coalitions. (In contrast, in the Open Membership game, stand-alone stability is only a necessary condition for a NE CS, because a player can join any existing coalition. But as in the Open Membership game, the grand coalition is a NE CS outcome if and only if it is stand-alone stable.)

Proposition 4.5: Suppose that $C^* \equiv \{\mathbf{k}^*_{m^*-1}, r^*\}$ is stand-alone stable, where $m^* = I(N/k^*)$ and $r^* = N - (m^* - 1)k^*$, $1 \leq r \leq k^*$. Further suppose that the size-k coalition is not stand-alone stable in any coalition structure, for all $k = k^* + 1, \ldots, N$. Then, in the Exclusive Membership game:

1. C^* is the most concentrated NE CS;
   Under $(P.1)-(P.3)$,
2. C^* is a CPNE CS;
3. If there is any other CPNE coalition structure, it has exactly m^* coalitions and is less concentrated than C^*; and
4. If $r^* = k^* - 1$ or k^*, then C^* is the unique CPNE CS.

The intuition for the result that C^* is a CPNE CS of the Exclusive Membership game is similar to the case of the Open Membership game. Notice that the results for the Exclusive Membership game do not require $(P.4)$. Also note the difference between $\{\mathbf{k}_{m-1}, r\}$ and $\{\mathbf{k}_{m-q}, \mathbf{k-1}_q\}$ in Propositions 4.4 and 4.5: whereas $\{\mathbf{k}_{m-1}, r\}$ is defined to be the *most* concentrated coalition structure with the size of the largest coalition equal to k, $\{\mathbf{k}_{m-q}, \mathbf{k-1}_q\}$ is defined to be the *least* concentrated coalition structure with m coalitions. As a result, C^* is (weakly) more concentrated than C^{**}: the most concentrated NE CS (which is the most concentrated CPNE CS) of the Exclusive Membership game is (weakly) more concentrated than the most concentrated NE CS (which is the unique CPNE CS) of the Open Membership game, as in Example 4.1. More generally, Yi and Shin (2000) show the following result.

Proposition 4.6: Under $(P.1)$–$(P.4)$, the unique CPNE CS of the Open Membership game is (weakly) less concentrated than *any* coalition-proof Nash equilibrium RJV structure of the Exclusive Membership game.

4.3.4: The simultaneous-move coalition unanimity game

Unlike the preceding games, the grand union is a stable outcome in this game, because no group of players can profitably deviate from it.

Proposition 4.7: Suppose that the aggregate payoff of the players is greater under the grand coalition than under any other coalition structure: $N\pi(N;\{N\}) \geq \Sigma_{i=1}^{m} n_i \pi(n_i;C)$ for all $C = \{n_1, n_2, \ldots, n_m\}$. Then, in the simultaneous-move Coalition Unanimity Game:

1. Under $(P.2)$, $\{N\}$ is *a* SNE CS.
2. Under $(P.1)$–$(P.3)$, if $\{N\}$ is stand-alone stable, it is the *unique* SNE CS.

Proof: See the Appendix.

The above proposition shows that the grand coalition is *always* a stable outcome in the Simultaneous-Move Coalition Unanimity game. This result might be somewhat surprising, because it might seem that it is 'hard' to form a coalition in the Coalition Unanimity game since the consent of all the potential members is required. This conjecture is wrong for the case of positive externalities. It actually becomes hard to *dissolve* a coalition. The players contemplating leaving the coalition would want the remaining members to stay together as a smaller coalition. Since the departure of some members of a coalition results in a complete dissolution of the coalition, members of a coalition find leaving it less attractive when coalition formation creates positive external effects on other players.

4.3.5 The infinite-horizon sequential-move coalition unanimity game

In the case of output cartels in the linear Cournot oligopoly model (whose per-member partition function is given in equation (4.4)), Bloch (1996) shows that the unique SPE CS of the Coalition Unanimity game is $C^u = \{k^u, 1, 1, \ldots, 1\}$, where $k^u = I[(2N+3-(4N+5)^{1/2})/2]$ is the size of the 'minimum' profitable cartel identified by Salant et al. (1983). In equilibrium, the first $N-k^u$ players announce 1 and the next player announces k^u. Since $k^u < N$ for $N \geq 6$, the grand coalition is not the equilibrium outcome of the Coalition Unanimity game for $N \geq 6$. (In this linear model, the only stand-alone stable coalition structure is $\{1, 1, \ldots, 1\}$. Thus, $\{1, \ldots, 1\}$ is the unique NE (and CPNE) CS in all three preceding games.)

Unlike the preceding games, however, it is hard to come to a sharp characterization of the SPE CS of the infinite-horizon Coalition Unanimity game with positive externalities. But in a special case that Yi (1997) examines, the unique SPE CS of the infinite-horizon Coalition Unanimity game is at least as concentrated as C^*, the most concentrated CPNE CS of the Exclusive Membership game.

Proposition 4.8: Suppose that $k^* \geq N/2$ in Proposition 4.5 so that $C^* = k^*, N-k^*\}$. Further suppose that $\pi(N-k^*;\{k^*,N-k^*\}) \geq \pi(1;\{N-2,1,1\})$. Under $(P.1)$–$(P.3)$, the SPE CS of the infinite-horizon Coalition Unanimity game is $\{k^u, N-k^u\}$, where $k^u \in \arg\max_{k^* \leq k \leq N} \pi(k;\{k,N-k\})$. Since $k^u \geq k^*$, the unique SPE CS of the infinite-horizon Coalition Unanimity game is (weakly) more concentrated than the most concentrated CPNE CS of the simultaneous-move Exclusive Membership game.

4.3.6 The equilibrium binding agreements game

Yi (1997) shows that under $(P.1)$–$(P.3)$, a stand-alone stable coalition structure is stable in the Equilibrium Binding Agreements game.

Proposition 4.9: Under $(P.1)$–$(P.3)$, a stand-alone stable coalition structure is a stable outcome in the Equilibrium Binding Agreements game.

Since C^*, the most concentrated CPNE CS of the simultaneous-move Exclusive Membership game, is stand-alone stable, it is also stable in the Equilibrium Binding Agreements game. Hence, we conclude that the Equilibrium Binding Agreements game can support a (weakly) more concentrated coalition structure as a stable outcome than does the Exclusive Membership game.

Like the infinite-horizon Coalition Unanimity Game, it is hard to obtain a general characterization result of the stable coalition structures in the Equilibrium Binding Agreements Game. Furthermore, it is not easy to obtain conditions under which one can compare the degree of concentration in these two games. For example, consider the linear Cournot cartel model which Bloch (1996) and Ray and Vohra (1997) examine. For $N=6$, $\{5,1\}$ is the unique subgame perfect equilibrium coalition structure of the infinite-horizon Coalition Unanimity game. $\{5,1\}$ is more concentrated than $\{3,2,1\}$, which is the most concentrated stable coalition structure in the Equilibrium Binding Agreements game. For $N=9$, $\{8,1\}$ is the unique equilibrium coalition structure of the infinite-horizon Coalition Unanimity game. But $\{9\}$ (which is more concentrated than $\{8,1\}$) is stable under the Equilibrium Binding Agreements rule, as shown by Ray and Vohra (1997).

In summary, the results in this section show the following pattern. In the case of positive externalities, the simultaneous-move Coalition Unanimity Game supports the grand coalition, which is the most concentrated coalition structure, as the equilibrium outcome. Other games of coalition formation typically do not support the grand coalition as stable outcomes. The infinite-horizon Coalition Unanimity Game and the Equilibrium Binding Agreements Game support more concentrated coalition structures as stable outcomes than does the Exclusive Membership game, which in turn supports more concentrated coalition structures as stable outcomes than does the Open Membership game. The equilibrium coalition structure in the Single Coalition Formation game is the least concentrated.

5. ECONOMIC COALITIONS WITH NEGATIVE EXTERNALITIES

5.1 Conditions on the Per-Member Partition Function: Negative Externalities

(N.1) $\pi(n_i;C)>\pi(n_i;C')$, where $\{n_i\}\subset C$, C' and $C'\backslash\{n_i\}$ can be derived from $C\backslash\{n_i\}$ by merging coalitions in $C\backslash\{n_i\}$.

If coalitions merge to form a larger coalition, *outside* coalitions not involved in the merger are worse off.

Condition (N.1) is the defining feature of coalition formation with negative external effects across coalitions. Notice that condition (N.1) is the opposite of condition (P.1) in the previous section (when we restrict condition (P.1) for the case of mergers of coalitions.) The next two conditions are about the *internal* effects of changes in the coalition structure (the effects on players involved in the changes in the coalition structure).

(N.2) $\pi(n_j;C)<\pi(k;C')$, where (1) $\{n_1,n_2, ..., n_j\}\subseteq C$; (2) $k=\Sigma_{i=1}^{j} n_i$ and $C' = C\backslash\{n_1,n_2, ..., n_j\}\cup\{k\}$; and (3) $n_i \geq n_j$ for $i=1, 2, ..., j-1$.

A member of a coalition becomes better off if his coalition merges with larger or equal-sized coalitions.

(N.3) $p\ \ \pi(n_j;C)<\pi\ \ (n_i+1;C')$, where $C'=C\ \backslash\{n_i,n_j\}\cup\{n_i+1,\ n_j-1\}$, $n_i\geq n_j\geq 2$.

A member of a coalition becomes better off if he leaves his coalition to join another coalition of equal or larger size.

Several remarks are in order. First, under (N.2), *all* coalition structures are stand-alone stable. However, we will see that stand-alone stability is not useful in determining equilibrium coalition structures in the case of negative externalities. Second, (N.3) is the opposite of (P.4) in the previous section. Third, (N.2) and (N.3) are distinct from each other, because (N.2) concerns the *merger* of coalitions whereas (N.3) concerns an *individual* change in coalition affiliation. Finally, (N.2) does not imply that the merger of coalitions necessarily benefits the members of the *larger* coalitions involved. For example, when two coalitions combine, members of the larger coalition may earn lower payoffs. Similarly, (N.3) does not imply that, when a member of a coalition joins a larger one, the *existing* members of the larger coalition necessarily become better off. (By symmetry, the merger of two *equal-sized* coalitions benefits all members. Similarly, the existing members of a coalition become better off by admitting a new member from another coalition of equal size.)

5.2 Economic Models of Coalition Formation with Negative Externalities

5.2.1 Joint ventures with efficiency gains

Consider a homogeneous-good Cournot oligopoly with inverse demand $P(X)$, where X is the industry output and $P'(X)<0$, $P''(X)\leq 0$ when $P(X)>0$. There are N ex-ante symmetric firms, which have access to a common production technology. Firm i's cost function is given by $c^i(x_i,\omega_i)=\mu(\omega_i)x_i$, $\mu(\omega_i)>0$ and $\mu'(\omega_i)<0$, where x_i is firm i's output, ω_i is firm i's stock of productive assets including intangible production know how. Notice that an increase in a firm's stock of research assets lowers the total cost and the marginal cost of production.

If a group of firms form a joint venture, they can combine their productive assets and realize higher efficiencies, since a member of a coalition can utilize the total pool of productive assets of the members. If there are synergy effects from pooling the expertise of the participating firms, the members of a coalition will gain a competitive advantage against competing firms (or coalitions). Bloch (1995) and Yi (1998a, 1998c) model this synergy effect by assuming that each firm initially has one unit of non-overlapping productive asset. By forming a coalition, the member firms gain access to the total pool of research knowledge of members. Hence, a member of a size-k coalition has access to k 'effective' units of research assets.

For the linear demand function $P(X)=A-X$, the per-member partition function is given by:

$$\pi(n_i;C)=(A-(N+1)\mu(n_i)+\Sigma_{j=1}^{m} n_j\mu(n_j))^2/(N+1)^2. \qquad (5.1)$$

It is straightforward to show that the above per-member partition function given in equation (4.1) satisfies (N.1)–(N.3). More generally, Yi (1998a) establishes the following result:

Lemma 5.1: Joint ventures with efficiency gains in the Cournot oligopoly with the inverse demand function $P(X)$, $P'(X)<0$, $P''(X)\leq 0$ when $P(X)>0$ and the cost function $c(x,\omega)=\mu(\omega)x$, $\mu'(\omega)<0$, satisfy $(N.1)$–$(N.3)$.

The intuition for Lemma 5.1 is as follows. When joint ventures (say the size-n_i and size-n_j ventures, $n_i \geq n_j$) merge, their members combine their productive assets and thus lower their marginal costs. As a result, they steal business from other firms, reducing other firms' profits [$(N.1)$]. This merger increases the profits of the smaller size-n_j venture, because their production costs decrease relative to other firms as well as in absolute terms [$(N.2)$]. (Due to the disparity in cost reduction, however, the members of larger size-n_i venture may earn lower profits.) If a member of a size-n_j venture joins a larger or equal-sized size-n_i venture, the deviator earns a higher profit, because its production costs decrease both relative to other firms and in absolute terms.

5.2.2 Customs unions

A customs union is a set of countries that abolish tariffs on imports from member countries, but set *common* external tariffs on imports from nonmember countries. Recall that members of a free-trade area also abolish tariffs on internal trade, but set *individual* external tariffs. Strikingly, when external tariffs are set for welfare maximization, this difference in how tariffs are determined changes the *sign* of the effect of the formation of a coalition on the welfare of nonmember countries: the formation of a customs union *reduces* the welfare of nonmember countries. Consider the model of intra-industry trade in Section 4.2.4. Now, instead of assuming that a member country of a trading bloc of size k maximizes its *own* welfare, assume that it maximizes the *aggregate* welfare of the member countries in setting its external tariffs. A member of the size-k customs union solves:

$$\underset{\{\tau_{ij}\}_{j=k+1}^{N},}{\text{Max}} \ \Sigma_{i=1}^{k} W^i \tag{5.2}$$

where $\tau_{ij}=0$ for $j=1, ..., k$. Yi (1996a) shows that the per-member partition function is given by:

$$W^C(n_i;C)=\frac{1}{2}-\frac{1}{(N+1)+(n_j+1)(2n_j+1)} + \Sigma_{j\neq i}^{m}\frac{n_j}{[(N+1)+(n_j+1)(2n_j+1)]^2}. \tag{5.3}$$

Lemma 5.2: Customs unions with the utility function $u(Q;\ M)=aQ-[1/2]Q^2+M$ and the cost function $c(q)=cq$ satisfy $(N.1)$–$(N.3)$.

The intuition why (N.1)–(N.3) hold is as follows. Suppose that two customs unions, of size-n_i and size-n_j, $n_i \geq n_j$, merge. Members of the merged customs union abolish tariffs among themselves and impose joint-welfare-maximizing tariffs on outsiders. As a result, terms of trade for outsiders deteriorate, reducing their welfare [(N.1)]. The members of the smaller customs union benefit from this merger, because they obtain a tariff-free access to n_i markets in return to granting members of the size-n_i customs union a tariff-free access to n_j markets, $n_i \geq n_j$ [(N.2)]. Now, suppose that a member of the size-n_j customs union leaves its customs union to join the size-n_i customs union, $n_i \geq n_j$. Essentially, this deviator gives up a tariff-free access to $n_j - 1$ countries in return for obtaining a tariff-free access to n_i countries. This deviator's welfare improves, since an increase in the number of markets with tariff-free access increases a country's welfare [(N.3)]. (As in joint ventures with complementary assets, the existing members of the large customs union need not benefit by admitting a member of a small customs union. The reason is that they gain tariff-free access to a single country in return for granting this new member tariff-free access to all existing member countries. Similarly, the members of a large customs union need not gain from the merger with a small customs union.)

It is striking that free-trade areas and customs unions (with the same utility and production functions) have *opposite* effects on the welfare of nonmember countries (Lemmas 4.4 and 5.2). This result points to the importance of the exercise of monopoly power by the bloc members in setting terms of trade with nonmember countries. If they do (as in the case of customs unions), nonmembers may suffer, but if they do not (as in free-trade areas), nonmembers may benefit.

5.3 Stable Coalition Structures with Negative Externalities

5.3.1 The open membership game

Yi (1997) shows that the grand coalition is the unique (pure-strategy) equilibrium outcome of the simultaneous-move Open Membership Game. Intuitively, the grand coalition is an NE CS, because by (N.2), any player who leaves it to form a singleton coalition becomes worse off. (That is, (N.2) implies that *all* coalition structures are stand-alone stable.) But a coalition structure with two or more coalitions is not an NE CS, because the member of the smallest coalition (including singleton coalitions, if any) can become better off by joining the largest coalition by (N.2) and (N.3). Here, I also show that it is *a* subgame-perfect equilibrium outcome of the sequential-move version of this game.

Proposition 5.1: Assume (N.2) and (N.3).

1. In the simultaneous-move Open Membership game, $\{N\}$ is the *unique* NE CS.
2. In the sequential-move Open Membership game, $\{N\}$ is *a* SPE CS.

Proof: See the Appendix.

Remark: It is straightforward to see that under (N.2), $\{N\}$ is the unique NE CS of the (Open Membership) simultaneous-move Single Coalition Formation game. A modification of the proof of the Proposition 5.1 (2) shows that $\{N\}$ is an SPE CS of the sequential-move Single Coalition Formation game. Hence, I do not separately report equilibrium structures of the Single Coalition Formation game.

5.3.2 The infinite-horizon sequential-move coalition unanimity game

The following definition proves useful in characterizing the equilibrium coalition structures.

Definition 5.1: k_0 is the largest integer which satisfies $\pi(k;C)\geq\pi(k-1;C')$, for *all* coalition structures C and C', $C' = C\backslash\{k\}\cup\{k-1,1\}$, and for *all* k, $2\leq k\leq k_0$.

The integer k_0 is the largest integer such that the existing members of a size-$(k-1)$ coalition, $k-1<k_0$, are made better off by merging with a singleton coalition, *holding the rest of the coalition structure fixed.* For example, in Bloch's (1995) linear model of joint ventures, $k_0=(N+3)/2$. In Yi's (1996a) linear-quadratic model of customs unions, $k_0\cong N^{2/3}$ for a large N.

Suppose that s_1, s_2, ..., s_m are the announcements of coalition sizes in the (generically) unique subgame perfect equilibrium of the Size Announcement game, and thus of the Coalition Unanimity game. s_i is the size of the i-th coalition to form in the equilibrium path, $i=1, 2, ..., m$. Yi's (1997) following result shows that the last coalition to form is uniquely the smallest, and that the second-to-last coalition to form is uniquely the second smallest. Thus, a symmetric coalition structure is not an equilibrium outcome. Furthermore, the second-to-last coalition has at least k_0 members so that the number of equilibrium coalitions does not exceed $I(N/k_0)$, where $I(r)$ is the closest integer greater than or equal to r.

Proposition 5.2:

1. Under (N.2), $s_m<s_j$, $j=1, ..., m-1$.
2. Under (N.1), $s_{m-1}\geq k_0$.

3. Under $(N.1)$ and $(N.2)$, $s_{m-1} < s_j, j=1, \ldots, m-2$.
4. Under $(N.1)$ and $(N.2)$, $m \leq I(N/k_0)$.

When $k_0 \geq N/2$, the task of identifying the equilibrium coalition structure of the Infinite Horizon Coalition Unanimity game becomes much simpler, since Proposition 5.2, (4) shows that the number of equilibrium coalitions is at most two. Instead of looking at all feasible coalition structures, one only needs to compare $Q(N/2)+1$ coalition structures which contain at most two coalitions, where $Q(r)$ is the integer part of r. For P_1, announcing k_0 dominates announcing k', $1 \leq k' < k_0$, because $\pi(k_0;\{k_0,N-k_0\}) \geq \pi(k';\{k',1,\ldots,1,N-k_0\}) > \pi(k';\{k',N-k'\})$ by the definition of k_0 and $(N.1)$. Thus, the unique subgame perfect equilibrium coalition structure of the Coalition Unanimity game is $\{k^u,N-k^u\}$, where $k^u \in \arg\max_{k_0 \leq k \leq N} \pi(k;\{k,N-k\})$: P_1 chooses the 'best' coalition structure from $\{k,N-k\}$, $k=k_0, k_0+1, \ldots, N$. For example, Yi (1998a) shows that $k_0 \geq (N+3)/2$ in the case of joint ventures for weakly concave inverse demand function $[P''(X) \leq 0]$ and the cost function with weakly increasing returns to scale in productive assets $[c(x,\omega)=\mu(\omega)x,\ \mu'(\omega)<0,\ \mu''(\omega) \leq 0]$.

It turns out that the grand coalition, which maximizes social welfare under reasonable conditions, is frequently not the equilibrium outcome of the Coalition Unanimity game. In the case of customs unions, Yi (1996a, p. 176) shows that two asymmetric coalitions form in equilibrium for $N \geq 5$. But the grand coalition (which maximizes world welfare) is the stable outcome under in the Open Membership game. In light of this result, Yi (1996a, 1996b) claims that the formation of welfare-maximizing customs unions is a stepping stone towards global free trade when membership of coalitions is open to outsiders, but can be a stumbling block when membership can be restricted (as in the Coalition Unanimity game).

In the case of joint ventures with efficiency gains, Bloch (1995) shows that $\{(3N+1)/4,\ (N-1)/4\}$ forms in equilibrium for the case of linear demand function $[P(X)=A-X]$ and linear cost function $[c^i(x_i,\omega_i)=(\bar{\omega}-\omega_i)x_i]$ for $N \geq 4$. (In this case, the per-member partition function is given by:

$$\pi(n_i;C) = [a + (N+1)n_i - \Sigma_{j=1}^{m} n_j^2]^2/(N+1)^2, \tag{5.4}$$

where $a = A - \bar{\omega}$.)

The social welfare loss from exclusivity can be substantial. For example, in this linear model with $A=6$ and $N=4$, Yi (1998a) shows that the total social surplus in the equilibrium structure of the Coalition Unanimity game [{3,1}] is 21.5 per cent less than the social surplus in the equilibrium structure of the Open Membership game [{4}].

Remark: The above comparison of social surplus under the two membership rules assumes that there are no *side payments* with respect to membership decisions. When unrestricted side payments are feasible, it is likely that the coalition structure that maximizes the aggregate payoff of all players will emerge as the stable outcome. Yi (1998a, 1998b) shows that the industry-profit maximizing joint venture structure in the linear model is given by $\{\bar{k},1,1,\ldots,1\}$, where $\bar{k} \cong [(3N+4) + \sqrt{64A/(N+2) + (9N^2 + 8N + 16}]/8$. $\bar{k} = N$ if and only if $A \geq [N^3 - N^2 - 7N + 8]/4$. Hence, the industry-profit maximizing joint venture structure need not be the grand coalition that maximizes total social surplus. (This difference comes from the inclusion of consumer surplus in total social surplus.) When membership is open to outsiders, the socially efficient grand coalition emerges as the equilibrium outcome. But when membership can be restricted, the grand coalition need not be the stable outcome with or without side payments.

5.3.3 Equilibrium binding agreements

Yi (1997) shows that a coalition structure with the size of the largest coalition is less than or equal to k_0 is stable in the Equilibrium Binding Agreements game. When $k_0 \geq N/2$, the following result identifies conditions under which $\{k_0, N-k_0\}$ is the most concentrated stable coalition structure in the Equilibrium Binding Agreements rule.

Proposition 5.3:

1. Under (*N*.1), $C = \{n_1, n_2, \ldots, n_m\}$, $n_i \leq k_0$ for $i = 1, \ldots, m$, is a stable coalition structure in the Equilibrium Binding Agreements game.
2. Under (*N*.1), $\{k_0, N-k_0\}$ is the most concentrated stable coalition structure in the Equilibrium Binding Agreements game if for all $k > k_0$, there exists $\hat{k}$, $N/2 \leq \hat{k} \leq k_0$, such that $\pi(k;\{k,N-k\}) < \pi(\hat{k};\{\hat{k},k-\hat{k},N-k\})$.
3. Under (*N*.1), $\{N\}$ is *not* stable under the Equilibrium Binding Agreements rule if $k_0 \geq N/2$ and if there exists $N/2 \leq \hat{k} \leq k_0$ such that $\pi(N;\{N\}) < \pi(\hat{k};\{\hat{k},N-\hat{k}\})$.

Proof: See the Appendix.

The intuition for the first part of Proposition 5.3 is as follows. By the definition of k_0, *if* other coalitions do not break apart, members of a coalition whose size is less than or equal to k_0 have no incentives to break apart their own coalition. But no other coalition breaks apart in response, because their own sizes are less than or equal to k_0. (A precise proof uses induction on the number of players.) In the second part, by (1), $\{\hat{k},k-\hat{k},N-k\}$ is stable in the Equilibrium Binding Agreements game. Since $\hat{k}$ players can

Table 3.1 Stable coalition structures in Bloch's (1995) linear model of joint ventures

Simultaneous-Move Open Membership	Infinite-Horizon Coalition Unanimity	Equilibrium Binding Agreements
$\{N\}$	$\{(3N+1)/4,(N-1)/4\}$	$\{(N+3)/2,(N-3)/2\}$

Note: For the Equilibrium Binding Agreements game, the most concentrated stable coalition structure is reported.

profitably leave the size-k coalition to form a size-$\hat{k}$ coalition which results in the coalition structure $\{\hat{k},k-\hat{k},N-k\}$, $\{k,N-k\}$ is not stable.

For example, in Bloch's (1995) linear model of joint ventures, a straightforward derivation shows that $\pi(k;\{k,N-k\})<\pi(k_0;\{k_0,k-k_0,N-k\})$ for all k, $k_0\leq k\leq N$. Since $k_0=(N+3)/2$, this linear model yields a sharp prediction about the ordering of stable coalition structures in the three membership rules. Table 3.1 shows that the equilibrium coalition structure of the simultaneous-move Open Membership game is more concentrated than the equilibrium coalition structure of the infinite-horizon Coalition Unanimity game, which in turn is more concentrated than any stable coalition structure of the Equilibrium Binding Agreements game.

Yi (1997) identifies conditions on the per-member partition function that generalizes the above result.

Proposition 5.4: Assume (N.1) and (N.2) and suppose that $k_0\geq N/2$. Consider $C=\{n_1,n_2,\ldots,n_m\}$, $n_1>k_0$. If there exists $\hat{k}$, $N/2\leq\hat{k}\leq k_0$, such that $\pi(n_1;C)<\pi(\hat{k};C')$, $C'=C\backslash\{n_1\}\cup\{\hat{k},n_1-\hat{k}\}$, then the unique subgame perfect equilibrium coalition structure of the Coalition Unanimity game is (weakly) more concentrated than any stable coalition structure under the Equilibrium Binding Agreements.

Intuitively, under the conditions of Proposition 5.4, $\{k^u,N-k^u\}$ $(=\{(3N+1)/4,(N-1)/4\}$ in the case of Bloch's linear model) is stable under the Coalition Unanimity game because, if $\hat{k}(=k_0=(N+3)/2$ in Bloch's linear model) members of the size-k^u coalition leave it to form a size-$\hat{k}$ coalition, the remaining members of the (previously) size-k^u coalition can 'credibly threaten' to form the size-$(N-\hat{k})$ coalition with the size-(N-k^u) coalition. By (N.1), this 'retaliation' reduces the payoff of the deviators. Under the conditions of in Proposition 5.4, this retaliation reduces the payoff of the deviators sufficiently enough to make the deviation not profitable. In contrast, $\{k^u,N-k^u\}$ is not stable under the Equilibrium Binding Agreements rule because $\hat{k}$ members of the size-k^u coalition can earn a higher payoff by breaking off to form a size-$\hat{k}$ coalition, without worrying about the response of the other players. Under the Equilibrium Binding Agreements rule, the remaining $k^u - \hat{k}$ members can only break up into smaller subcoalitions but cannot merge with the other coalition in response to the deviation of $\hat{k}$ leading perpetrators. However, if the remaining members (or members of other coalitions) do break up into smaller subcoalitions, the leading perpetrators become even better off by (N.1).

5.3.4 The simultaneous-move exclusive membership game

Not many results are known for the Exclusive Membership game in the case of negative externalities. However, it is frequently the case that the grand coalition is often not a stable outcome. Under (N.2), *all* coalition structures can be supported as Nash equilibrium outcomes by letting each player announce the list of their coalition members (and only them). Any player who deviates forms a singleton coalition. However, under (N.2), that deviator earns a lower payoff. Hence, $\{N\}$ is trivially a stable outcome under the Nash criterion. However, if one allows group deviations, $\{N\}$ is typically not stable. For example, in Bloch's (1995) linear model with $N=5$, $k_0 = k^u = 4$: we have $\pi(4;\{4,1\}) > \pi(5;\{5\})$, $\pi(3;\{3,1,1\})$, $\pi(2;\{2,1,1,1\})$ and $\pi(1;\{1,1,1,1,1\})$. In this case, $\{4,1\}$ is the unique coalition-proof Nash equilibrium (indeed, the unique strong Nash equilibrium) outcome of the Exclusive Membership game. (Let the P_1, P_2, P_3, P_4 announce $\{P_1, P_2, P_3, P_4\}$ and P_5 announce $\{P_5\}$. No group of players can make a profitable deviation.) One can also show that $\{4,1\}$ is the unique subgame-perfect equilibrium outcome of the sequential-move Exclusive Membership game.

Remark: In this example, no coalition-proof Nash equilibrium coalition structure exists in the simultaneous-move Open Membership game: from $\{5\}$, four players can make a profitable and self-enforceable deviation to $\{4,1\}$. However, $\{4,1\}$ is not stable because the player in the singleton coalition can profitably join the size-4 coalition (by (N.2)). This nonexistence problem poses a tricky question in the Open Membership game. However, if players are 'far-sighted', then one can say that $\{5\}$ is stable in the Open Membership game, because the four players who see the opportunity of a profitable deviation to $\{4,1\}$ will be deterred from forming the size-4 coalition, because they foresee that their deviation will be neutralized by the remaining player who can join their coalition. Hence, I do not examine group deviations in the Open Membership game for the case of negative externalities. (No such problems arise in the case of positive externalities in the previous sections.) Additional support for asserting that the grand coalition is stable in the Open Membership game comes from Proposition

5.1, which shows that the grand coalition is a subgame-perfect equilibrium outcome of the sequential-move Open Membership game.

5.3.5 The simultaneous-move coalition unanimity game

As in the Exclusive Membership game, the grand coalition is a Nash equilibrium outcome, but not stable against group deviations.

Proposition 5.5:

1. Suppose that $\pi(N;\{N\})>\pi(1;\{1, 1, ..., 1\})$. Then the grand coalition is a Nash equilibrium outcome of the simultaneous-move Coalition Unanimity game.
2. Suppose that there exists $\hat{k}\leq k_0$ such that $\pi(N;\{N\})<\pi(\hat{k};\{\hat{k}, 1, ..., 1\})$. Then the grand coalition is *not* a coalition-proof Nash equilibrium outcome of the simultaneous-move Coalition Unanimity game.

In summary, the results in this section show the following pattern. In the case of negative externalities, the Open Membership Game supports the grand coalition. Other games of coalition formation typically do not support the grand coalition as stable outcomes. The infinite-horizon Coalition Unanimity Game supports a more concentrated coalition structure as a stable outcome than does the Equilibrium Binding Agreements. (The characterization of stable coalition structures in the Exclusive Membership Game and the simultaneous-move Coalition Unanimity Game await further work.) Notice that this pattern is the exact *opposite* of the pattern in the case of positive externalities. There, the equilibrium coalition structure of the Open Membership Game was the *least* concentrated among the five general coalition formation games. Here, it is the *most* concentrated among the general coalition formation games.

6 CONCLUDING REMARKS

In this survey, I have examined equilibrium coalition structures when coalition formation creates externalities on nonmembers. I have classified various economic coalitions either as coalitions with positive externalities or as coalitions with negative externalities and then examined stable coalition structures under several noncooperative games of coalition formation. The main result is that the grand coalition is rarely an equilibrium outcome in the case of positive externalities due to free-riding problems. In the case of negative externalities, the grand coalition is the stable outcome in the Open Membership game, but typically not in other games. In the case of negative externalities, members of a large coalition have *strategic* incentives to limit their membership ranks in order to gain competitive edge against other players.

I conclude this survey by remarking on some other approaches to coalition formation that I have not covered in the main part of the paper and by suggesting some thoughts on the direction of future research.

Other Approaches to Coalition Formation

In addition to Γ and Δ games, Hart and Kurz (1983) examine stable coalition structures under the concepts of α and β cores. For a survey of stable coalition structures using core-related concepts, see Bloch (1998). Aumann and Myerson (1988) and Jackson and Wolinsky (1996) examine stable and efficient social networks in a link formation game, in which players form coalitions by linking with other players. Espinosa and Inarra (2000) and Horn and Persson (2001) examine stable cartel structures in a Cournot oligopoly under the concept of the von Neumann and Morgenstern stable set. Kamien and Zang (1990) analyse an acquisition game in which firms form coalitions form through the process of buying and selling.

'Hybrid' External Effects

Unlike in the models of economic coalitions surveyed in this chapter, the formation, expansion or merger of a coalition can have positive external effects on some nonmember players and negative effects on others. Alternatively, the formation of a coalition can have either positive or negative external effects depending on the number and sizes of other coalitions. An analysis of such a 'hybrid' case is a topic of future research.

Heterogeneous Players

I have restricted my survey to the case of ex-ante symmetric players. This symmetry assumption is common in many papers on the endogenous formation of coalitions. When heterogeneous players are introduced, the analysis is typically done in a setting with a small number of players or only one nondegenerate coalition is allowed. For example, Cassela (1992) examined a currency union formation game among two asymmetrically sized countries. Kennan and Riezman (1990) and Krishna (1998) examined a trading-bloc formation game among three countries of different sizes. Botteon and Carraro (1997) analysed stable environmental coalitions among five countries. Donsimoni et al. (1986) examined the Single Cartel Formation game among *n* heterogeneous firms. Burbidge et al. (1997) reported some results about the instability of the grand coalition among *n* heterogeneous players.

But so far there is not much result on the existence and characterization of stable coalition structures among heterogeneous players. (See Ray and Vohra (1999) for an important contribution to the existence question.) The difficulty arises from the fact that when players are not symmetric, it is no longer possible to identify a coalition by its size. As hard as the analysis may be, heterogeneity of players raises the interesting and important issue of the composition of coalitions: do coalitions in a stable coalition structure (assuming that one exists) consist of similar players or dissimilar players or both? How are the coalition payoffs divided among the members? One way to begin the analysis in this direction might be to assume just two types of players and see if equilibrium coalitions consist of the same types or of different types and how the coalition payoffs are divided among members. Recently, Belleflamme (2000) made a start in examining stable coalition structures among heterogeneous players, albeit under the restrictive assumption that at most two coalitions can form.

Multiple Coalition Membership/Coalition dynamics

One of the simplifying assumptions of the current literature is that a player can only belong to one coalition. However, in reality, a player can belong to several coalitions at the same time. For example, the US is a member of both the North American Free-Trade Agreements zone and the Asia Pacific Economic Cooperation zone.

In addition, the current literature does not address the issue of coalition dynamics. Developing a dynamic model of coalition formation, expansion, dissolution and mergers awaits future research.

NOTES

1. Of course, endogenous formation of coalitions is not limited to the economic arena. In international relations, the Nuclear Non-Proliferation Treaty is a good example of endogenous coalitions: since it is up to individual countries to ratify the treaty, the number of signatories of the treaty is endogenously determined. In politics, coalitional governments are a classical example of endogenous coalitions.
2. Thrall and Lucas (1963) is an early attempt to formulate the partition function approach.
3. There are some noteworthy predecessors to this work, including d'Aspremont et al. (1983), Hart and Kurz (1983, 1984) and Economides (1986). More remark on these papers follow in the main text.
4. In my (somewhat uncharitable) view, I regard the characteristic function approach to modeling settings of strategic play as the *Procrustean bed.*
5. See Greenberg (1995) for a survey of coalition structures based on the characteristic function approach.
6. The implicit assumption in using the coalition structure is that one player can belong to only one coalition.
7. If the second-stage game has multiple Nash equilibrium outcomes, the analysis of

stable coalition structures becomes problematic. As a simple example, consider the following two-player game. If the two players form a coalition, there is a unique Nash equilibrium outcome in which each player earns $3. If they do not form a coalition, there are two pure-strategy Nash equilibria (and a mixed-strategy equilibrium). In one pure-strategy Nash equilibrium, player 1 earns $4 and player 2 earns $0 and in the other equilibrium, their payoffs are reversed. In this case, the stability of the grand coalition depends on the expectation of the players. If player 1 expects that when he leaves the grand coalition, the favorable Nash equilibrium will arise (the 'optimistic' scenario), then he will leave the grand coalition, but if he expects the unfavorable equilibrium (the 'pessimistic' scenario), he will stay in the coalition. The uniqueness assumption allows one to avoid this complication. The uniqueness assumption is common in most models that I review in this paper.

8. Thus, the prediction about equilibrium coalition structures is unique up to the permutation of the players.
9. In the case of MCC, however, the organizers did not invite AT&T and IBM to join, primarily due to antitrust concerns (Joint Economic Committee, 1984).
10. As one can see, there are many other strategy profiles that support the coalition structure {2,1,1} as the outcome. Hence, any claim about the uniqueness applies to the equilibrium outcome and not to the strategies.
11. Hart and Kurz's (1983) original name is 'game Δ'. In order to contrast this game to the Open Membership game, this game is renamed the Exclusive Membership game.
12. If there is a tie, take the one with the smallest index.
13. Hart and Kurz also examined this game, which they call 'game Γ'. I call this game the 'Coalition Unanimity' game because the formation of a coalition requires the unanimous approval of *all* prospective members of the coalition.
14. Von Neumann and Morgenstern called the players who form a coalition by announcing exactly the same list of players a 'ring'. And a player who forms a one-player coalition is called a 'solo set'.
15. See Hart and Kurz (1983) for more discussion on this issue.
16. (*P*.4) can be weakened as in Yi and Shin (2000).
17. There is now a voluminous literature on cooperative R&D. Katz (1986) is the seminal paper. Kamien and Zang (1993) allow for competing coalitions, but they assume symmetric coalition structures and do not examine endogenous coalition formation.
18. Since Viner (1950), the international trade literature has focused on the welfare effects of the formation of trading blocs. See Baldwin and Venables (1995) and Ethier (1998) for recent surveys. Some recent papers that emphasize coalition formation are Riezman (1985), Krugman (1991), Bond and Syropoulos (1996) and Baldwin (1995). Riezman examines stable structures of trading blocs using a variant of the core concept. Krugman examines the welfare effects of the symmetric expansion of symmetric customs unions. Bond and Syropoulos show the instability of symmetric structure of customs unions, but do not examine equilibrium structures. Baldwin examines a variant of the (Open Membership) Single Coalition Formation game and shows that the formation of a regional bloc enhances non-members' incentives to join the bloc.
19. Yi (1996a) considers a more general utility function that incorporates imperfect substitutes.
20. While Kohler (2002) does not explicitly examine other conditions on the per-member partition function with positive externalities in the current paper, it seems that a singleton country earns a higher profit than members of the nondegenerate union, so that a version of condition (*P*.2) holds.
21. Coalition-proof Nash equilibrium (Bernheim, Peleg and Whinston, 1987) imposes a certain *internal consistency* requirements on permissible group deviations. Instead of providing the formal definition of the coalition-proof Nash equilibrium, for the current paper, it suffices to require that a group deviation constitute a *Nash* equilibrium among the deviators, holding the strategies of other players fixed.
22. One can show that {2,2} is the unique SPE CS of the sequential-move Open Membership game.

23. However, all CPNE coalition structures have the same number of coalitions. See Proposition 4.5.
24. Thus, {3,1} is an SNE CS in this example. However, the existence of a SNE CS is not guaranteed even in the Exclusive Membership game. For example, if a player who forms *s* singleton coalition in {2,1,1} earns 8 instead of 6, then no SNE CS exists in both the Open Membership and the Exclusive Membership games. Notice that {2,2} continues to be a CPNE CS in both games.
25. One can show that {3,1} is the unique SPE CS of the sequential-move Exclusive Membership game.
26. If $\pi(k_s; \{k_s, \mathbf{1}_{N-k_s}\}) = \pi(1;(k_s; \{k_s - 1, \mathbf{1}_{N-k_{s+1}}\})$ and if $\{k_s - 1, \mathbf{1}_{N-k_{s+1}}\}$ is stand-alone stable, then $\{k_s - 1, \mathbf{1}_{N-k_{s+1}}\}$ is also a CPNE CS. However, a slight perturbation of payoffs will remove the multiplicity. From now on, we ignore such ties in payoffs.

REFERENCES

Aumann, R. and R. Myerson (1988), 'Endogenous formation of links between players and of coalitions: an application of the Shapley value', in L. Shapley (ed.), *The Shapley Value*, Cambridge: Cambridge University Press (1989).

Baldwin, R. (1995), 'A domino theory of regionalism', in R. Baldwin, P. Haaparanta and J. Kiander (eds), *Expanding European Regionalism: The EU's New Members*, Cambridge: Cambridge University Press (1995).

Baldwin, R. and A.J. Venables (1995), 'Regional economic integration', in G. Grossman and K. Rogoff (eds), *Handbook of International Economics*, Vol. 3, Amsterdam: Elsevier.

Belleflamme, P. (2000), 'Stable coalition structures with open membership and asymmetric firms', *Games and Economic Behaviour*, **30**(1), 1–21.

Bernheim, B.D., B. Peleg and M.D. Whinston (1987), 'Coalition-proof Nash equilibria: 1. concepts', *Journal of Economic Theory*, **42**(1) 1–12.

Bloch, F. (1995), 'Endogenous structures of association in oligopolies,' *Rand Journal of Economics*, **26**(3) 537–56.

Bloch, F. (1996), 'Sequential formation of coalitions with fixed payoff division', *Games and Economic Behavior*, **14**(1) 90–123.

Bloch, F. (1997), 'Noncooperative models of coalition formation in games with spillovers', in C. Carraro and D. Siniscalco (eds), *New Directions in the Economic Theory of the Environment*, Cambridge: Cambridge University Press.

Bond, E.W. and C. Syropoulos, (1996), 'The size of trading blocs: market power and world welfare effects', *Journal of International Economics*, **40**(3–4) 417–37.

Botteon, M. and C. Carraro (1988), 'Environmental coalitions with heterogeneous countries: burden-sharing and carbon leakage', in A. Ulph (ed.), *Environmental Policy, International Agreements and International Trade*, Oxford: Oxford University Press.

Burbidge, J.B. et al (1999), 'A coalition-formation approach to equilibrium federations and trading blocs', *American Economic Review*, **87**(5) 940–56.

Carraro, C. (1997), 'The structure of international environmental agreements', unpublished manuscript.

Carraro, C. and F. Moriconi (1998), 'Endogenous formation of environmental coalitions', unpublished manuscript.

Carraro, C. and D. Siniscalco (1993), 'Strategies for the international protection of the environment', *Journal of Public Economics*, **52**(3), 309–28.

Cassela, A. (1992), 'Participation in a currency union', *American Economic Review*, **82**(4), 847–63.

d'Aspremont, C. and A. Jacquemin (1988), 'Cooperative and noncooperative R&D in an oligopoly with spillovers', *American Economic Review*, **78**(5), 1133–7.

D'Aspremont, C.A., A. Jacquemin, J.J. Gabszewicz and J. Weymark (1983), 'On the stability of collusive price leadership', *Canadian Journal of Economics*, **16**(1), 17–25.

Deneckere, R. and C. Davidson (1985), 'Incentives to form coalitions with Bertrand competition', *Rand Journal of Economics*, **16**(4), 473–86.

Donsimoni, M.P. et al (1986), 'Stable cartels', *International Economic Review*, **27**(2), 317–27.

Economides, N.S. (1986), 'Non-cooperative equilibrium coalition structures', Columbia University Discussion Paper Series, No. 273.

Espinosa, M.P. and E. Inarra (2000), 'Von Neumann and Morgenstern stable sets in a Cournot merger system', *International Game Theory Review*, **2**(1), 29–45.

Ethier, W.J. (1988), 'The new regionalism', *Economic Journal*, **108**(449), 1149–1161.

Greenberg, J. (1995), 'Coalition structures', In (R.J. Aumann and S. Hart (eds.) *Handbook of Game Theory with Economic Applications*, Vol. 2, Amsterdam: North-Holland.

Hart, S. and M. Kurz (1983), 'Endogenous Formation of Coalitions', *Econometrica*, **51**(4), 1047–64.

Hart, S. and M. Kurz (1984), 'Stable Coalition Structures', in M.J. Holler (ed.) *Coalitions and Collective Action*, Wurzburg, W. Germany and Vienna: Physica.

Heal, G. (1994), 'The Formation of Environmental Coalitions', in C. Carraro (ed.), *Trade, Innovation, Environment*, Dordrecht: Kluwer Academic.

Horn, H. and L. Persson (2001), 'Endogenous Mergers in Concentrated Markets', *International Journal of Industrial Organization*, **19**(8), 1213–1244.

Jackson, M.O. and A. Wolinsky (1996), 'A strategic model of social and economic Networks', *Journal of Economic Theory*, **71**(4), 44–74.

Joint Economic Committee (1984), *Congressional Hearings on Antitrust Policy and Joint Research and Development Ventures*, Washington: U.S. Government Office.

Kamien, M. and I. Zang (1990), 'The limits of monopolization through acquisition', *Quarterly Journal of Economics*, **105**(2), 465–99.

Kamien, M. and I. Zang (1993), 'Competing research joint ventures', *Journal of Economics and Management Strategy*, **2**(1), 23–40.

Katz, M.L. (1986), 'An analysis of cooperative research and development', *Rand Journal of Economics*, **17**(3), 527–43.

Kennan, J. and R. Riezman (1990), 'Optimal tariff equilibria with customs unions', *Canadian Journal of Economics*, **23**(1), 70–83.

Kohler, M. (1997), 'Coalition formation in international monetary policy games', *Journal of International Economics*, **56**(2), 371–385.

Krishna, P. (1998), 'Regionalism and multilateralism: a political economy approach', *Quarterly Journal of Economics*, **113**(1), 227–51.

Krugman, P.R. (1991), 'Is bilateralism bad?' in E. Helpman and A. Razin (eds), *International Trade and Trade Policy*, Cambridge: MIT Press, pp. 9–24.

Poyago-Theotoky, J. (1995), 'Equilibrium and optimal sizes of a research joint venture in an oligopoly with spillovers', *Journal of Industrial Economics*, **43**(2) 209–26.

Ray, D. and R. Vohra (1999), 'A theory of endogenous coalition structures', *Games and Economic Behavior*, **26**(2), 286–336.

Ray, D. and R. Vohra (1997), 'Equilibrium binding agreements', *Journal of Economic Theory*, **73**(1), 30–78.

Riezman, R. (1985), 'Customs unions and the core', *Journal of International Economics*, **19**(3–4), 355–65.

Salant, S.W., S. Switzer and R.J. Reynolds (1983), 'Losses from horizontal mergers: the effects of an exogenous change in industry structure on Cournot-Nash equilibrium', *Quarterly Journal of Economics*, **93**(2), 185–99.

Spence, A.M. (1984), 'Cost reduction, competition, and industry performance'. *Econometrica*, **52**(1), 101–21.

Thrall, R. and W. Lucas (1963), 'N-person games in partition function form', *Naval Research Logistics Quarterly*, **10**, 281–98.

Viner, J. (1950), The Customs Union Issue, New York: Carnegie Endowment for International Peace.

von Neumann, J. and O. Morgenstern (1944), *Theory of Games and Economic Behavior*, Princeton: Princeton University.

Yi, S-S. (1996a), 'Endogenous formation of customs unions under imperfect competition: open regionalism is good', *Journal of International Economics*, **41**(1–2), 153–77.

Yi, S-S. (1996b), 'Open regionalism and world welfare', *Eastern Economic Journal*, **22**(4), 467–75.

Yi, S-S. (1997), 'Stable coalition structures with externalities'. *Games and Economic Behavior*, **20**(2), 201–37.

Yi, S-S. (1998a), 'Endogenous formation of joint ventures with efficiency gains', *Rand Journal of Economics*, **29**(3), 610–31.

Yi, S-S. (1998b), 'Endogenous formation of joint ventures with efficiency gains: further results', *Sogang Economic Papers*, **27**(2), 261–82.

Yi, S-S. (1998c), 'Industry profit-maximizing joint-venture structure in a linear Cournot oligopoly', *Economics Letters*, **58**(3), 361–6.

Yi, S-S. (1999), 'Equilibrium cartel structures in cournot oligopoly', unpublished manuscript, Sogang University.

Yi, S-S. (2000), 'Free-trade areas and welfare: an equilibrium analysis', *Review of International Economics*, **8**(2), 336–47.

Yi, S-S. and H.S. Shin (2000), 'Endogenous formation of research coalitions with spillovers', *International Journal of Industrial Organization*, **18**(2), 229–56.

APPENDIX

Proof of Proposition 4.6

1. I claim that $\alpha = (\alpha^1, \alpha^2, ..., \alpha^N)$, where $\alpha^1 = \alpha^2 = ... = \alpha^N = P = \{P_1, P_2, ..., P_N\}$ constitutes an SNE. Suppose that a group of players, T, deviate from α. Let $C = \{n_1, n_2, ..., n_m\}$, $n_1 \geq n_2 \geq ... \geq n_m$, be the resulting coalition structure. In the simultaneous-move Coalition Unanimity game, all the players in $P \backslash T$ become singleton coalitions in the new coalition structure. Thus, some deviators belong to the biggest size-n_1 coalition. By $(P.2)$, $\pi(n_1;C) \leq \pi(n_i;C)$ $\forall i = 2, ..., m$. Since $N\pi(N;\{N\}) \geq \Sigma_{i=1}^{m} n_i \pi(n_i;C)$, we obtain $\pi(N;\{N\}) > \pi(n_1;C)$: these n_1 deviators are worse off.
2. If $\{N\}$ is stand-alone stable, then $\pi(N;\{N\}) \geq \pi(1;\{N-1,1\}) > \pi(k;\{k,N-k\}) > \pi(k;\{k\} \cup D)$, where D is a coalition structure that can obtained by breaking up $\{N-k\}$. The first inequality follows from stand-alone stability of $\{N\}$, the second from $(P.2)$ and $(P.3)$ and the third from $(P.1)$. Thus, if the grand coalition is stand-alone stable, it has a higher per-member profit than any coalition in any other coalition structure. $\{N\}$ is the unique SNE CS, since all players make a profitable group deviation to the grand coalition from any other coalition structure. **Q.E.D.**

Proof of Proposition 5.1 (2)

Consider the following strategy profile:

- P_1: Announce any address.
- $P_2, ..., P_N$: Choose the most frequently announced address. If there is a tie, then pick an address *different* from the one chosen by the country who created the tie most recently.

The above strategy profile supports $\{N\}$ as the equilibrium outcome. It is obvious that for P_N the above strategy is optimal for any given history. Now suppose that the claim is true for $P_N, P_{N-1}, ..., P_{N-k+2}$. Suppose that $N-k$ countries before P_{N-k+1} have announced t addresses. Without loss of generality, suppose that a_i has been announced f_i times, $f_i \geq f_{i+1}$, $i = 1, 2, ..., t-1$. If $f_1 = f_2$, then label the addresses so that a_1 is *not* the address chosen by the player who created the tie most recently. We need to show that announcing a_1 is *an* optimal strategy for P_{N-k+1}. If P_{N-k+1} announces

a_1, then a_1 becomes the *unique* most frequently announced address for P_{N-k+2}. By inductive hypothesis, P_{N-k+2} (and all subsequent countries) announce a_1 along the unique subgame perfect equilibrium path of the continuation game. P_{N-k+1}'s welfare is then $W(f_1+k;\{f_1+k,f_2, ..., f_t\})$. Suppose that P_{N-k+1} announces another equally popular address a_i, $i>1$, $f_i=f_1$. Then a_i becomes the *unique* most frequently announced address, and all subsequent countries will also announce a_i. P_{N-k+1}'s welfare is the same as above. Hence, P_{N-k+1} is *indifferent* between a_1 and any other equally popular address a_i, $i>1, f_i=f_1$. Now suppose that P_{N-k+1} announces a less popular address $a_j, f_j<f_1$. (a_j can be a new address.) Suppose that $f_j+1<f_1$: a_j is *not* one of the most popular addresses for P_{N-k+2}. By hypothesis, P_{N-k+2} chooses a_1 (or any other equally popular address which is not chosen by the country who created the tie most recently). P_{N-k+1}'s welfare is $W(f_j+1; \{f_1+k-1,f_2, ..., f_j+1, ..., f_t\})$, which is smaller than $W(f_1+k;\{f_1+k,f_2, ...,f_j, ...,f_t\})$ by (N.2) and (N.3). Finally, suppose that $f_j+1=f_1$: a_j is one of the most popular addresses for P_{N-k+2}. Then, P_{N-k+2} is indifferent between a_1 and a_j. By hypothesis, however, P_{N-k+2} breaks the tie against P_{N-k+1}, since P_{N-k+1} created the tie most recently. Once again, P_{N-k+1}'s welfare is $W(f_j+1;\{f_1+k-1,f_2, ..., f_j+1, ..., f_t\})$, which is smaller than $W(f_1+k;\{f_1+k,f_2, ...,f_t\})$, P_{N-k+1}'s welfare if it chooses a_1.

Q.E.D.

Proof of Proposition 5.3 (2)

By construction, $k_0 \geq \hat{k}$, $N-\hat{k}$. By the first part of the Proposition (which Yi (1997) proves), $\{\hat{k},k-\hat{k},N-k\}$ is stable in the Equilibrium Binding Agreements game. Since $\hat{k}$ players can profitably leave the size-k coalition to form a size-$\hat{k}$ coalition which results in the coalition structure $\{\hat{k},k-\hat{k},N-k\}$, $\{k,N-k\}$ is not stable. **Q.E.D.**

Proof of Proposition 5.5

1. Consider the strategy profile that supports $\{N\}$ as the outcome: each player announces the set of all N players. If *any* player deviates, then the remaining $N-1$ players dissolve the coalition and become singleton coalitions. Hence, the resulting coalition structure is $\{1,1, ..., 1\}$ and the deviator is worse off.
2. Let $\hat{k}$ players instead announce a list that consists of them (and them only). By the rule of the game, the resulting coalition structure is $\{\hat{k},1,1, ..., 1\}$ and the deviators are better off. Next, by the definition of k_0, there is no further profitable deviation (from the original deviation)

for the $\hat{k}$ players, because given the strategies of the other $N-\hat{k}$ players, the only feasible deviation in this game is by forming a *smaller* coalition among some of the deviators. Since $\hat{k} \leq k_0$, such further deviation is not profitable. Hence, the original deviation is self-enforceable.

Q.E.D

4. Farsightedness in coalition formation

Marco Mariotti and Licun Xue

1. INTRODUCTION

The main theme of this chapter is the formalization of the concept of 'farsightedness' in the behaviour of coalitions. Loosely speaking, a coalition is farsighted when it looks ahead at the ultimate consequences of its actions. If a subcoalition breaks up from a larger coalition, will this cause further breakups? And how will the members who are excluded from the deviating coalitions react? These are the sort of questions that are addressed in the literature we survey. As an example, the most popular cooperative solution concept, the Core, seems to embody a very limited amount of farsightedness: a coalition will deviate from a given *status quo* if it perceives the possibility of an immediate improvement, disregarding the possible further developments of play. In fact, things are not so simple, for even the Core can be shown to embody some amount of farsightedness (Ray, 1989). One could analyse in turn the behavioural assumptions implicit in other classical solution concepts, such as for instance the Bargaining Set for cooperative games or the Strong Nash Equilibrium for games in strategic form. But, rather than proceeding case by case, we study here some recent attempts at dealing with the issue of farsightedness in a general way.

The lion's share in this chapter is taken by Greenberg's (1990) Theory of Social Situations (TOSS in short), for two reasons. Firstly, it is the quintessential general framework, which provides a unified language to treat the issues of interest here (and indeed most other game theoretic situations). In fact, TOSS is a valuable tool to pinpoint the (often implicit) behavioural assumptions of several existing solution concepts. Secondly, TOSS has been rather influential, spawning a literature that aims to extend, modify and apply the original theory. Although the resulting contributions sometimes end up looking rather different from Greenberg's formulation, their conceptual relatedness is obvious. Besides, they can often be formally reconducted to TOSS. We discuss TOSS and some subsequent results obtained by Greenberg and others in section 2.

Because of space limitations, our survey beyond TOSS is far from being comprehensive. In fact, we focus on just a few of the concepts that have been proposed in the last decade. We think, however, that this will suffice to give the reader a flavour of the style and direction of the analysis involved.

In section 3 we present Chwe's (1994) work. He considers a class of social environments that, although less general than those allowed by TOSS, is sufficiently flexible to integrate the presentation of some negotiation processes associated with cooperative, strategic and extensive form games. Chwe's main objective is to offer a notion of 'consistency' in the vein of the von Neumann and Morgenstern Stable Set, but which both captures foresight and is likely to be nonempty. Chwe's inclusive solution, the Largest Consistent Set, can be derived by using Greenberg's framework.

By inspecting the situation underlying Chwe's notion, Xue (1998) shows that Chwe's solution captures only a limited aspect of foresight. He then proposes a solution concept that captures 'perfect foresight' using Greenberg's framework. Xue's approach centers around the graph-theoretic notion of a 'path' and attempts to embody in a more complex environment the logic of subgame perfection used in extensive form games. This approach is considered in section 4.

In section 5 we discuss yet another approach proposed in Mariotti (1997), which attempts to integrate some of Greenberg's ideas with the standard notion of a 'strategy' in order to capture farsightedness. As in Xue's work here, too, one tries to transfer the logic of subgame perfection to the more complex environment. The original work was formulated in terms of Greenberg's Coalition Contingent Threat Situation for games in strategic form. In this chapter we provide a version of the same concepts which applies at a similar level of generality of Chwe's and Xue's approaches.

Section 6 concludes.

2. THE THEORY OF SOCIAL SITUATIONS

When von Neumann and Morgenstern (1944) laid out the foundations of game theory, they proposed the 'Stable Set' as the main solution concept for situations in which the participants can form coalitions by freely communicating and making binding agreements. The idea of a Stable Set fell relatively out of favour in the subsequent developments of game theory. However, Greenberg's TOSS revived some of the original motivations and even terminology of von Neumann and Morgenstern. TOSS is a much more general theory of social behaviour than that contained in *Theory of Games and Economic Behaviour (TGEB)*, but it revolves around the same central idea of 'stable standards of behaviour' as regulatory of strategic behaviour.

In TGEB a standard of behaviour amounts simply to a set of utility imputations. According to von Neumann and Morgenstern, a standard of behaviour, viewed as a solution to the game, must satisfy two requirements: (i) it is 'free from inner contradictions' (internal strategy), and (ii) it can 'be used to discredit any non-conforming procedure' (external stability) (TGEB, p. 41). Greenberg introduced a far more encompassing notion of standard of behaviour to which these two requirements, expressing the features of stability a 'social norm' should possess, can be applied.

TOSS aims to offer a unified approach to the study of strategic interactions. This approach supersedes the classical distinction between 'noncooperative' and 'cooperative' (or other) descriptions of social environments. A social environment is represented as a 'situation' which specifies *all* relevant information: for example, the beliefs of the players, the institutional setting such as the availability of binding agreements and social and legal restrictions on the formation of certain coalitions, and the details of negotiation process. In TOSS a unified solution concept is used for all such situations, by employing the stability criteria mentioned above. It is this separation between the solution concept and the description of the social environment that so often makes TOSS a useful language to address the issue of farsightedness. Behavioural assumptions additional to those implicit in stability are brought automatically to the fore once a given solution concept is expressed in TOSS language. In this sense, stability (a property that social norms are assumed to possess) becomes a benchmark against which to 'measure' other behavioural assumptions.

These observations can provide a response to the criticism that TOSS, being able to incorporate most existing solution concepts, is 'too' general, to the point of being empty as a solution concept itself. According to this criticism, 'anything' can be obtained as solution in TOSS, provided the appropriate social environment (situation) is specified. In our view, on the contrary, it is precisely *because* TOSS is so general that it is useful. The pertinent criticism against TOSS should rather concern the issue whether stability (in the technical sense) is a necessary characteristic of social norms.

2.1 Definitions

2.1.1 Situation

We start by introducing the first main ingredient of TOSS, namely the notion of a 'situation'. This notion in turn involves two elements: a set of 'positions' and an 'inducement correspondence'. A *position* describes the 'current state of affairs'. In particular, it specifies a set of individuals, the set of all possible outcomes, and the preferences of the individuals over this set of outcomes. Formally:

Definition 1: *A position, G, is a triple* $G=(N(G), X(G), \{u_i(G)\}_{i\in N(G)})$, *where* $N(G)$ *is the set of players,* $X(G)$ *is the set of all feasible outcomes, and* $u_i(G)$ *is the utility function of player i in position G over the outcomes*[1], *that is,* $u_i(G): X(G)\to\Re$. *Thus, for all* $x, y\in X(G)$, *and for all* $i\in N(G)$, $u_i(G)(x) > u_i(G)(y)$ *if and only if i prefers, in position G, the outcome x over the outcome y.*

In the theory, given a position, any feasible alternative can be 'proposed'. Although 'proposed' is the term used by Greenberg, a more indicative term could be 'under consideration'. The crucial point is that in a position a feasible alternative becomes – through some procedure which may or may not be one of negotiation – the current *status quo*. All the individuals active in the position can consider whether to accept or not the proposed *status quo*. An *inducement correspondence* specifies what it is feasible for any coalition (a set of players) to do if it decides to reject the proposed alternative. Consider a position G and suppose that an outcome $x^*\in X(G)$ is proposed. For a coalition $S\subset N(G)$ to be able to decide whether to accept or reject the proposed outcome, it must know (at least) the courses of action that are available. To be more specific, S has to know the set of positions it can 'induce' it if rejects x^*.

Definition 2: *Let* Γ *be a set of positions and let:*

$$\Omega = \{(G, x, S) \mid G\in\Gamma,\ x\in X(G),\ S\subset N(G)\}.$$

An inducement correspondence is a mapping:

$$\gamma:\Omega\to\Gamma,$$

that specifies, for each $G\in\Gamma$, $x\in X(G)$, *and* $S\subset N(G)$, *a subset of* $\gamma(S, G, x)\subset\Gamma$.

A *situation* is a pair (γ, Γ), where Γ is a set of positions, and γ is the inducement correspondence. A situation provides a *complete* description of a social environment. In particular, it specifies who can do what at every stage or the detailed 'rules of the game'.

The requirement that Γ is closed under γ guarantees that 'the rules of the game' specify what can happen from any admissible (possibly itself an induced) position $G \in \Gamma$, when a feasible outcome $x \in X(G)$ is proposed. One additional requirement imposed on the inducement correspondence, γ, is that the set of players of each position that a coalition S can induce, includes the players in S. Formally, it is assumed:

Let (γ, Γ) be a situation. For all $G \in \Gamma$, $S \subset N(G)$, and $x \in X(G)$, if $H \in \gamma(S,G,x)$, then $S \subset N(H)$.

Note that γ may still assign the empty set to some (or even all) coalitions – some (or all) coalitions may be unable to induce any position at all. Think, for example, of the terminal nodes of an extensive form game.

2.1.2 Standards of behaviour

A situation specifies what it is feasible. We now move to the description of *behaviour*, namely a choice out of the feasible set of outcomes. This is done through the concept of 'standard of behaviour'.

Given the description of the social environment as a situation, a standard of behaviour specifies the 'solution' to every position in Γ. More precisely, consider a situation (γ, Γ) and a position $G \in \Gamma$. A natural question is: What is the set of outcomes that it is 'reasonable' to expect at G? That is, what is the set that consists of all the feasible outcomes in $X(G)$ from which no coaliation in $N(G)$ will choose to induce another position? This subset of $X(G)$ (whatever it may be) is called a 'solution for G' and denoted by $\sigma(G)$.

Equipped with the concept of a solution for a given G, it is clear that a formal object linking *any* position to its solution must be introduced. This is because, given any position G, the acceptability of an outcome x^* in $X(G)$ depends on the outcomes that are believed to be accepted in the positions that can be induced from G when x^* is proposed. Consider for example $H \in \gamma(S, G, x^*)$. For members of S to be able to decide whether to reject x^* and induce H, they must have information about the outcomes that are expected to result once position H is induced. This discussion motivates the following definition.

Definition 3: *Let Γ be a collection of positions. A standard of behaviour (SB) for Γ is a mapping σ that assigns to every position $G \in \Gamma$ a solution $\sigma(G) \subset X(G)$.*

An SB σ for Γ is any arbitrary mapping which specifies a solution for every position. Greenberg views an SB as a particular 'theory in the social sciences', namely a theory of social behaviour, given a social environment specified by a situation.

The next step is to impose some restrictions on σ. This is where the notion of stability comes in. As von Neumann and Morgenstern required stability of their solution, so it is required in TOSS that σ be 'free of inner contradictions' and that it can 'be used to discredit any non-conforming procedure'. As we saw above, these two properties are termed 'internal stability' and 'external stability', which we shall define formally.

2.1.3 Stability

Consider a situation (γ, Γ), and let σ be an SB for Γ. The first fundamental assumption is that rational behaviour entails internal stability of σ as explained below.

Imagine that a way of comparing *sets* of outcomes with outcomes has been defined (recall that a solution is a subset and generally not a singleton). If all players adopt the recommendations made by σ, any group of players, S, will reject an outcome, $x \in X(G)$ if it can induce a position $H \in \gamma(S, G, x)$, whose solution $\sigma(H)$ all members of S prefer to x.

So, this principle provides a justification for rejecting outcomes. Formally:

Definition 4: *Let σ be an* SB *for situation* (γ, Γ). *σ is internally stable for* (γ, Γ) *if for all $G \in \Gamma$, whenever there exists a coalition $S \subset N(G)$ and a position $H \in \gamma(S, G, x)$ such that the members of S prefer $\sigma(H)$ to x, it is the case that $x \notin \sigma(G)$.*

The next assumption is that rational behaviour entails external stability: the rejection of x can be justified *only* by an objection in terms of the 'solution' outcomes in $\sigma(H)$, and not any other outcome in the set of feasible ones, $X(H)$. The underlying logic is that outcomes belonging to $X(H) \backslash \sigma(H)$ have no validity as objections because, not being part of the solution set, they cannot form the basis for an agreement between the members of a rejecting coalition.

This prevents the exclusion of certain outcomes from σ from being arbitrary. This principle limits the justifications for rejecting outcomes to those expressed by internal stability. Formally:

Definition 5: *Let σ be an* SB *for situation* (γ, Γ). *σ is externally stable for* (γ, Γ) *if for all $G \in \Gamma$, whenever there exists no coalition $S \subset N(G)$ and a position $H \in \gamma(S, G, x)$ such that the members of S prefer $\sigma(H)$ to x, it is the case that $x \in \sigma(G)$.*

Definition 6: *Let σ be an* SB *for situation* (σ, Γ). *σ is stable if it is both internally and externally stable.*

Stability is the only requirement imposed on SB. The above two definitions are incomplete in that it has not yet been specified how the members of a coalition S compare $\sigma(H)$ and x. This difficulty is resolved in the original formulation of TOSS by considering only two extreme behavioural assumptions (formally defined at the end of this subsection): optimistic and conservative behaviour. Though these assumptions yield several interesting results, the investigation of alternative behavioural assumptions may prove to be valuable. For example, Greenberg's (1994) definition of stable value for cooperative games with transferable utilities, a uniform probability distribution is used to evaluate the solution of a position. In general, it is clear that any particular specification of a method, or set of methods, to compare sets of outcomes with outcomes is not an integral part of the TOSS, but rather a part of the description of the social environment. Indeed, one might even conceive of a separate such method of evaluation for each player. This is to be contrasted with Chwe's approach in the next section, where a particular assumption of 'conservative' behaviour is built in the formal definition of his solution concept.

The two extreme behavioural assumptions introduced by Greenberg (1990) are as follows:

Optimistic Behaviour: A coalition S prefers $\sigma(H)$ to $x \in X(G)$ if *there exists* an outcome $y \in \sigma(H)$ that all members of S prefer to x, that is, $u_i(H)(y) > u_i(G)(x)$ for all $i \in S$.

Conservative Behaviour: A coalition S prefers $\sigma(H)$ to $x \in X(G)$ if *all* outcomes in $\sigma(H)$ make all members of S better off, that is, for all $y \in \sigma(h)$, $u_i(H)(y) > u_i(G)(x)$ for all $i \in S$.

If an SB is stable under the assumption of optimistic behaviour, the SB is called Optimistic Stable Standard of Behaviour (OSSB) and if an SB is stable under the assumption of conservative behaviour, the SB is called Conservative Stable Standard of Behaviour (CSSB). In some important situations, such as the Coalitional Contingent Threat Situation defined below, these two notions may coincide.

2.2 Some Results

2.2.1 OSSB and von Neumann and Morgenstern stability

As we have explained before, the terms 'standard of behaviour' and 'stability' have been borrowed from von Neumann and Morgenstern's seminal work. In fact, the OSSB can be formally derived from von Neumann and Morgenstern's (vN-M) Abstract Stable Set for some 'associated abstract system'. Recall that *an abstract system* is a pair $(D, <)$, where D is an arbitary nonempty set, and $<$ is a binary relation on D, called the dominance relation. For $a, b, \in D$, $b<a$ is interpreted to mean that a dominates b.

Definition 7: *Let* $(D,<)$ *be an abstract system and* $A \subset D$. *A is vN-M internally stable if* $x \in A$ *implies that there does not exist* $y \in A$ *such that* $x \not< y$; *A is vN-M externally stable if* $x \in D \setminus A$ *implies that there exists* $y \in A$ *such that* $x<y$; *A is vN-M stable if it is both vN-M internally and externally stable.*

We can formally define an abstract system $(D,<)$ associated with a situation (γ, Γ) as follows:

$$D \equiv \{(G, x) | G \in \Gamma \text{ and } x \in X(G)\},$$

and, for (G, x) and (H, y) in D, $(G, x)<(H, y)$ if and only if there exists an $S \subset N(G)$ such that $H \in \gamma(S, G, x)$, and for all $i \in S$, $u_i(H)(y)>u_i(G)(x)$. Also, let us define the graph C of an SB σ by:

$$C \equiv \{(G, x) | G \in \Gamma \text{ and } x \in \sigma(G)\}.$$

We can now state the following fundamental result, due to Shitovitz (see Greenberg (1990)).

Theorem 1: *Let* (γ, Γ) *be a situation. The mapping* σ *is an OSSB for* (γ, Γ) *if and only if its graph is a vN-M abstract Stable Set for the system* $(D,<)$ *that is associated with* (γ, Γ).[2]

Theorem 1 draws a formal relationship between OSSB[3] and the abstract Stable Set. This is of great practical use in applications because it allows one to apply known results from works on abstract Stable Sets to the theory of social situations. We mention in particular the following theorem due to von Neumann and Morgenstern (1947). To state it we need an additional definition.

Let $(D,<)$ be an abstract system. The dominance relation, $<$, is called *acyclic* if there is no *finite* sequence, a_j, $j=1, 2, ..., J$, of elements in D, such that for all $j=1, 2, ..., J$, $a_j< a_{j+1}$, where $a_{J+1}=a_1$. The dominance relation, $<$, is called *strictly acyclic* if there exists no *infinite* sequence, a_j, of elements in D, such that $a_j< a_{j+1}$, for all j, $j=1, 2,...$.[4]

Theorem 2: *Let* $(D, <)$ *be an abstract system, where the dominance relation* $<$ *is strictly acyclic. Then there exists a unique vN-M (abstract) Stable Set for the system* $(D,<)$.

This result can be proved by using transfinite induction.

Form Theorems 1 and 2 the following basic existence result, also proved by Shitovitz (1987), follows:

Theorem 3: *Let* (γ, Γ) *be a situation such that* Γ *contains a finite number of positions, and each positon* $G \in \Gamma$ *contains a finite number of outcomes. Assume, in addition, that the inducement correspondence is such that for all* $G, H \in \Gamma$, $x \in X(G)$ *and* $S \subset N(G)$, *if* $H \in \gamma(S, G, x)$ *then* $N(H) = S$. *Then,* (γ, Γ) *admits a unique OSSB.*

It is important to note that a stable SB under behavioural assumption other than optimism cannot, in general, be formally derived from a vN-M abstract Stable Set. This is but one feature illustrating the greater generality of TOSS. This kind of result proves to be very useful in comparing different notions in coalitional analysis, as while most notions involve *implicit* assumptions about the negotiation process and behaviour, TOSS does not address foresight directly.

2.2.2 Some properties of OSSB and CSSB

We proceed to state some properties of OSSB and CSSB. Observe that by external stability, an OSSB or a CSSB cannot be identically empty-valued. That is, if σ is an OSSB or CSSB for a situation (γ, Γ), then there exists at least one position $G \in \Gamma$ such that $\sigma(G) \neq \theta$. σ is said to be *nonempty-valued* if $\sigma(G) \neq \theta$ for all $G \in \Gamma$. Let σ and σ' be two SB's for a situation (γ, Γ). Say σ *includes* σ' if $\sigma(G) \supset \sigma'(G)$ for all $G \in \Gamma$. Greenberg, Monderer, and Shitovitz (1996) proved the following result:

Theorem 4: *Let* (γ, Γ) *be a situation and let* Σ *be the set of all conservative internally stable nonempty-valued* SB*'s. Then* Σ *admits a largest element,* σ^L, *with respect to the inclusion order defined above. Moreover,* σ^L, *is the largest nonempty-valued CSSB.*

Note that if an optimistic internally stable SB in nonempty-valued, then it is also conservative internally stable. Hence we have the following corollary:

Corollary 5: *If* σ *is a nonempty-valued OSSB, then there exists a CSSB that includes it. In particular, every nonempty-valued OSSB is included in the largest nonempty-valued CSSB.*

2.3 Applications

TOSS can be used to 'derive', namely express in a new language, existing solution concepts. This is accomplished by identifying the situations underlying those solution concepts. Since a standard of behaviour is only constrained by the requirement of stability, and a situation entails a complete specification of all other aspects of the negotiation and reasoning process, one can often uncover subtle or hidden assumptions imposed by an existing solution concept. This can, in turn, point to possible desirable modifications of this solution concept and suggest new concepts. Such an approach will be apparent in the next two sections.

In what follows, we shall use two examples, useful for later reference, to illustrate applications of TOSS.

2.3.1 The von Neumann and Morgenstern (vN-M) situation

Let (N, v) be a finite game in characteristic function form, with $v(S)$ a compact nonempty subset of (the Euclidean space) $\Re^S$.

Definition 8: *A* Stable Set, *or a* vN-M solution, *for the cooperative game (N, v) is a set A which is a subset of $v(N)$ and satisfies the following: $y \in A$ if, and only if, there exist no coalition $S \subset N$ and a payoff $x \in A$ such that $x_S \in v(S)$ and $x_S \gg y_S$.*

The negotiation process underlying vN-M solution is one where coalitions make 'tender threats' which other coalitions can, in turn, counter by other tender threats. That is, every offer in $v(N)$ that is being made can be objected to by some coalition which offers a new payoff in $v(N)$, which, in turn, can be objected to by any other coalition, and so on.

The situation $(\hat{\gamma}, \hat{\Gamma})$ that describes this negotiation process for the cooperative game (N, v) is constructed by defining, for each $S \subset N$, the position $\hat{G}^S = (N, \hat{v}(S), \{u_i(\hat{G}^S)\}_{i \in N})$ as follows. The set of players in position $\hat{G}^S$ is the set N. The set of outcomes, $\hat{v}(S)$, in that position contains all those payoffs that are feasible for the grand coalition and whose projection on S yields a payoff that is feasible for coalition S, that is $\hat{v}(S) = \{x \in v(N) | x_S \in v(S)\}$. Finally, for all $i \in N$ and $x \in \hat{v}(S)$, $u_i(\hat{G}^S)(x) = x_i$. Next, define the situation $(\hat{\gamma}, \hat{\Gamma})$ by $\hat{\Gamma} = \{\hat{G}^S | S \subset N\}$ and, for all $\hat{G}^S \in \hat{\Gamma}$, $x \in X(\hat{G}^S)$, and $T \subset N$, $\hat{\gamma}(T, \hat{G}^S, x) = \{\hat{G}^T\}$. This says that a coalition T can counter-propose the payoff y, $y \in \hat{v}(T)$ independently of the currently proposed payoff, x and of whichever coalition proposes it.

The crucial relationship (credited to P. De Marzo, 1986 in Greenberg (1990)) between an OSSB for the vN-M situation $(\hat{\gamma}, \hat{\Gamma})$, and a vN-M solution for the game (N, v), is stated below:

Theorem 6: *Let (N, v) be a cooperative game. The* SB σ *is an OSSB for* $(\hat{\gamma}, \hat{\Gamma})$ *if, and only if,* $\sigma(\hat{G}^N) \equiv \sigma(G^N) \equiv A$, *where A is a vN-M solution for the game (N, v), and for all* $\hat{G}^S \in \hat{\Gamma}, : \sigma(\hat{G}^S) \equiv A \cap \hat{v}(S)$.

This result holds, with the appropriate reformulation of the definitions, for games with an infinite number of players.

2.3.2 The coalitional contingent threat situation

A game in strategic form is a triple $(N, \{Z_i\}_{i \in N}, \{u_i\}_{i \in N})$, where N is the set of players, Z_i is the nonempty strategy set of player i, and $u_i: Z_N \to \Re$ is player i's payoff function, where, for $S \subset N$, Z_S denotes the Cartesian product of Z_i over $i \in S$.

Consider the following negotiation process. An n-tuple of strategies $\zeta \in Z_N$ is proposed to the players. If all individuals *openly* agree to play ζ, then ζ will be played. If a coalition $S \subset N$ objects to the specified choice of ζ_S, he has to declare that if all other players will stick to the specified n-tuple of strategies ζ (hence the term 'contingent threats'), then it will employ the strategy $\rho_S \in Z_S$ instead of ζ_S. The new revised proposal then becomes $\xi = (\zeta_{N \setminus S}, \rho_S)$, from which another coalition, T, can in turn openly threaten to deviate, and the process continues in this manner.

The foregoing process is described by the following coalitional contingent threats situation (γ, Γ).[5] For $\zeta \in Z_N$, let G_ζ denote the position where the set of players is N, the set of outcomes consists of the single N-tuple of strategies ζ, and the utility level player $i \in N$ derives from ζ is $u_i(\zeta)$. that is:

$$G_\zeta \equiv (N, \{\zeta\}, \{u_i\}_{i \in N}).$$

The set of positions in the coalitional contingent threats situation (γ, Γ) is:

$$\Gamma \equiv \{G^N\} \cup \{G_\zeta \mid \zeta \in Z_N\},$$

and the inducement correspondence γ is given by: For all $G \in \Gamma$, $\zeta \in Z_N$, and $S \subset N(G)$,

$$\gamma(S \mid G, \zeta) \equiv \{G_\xi \mid \xi = (\xi_S, \zeta_{N \setminus S}), \xi_S \in Z_S\}.$$

Since the set of outcomes at each position is a singleton, a standard of behaviour in this situation is an OSSB if, and only if, it is a CSSB. Moreover, an OSSB (CSSB) contains the set of strong Nash equilibria. In the rest of this chapter, the coalitional contingent threat situation will be variously modified to capture foresight of the players.

3. THE LARGEST CONSISTENT SET

3.1 Definitions and Some Results

Chwe (1994) uses an alternative, simpler description of a social environment than the one considered so far. Consider a set of individuals, N, who are faced with a feasible set of alternatives Z. Each individual $i \in N$ has a strict preference relation $<_i$ on Z. What coalitions can do if and when they form is specified by $\{\xrightarrow{S}\}_{S \subset N}$, where $\{\xrightarrow{S}\}$, $S \subset N$, is an 'effectiveness relation' on Z and $a \xrightarrow{S} b$, where $a, b \in Z$, means that coalition $S \subset N$ can replace a by b.[6] Restrictions on coalition formulation, if there are any, are also reflected in $\{\xrightarrow{S}\}_{S \subset N}$ (which is a collection of partial relations). Thus, a social environment (see also Rosenthal, 1972) is represented by $\mathcal{G} = (N, Z, \{<_i\}_{i \in N}, \{\xrightarrow{S}\}_{S \subset N})$. Here are some examples to illustrate the flexibility and generality of $\mathcal{G}$.

Example 1: *The coalitional contingent threat situation associated with a strategic form game can be represented by* $\mathcal{G}$. *Let* $Z = Z_N$. *Thus, for all* $a, b \in Z$, $a \xrightarrow{S} b$ *if and only if* $a_{-S} = b_{-S}$. *If coalitions cannot form, then for every* $i \in N$, *and* $a, b \in Z$, $a \xrightarrow{\{i\}} b$ *if and only if* $a_{-i} = b_{-i}$, *and* $a <_i b$ *if and only if* $u_i(a) < u_i(b)$. *This corresponds to the 'individual contingent threat situation'.*

Example 2: *One way to represent a cooperative game by* $\mathcal{G}$ *is as follows. Let* Z *be the set of imputations (efficient and individually rational payoff vectors in* $v(N)$*). For* a, $b \in Z$ *and* $S \subset N$, $a \xrightarrow{S} b$ *if, and only if,* $b_S \in v(S)$. *This bears a similarity with the vN-M situation.*

Although $\mathcal{G}$ describes the *primitives* of a social environment, its description of the social environment is incomplete, in comparison with a *situation*. Indeed, we can apply different solution concepts to $\mathcal{G}$, each of which embeds different 'rules of the game'. For example, the vN-M solution for cooperative games can be generalized to more complex social environments as studied in this chapter. That is, one can apply the notion of 'vN-M abstract Stable Set' to the study of social environment represented by $\mathcal{G}$. To this end, we introduce the following definition:

Let V be an (abstract) Stable Set for $(Z, >)$. If $x \in Z$ is the *status quo*, the set of 'predicted outcomes' is given by $\{y \in V \mid y = x$ or $y > x)$. That is, if some $x \in V$ is the *status quo*, it will prevail; however, if some $x \in Z \backslash V$ is the *status quo*, then some $y \in V$ such that $y > x$ will prevail.

The following dominance relation on Z is similar to the one used in the definition of vN-M solution for cooperative games:

Definition 9: *For $a, b \in Z$, b is said to dominate a, or $b > a$, if there exists a coalition $S \subset N$ that can replace a by b, that is, $a \xrightarrow{S} b$, and all members of the acting coalition S prefer b to a, that is, $a <_i b$ for all $i \in S$.*

Let V be stable for $(Z, >)$. If $\mathcal{G}$ represents a cooperative game, then V is equivalent to the vN-M solution for this cooperative game. However, Harsanyi (1974, p. 10) criticizes the vN-M solution for its failing to incorporate foresight. Such a criticism applies also to an abstract Stable Set V for $(Z, >)$, which can be illustrated by an (extremely) simple example, where $N = \{1, 2\}$, $Z = \{a, b, c\}$, player 1 can replace a by b, that is $a \xrightarrow{S} b$, and player 2 can replace b and c, that is, $b \xrightarrow{S} c$. This example is depicted below where the vector attached to each alternative is the payoff vector derived from that alternative if it prevails.

$$a_{(1,1)} \xrightarrow{\{1\}} b_{(0,0)} \xrightarrow{\{2\}} c_{(2,2)}. \tag{3.1}$$

The unique Stable Set for $(Z, >)$ is $V = \{a, c\}$. According to the definition of V, player 1 will not replace a by b, since b itself is not stable (and hence will be replaced). But if he is farsighted, he should and will replace a by b, precisely because player 2 (who is rational) will subsequently replace b by c. That is, farsighted players do not just look at the next step. For this reason, Harsanyi suggests (within the framework of cooperative games) to replace the (direct) dominance relation $>$ by some 'indirect dominance', which captures the fact that farsighted individuals consider the *final* outcomes that their actions may lead to. Chwe (1994) formalized a version of Harsanyi's indirect dominance when applied to $\mathcal{G}$. An alternative b is said to indirectly dominate another alternative a if b can replace a in a sequence of 'moves', such that at each move the active coalition prefers (the final alternative) b to the alternative it faces at that stage. Formally:

Definition 10: *For $a, b \in Z$, b indirectly dominates a, or $b \gg a$, if there exist $a_0, a_1, \ldots, a_m$ in Z, where $a_0 = a$ and $a_m = b$, and coalitions $S_0, S_1, \ldots, S_{m-1}$ such that for $j = 0, 1, \ldots, m-1$, $a_j \xrightarrow{S_j} a_{j+1}$ and for all $i \in S_j, a_j <_i a_m$.*

Now, given the indirect dominance relation $\gg$, one can consider the (abstract) Stable Set for $(Z, \gg)$. For equation 4.1, the unique Stable Set for $(Z, \gg)$ is $H = \{c\}$, which captures foresight of the individuals in this example: if a is the *status quo*, c is the only predicted outcome. As noted by Chwe (1994, p. 6), however, the Stable Set for $(Z, \gg)$ can be too 'exclusive' in that its exclusion of some alternatives may not be consistent with rationality and foresight. To rectify this, Chwe suggests a new solution concept – 'the Largest Consistent Set'. In the definition of (the largest) consistent set, a coalition rejects or deviates from an alternative only if its deviation leads *only* to alternatives that benefit its members. (In contrast, the Stable Set for $(Z, \gg)$ entails that a coalition deviates as long as this deviation might lead to *some* alternative that benefits its members.) The Largest Consistent Set has the merits of 'ruling out with confidence' and being nonempty under weak condition. It turns out, however, that the Largest Consistent Set may be too inclusive. We shall illustrate these issues by the example in equation 4.2 in the next section. But first let us introduce the formal definition of the Largest Consistent Set.

Definition 11: *Consider a social environment* $\mathcal{G}$. *A subset* $Y \subset Z$ *is consistent if* $a \in Y \Leftrightarrow$ *for every* $d \in Z$ *and* $S \subset N$ *such that* $a \xrightarrow{S} d$, *there exists* $e \in Y$, $e = d$ *or* $e \gg d$, *such that* $a \not<_s e$. *The Largest Consistent Set (LCS) is the unique maximal consistent set with respect to set inclusion.*

Chwe proved that if Z is countable and contains no infinite sequence $a_1, a_2, \ldots$ such that $i<j$ implies $a_i \ll a_j$, then LCS is nonempty. Xue (1997) extends this result by removing the countability condition. Chwe also applies his notion to 'coalitional contingent threat situation', voting games and other contexts.[7]

3.1.1 LCS and TOSS

As shown by Chwe (1994), the notion of consistent set can be cast within the framework of TOSS, thereby revealing how individuals view and use their alternatives. In particular, the negotiation/reasoning process underlying Chwe's consistent set is described by situation (γ, Γ) defined as follows:

For $a \in Z$, define a position $G_a = (N, X_a, (<_i)_{i \in N})$ where:

$$X_a = \{a\} \cup \{b \in Z | a \ll b\},$$

and $\Gamma = \{G_a | a \in Z\}$. For $G_a \in \Gamma$, $x \in X_a$ and $S \subset N$, $\gamma(S|G_a, x) = \{G_y | x \xrightarrow{S} y\}$.

Chwe (1994, Proposition 4) showed that the CSSB for the 'Chwe situation' is formally related to his consistent set. This formal relationship can be stated in the following proposition (see Xue, 1997).

Proposition 7: *For* $Y \subset Z$, *define an* SB ψ *for the 'Chwe situation' by* $\psi(X_a) = X_a \cap Y$ *for all* $a \in Z$. *Then,* ψ *is a CSSB if, and only if,* Y *is consistent and* ψ *is nonempty-valued. In particular,* ψ *is the largest (nonempty-valued) CSSB if and only if* Y *is the LCS and* ψ *is nonempty-valued.*

4. A 'PATH' APPROACH

4.1 Paths and Perfect Foresight

According to Chwe (1994), the set of 'predicted outcomes', when $x \in Z$ is the *status quo*, is given by $\{y \in LCS | y = x \text{ or } y \gg x\}$. We now proceed to illustrate that the Stable Set for $(Z, \gg)$ can be too exclusive while the LCS can be too inclusive. Consider the social environment where $N = \{1, 2\}$, $Z = \{a, b, c, d\}$, and the 'effectiveness relations' as well as the payoffs are depicted in equation 4.2:

$$
\begin{array}{lll}
a_{(6,0)} & & \\
\{1\}\downarrow & & \\
b_{(7,4)} & \xrightarrow{\{2\}} & c_{(5,10)} \\
\{1,2\}\downarrow & & \\
d_{(10,5)} & &
\end{array}
\qquad (4.2)
$$

Assume that the *status quo* is a. If a prevails, the payoffs are 6 and 0 for players 1 and 2 respectively. Player 1 can replacy a by b, which, if prevails, yields a payoff of 7 to player 1 and 4 to player 2. Once b becomes the (new) *status quo*, there are two possibilities: either player 2 can replace b by c, or players 1 and 2 together can replace b by d. Applying the definition of indirect dominance gives:

$$b \gg a,\ d \gg b,\ c \gg b, \text{ and } d \gg a.$$

As a result, the unique Stable Set for $(Z, \gg)$ is $H = \{c, d\}$. a is excluded from H since $d \gg a$ and $d \in H$. Note that $c \in H$ but $c \not\gg a$. Therefore, if a is the *status quo*, the unique predicted outcome is d. But clearly, to reach d from a requires player 1 first to replace a by b, and once b is reached, player 1 will not join player 2 to replace b by d; instead, player 2 will replace b by c. Hence given that players are farsighted, in contemplating a deviation from a, player 1 should anticipate the final outcome (c, in this case) that will arise, and thereby will not replace a by b.

The LCS solves the exclusion of a. Indeed, $LCS = \{a, c, d\}$. Therefore, when a is the *status quo*, the set of predicted outcomes is $\{a, d\}$. But there remains a problem: when a is the *status quo*, one of the 'predicted' outcomes according to the LCS is d, resulting in the same difficulty as was discussed above. The above analysis illustrates several aspects of perfect foresight.

- A farsighted player considers only the final outcomes that might result when making choices. Indeed, player 1, in contemplating a deviation from a, does not make his decision by comparing a with b.
- Even though, as stated in (1), it is only the final outcomes that matter, a player with perfect foresight considers also how, if at all, these final outcomes can be reached. In out example, it is feasible to reach d from a, but rational players would not follow the 'path' (a, b, d). (Were b reached, player 2 would deviate and implement c.) To capture perfect foresight, we must, therefore, consider deviations 'along the way' to the final outcomes.
- The exclusiveness of the Stable set for $(Z, \gg)$ and inclusiveness of the LCS are not isolated events. They both stem from the fact that indirect dominance defined on Z fails to capture perfect foresight since it ignores the possible deviations along the way from one alternative (for example, a) to another (for example, d).

On the basis of these considerations Xue (1998) suggests that, in order to model perfect foresight, one needs to consider the 'graph' of a social environment and use 'paths' as the building blocks in the formalization of foresight. The social environment depicted in equation 4.2 has been represented intentionally in a graph form to stress this point. Viewing a social environment as a graph has been overlooked in the literature on foresight, since its necessity is not obvious, particularly when $\mathcal{G}$ represents a normal form game, a cooperative game, or a social environment of more complex structure.

We now formalize perfect foresight by considering the 'graph' of $\mathcal{G}$. To this end, we introduce the following definitions:

Definition 12: *The directed graph generated by $\mathcal{G}$, denoted $\phi(\mathcal{G})$, consists of the set of vertices (nodes) Z and a collection of arcs where for every $a, b \in Z$, ab is an arc if, and only if, there exists $S \subset N$ such that $a \xrightarrow{S} b$. If ab is an arc, b is said to be adjacent to a and a adjacent to b. A path is a sequence of vertices $(v_1, v_2, \ldots, v_k)$, where for all $j = 1, 2, \ldots, k-1$, v_jv_{j+1} is an arc, that is, there exists a coalition $S_j \subset N$ such that $v_j \xrightarrow{S_j} v_{j+1}$. The length of this path is $k-1$. $\phi(\mathcal{G})$ is said to be acyclic if every path consists of distinct vertices. $\phi(\mathcal{G})$ is said to be bounded if there exists a finite integer J such that every path has a length that does not exceed J.*

The following notations are introduced to facilitate the subsequent analysis. If $a \in Z$ is a vertex that lies on the path α, we shall write $a \in \alpha$. For a path α, let $\alpha|_b$, where $b \in \alpha$, denote its continuation from b (and including b) and let $t(\alpha)$ denote its terminal node (that is, the last node that lies on α).

Also, let Π be the set of all paths and for $a \in Z$, let Π_a denote the set of paths that originate from a (including a itself). The preferences over paths in Π are the preferences over their terminal nodes, that is, for any two paths α and β, $\alpha <_i \beta$ if and only if $t(\alpha) <_i t(\beta)$. Also, we write $\alpha <_S \beta$ if $t(\alpha) <_S t(\beta)$, that is, if $t(\alpha) <_i t(\beta)$ for all $i \in S$.

For every $a \in Z$, Π_a specifies the set of 'feasible outcomes' when a is the *status quo* (or under consideration). Note that $\mathcal{G}$ is far more general than an extensive form game: at every node, more than one coalition may act, and $\phi(\mathcal{G})$, the graph of $\mathcal{G}$, need not by acyclic (such is the case, for example, when $\mathcal{G}$ represents a cooperative game or a normal form game).

We shall retain the assumptions of Chwe (1994) that actions are public and payoffs are derived at a *status quo* only if no coalition wishes to replace it. Consider, for example, a duopoly pricing model. Then the assumption of public actions amounts to the requirement that price changes are *instantly* detected while payoffs are derived only if prices are 'stable' in that no firm will wish to change its price. Public actions can also represent objections and counter-objections in an open negotiation, in which case our analysis identifies those agreements that are acceptable to rational (and far-sighted) individuals.

In the analysis that follows, perfect foresight is captured *explicitly* by the following situation, which we shall henceforth refer to as 'the situation with perfect foresight': Assume that alternative $a \in Z$ is the *status quo*. Then the associated position is $G_a = \{N, \Pi_a, (>_i)_{i \in N}\}$. Thus, the set of positions is given by:

$$\Gamma^* = \{G_a | a \in Z\}.$$

Consider a path $\alpha \in \Pi_a$ and some node $b \in \alpha$ and assume that a coalition $S \subset N$ can replace b by some alternative c that does not lies on α, that is, $b \xrightarrow{S} c$ and $c \notin \alpha$. In doing so, S is aware that the set of feasible paths from c is Π_c. Thus, the inducement correspondence γ^* is given by: For all $G_a \in \Gamma^*$, $\alpha \in \Pi_a$, and $S \subset N$,

$$\gamma^*(S, G_a, \alpha) = \{G_a | b \in \alpha \text{ and } b \xrightarrow{S} c\}.$$

A stable standard of behaviour σ for (Γ^*, γ^*) specified, for every $\alpha \in Z$, the set of paths Π_a that might be followed by rational and farsighted individuals.

4.1.1 Properties

It is easy to verify that for the social environment depicted in equation 4.2, the situation with perfect foresight admits a unique OSSB which coincides with the unique CSSB. Denoting this SB by σ, we have $\sigma(G_b) = \{(b, c)\}$[8] and $\sigma(G_a) = \{a\}$. Hence, coalition $\{1, 2\}$ will never form. Moreover, if a is the *status quo*, a (and only a) will prevail. Thus, the unique (optimistic or conservative) stable SB gives rise to the outcome conforming to perfect foresight.

For an arbitrary social environment $\mathcal{G}$, the notion of (optimistic or conservative) stable SB is used in the same fashion. In particular, a stable SB enables us to answer the following questions:

- Which outcomes in Z are 'stable' in that they will prevail? That is, which outcomes, if it happens to be the *status quo*, will not be replaced by farsighted rational individuals?
- How are stable outcomes reached from 'non-stable' outcomes?
- Which coalitions might form in the process of replacing a non-stable outcome with a stable one?

Before we answer these questions, we shall establish a few important properties of a stable SB. The first lemma shows that predictions by a stable SB are consistent, that is a 'stable path' satisfies a 'truncation property': the continuation of a 'stable path' is stable at any stage along the way. The second lemma guarantees that the existence of a stable SB implies the existence of stable outcomes in Z. Formally:

Lemma 8: *Assume that σ is a stable* SB, *and that $\alpha \in \sigma(G_a)$. Then, for all $b \in \alpha$, $\alpha|_b \in \sigma(G_b)$.*

Lemma 9: *If σ is a stable* SB, *then there exists at least one $a \in Z$ such that $a \in \sigma(G_a)$.*[9]

Let σ be an OSSB/CSSB for the situation with perfect foresight. Then the set of *stable outcomes under optimism/conservatism* is given by $E_\sigma = \{a \in Z | a \in \sigma(G_a)\}$. Each alternative $a \in E_\sigma$ is stable under optimism/conservatism in the sense that it will prevail if it is the *status quo*. Put differently, no coalition (who behaves optimistically/conservatively) with the power to replace a by another alternative would (eventually) benefit by doing so. Moreover, every outcome that belongs to $Z \backslash E_\sigma$ is an *unstable outcome*. Whenever such an outcome is the *status quo*, there is at least one coalition that can and will (eventually) benefit from replacing it.

The above assertion relies on the existence of a stable SB. Thus, it is important to investigate the existence of a stable SB. One simple sufficient condition is as follows (for more general results, see Xue (1998)):

Proposition 10: *Assume that $\phi(\mathcal{G})$ is a bounded acylic graph.*[10] *Then there exists a unique OSSB and a unique CSSB.*

In our analysis, foresight is formalized by considering the graph of the social environment. There is an intimate connection between our notion and subgame perfection in extensive form games of perfect information – a special class of directed graphs. Indeed, if $\mathcal{G}$ represents an extensive form game of perfect information, there is an equivalence between the CSSB for the situation with perfect foresight and the notion of subgame perfection. Consequently, our analysis extends the notion of subgame perfection to social environments with diverse coalitional interactions.

Proposition 11 provides a formal result on the relationship between the largest CSSB for the situation with perfect foresight and the largest CSSB (hence the LCS) for the Harsanyi–Chwe situation.

Proposition 11: *Let $\mathcal{G}$ be a social environment. Let ψ^{ℓ} be the largest CSSB for the Harsanyi–Chwe situation and σ be a nonempty-valued CSSB for the situation with perfect foresight such that for every $a \in Z$, $\alpha \in \sigma(a)$, where $t(\alpha) \neq a$ implies $t(\alpha) \gg a$. Then for all $a \in Z$, $\alpha \in \sigma(a)$ implies $t(\alpha) \in \psi^{\ell}(\alpha)$, that is, σ 'refines' ψ^{ℓ}.*

The notion of perfect foresight can also be applied to normal form games. If $\mathcal{G}$ represents the coalitional contingent threat situation, we have the following results:

Proposition 12: *Let a be a strict Strong Nash Equilibrium for a finite normal form game G and assume that $\mathcal{G}$ represents the coalitional contingent threat situation. Then a belongs to the set of stable outcomes under conservatism as defined by the largest CSSB for the situation with perfect foresight.*

The set of stable outcomes, however, may also include strategy profiles that are not Nash equilibria. By modifying the approach presented here, Xue (2000) defines the notion of 'negotiation-proof Nash equilibrium', which rectifies myopia and nestedness embedded in the notion of coalition-proof Nash equilibrium.

5. A STRATEGIC APPROACH

5.1 General Definitions

When discussing the stability of outcomes with respect to coalitional deviations, we normally use expressions such as 'coalition *S* would deviate' without specifying how exactly the *individual* members of the (prospective) coalition plan and implement the deviation. In other words, we treat each possible coalition, rather than each of the individual players, as the fundamental decision unit. Importantly, this is true even when considering games described in strategic form, in which coalitions are not primitives of the analysis (think of the concepts of a Strong Nash Equilibrium or the Coalition Proof Nash Equilibrium). Attributing a will and decision power directly to coalitions suggests that one could explicitly define a non-cooperative game with coalitions *as players*. The advantage of doing this is that one can then adapt the standard tools and equilbrium concepts used in non-cooperative game theory to capture the ideas of farsightedness and consistency (think of subgame perfection, for example). In particular, one can define *strategies* for coalitions. Consistency and farsightedness will be expressed by a *strategic equilibrium* notion. The dual nature of non-cooperative strategies as both prescription and expectation of behaviour also allows us to throw some light on the problem pointed out by Luce and Raiffa (1957).

> Presumably, an adequate descriptive theory will incorporate the expectations of each potential coalition as to the reactions of the remaining players if that coalition should actually form. How these expectations should be calculated is far from clear. (p. 191)

At a strategic equilibrium expectations are endogenously determined as equilibrium expectations.

This line of enquiry has been pursued in Mariotti (1997) with the definition of a 'Coalitional Equilibrium'. The original paper proposed this concept in the context of an underlying non-cooperative game described in strategic form. Here, we first generalize the basci ideas to make them coherent within the context of this chapter. Later we will move to strategic form games.

Given are: a finite set of outcomes Z; a set of players N; a set of feasible coalitions Σ, with $S \subset N$ for all $S \in \Sigma$; $|N|$ preference relations $\succeq_i$, one for each player i, on subsets of Z; a (possibly empty) effectiveness correspondence $r : Z \times \Sigma \rightarrow \mathrm{Z}$. In this last defintion, $b \in r(a, S)$ denotes the fact that coalition S can move the *status quo* from a to b. Therefore, this is simply a notationally different way of expressing a set of effectiveness relations.

We assume that preferences satisfy the following: $B \succ_i \emptyset$ for all nonempty $B \subseteq Z$; $B \succeq_i C$ if $\{b\} \succeq_i \{c\}$ for all $b \in B$, $c \in C$. The same observations made for Greenberg's TOSS apply here: any further specification of a preference relation on sets of outcomes is not part of the solution concept, but rather part of the description of the social environment under consideration.

Imagine the following procedure, inspired by Greenberg's (1990) *coalitional contingent threat situation* defined in section 2. At each stage an outcome a is under proposal. Any coalition S may potentially induce a new outcome b provided that $b \in r(a, S)$. Once at b, any other coalition T may induce $c \in r(b, T)$, and so on. The process continues in this way until there is an outcome from which nobody wishes to deviate.

A *history* is a finite sequence of pairs $\{(S^n, a^n)\}_{n=1,..,K}$ such that for all n: (i) $a^n \in Z$ and $S^n \in \Sigma$; (ii) $a^{n+1} \in r(a^n, S^n)$. A composite history obtained by adding to h an additional element (S, a) is written $h \oplus (S, a)$.

An initial history at a *status quo*, a is represented by $\{\emptyset, a\}$. Let $\mathcal{H}$ be the set of all histories. Given $h \in \mathcal{H}$ with $h = \{(S^n, a^n)\}_{n=1,..,K}$, let $\lambda(h) = a^K$. An *S-strategy* is a map $\alpha_S : \mathcal{H} \rightarrow Z$ with the property that, for all $h \in \mathcal{H}$, $\alpha_S(h) \in r(\lambda(h), S)$. An S-strategy defines what each coalition would do, after each history, *if* it could move. Let Ω_S be the set of all S-strategies, and let $\Omega = \Pi\Omega_S$ (assume an ordering to list coalitions).

Given $h \in \mathcal{H}$ and $\alpha \in \Omega$, we say that $b \in Z$ is *reachable* from h via α if there exists a history $h' = \{(T^n, C^n)\}_{n=1,..,K'}\}$, called a *reaching history* for b, with the following properties: (i) $c^1 = \alpha_{T1}(h)$; (ii) for all n, $c_n = \alpha(h \oplus (T^1, c^1) \oplus \ldots \oplus (T^{n-1}, c^{n-1}))$; (iii) $b = c^{K'}$. That is, there must be a sequence of coalitions whose S-strategies lead, starting from history h, to the outcome b.

Given $h \in \mathcal{H}$ and $\alpha \in \Omega$, we say that $b \in Z$ is *terminal* from h via α if (i) b is reachable from h via α; (ii) for all reaching histories h' for b, for all $S \in \Sigma$, $\alpha_S(h \oplus h') = b$. That is, after reaching b no coalition wants to move. Let $\tau(h, \alpha) = \{b \in Z | b \text{ is terminal from } h \text{ via } \alpha\}$. Clearly, $\tau(h, \alpha)$ may be empty. By our assumption on preferences, this case is at the bottom of the preference ranking for all players. This means that infinite histories are worse than any other set of outcomes. Players only care about the final outcome and do not mind how many moves it takes to get there.

We can now define our equilibrium notion.[11] A *Coalitional Equilibrium* (CE) is a pair $(a^*, \alpha^*) \in Z \times \Omega$ such that for all $h \in \mathcal{H}$: (i) if $\lambda(h) = a^*$, a^* is terminal from h via a^*; (ii) for all $S \in \Sigma$ there is no $\alpha_S \times \Omega_S$ such that $\tau(h, (\alpha_S, \alpha^*_{-S})) \geq_i \tau(h, \alpha^*)$ for all $i \in S$; (iii) if for some $S \in \Sigma$ $\alpha^*_S(h) \neq \lambda(h)$ then $\tau(h, \alpha^*) \geq_i \{\lambda(h)\}$ for all $i \in S$. If (a^*, α^*) is a CE, say that a^* is an *equilibrium point supported by* α^*.

In applications, it is often much easer to consider the stationary version of the concept, in which S-strategies are only conditional on the current *status quo*, independently of the history that led to it. A stationary S-strategy is thus a map σ_S from the set of outcomes to itself. A *stationary Coalitional Equilibrium* is a CE in which coalitions are restricted to play only stationary strategies.

Part (i) of the definition of a CE simply states the stationarity of the outcome a^* when the S-strategy profile α^* is played. Part (ii) is analogous to the definition of a subgame perfect equilibrium in an extensive form game: after no history can a coalition deviate from the equilibrium S-strategy and improve. However, the definition is adapted to take into account the fact that an S-strategy profile may not lead to a unique outcome. A further difference with a standard extensive form is that here we are not dealing with a tree. There may be a combination of S-strategies that generate infinite cycles. Condition (iii) implies that an equilibrium S-strategy profile always leads to a terminal outcome. The interpretation of this condition is that, at any history, the coalition that has the power to move has the option of implementing the *status quo*.

Some remarks on the correct interpretation of a strategy and an equilibrium are in now order. It does not seem plausible to assume that all coalitions (most of which may not even ever actually form!) *plan* behaviour before playing the game. The proper interpretation of a profile of S-strategies is as a set of common expectations regarding contingent coalitional behaviour: an S-strategy expresses what it is commonly expected that coalition S would do, after any history, if it formed and thus obtained the power to move. Given such expectations, the idea is that any coalition is assumed to exploit an improvement opportunity, at any history, with a (one-step, as shown below) deviation. So, for expectations to be consistent with optimality of behaviour, we need that strategies form an equilibrium. An outcome is an equilibrium outcome if it is consistently expected that no coalition will want to depart from it. This addresses the problem raised in the previous quotation by Luce and Raiffa.

5.2 Some Basic Results and Obervations

We first observe that the 'one-deviation property' applies in this context. If a coalition can improve on a given S-strategy α_S, then it can do so by using a strategy that differs from α_S only in the actions prescribed at one history. The reason for this result is that infinite histories have less value than any other history; then, standard arguments can be applied.

Next, we turn to the issue of stationarity.

Proposition 13: *Any stationary CE is also a CE.*

This again follows from standard arguments, presented for example in Harsanyi (1974). Although it is reassuring to know that the restriction to stationarity does not create new equilibria, the only justification for this restriction is simplicity of computation.

Nonstationary equilibria sometimes must be invoked to guarantee existence, as the following simple example shows:

Example 3: *$N=\{1, 2, 3\}$. $Z=\{a, b, c\}$, $\{b\}=r(\{1\}, a)$, $\{c\}=r(\{2\}, b)$, $\{a\}=r(\{3\}, c)$ and $r(S, x)$ is empty otherwise. $\{b\}>_1\{a\}>_1\{c\}$, $\{c\}>_2\{b\}>_2\{a\}$, $\{a\}>_3\{c\}>_3\{b\}$. There is no need to specify preferences on other subsets.*

In this example each play *i* can move to the next outcome in the cycle, which is his favourite. But this is threatened by the next player having the power to move to *his* best outcome, which is *i*'s worst outcome. There is no stationary CE. To see this informally, suppose for instance that *a* was an equilibrium point. Then *b* cannot be an equilibrium point: otherwise 1 would move to it. But in a CE 3 must move from *c* to *a*, given that *a* is an equilibrium point. So 2 would not move from *b* to *c* and *b* would also be an equilbirum point, a contradiction. An analogous argument shows that *b* or *c* cannot be equilibrium points either.

But consider non-stationary strategies constructed as follows. A player stays at the *status quo* at any initial history (that is, of the type $(x, \emptyset)$). At non-initial histories, the initial mover is 'punished' by the other two players by implementing his worst outcome. For example, a history with outcome sequence *ab* must have 1 as the first mover. Then at this history 2 moves to *c* and 3 stays at *c*. If some player deviates from this punishment pattern, he is punished in the same way if possible (in the case above, if 2 fails to move to *c* he cannot be punished – but observe that 2's deviation would clearly be non-optimal). And so on. So, for example, suppose that the history with sequence of outcomes *abc* (player 1 to be punished) is followed by *a* (player 3 has moved to *a* instead of punishing 1 by staying at *c*), so that we are at the history with action sequence *abca* and it is 1's turn to move. According to the strategies described, what happens is that 1 moves to *b* and 2 stays at *b*, implementing 3's worst outcome.

It is not difficult to see that the strategy profile sketched above constitutes a CE. Play does not move from *a*, *b* and *c* when starting at those outcomes.

This type of 3-cycle example is notorious for generating existence problems. For instance, there is no von Neumann–Morgenstern Stable Set in the associated abstract system. Using a non-stationary CE allows one to glean some insight in the complex social behaviour and expectations which may occur in this situation. For comparison, the LCS includes the same set of outcomes, but little light is shed on the expectations sustainging those outcomes.

In general, existence of a CE is hard to establish, although there are no examples of non-existence. Existence results can be obtained for some limited case. For instance, existence of a (stationary) CE is guaranteed whenever the effectiveness correspondence is such that all possible histories are acyclic, in the sense that they cannot reach the same outcome twice (but possibly involve the same coalition moving more than once). To see this, note that this form of acyclicity implies that there exist outcomes from which no coalition can move. The equilibrium S-strategies can then be constructed by backward induction, starting at these outcomes. Another existence result is given in the next subsection.

To give the flavour of the characterization results possible in this framework, we sketch one on Pareto optimality, which generalizes Proposition 4.2 in Mariotti (1997).

Proposition 14: *Suppose thar $r(\{N\}, a) = Z$ for all $a \in Z$. Let (a^*, α^*) be a stationary* CE *such that a^* is the unique equilibrium point supported by α^*, in the sense that if (a^{**}, α^*) is also a* CE*, then $a^* = a^{**}$. Then a^* is Pareto optimal in Z, in the sense that there is no other outcome b such that all players prefer $\{b\}$ to $\{a\}$.*

The first assumption in the statement says that the grand coalition can move to any outcome from any outcome. To see that the result holds, suppose that a^* was Pareto dominated, in the sense described in the statement, by another outcome b. Then, for it to be optimal for the grand coalition not to move to b from a^*, it must be the case that α^* prescribes some coalition S to move from b. Condition (iii) in the defintion of a CE implies that this leads to a terminal point c preferred by S to $\{b\}$. But such a terminal point c is clearly an equilibrium point, so by uniqueness $c = a^*$. This yields the contradiction that the members of S prefer $\{a^*\}$ to itself.

A similar argument shows that in unanimity games (where all players agree on what is the best outcome), the unique equilibrium point is the unanimous best outcome.

5.3 Strategic Form Games

More precise results can be obtained in specific contexts. The original version of a CE was proposed in the context where the underlying strategic situation is described by means of a strategic form game $F = (N, \{Z_i\}_{i \in N}, \{u_i\}_{i \in N})$ where Z_i is the strategy space of player i and u_i his utility function. Therefore, the outcome space Z is the Cartesian product of the Z_i. The preference relation $\gtrsim_i$ was assumed to be as follows: $B \succeq_i C$ if there exists $b \in B$ such that $u_i(b) \geq u_i(c)$ for all $c \in C$. Then, one can prove:

Proposition 15: *Any stationary Coalitional equilibrium point yields each player more than his maximum value.*

Proposition 16: *Let F be a two-player game such that: (i) the Pareto frontier is strictly decreasing and (ii) there exists a Pareto efficient outcome* a^* *that dominates the pair of maximin values. Then a stationary Coalitional Equilibrium exists, with* a^* *as an equilibrium point.*

These two results apply directly to the simple but interesting example of the Prisoner's Dilemma game. Proposition 15 tells us that {Cooperate, Defect} and {Defect, Cooperate}, which yield one of the player his lowest, and individually irrational, payoff, cannot be equilibrium points. Proposition 16 tells us that {Cooperate, Cooperate) can be supported as an equilibrium point. Proposition 14 tells us that {Defect, Defect} cannot be the unique equilibrium point. Finally, it is not difficult to see that {Cooperate, Cooperate} and {Defect, Defect} cannot coexist as equilibrium points. We can conclude that {Cooperate, Cooperate} is the unique equilibrium point. The reason why it is claimed that this game is not trivial is that other solution concepts yield different results. For example, the Strong Equilibrium Set, the Optimistically Stable Standard of Behaviour of the coalitional contingent threat situation and the von Neumann–Morgenstern Stable Set of the associated abstract situation are all empty. The Coalition Proof Nash Equilibrium is {Defect, Defect}. The Largest Consistent Set is {Cooperate, Cooperate}. One concludes that, even in such simple games, what outcome or set of outcomes prevails is very senstive to exactly how farsighted players are assumed to be and to the details of the negotiation procedure.

Another interesting example is the following:[12]

	L	R	L	R
T	2, 2, 2	0, 0, 0	0, 0, 0	4, 4, 1
B	0, 0, 0	0, 0, 0	0, 0, 0	3, 3, 3.
	L		R	

Here there are two stationary Coalitional Equilibria, one with $\{(B, R, R)\}$ as the unique equilibrium point, the other with $\{(T, R, R)\}$ as the unique equilibrium point. For comparison, the Largest Consistent Set is:

$$\{(T, L, L), (B, R, R), (T, R, R)\}.$$

Let us try to understand these different results in terms of the expectations the player must have. In particular, observe that though (T, L, L) is included in the LCS it cannot be a Coalitional equilibrium point. Why? Because if it was, this would imply that (B, R, R) is not an equilibrium point (deviation by the grand coalition). In turn, the only explanation for this is that it is a common expectation that Row would deviate to (T, R, R), and so that $(T,$

R, *R*) is also an equilibrium point. But this is not a consistent expectation, because there is nothing to stop Box in deviating to (*T*, *R*, *L*). In particular, this deviation cannot be deterred by the fear or returning to (*T*, *R*, *R*) (via (*B*, *R*, *R*)): for in this case Column would upset the stability of (*T*, *L*, *L*) by moving to (*T*, *R*, *L*).

It is clear from this analysis that the inclusion of (*T*, *L*, *L*) in the LCS can only be supported by expectations which are inconsistent across players about what happens at (*T*, *R*, *L*): on the one hand, for Column to stay at (*T*, *L*, *L*) he must think that play would lead back from (*T*, *R*, *L*) to (*T*, *L*, *L*) after his deviation; but, on the other hand, for Box to stay at (*T*, *R*, *R*) he must think that play would lead back from (*T*, *R*, *L*) to (*T*, *R*, *R*) after his deviation.

6. CONCLUDING REMARKS

We have presented a selective survey of what we believe is an important issue, the formalization of farsightedness in coalition formation. This issue has not played a dominant role in the literature so far. By contrast, consider extensive form games, where the aspect of farsightedness of individual players is recognized as crucial, and is taken into account when using concepts such as subgame perfection, sequentiality, and so on.[13]

As we have discussed, in the literature considered in this chapter there isn't yet a single equilibrium concept on which consensus has been reached. We have argued, however, that Greenberg's Theory of Social Situations provides a useful unifying framework to study the issue, and we have examined in depth some subsequent contributions which in one way or the other are related to that theory. Other approaches and insights are offered, for example, by Arce (1996), Chakravorti (1999), Diamantoudi (2000), Konishi and Ray (2000), Li (1992) and Suzuki and Muto (2000). Applications to the study of International Environmental Agreements are provided, for example, in Ecchia and Mariotti (1997, 1998).

What has been offered so far is an increased understanding of (the implicit assumptions underlying) existing solution concepts, as well as some proposals for improvement. But this is doubtless an exciting area of research in which much work is ongoing and much still remains to be done.

NOTES

1. Here we keep with Greenberg's formulation by using a utility function, although a preference relation is all that is needed to define the primitive of TOSS.
2. The comparison between OSSB and vN-M abstract stable sets has to involve the graph

of the SB, since the stability of an SB is imposed on the *mapping*, σ, whereas in vN-M, the stability is required of a *set*.
3. The notion of CSSB, on the other hand, cannot be formally related to a vN-M abstract stable set. However, using the notion of 'F-stability', Rothblum obtained a partial analog of this theorem for CSSB (see, Greenberg, 1990, section 11.8.)
4. Observe that strict acyclicity implies acyclicity.
5. If only individuals can make contingent threats, then resulting situation is called the 'individual contingent threat situation' (see Greenberg, 1990).
6. It is reasonable, but not necessary, to assume $a \xrightarrow{T} a$ where T is the union of all the coalitions that can replace a by some other alternatives.
7. See Page, Wooders, and Kamat (2001) for an application of Chew's notion of farsighted stability to network formation.
8. Recall that (b, c) is the path that originates from b and terminates at c.
9. Recall that for the social environment depicted in equation 4.2, there exists a unique OSSB σ which coincides with the unique CSSB and $a \in \sigma(G_a)$.
10. Equations 4.1 and 4.2, for example, are both bounded acyclic graphs.
11. The terminology used here differs slightly from that in Mariotti (1997). A Coalitional Equilibrium was called there a Full Coalitional Equilibrium.
12. Taken from Mariotti (1997).
13. Similarly, Brams' (1994) Non Myopic Equilibrium is motivated by the desire to endow with farsightedness players acting in situations which are described as strategic form games.

REFERENCES

Arce M., D.G. (1996), 'On the policing properties of coalition-proof versus farsighted strong equilibria', *mimeo*.

Bernheim, B.D., B. Peleg and M.D. Whinston (1987), 'Coalition-proof Nash equilibria. I. concepts', *Journal of Economic Theory*, **42** (1), 1–12.

Brams, S. (1994), *Theory of Moves*, Cambridge: Cambridge University Press.

Chakravorti, B. (1999), 'Far-sightedness and the voting paradox', *Journal of Economic Theory*, **84** (2), 216–26.

Chwe, M. S.-Y. (1994), 'Farsighted coalitional stability', *Journal of Economic Theory*, **63** (2), 299–325.

Diamantoudi, E. (2000), 'Cartel stability revised', *mimeo*, University of Aarhus.

Ecchia, G. and M. Mariotti (1997), 'The stability of international environmental coalitions and farsighted countries: some theoretical observations', in C. Carraro (ed.), (1997), *International Environmental Agreements: Strategic Policy Issues*, Cheltenham: Edward Elgar.

Ecchia, G. and M. Mariotti (1998), 'Coalition formation in international environmental agreements and the role of institutions', *European Economic Review*, **42** (3), 573–82.

Greenberg, J. (1990), *The Theory of Social Situations*, Cambridge: Cambridge University Press.

Greenberg, J. (1994), 'Coalition structures' in R. Aumann and S. Hart (eds), *Handbook of Game Theory*, Amsterdam: North Holland.

Greenberg, J., D. Monderer and B. Shitovitz (1996), 'Multistage situations', *Econometrica*, **64** (6), 1415–37.

Harsanyi, J.C. (1974), 'An equilibrium-point interpretation of stable sets and a proposed alternative definition', *Management Science*, **20** (4), 1472–95.

Konish, H. and D. Ray (2000), 'Coalition formation as a dynamic process', *mimeo*, Boston College.
Li, S. (1992), 'Far-sighted strong equilibrium and oligopoly', *Economic Letters*, **40** (1), 39–44.
Luce, R.D. and H. Raiffa (1957), *Games and Decisions*, New York, NY: John Wiley.
Mariotti, M. (1997), 'A theory of agreement in strategic form games', *Journal of Economic Theory*, **74** (1), 196–217.
Page, F., M.H. Wooders and S. Kamat (2001), 'Networks and farsighted stability', *mimeo*.
Ray, D. (1989), 'Credible coalitions and the core', *International Journal of Game Theory*, **18** (2), 185–87.
Rosenthal, R.W. (1972), 'Cooperative games in effectiveness form', *Journal of Economic Theory*, **5** (1), 88–101.
Suzuki, A. and S. Muto (2000), 'Farsighted stability in an *n*-person prisoner's dilemma', *mimeo*, Yamagata University.
von Neumann, J. and O. Morgenstern (1947) *Theory of Games and Economic Behavior*, Princeton, NJ: Princeton University Press, first edition 1944, second edition 1947.
Xue, L. (1997), 'Nonemptiness of the largest consistent set', *Journal of Economic Theory*, **73** (2), 453–59.
Xue, L. (1989), 'Coalitional stability under perfect foresight', *Economic Theory*, **1** (3), 603–627.
Xue, L. (2000), 'Negotiation-proof Nash equilibrium', *International Journal of Game Theory*, **29** (3), 339–57.

5. Stable coalitions

Carlo Carraro and Carmen Marchiori

1. INTRODUCTION

Coalitions are a widespread phenomenon in old and modern societies. Households can be seen as coalitions, as well as nations or research joint ventures. In industrial economics, cartels have been interpreted as coalitions, whereas in environmental economics, agreements among several nations to protect the international environment have also been described as coalitions.

In recent years, the problem of global public goods, such as the international environment, but also peace or crime control, has become increasingly important. Transnational externalities, being related to knowledge, information, migrations, pollution, crime and similar flows, play a major role in international politics. Their importance and close link to economic development may affect growth and welfare at a macroeconomic level. Hence the need for global policies to correct their undesired effects. In the present institutional setting – with no supranational governing bodies – global externalities cannot be corrected by global institutions, which do not exist, but need to be corrected by voluntary agreements among sovereign states and/or by voluntary initiatives undertaken by firms, industries, households, NGOs and so on. This situation requires international cooperation among nations and/or agents.

To analyse the emergence of international cooperation, economists have used a fairly new game-theoretic approach, in which cooperation is the outcome of a non-cooperative strategic behaviour of the players involved in the negotiations. This approach has been proposed both in games without spillovers (Le Breton and Weber, 1993; Konishi, Le Breton and Weber, 1997) and in games with positive or negative spillovers (Bloch, 1996, 1997; Carraro and Siniscalco, 1993; Yi, 1997).[1]

The game is therefore a two-stage game: in the first stage, countries/agents decide non-cooperatively whether or not to sign the agreement (join the coalition) given the adopted burden-sharing rule; in the second stage, countries/agents set their policy/decision variables by maximizing their welfare function given the decision taken in the first stage and the adopted burden-sharing rule. Signatories, that is, those countries/agents which decide non-cooperatively to sign the agreement/join the coalition, act cooperatively (that is, they maximize a joint welfare function), whereas non-signatories play a non-cooperative Nash game against the group of signatories. These behavioural assumptions are quite standard and formalized in the concept of PANE equilibrium by Chander and Tulkens (1995, 1997).[2]

This chapter aims at analysing the above game from different viewpoints. The ultimate goal is to determine the stable coalition structures of the game and whether a non-trivial coalition emerges at the equilibrium. This can be the grand coalition or, more frequently, a partial coalition whose members are a subset of all players of the game. More importantly, we would also like to examine how the stable coalition structures change when assumptions on the rules of the game change. In particular, we will account for simultaneous vs. sequential games, linear vs. circular orders of moves, open vs. exclusive vs. coalition unanimity membership rules, orthogonal vs. non-orthogonal free-riding, monotonic vs. humped-shaped payoff functions, Nash vs. rational conjectures. In all cases, the equilibrium concept used to analyse the emergence of cooperation is strictly non-cooperative. Moreover, we focus on coalition structures in which only one non-trivial coalition belongs to the equilibrium. This case is the one most frequently considered in the economic literature, because in most situations a single agreement is proposed and countries/agents decide whether or not to sign it.[3]

As a consequence, one of the outcomes of this chapter is a sort of taxonomy of equilibria of the non-cooperative game in which countries decide whether or not to join a coalition. This taxonomy will hopefully include all cases already discussed in the economic literature and also provide a consistent analysis of new types of coalition games. Note that the economic situation which provides a background and a justification to our analysis is mostly the provision of global public goods and the management of global commons. However, our results can be applied to several other situations, both in economics and political science.

The structure of this chapter is as follows. Section 2 provides the main definitions and assumptions. Section 3 defines the concepts of spillovers and free-riding which will be considered in the subsequent analysis and introduces our definitions of profitability and free-riding functions. Sections 4 and 5 identify the stable coalition structures and how stable coalitions change according to the rules of the game. Some concluding remarks are provided in section 6.

2. ASSUMPTIONS AND DEFINITIONS

Assume negotiations take place among n countries/agents, $n \geq 3$, each indexed by $i=1, ..., n$. Countries/agents play a two-stage game. In the first stage – the *coalition game* – they decide non-cooperatively whether or not to sign the agreement (that is, to join the coalition c of cooperating countries). In the second stage, they play a non-cooperative *policy game* in which countries/agents who have signed the agreement play as a single player against non-signatories. Signatories divide the resulting payoff according to a given burden-sharing rule (any of the rules derived from cooperative game theory). As said, these behavioural rules coincide with those underlying the concept of γ-equilibrium in Chander and Tulkens (1995, 1997).

This two-stage game can be represented as a *game in normal form* denoted by $\Gamma=(N, \{X_i\}_{i \in N}, \{u_i\}_{i \in N})$, where N is a finite set of players, X_i the strategy set of player i and u_i the payoff function of player i, assigning to each profile of strategies a real number, that is, $u_i : \Pi_{i \in N} X_i \rightarrow R$. The payoff function is a twice continuously differentiable function.

A *coalition* is any nonempty subset of N. A *coalition structure* $\pi = \{C_1, C_2, ..., C_m\}$ is a partition of the player set N, that is, $C_i \cap C_j = \emptyset$ for $i \neq j$ and $\cup_{i=1}^{m} C_i = N$. In international games, as well as in many other games, the formation of coalitions creates externalities. Hence the appropriate framework to deal with this situation is a *game in partition function form*, in which the payoff of each player depends on the entire coalition structure to which he or she belongs (Bloch, 1997; Ray and Vohra, 1999). This is why we convert the game in normal form into a game in partition function.

Denote by Π the set of all feasible coalition structures. A *partition function* P: $\Pi \rightarrow R$ is a mapping which associates to each coalition structure π a vector in $\Re^{|\pi|}$, representing the worth of all coalitions in π. In particular, $P(C_i; \pi)$ assigns to each coalition C_i in a coalition structure π a worth. When the rule of payoff division among coalition members is fixed, the description of gains from cooperation is done by a *per-member partition function* p: $\Pi \rightarrow \Re^n$, a mapping which associates to each coalition structure π a vector of individual payoffs in $\Re^n$. In particular $p(C_i; \pi)$ represents the payoff of a player belonging to the coalition C_i in the coalition structure π.

Under suitable assumptions (A.1 and A.2 below), the second stage of the game can be reduced to a partition function (Yi, 1997; Bloch 1997). Therefore, the study of coalition stability consists of the study of the first stage of the game, that is, the one in which players decide whether or not to sign the agreement. A necessary assumption for the second stage of the game to be reduced to a partition function is the following one:

A.1 (Uniqueness): *The second stage game, in which all players decide simultaneously, has a unique Nash equilibrium for any coalition structure.*

Moreover, in order to convert the strategic form into a partition function one, the competition among the various coalitions must be specified. As said, the most common, and perhaps the most natural assumption, is:

A.2 (PANE): *Inside each coalition players act cooperatively in order to maximize the coalitional surplus, whereas coalitions (and singletons) compete with one another in a non cooperative way.*

The partition function is then obtained as a Nash equilibrium payoff of the game played by coalitions and singletons. Formally, for a fixed coalition structure $\pi = \{C_1, C_2, ..., C_m\}$, let x^* be a vector of strategies such that:

$$\forall C_i \in \pi, \quad \sum_{j \in C_i} u_j(x^*_{C_i}, x^*_{N/C_i}) \geq \sum_{j \in C_i} u_j(x_{C_i}, x^*_{N \setminus C_i}) \quad \forall x_{C_i} \in \times_{j \in C_i} X_j.$$

Then define:

$$P(C_i; \pi) = \sum_{j \in C_i} u_j(x^*).$$

In order to simplify the derivation of the partition function, we introduce a further assumption:

A.3 (Symmetry): *All players are ex-ante identical, which means that each player has the same strategy space in the second stage game.*

This assumption allows us to adopt an equal sharing payoff division rule inside any coalition, that is, each player in a given coalition receives the same payoff as the other members.[4] Furthermore, the symmetry assumption implies that a coalition C_i can be identified with its size c_i and a coalition structure can be denoted by $\pi = \{c_1, c_2, ..., c_m\}$, where $\Sigma_i c_i = n$. As a consequence, the players' payoff depends only on the coalition sizes and not on the identities of the coalition members. The per-member partition function (partition function hereon) can thus be denoted by $p(c_i; \pi)$, which represents the payoff of a player belonging to the size-c_i coalition in the coalition structure π.

We also assume:

A.4 (Single coalition): *Coalition structures are characterized by a single coalition. Non-cooperating players behave as singletons.*

This assumption, which is adopted in most analyses of international games, allows us to further simplify previous definitions. A coalition structure can indeed be denoted by $\pi = \{c, 1_{(n-c)}\}$ and the per-member partition function becomes $p(c; \pi)$.

Let us now identify the main features of the game. The decision process through which a coalition forms can be modelled either as a *simultaneous* game, in which all players announce at the same time their strategic choice, or as a *sequential* one, in which each player can announce his or her strategy according to an exogenous order of moves. In this chapter, we will consider both a *linear* and a *circular* order of moves. In the three cases – simultaneous, linear sequential, circular sequential – the ruling solution concept is (almost always) some variant of the non-cooperative Nash equilibrium, because we focus mainly on coalition stability in games where self-interested players can only agree on strategy profiles consistent with the best-reply property.

Our classification of coalition games also includes three different membership rules: the open membership rule, the exclusive membership rule and the coalition unanimity rule. In the *open membership game*[5] (d'Aspremont et al., 1983; Carraro and Siniscalco, 1993; Yi and Shin, 1994) each player is free to join and to leave the coalition without the consensus of the other coalition members. The decision process can be thought of as if each player announces a message. In this game, all players who announce the same message form a coalition. This open membership rule thus implies that a coalition accepts any new player who wants to join it.

By contrast, in the *exclusive membership game*[6] (Yi and Shin, 1994) or *game* Δ[7] (Hart and Kurz, 1983), each player can join a coalition only with the consensus of the existing members, but is free to leave the coalition. In this decision process, each player's message consists in a list of players with whom he or she wants to form a coalition. Then players who announce the same list form a coalition, which is not necessarily formed by all players in the list.

Finally, in the *coalition unanimity game*[8] (Chander and Tulkens, 1993; Yi and Shin, 1994; Bloch, 1997) or *game* Γ (Hart and Kurz, 1983),[9] no coalition can form without the unanimous consensus of its members. This implies that players are not free either to join the coalition or to leave it. In this decision process, players' messages consist in a list of players as in the previous one. However, if a coalition is formed, it is necessarily composed of all players in the list and as soon as a player defects the coalition breaks up into singletons.

Another feature of the game with important implications on the equilibrium coalition structure is the form of per-member partition function. It is also useful to simplify the distinction between the membership rules described above. Two cases will be considered. In the first one, the per-member partition function is positively sloped and *monotonic,* whereas in the second one it is *humped-shaped.* In the monotonic case, and above a minimum coalition size c^m (see below), the per-member partition function increases monotonically with respect to the number of signatories of the agreement. Formally, $p(c; \pi)$, where $\pi = \{c, 1_{(n-c)}\}$, is an increasing function of c for all $c \geq c^m$, $c^m \geq 2$. In the humped-shaped case, and above a minimum coalition size c^m, there is an optimal size $c^\circ < n$ at which the per-member partition function is maximized. Formally, $p(c; \pi)$, where $\pi = \{c, 1_{(n-c)}\}$, increases with c in the interval $[c^m, c^\circ]$ and decreases with c for $c^\circ < c \leq n$.

As a consequence, in the monotonic case the open membership and the exclusive membership rules are equivalent, because no players in the coalition have an incentive to ban the entry of other players. The analysis of coalition stability is thus limited to two rules (open membership and coalition unanimity). By contrast, when the per-member partition function is humped-shaped, we need to consider all three rules because, for $c > c^\circ$, coalition members have an incentive to prevent other players from joining the coalition.

Both in the case of monotonic and humped-shaped per-member partition function, we make a final assumption which simplifies our analysis:

A.5 (Marginal gains): *The marginal per-member partition function* $\partial p(c; \pi)/\partial c$ *is smaller than* $\partial p(1; \pi)/\partial c$ *– the marginal payoff function of free-riders – for all* $2 \leq c \leq n$.

This assumption is based on the idea that even when members of a coalition increasingly gain from additional memberships, the marginal gain of free-riders is even larger. The intuition is as follows. Even when cooperating players gain from increasing the coalition size, they still pay a cost to obtain the coalition benefits. By contrast, free-riders obtain the same benefits (as said in the Introduction, we are focusing mainly on the case of global public goods) without paying any costs. Assuming an increasing cost function, the marginal gain for coalition members provided by an additional player in the coalition is equal to the additional benefit minus the additional cost. In the case of free-riders, the marginal gain is larger because it is equal to the additional benefit without any costs.

Note that Assumption 5 implies that if $p(c; \pi)$ is monotonically increasing, then $p(1; \pi)$ is also monotonically increasing. If $p(c; \pi)$ is positive for all $c \in [2, n]$, then $p(1; \pi)$ is also positive for all $c \in [2, n]$.

Another important element of our taxonomy is the type of conjecture formed by players when taking their decision about joining or leaving a coalition. We consider two cases. The usual *Nash conjecture* for which a

Table 5.1 Coalition games: taxonomy

	Open membership (monotonic or humped-shaped payoff)	**Exclusive membership** (humped-shaped payoff)	**Coalition unanimity** (monotonic or humped-shaped payoff)
Simultaneous game (orthogonal or negatively sloped reaction funct.)	Nash or Rational conjectures	Nash or Rational conjectures	Nash
Linear sequential game (orthogonal or negatively sloped reaction funct.)	Subgame perfect	Subgame perfect	Subgame perfect
Circular sequential game (orthogonal or negatively sloped reaction funct.)	Subgame perfect	Subgame perfect	Subgame perfect

player i takes his decision given the other players' decisions, which are assumed not to change as a consequence of player i's decision. This implies that when a player decides to defect from a coalition, he or she conjectures that the other players will keep cooperating. By contrast, in the *rational conjecture* case, a player leaving a coalition can rationally predict the consequences of his or her decision and therefore how many players will then decide to join or leave the coalition as a consequence of his or her decision to leave the coalition.

In our taxonomy, we do not discuss the case in which spillovers from one coalition to another coalition are positive and one in which they are negative.[10] We focus only on positive spillovers. As said above, many economic problems are characterized by the incentive to free-ride on the other players' cooperative behaviour. In other words, a coalition provides *positive spillovers* to the other players or coalitions. The case of positive spillovers is also one in which coalitions are most likely to be unstable. Hence, it provides a benchmark for all other possible assumptions on coalition spillovers.

Table 5.1 summarizes the taxonomy that we adopt to survey the main contributions to the theory of coalition stability and to provide new results. For each combination of the three main features of the game – order of moves, membership rules, conjectures – we discuss the case in which the players' reaction functions are *orthogonal* vs. the case in which they are *negatively sloped*. The orthogonal case is particularly important in international environmental games because it implies that free-riders enjoy the cleaner environment produced by the emission abatement carried out in some countries, but do not expand their own emissions. By contrast, the non-orthogonal case is the one in which market mechanisms induce the so-called 'leakage' problem, that is, free-riders benefit twice from the other countries' cooperation, both because they get a cleaner environment and because they can increase their degree of exploitation of natural resources.

3. SINGLE COALITION GAMES WITH POSITIVE SPILLOVERS

As assumed above, in this section we consider the situation in which countries are proposed to sign a *single agreement*. From a game-theoretic viewpoint, this implies that only one coalition can be formed, the remaining defecting players playing as singletons. The first stage of the game is therefore a binary choice game (joining the coalition or behaving as a lone free-rider) and the outcome of this interaction is a single coalition structure $\pi = \{c, 1_{(n-c)}\}$.

In this setting, we can provide a formal definition of positive spillovers and free-riding.

Positive spillovers: In any single coalition structure, if some players form a coalition, the other players are better off. Then the partition function of any player outside the coalition – the non-member partition function – is increasing in c for all values of c. Formally, $p(1; \pi)$, where $\pi = \{c, 1_{(n-c)}\}$, is an increasing function of c.

The existence of positive spillovers creates an incentive to free ride on the coalition decision to cooperate. In particular, two different free-riding behaviour patterns may emerge according to the slope of players' reaction functions (Carraro and Siniscalco, 1993).

Orthogonal free-riding: When players' reaction functions in the policy game are orthogonal, free-riders benefit from the cooperative abatement of the coalition, but have no incentive to damage it (in international environmental games, there is no 'leakage').

Non orthogonal free-riding: When players' reaction functions in the policy game are non-orthogonal, that is, in an environment in which there is a greater interdependence between countries' policy strategies, free-riders can damage the coalition (for example, in environmental games, by increasing emissions whenever cooperating countries reduce their own). In this case, free-riding can lead to decreasing returns from cooperation (in particular for small coalitions). This implies that a small number of cooperators may break loose from cooperation, because of the strategy adopted in the free-riding countries/agents. Let c^m be the size a coalition has to reach in order to start benefiting from cooperation and to obtain an increasing benefit as the coalition becomes larger and larger.[11]

As stated in the Introduction, this chapter focuses on coalition games characterized by positive spillovers and incentives to free ride, a framework that is useful for analysing many international economic and political problems. Given these features of the n-player coalition game, let us characterize its equilibrium. As said, players decide independently and non-cooperatively whether or not to join the coalition. An obvious necessary condition for the existence of a coalition is its profitability.

Profitability: A coalition c is profitable if each cooperating player gets a payoff larger than the one he or she would get when no coalition is formed. Formally:

$$p(c;\ \pi) > p(1;\ \pi^S), \tag{5.1}$$

for all players in the coalition c, where $\pi = \{c, 1_{(n-c)}\}$ and $\pi^S = \{1_n\}$.

Figure 5.1 shows the profitability function $P(c) = p(c;\ \pi) - p(1;\ \pi^S)$ for the two types of free-riding behaviour that we consider in this chapter. Notice that, in the presence of non-orthogonal free-riding, $P(c)$ is positive for values of c above c^m. In a similar way, we can define the gain from free-riding on the coalition cooperative behaviour. If a coalition c forms, a free-rider achieves $Q(c) = p(1;\ \pi) - p(1;\ \pi^S)$, where $Q(c)$ is the free-riding function. This is shown in Figure 5.2, where two cases are identified. The case in which free-riding is orthogonal and fixed abatement costs are low, and the case in which free-riding is strongly non-orthogonal, thus inducing decreasing returns from free-riding.[12]

From equation 5.1, the value of the minimal profitable coalition size c^m can easily be derived. Indeed, c^m is the value of c at which $P(c)$ becomes positive. This value depends on the strategic interaction between the coalition and the singleton players. In particular, with orthogonal free-riding, any coalition size is profitable and c^m is simply 2, that is, $P(c)$ is non-negative for all $c \geq 2$ (Carraro and Siniscalco, 1992). By contrast, with non-

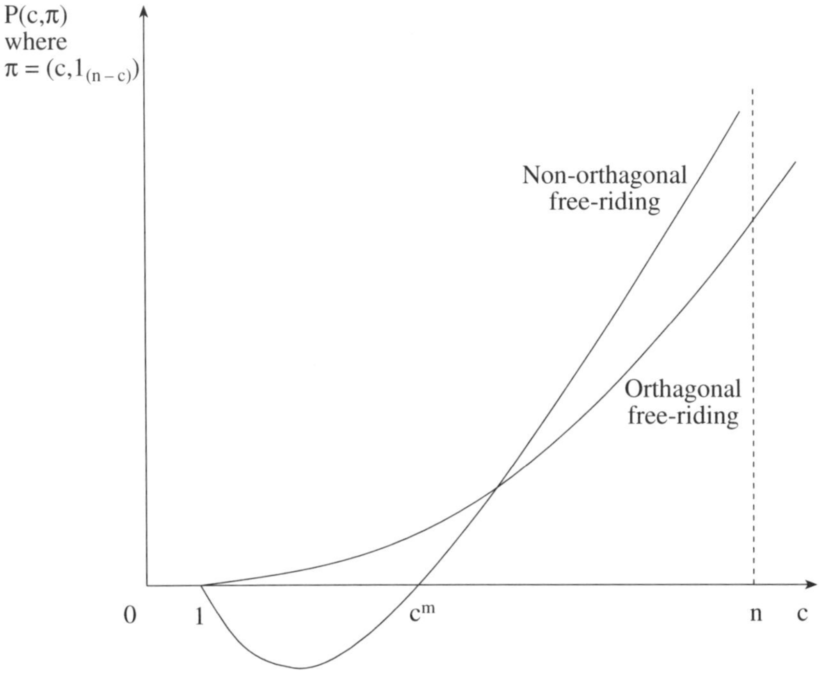

Figure 5.1 Member partition function

orthogonal free-riding, the coalition has to reach a minimal size by which it can offset the damaging action undertaken by free-riders. This size, denoted by c^m, is generally larger than two (see Figure 5.1). In the sequel, we assume $c^m \leq n$, that is, the grand coalition n is profitable.

The profitability condition defined above is only a necessary condition for an equilibrium coalition to form. In order to completely characterize the equilibrium of the game, we need to introduce the concept of stability. This concept differs with the rules of the game. Therefore, in the following sections we will introduce a definition of stability for each set of rules. Let us start the analysis with simultaneous coalition games.

4. SIMULTANEOUS GAMES

Let us assume that in the first stage of the game all players decide simultaneously whether or not to join the coalition. Let us then analyse the equilibria of the coalition game for three different membership rules. In all propositions below, Assumptions 1–5 will be used.

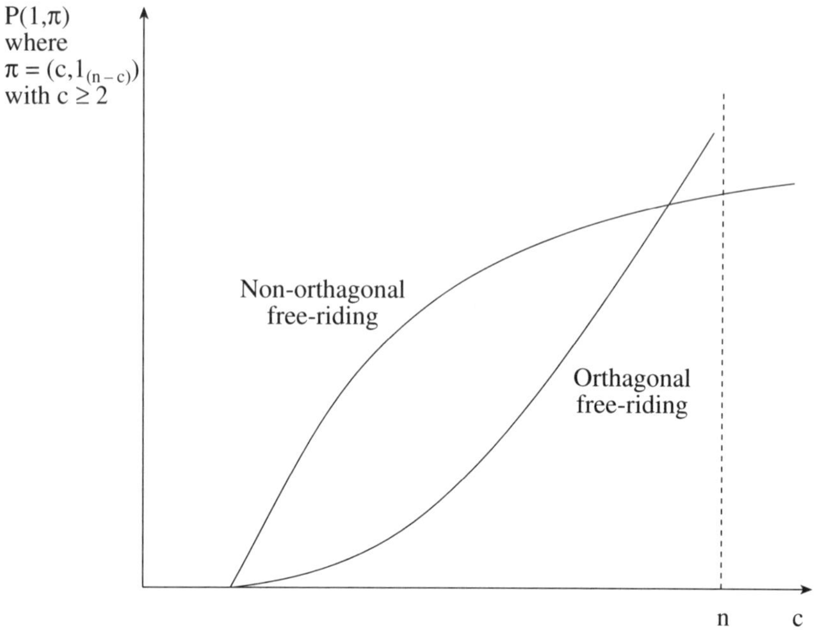

Figure 5.2 Non-member partition function

4.1 Open Membership

This is the membership originally adopted in the cartel stability literature (d'Aspremont et al., 1983; d'Aspremont and Gabsewicz, 1986) and in the environmental literature on international agreements (Hoel, 1991; Carraro and Siniscalco, 1992, 1993; Barrett, 1994). Under this rule, there is no restriction to entry and exit of players from the coalition. Moreover, let us assume that:

4.1.1 Nash conjectures

In the first stage of the game, each player outside the coalition takes as given the decision of the other players or coalition; each player inside the coalition maximizes the joint welfare taking as given the decision of the free-riders. The equilibrium of the coalition game is thus a Nash equilibrium, completely characterized by the following condition:

Nash stability (d'Aspremont et al., 1983): A coalition is stable if it is both internally and externally stable. It is internally stable if no cooperating player is better off by defecting in order to form a singleton. Formally:

$$p(c;\ \pi) \geq p(1;\ \pi'), \tag{5.2a}$$

where $\pi = \{c, 1_{(n-c)}\}$ and $\pi' = \pi \backslash \{c\} \cup \{c-1,\ 1\}$ for all $i \in c$.[13] It is externally stable if no singleton is better off by joining the coalition c. Formally:

$$p(1;\ \pi) > p(c';\ \pi'), \tag{5.2b}$$

where $\pi = \{c, 1_{(n-c)}\}$ and $\pi' = \pi \backslash \{c, 1\} \cup \{c'\}$ and $c' = c+1$ for all $i \notin c$.

The stability function (*Carraro and Siniscalco, 1992*): The stability function is a useful tool to identify the size of a (Nash) stable coalition, that is, the equilibrium of the simultaneous coalition game with open membership. Let:

$$L(c) = p(c;\pi) - p(1;\pi') = P(c) - Q(c-1) \tag{5.3}$$

be the stability function, where $\pi = \{c, 1_{n-c}\}$, $\pi' = \{c', 1_{n-c'}\}$ and $c' = c-1$.

When positive, the stability function shows that a singleton has an incentive to join the coalition c. When negative, it signals an incentive to free-ride on the coalition action. The stable coalition size is the one where no cooperating player is willing to defect and no free-rider is willing to join the coalition. Hence, as formally shown below, it coincides with the largest integer c^* below the value of c for which $L(c) = 0$ and $L'(c) \leq 0$.

A few diagrams will help us to identify possible equilibrium coalition sizes. By definition, the function $Q(c-1)$ is equal to the non-cooperative payoff when $c = 2$, whereas the member partition function $P(c)$ is equal to the non-cooperative payoff when $c = 1$. Figures 5.3, 5.4, 5.5 and 5.6 show the functions $P(c)$ and $Q(c-1)$ and the resulting function $L(c)$ for different marginal incentives to cooperate and free-ride (using Assumption 5). These Figures capture four main situations that are likely to occur, but are certainly not exhaustive of all possible cases. Their analysis is, however, helpful in understanding which mechanisms support a stable coalition.

Stability function with orthogonal free-riding: Consider first Figure 5.3, that is, the case in which the profitability function is monotonic. This case has been studied in several environmental economics contributions (Cf. Carraro and Siniscalco, 1992; Chander and Tulkens, 1997) and in simple models of public goods provision (Yi, 1997). In this case, the game is characterized by positive spillovers. There is no feedback because there is no leakage. As a consequence, both the per-member function and the non-member one are monotonically increasing for all values of c. The two curves – $P(c)$ and $Q(c-1)$ – intersect at $c^* < n$, that is, the stability function

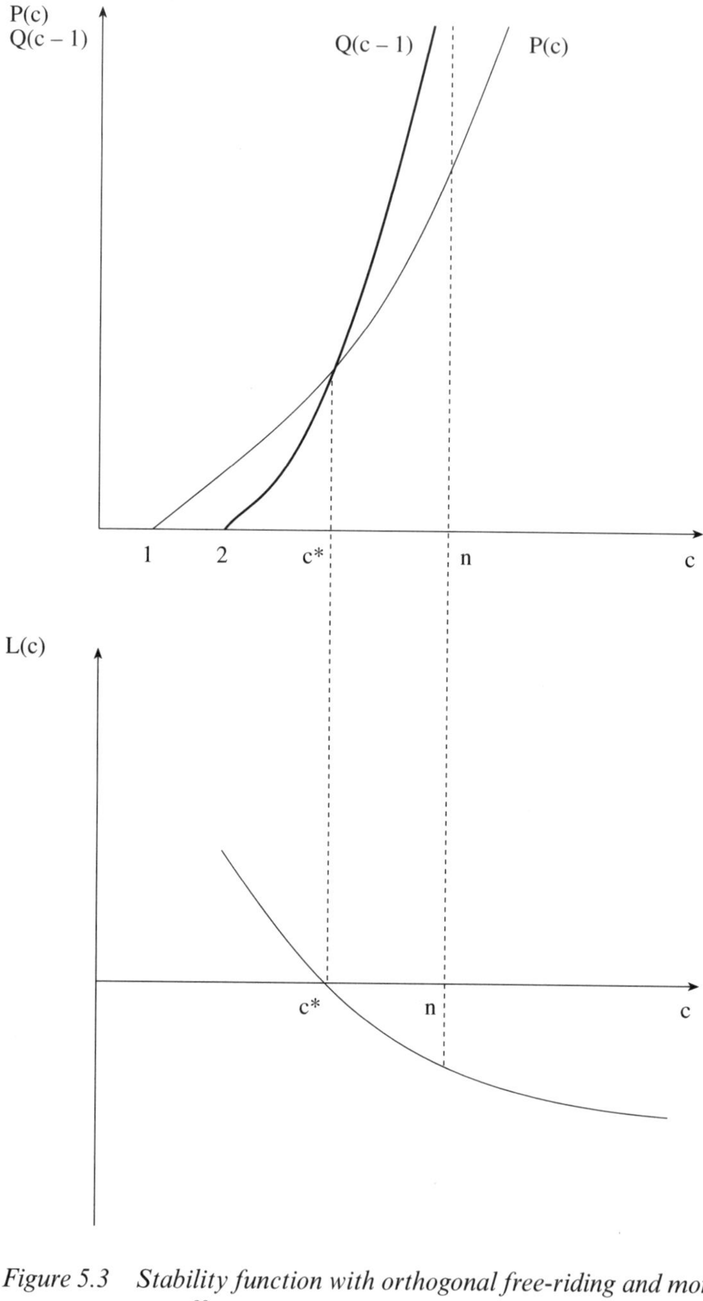

Figure 5.3 Stability function with orthogonal free-riding and monotonic payoff

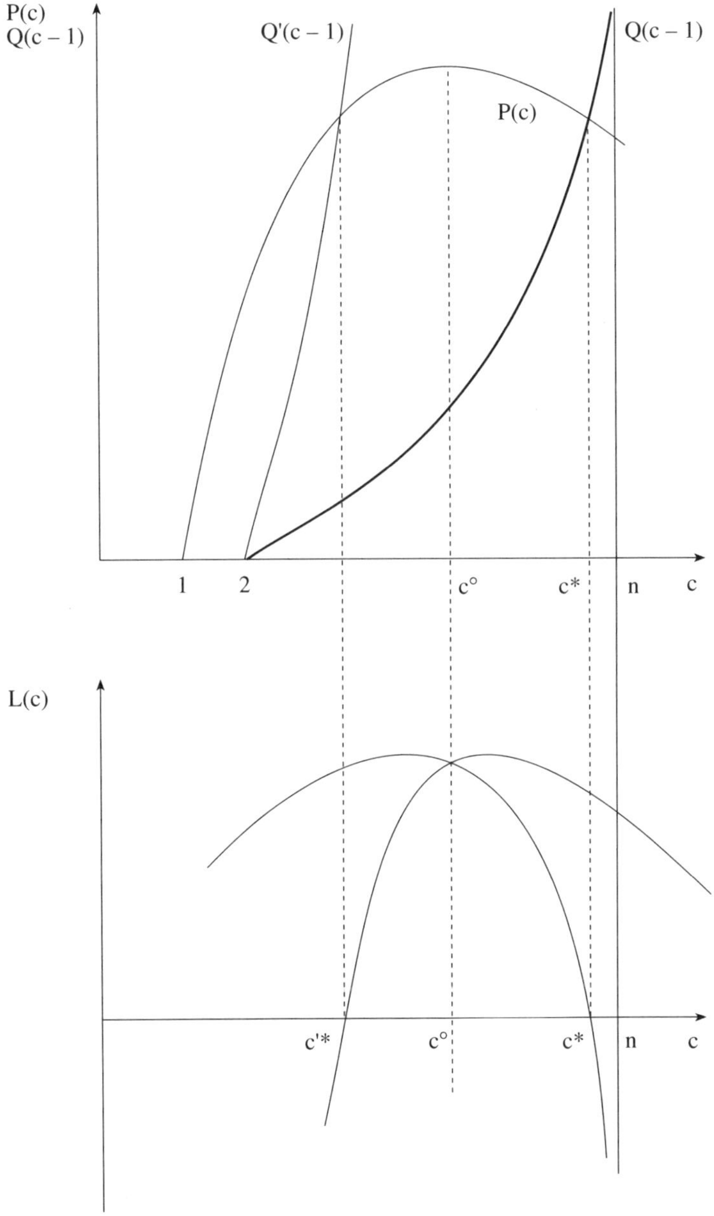

Figure 5.4 Stability function with orthogonal free-riding and humped-shaped payoff

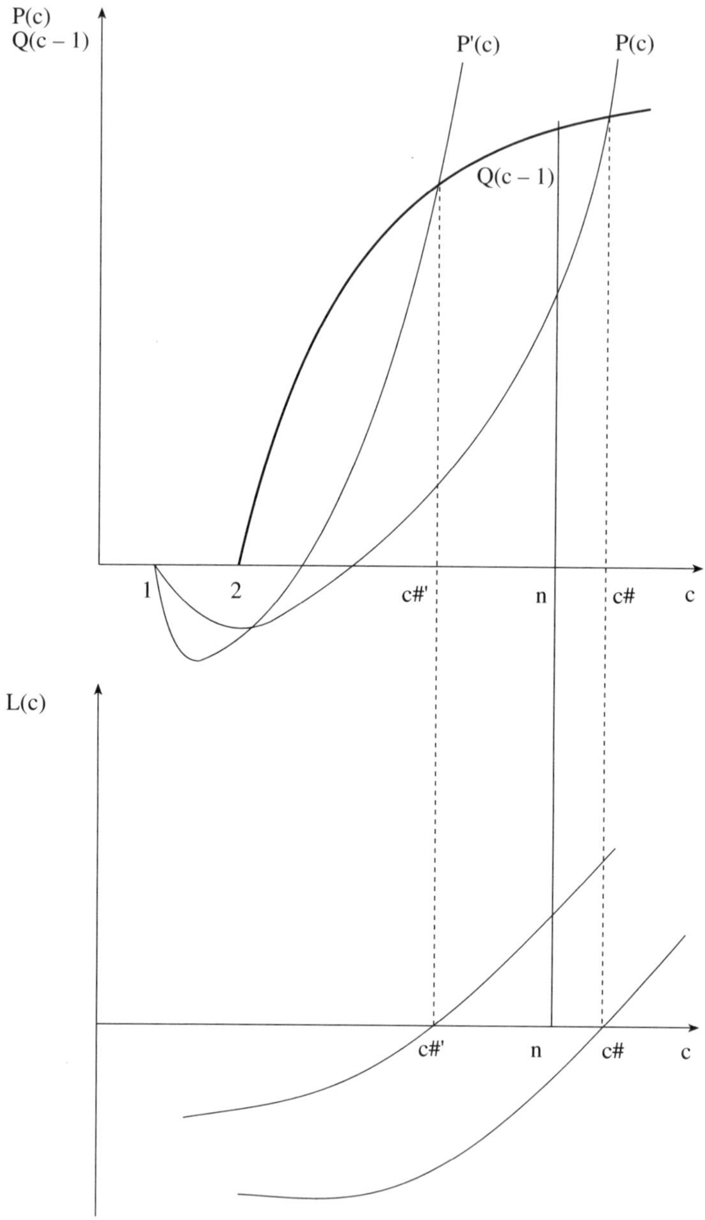

Figure 5.5 Stability function with non-orthogonal free-riding and monotonic payoff

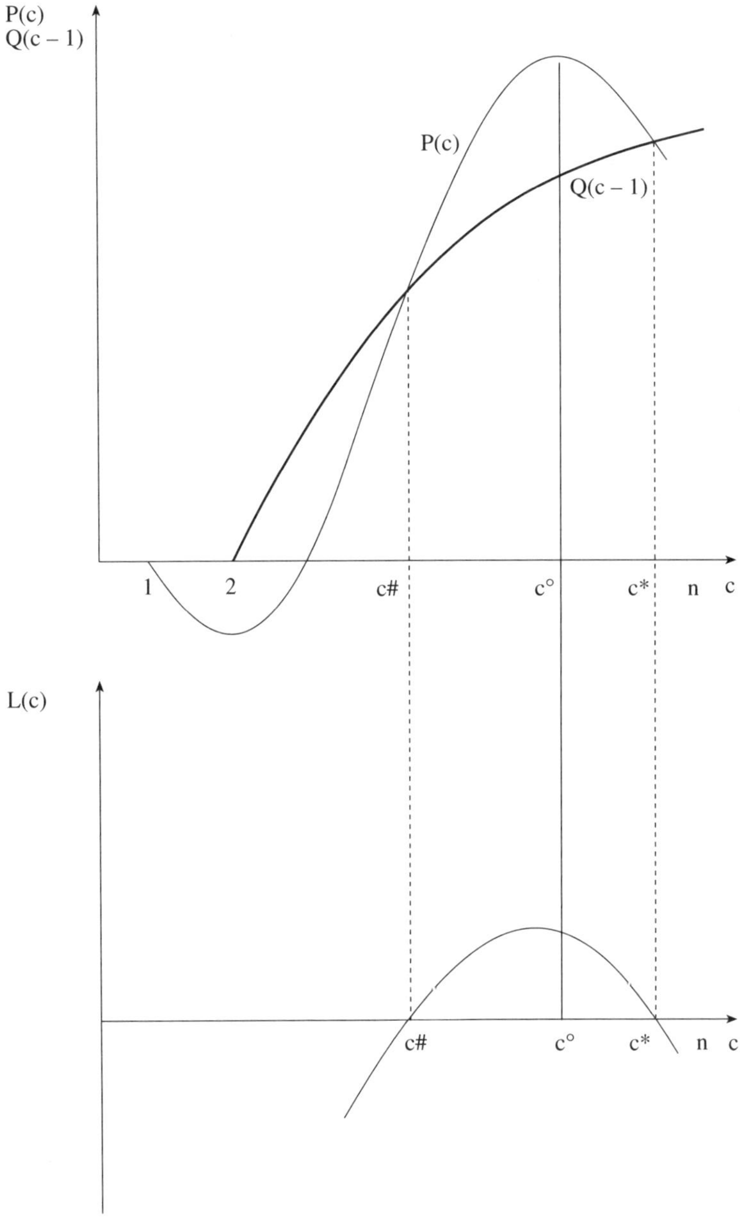

Figure 5.6 Stability function with non-orthogonal free-riding and humped-shaped payoff

$L(c)$ becomes negative for coalition sizes above c^*. The coalition size c^* defines the Nash-stable coalition (see Proposition 1). If c^* is larger than one, the stable coalition structure is non-trivial.

In Figure 5.3, fixed abatement costs are implicitly assumed to be low. The presence of high fixed abatement costs to be shared among coalition members implies that the profitability function increases at decreasing rates (Heal, 1994). It is therefore concave, rather than convex. In this case (Figure 5.4), the intersection between the profitability and free-riding function can take place at values of c^* close to n and even above n, thus implying that the grand coalition can be stable ($P(n) > Q(n-1)$).[14] This case has been proposed by Heal (1994) to show that a large coalition, or even the grand coalition, can emerge as the equilibrium outcome of the non-cooperative coalition game.

Stability function with non-orthogonal free-riding: In this case, cooperation may not be profitable because free-riders offset the cooperative effort of cooperators (Botteon and Carraro, 1997a). This is particularly true for small coalitions, when the number of free-riders is large and the number of cooperators is low. As a consequence, the function $P(c)$ is first decreasing and then increasing and becomes positive for $c > c^m$ (see Figure 5.1). By contrast, the function $Q(c-1)$ is always increasing but at a decreasing rate. In environmental games, the economic mechanism (for example, lower energy prices) behind the leakage effect usually exhibits decreasing returns, that is, free-riders can damage cooperators at a decreasing rate, thus implying a concave, rather than convex, non-member partition function (see Figure 5.2). The resulting stability function $L(c)$ is shown in Figures 5.5 and 5.6. In Figure 5.5 the profitability function is monotonic, in Figure 5.6 it is humped-shaped. Notice that if $P(c)$ and $Q(c-1)$ intersect at $c^{\#} < n$, then a stable coalition may exist. However, $L(c^{\#}) \geq 0$, which implies that $c^{\#}$ does not satisfy the stability condition (equation 5.2b), namely other players would like to join the coalition. Therefore, in the case of Figure 5.5, the grand coalition could be the stable one (see Proposition 2a below). In the case of Figure 5.6, the stable coalition under open membership is c^* (see Proposition 2b).[15]

Let us now move to a formal analysis that enables us to prove the conclusions achieved by using the simple geometry of coalition stability. Let c^* be the largest integer smaller than or equal to the value of c which satisfies:

$$L(c) = 0 \quad \text{and} \quad L'(c) < 0. \tag{5.4a}$$

For convenience, let $c^* = 1$ when $L(c) < 0$ for all $1 < c \leq n$. Moreover, let $c^{\#}$ be the largest integer smaller than or equal to the critical size c which satisfies:

$$L(c)=0 \quad \text{and} \quad L'(c)>0 \tag{5.4b}$$

Proposition 1 (Carraro and Siniscalco, 1993; Barrett, 1994): In a game with Nash conjectures and open membership, in which the reaction functions are orthogonal, the stable coalition structures are:

- $\pi^* = \{c^*, 1_{(n-c^*)}\}$ when $1 < c^* < n$; and
- the grand coalition structure $\pi^n = \{n\}$ when $c^* \geq n$, that is, $L(c)>0$ for all $c \in [2, n]$;

both when the per-member partition function is monotonic and when it is humped-shaped (Figures 5.3 and 5.4).

Proof: Under orthogonal free-riding $c^m = 2$, because cooperators are not damaged by free-riders. Therefore, the profitability condition is satisfied for all coalitions $c \in [2, n]$. However, when $1 < c^* < n$, only c^* satisfies the stability conditions. Indeed, if c belongs to $(1, c^*)$, a singleton's best-reply is to join the coalition c. If c belongs to (c^*, n), the best-reply of a cooperating player is to defect. Therefore, only when $c = c^*$, no player wants to change his or her strategy. Hence, the coalition c^* is stable. By contrast, the stable coalition structure of the game coincides with the grand coalition when $c^* \geq n$, that is, $L(c)>0$ for all $c \in [2,n]$. In this case, no player wants to join the coalition when $c = n$; for all c such that $1 < c < n$, a singleton's best-reply is always to join the coalition. Finally, notice that $L(c)<0$ for all c belonging to $[2, n]$ cannot occur because both $P(c)$ and $Q(c-1)$ are monotonically increasing and $P(c)$ is defined in the interval $[1,n]$, whereas $Q(c-1)$ is defined in the interval $[2,n]$ (see Figures 5.3 and 5.4). Therefore, using Assumption 5, they can only intersect for $c>2$. If the two curves do not intersect, $P(c) > Q(c-1)$, that is, $L(c)>0$; otherwise, there exists a value of c, say c', for which $L(c)=0$ in the interval $[2,n]$. The stable coalition is defined by the largest integer smaller than or equal to c'.

Proposition 2.a (Carraro and Siniscalco, 1993): In a game with Nash conjectures and open membership, in which the profitability function is positive and monotonic for $c \geq c^m$, and free-riding is non-orthogonal (Figure 5.5), the stable coalition structures are:

- the singleton structure $\pi^S = \{1_n\}$ when $c^\# > n$; and
- the grand coalition structure $\pi^n = \{n\}$ when $c^m \leq c^\# \leq n$.

Proof: In the presence of non orthogonal free-riding, by definition of c^m, the profitability condition is satisfied for all $c^m \leq c \leq n$. As for stability, when

$c^{\#} > n$, the internal stability condition is not satisfied for all c belonging to $[2, n]$. Therefore, the stable coalition structure is $\pi^S = \{1_n\}$. When $c^m \leq c^{\#} \leq n$ the internal stability condition is not satisfied for $c < c^{\#}$, whereas the external stability condition is not satisfied for all c in the interval $(c^{\#}, n)$, that is, there is an incentive for free-rider to join a coalition c for all $c \geq c^{\#}$. Hence, no player wants to defect and no player wants to enter the coalition only when $c = n$. As a consequence, $\pi^n = \{n\}$ is the stable coalition structure.

Proposition 2.b: In a game with Nash conjectures and open membership, in which the profitability function is positive for $c \geq c^m$ and humped-shaped, and free-riding is non-orthogonal (Figure 5.6), the stable coalition structures are:

- the singleton structure $\pi^S = \{1_n\}$ when $c^{\#} > n$; and
- $\pi^* = \{c^*, 1_{(n-c^*)}\}$ when $c^m \leq c^{\#} \leq c^* \leq n$.

Proof: Same as for Proposition 2a. The only difference is that, when $c^m \leq c^{\#} \leq c^* \leq n$, there is no incentive to join a coalition $c > c^*$, that is, when $c > c^*$, the best reply of a cooperating player is to defect. There is also an incentive to defect for all $c < c^{\#}$. External stability is not met for $c^{\#} \leq c < c^*$. Therefore, the stable coalition is c^*.

It is important to stress that the above results identify the stable coalition structures but do not describe the mechanisms through which these equilibria are reached. For example, to achieve the stable grand coalition in the case of non-orthogonal free-riding, an adequate minimum participation constraint may be necessary.[16] This minimum participation constraint coordinates the decision of all players in a way to provide all players with the incentive to join the coalition.

A simple numerical example can also help understanding the above analysis of stable coalitions. Table 5.2 shows the payoff that can be obtained by defectors and cooperators under different coalition structures and assuming orthogonal free-riding. In each row, the payoff of singletons is shown first. The values in Table 5.2 are computed using the simple model proposed in Carraro and Siniscalco (1992) and then used by Barrett (1994) and Chander and Tulkens (1997) – even though Barrett (1994) adopts different rules of the game.

Let us first consider the structure of incentives that characterizes this game. It can be summarized by the following three facts:

- *Fact 1*: the profitability condition is satisfied for all $c \geq 2$.
- *Fact 2*: the coalition is internally stable for all $c \leq 3$.
- *Fact 3*: the coalition is externally stable for all $c \geq 3$.

Table 5.2 A single coalition game with orthogonal free-riding

Coalition structure	Per-member partition function					
1,1,1,1,1,1	0	0	0	0	0	0
1,1,1,1,2	2	2	2	2	0.5	0.5
1,1,1,3	6	6	6	2	2	2
1,1,4	12	12	4.5	4.5	4.5	4.5
1,5	20	8	8	8	8	8
6	12.5	12.5	12.5	12.5	12.5	12.5

Table 5.3 A single coalition game with non-orthogonal free-riding

Coalition structure	Per-member partition function					
1,1,1,1,1,1	1/49	1/49	1/49	1/49	1/49	1/49
1,1,1,1,2	1/36	1/36	1/36	1/36	1/72	1/72
1,1,1,3	1/25	1/25	1/25	1/75	1/75	1/75
1,1,4	1/16	1/16	1/64	1/64	1/64	1/64
1,5	1/9	1/45	1/45	1/45	1/45	1/45
6	1/24	1/24	1/24	1/24	1/24	1/24

As a consequence, the stable coalition structure of this game is $\pi^* = \{3,1,1,1\}$. Consider indeed any coalition structure in which the coalition is larger than three. By Fact 2, the best-reply of one of the coalition members is to defect from the coalition. On the other hand, consider any coalition structure in which the coalition is smaller than three. Then, by Fact 3 the best-reply of one of the players outside the coalition is joining the coalition. Fact 1 guarantees that the stable coalition is also profitable.

Now consider the case in which free-riding is non-orthogonal. The values of countries' payoff are summarized in Table 5.3. Again the incentive system is summarized by the following three facts:

- *Fact 1*: the profitability condition is satisfied for all $c \geq 5$.
- *Fact 2*: the coalition is internally stable for all $c < 1$.
- *Fact 3*: the coalition is externally stable for all $c \geq 1$.

As a consequence, the stable coalition structure is $\pi^* = \{1,1,1,1,1,1\}$. Consider indeed any coalition structure in which the coalition is larger than one. By Fact 2, the best-reply of any coalition member is to defect until the singleton structure is reached. Furthermore, by Fact 3 no singleton would be better off by joining the coalition in any coalition structure.

What are the implications of the above results? First, the game structure which captures countries' interactions is not a prisoners' dilemma, but rather a chicken game in which at least two groups of players (and two roles: signatories and defectors) co-exist (Carraro and Siniscalco, 1993). This has an important implication. If a stable coalition exists, the outcome of the game is not the one in which no cooperation takes place (no countries sign the agreement). At the equilibrium, there are two groups of countries, signatories and defectors, where the size of the group of signatories crucially depends on the slope of countries' reaction functions.

4.1.2 Rational conjectures

As well-known in oligopoly theory, the assumption of Nash conjectures is crucial in determining the feature of the equilibrium of the game. This is why several authors, starting from Bresnaham (1981), have proposed different assumptions on players' conjectures when they take their decision. Without entering into the debate on the validity of replacing the Nash assumption with alternative types of conjectures, we would like to consider the possibility, proposed for example in Chew (1994), Ray and Vohra (1999) and Mariotti (1997), that a cooperator anticipates the reaction of the other players when leaving a coalition. For example, other cooperators may defect, or a free-rider may decide to join the coalition and replace the cooperator who defected. Similarly, a free-rider anticipates the reaction of the other players when he or she decides to join a coalition, and so on. We assume that players' conjectures are rational, that is, that each player correctly anticipates the reaction of the other players to his or her decision.

In this context, we need to re-define the equilibrium conditions of the game, that is, the stability and profitability conditions. Whereas profitability is not modified by the introduction of rational conjectures, stability becomes as follows:

Rational conjecture stability (*Carraro and Moriconi, 1998*). A coalition is stable if it is internally and externally stable. It is internally stable if no cooperating player would be better off in the coalition structure induced by his defection. Formally:

$$p(c;\pi)\geq p(1;\pi'), \tag{5.5a}$$

for all players in the coalition c, where $\pi=\{c,1_{(n-c)}\}$, $\pi'=\pi\backslash\{c\}\cup\{c', 1_{(k+1)}\}$ and $c'=c-k-1$, where k is the number of defections following i's defection ($k+1$ defections including i). It is externally stable if no singleton would be better off in the coalition structure induced by his accession to the coalition. Formally:

$$p(1;\pi) \geq p(c''; \pi'') \tag{5.5b}$$

for all players which do not belong to c, where $\pi'' = \pi \backslash \{c, 1_{(k'+1)}\} \cup \{c''\}$, $c'' = c + k' + 1$, and k' is the number of accessions following i's accession ($k' + 1$ accessions including i).

Given this definition, and assuming the profitability condition to be met for simplicity's sake, the stable coalitions of the game are defined by the following proposition:

Proposition 3 (Carraro and Moriconi, 1998): In a game with rational conjectures and open membership, in which free-riding is orthogonal, the stable coalitions are:

- the grand coalition $c = n$, when $c^* \geq n$; and
- a sequence of coalitions c^*, c^{**}, c^{***} ... , where $c^{***} > c^{**} > c^*$ and $P(c^{**}) \geq Q(c^*)$, $P(c^{***}) \geq Q(c^{**})$, ... , when $1 < c^* < n$, n is sufficiently large, and the per-member partition function is either monotonic or humped-shaped.

Proof: When $c^* \geq n$, the equilibrium coalition of the game is the grand coalition. As $P(c) \geq Q(c-1)$ for all $c \leq n$, there is no incentive to defect, that is, the internal stability condition is met for all $c \leq n$. In addition, there is an incentive to join the coalition for all $c \leq n$. Hence the stable coalition is $c = n$.

When $c^* < n$, and n is sufficiently large, we have a sequence of stable coalitions $c^* < c^{**} < c^{***}, \ldots, < n$. If $c < c^*$, a singleton's best-reply is always to join the coalition until c^* is reached. And no $c^* + 1$ player wants to join c^*. Therefore, c^* is stable as in Proposition 1. However, other coalitions $c > c^*$ can be stable outcomes of the game. With rational conjectures, a cooperating player i anticipates the reaction of the others when leaving a coalition. In particular, a cooperating player of a coalition $c^{**} > c^*$ knows that if he or she defects from c^{**}, other k players will defect. If the conjecture is rational, player i knows that defections will continue until c^* is reached. Hence, the rational conjectures are $k = c^{**} - c^* - 1$ and $k' = 0$. Player i compares $P(c^{**})$ – the cooperative payoff in c^{**} – with $Q(c^*)$, the free-riding payoff in the equilibrium coalition resulting from his or her deviation. If the former payoff is smaller than the latter, the cooperating player i defects. Otherwise, the coalition c^{**} is stable. Therefore, the coalition c^{**} is stable if $P(c^{**}) \geq Q(c^*)$ where $c^{**} = c^* + k + 1$. When $P(c)$ is monotonic, and if n is sufficiently large, it is always possible to identify a coalition size c^{**} such that $P(c^{**}) \geq Q(c^*)$. Therefore, a stable coalition c^{**} exists. Given c^{**}, and n sufficiently large, it is also possible to identify a coalition size c^{***} such that $P(c^{***}) \geq Q(c^{**})$. Hence, c^{***} is stable. And so on.

When $P(c)$ is humped-shaped, the above argument holds for values of c below the maximand of $P(c)$ and also when this maximand is large enough (which implies that n is large enough).

Proposition 4.a: In a game with rational conjectures and open membership in which the profitability function is positive and monotonic for $c \geq c^m$ and free-riding is non-orthogonal, the stable coalitions are:

- a sequence of coalitions c^m, c^{**}, c^{***} ..., where $c^m < c^{**} < c^{***} < \dots$, and $P(c^m) \geq P(0)$, $P(c^{**}) \geq Q(c^m)$, $P(c^{***}) \geq Q(c^{**})$, ..., when $c^{\#} > n$ and n is sufficiently large; and
- when instead $c^m < c^{\#} \leq n$, the stable coalitions are a sequence of coalitions c^m, c^{**}, c^{***} ... where $c^m < c^{**} < c^{***} < \dots < c^{\#}$, and $P(c^m) \geq P(0)$, $P(c^{**}) \geq Q(c^m)$, $P(c^{***}) \geq Q(c^{**})$, ..., and the grand coalition $c = n$.

Proof: If $c^{\#} > n$, no coalition $c \leq n$ is internally stable. Therefore the rational conjecture of players belonging to the coalition c is $k = c - 1$ and $k' = 0$, that is, the singleton coalition forms. The smallest coalition which satisfies the condition that the payoff of a cooperating player is larger than the payoff he or she would achieve when free-riding from the coalition resulting from his or her defection is c^m, because, by definition of c^m, $P(c^m) \geq P(0) = Q(0)$. Therefore c^m is stable. However, if n is sufficiently large, another coalition size c^{**} exists such that $P(c^{**}) \geq Q(c^m)$; c^{**} is stable because a defector from c^{**} rationally conjectures $k = c^{**} - c^m - 1$ and $k' = 0$. Therefore when deciding whether or not to defect, the cooperating player compares $P(c^{**})$ – the payoff when cooperating in c^{**} – with $Q(c^m)$, his or her payoff when free-riding on the coalition resulting from his or her defection. Since $P(c^{**}) \geq Q(c^m)$, c^{**} is stable. In a similar way, if n is sufficiently large it is possible to show the stability of c^{***}, c^{****} and so on.

If $c^m < c^{\#} \leq n$ and $c^m < c^{**} < c^{***} < \dots < c^{\#}$, again the rational conjectures of players in $c < c^{\#}$ is that the singleton structure would emerge at the equilibrium following a player's defection. Therefore, the previous argument holds again if $c^{\#}$ is large enough, which implies that n *is* large enough. In addition, if a player belongs to c^{**} or c^{***} where $c^{\#} \leq c^{**} < c^{***} < \dots \leq n$, his or her rational conjecture is that entry will follow until the grand coalition forms, that is, $k = 0$ and $k' = n - c - 1$. Therefore, given the monotonicity of the payoff function, the stable coalition is $c = n$.

Proposition 4.b: In a game with rational conjectures and open membership, in which the profitability function is positive for $c \geq c^m$ and humped-shaped, and free-riding is non-orthogonal, the stable coalitions are:

- a sequence of coalitions c^m, c^{**}, $c^{***}\dots$, where $c^m < c^{**} < c^{***} < \dots$, and $P(c^m) \geq P(0)$, $P(c^{**}) \geq Q(c^m)$, $P(c^{***}) \geq Q(c^{**})$, … , when $c^{\#} > n$ and n is sufficiently large; and
- when instead $c^m < c^{\#} < c^* \leq n$, the stable coalitions are a sequence of coalitions c^m, c^{**}, c^{***} … where $c^m < c^{**} < c^{***} < \dots < c^{\#}$, and $P(c^m) \geq P(0)$, $P(c^{**}) \geq Q(c^m)$, $P(c^{***}) \geq Q(c^{**})$, … , and the coalition structure $\pi^* = \{c^*, 1_{(n-c^*)}\}$.

Proof: Same as for Proposition 4a. The only difference is that when $c^m < c^{\#} < c^* \leq n$ and $c > c^*$, the incentives for players in c are the same as those of Proposition 3. Hence, the same argument applies.

The examples of Tables 5.2 and 5.3 can be useful to understand the implications of the introduction of rational conjectures in the coalition game. Consider first the case of orthogonal free-riding (Table 5.2). The starting point is again Facts 1 to 3. If the coalition structure contains a coalition c whose size is smaller than three, singletons have an incentive to join the coalition until the size-3 coalition is reached. As a consequence, the rational conjectures are $k=0$, $k'=3-c+1$ and the stable outcome is $\pi^* = \{1,1,1,3\}$. Once the structure $\{3,1,1,1\}$ is implemented, if a country defects, a singleton has an incentive to join the coalition. The rational conjectures are $k=0$, $k'=1$ and the equilibrium is again $\pi^* = \{1,1,1,3\}$.

If the coalition structure is $\pi' = \{1,1,4\}$, a coalition member is willing to defect. If a country defects the structure $\pi^* = \{1,1,1,3\}$ is reached. Since π^* is a stable coalition structure, it turns out that the rational conjectures are $k=0$ (no additional defections) and $k'=0$ (no accession to replace the defector). Hence, one of the cooperating countries, by comparing $p(4; \pi')$ and $p(1; \pi^*)$, decides to defect. Therefore, π' is not a stable structure (the stable structure is again π^*).

If the coalition structure is $\pi^{**} = \{1,5\}$, again a cooperating player has an incentive to defect. If he or she defects, the structure π' is reached; but this structure is not stable as previously shown. Hence the rational conjectures are $k=1$ (one more country will defect) and $k'=0$ (no accession to replace the two defectors). Moreover, $p(5; \pi^{**}) > p(1;\pi^*)$. Therefore, by comparing $p(5; \pi^{**})$ with $p(1;\pi^*)$, no country belonging to $c=5$ decides to defect. As a consequence, the structure π^{**} is stable and a coalition $c^{**}=5$ forms.

If the coalition structure is $\pi'' = \{6\}$, a cooperating country is willing to defect. If it defects, the stable structure $\pi^{**} = \{1,5\}$ is reached. Then, the rational conjectures are $k=0$ (no further defection) and $k'=0$ (no accession to replace the defector). By comparing $p(6; \pi'')$ and $p(1; \pi^{**})$ a coalition member decides to defect. Hence the grand coalition is not stable in this game.

The conclusion is therefore as follows. When players choose their strategies by adopting rational conjectures, the stable coalition structure of the game summarized by Table 5.1 is either the basic coalition structure $\pi^* = \{1,1,1,3\}$ or the coalition structure $\pi^{**} = \{1,5\}$.

Now consider Table 5.3, where the game with non-orthogonal free-riding is shown. If the coalition structure is such that the coalition size is smaller than 5, by Fact 2 no singleton wants to join the coalition. On the other hand, by Fact 1 each cooperating country has an incentive to defect and to implement the singleton structure. Hence, for all coalition structures containing a coalition $c<5$, the rational conjectures are $k=c-1$ (all countries decide to defect) and $k'=0$ (no accession to replace the defectors). However, $P(c)<P(0)$ for $c<5$ by Fact 1 and no stable coalition forms, that is, the stable coalition structure is the singleton structure.

If the coalition structure is $\pi^{**} = \{1,5\}$, each country belonging to c has an incentive to defect, but its defection would induce a coalition structure in which $c<5$ and then the singleton coalition structure as argued above. Hence, in this case the rational conjectures are $k=5-1$ (a defection from c would lead all other countries to defect) and $k'=0$ (because no singleton has an incentive to join any coalition). This implies that each coalition member decides whether or not to cooperate by comparing his or her payoff $p(5; \pi^{**})$ with his or her payoff in the singleton structure $p(1; \pi^s)$. As a consequence, the coalition structure π^{**} is stable.

Finally, if the coalition structure is the grand coalition $\pi'' = \{6\}$, by Fact 1 a cooperating country has an incentive to defect. If it does defect, the coalition structure π' (which is stable as discussed above) is formed. Then in this case the rational conjectures are $k=0$ (no further defection) and $k'=0$ (no accession to replace the defector). As a consequence, one of the cooperating countries, by comparing $p(6; \pi'')$ and $p(1; \pi^*)$, decides to defect. The grand coalition is not stable.

Therefore, in the case of Table 5.3 (non-orthogonal free-riding) with rational conjectures there are again two stable coalition structures: the trivial coalition structure $\pi^s = \{1,1,1,1,1,1\}$ and the structure $\pi^* = \{1,5\}$.

4.2 Exclusive Membership

In the *exclusive membership game* (Yi and Shin, 1994) or *game* Δ (Hart and Kurz, 1983), each player can join a coalition only with the consensus of the existing members, but is free to leave the coalition. In this decision process, each player's message consists in a list of players with whom he or she wants to form a coalition. Players who then announce the same list form a coalition, which is not necessarily formed by all players in the list. In order to capture the intuition which lies behind the exclusive membership game, the following *optimality criterion* is introduced:

Optimality: A coalition denies membership to an outside player only if this new accession is not profitable for the coalition. Hence, a coalition accepts a new member only if all its members would be better off in the larger coalition. A coalition is optimal when there is no incentive to accept additional members or to exclude existing members.

In order to determine the equilibrium coalitions under exclusive membership, we need to modify the stability condition which characterizes the equilibrium of the game as follows:

Exclusive membership stability (Yi and Shin, 1994): A coalition is stable if the two following conditions are satisfied:

- No cooperating player is better off by defecting (internal stability). Formally:

$$p(c;\, \pi) \geq p(1;\, \pi'), \tag{5.6}$$

  where $\pi = \{c, 1_{(n-c)}\}$ and $\pi' = \pi \backslash \{c\} \cup \{c-1,\, 1\}$ for all $i \in c$.
- The coalition is optimal, that is, no cooperating player has an incentive to increase or reduce the coalition size.

4.2.1 Nash conjectures

The analysis focuses on the case in which the profitability function is humped-shaped. In the case of monotonic payoff functions, the results coincide with those obtained in the case of open membership, because the optimal coalition is the grand coalition in both cases.

Proposition 5: In a game with Nash conjectures and exclusive membership, in which the profitability function is humped-shaped and free-riding is orthogonal, the stable coalition structures are:

- $\pi^* = \{c^*,\, 1_{n-c^*}\}$, when $c^* < c^\circ$; and
- $\pi^\circ = \{c^\circ,\, 1_{n-c^\circ}\}$, when $c^* \geq c^\circ$;

where c° is the maximand of $P(c)$.

Proof: First, consider the case $c^* < c^\circ$. A coalition structure in which $c > c^*$ cannot be an equilibrium because the best-reply of a cooperating player is always to leave the coalition. A coalition structure in which $c < c^*$ is internally stable (equation 5.6 is met), and no cooperating player has an incentive to ban new accessions. Therefore, the equilibrium of the game is $\pi^* = \{c^*,\, 1_{n-c^*}\}$. The coalition c^* is the internally stable coalition that maximizes the per-member payoff.

Table 5.4. A single coalition game with humped-shaped payoff function and non-orthogonal free-riding

Coalition structures	Per-member partition function					
1,1,1,1,1,1,	0	0	0	0	0	0
1,1,1,1,2	0.7	0.7	0.7	0.7	2.7	2.7
1,1,1,3	2	2	2	4.4	4.4	4.4
1,1,4	4.2	4.2	5	5	5	5
1,5	6	4.4	4.4	4.4	4.4	4.4
6	2.7	2.7	2.7	2.7	2.7	2.7

Consider the case $c^* \geq c°$. All coalitions $c' > c^*$ do not satisfy equation 5.6. All coalitions c' such that $c° < c' \leq c^*$ satisfy equation 5.6, but cooperating players agree that a smaller coalition would provide a larger payoff because $P(c') < P(c°)$ by definition of $c°$. All coalitions c'' such that $c'' < c°$ satisfy equation 5.6, but cooperating players agree that a larger coalition would provide a larger payoff because $P(c'') < P(c°)$ by definition of $c°$. Therefore, the stable coalition structure is $\pi° = \{c°, 1_{n-c°}\}$.

Let us use again a simple model with orthogonal free-riding to illustrate this result.[17] The simplest way to obtain a humped-shaped stability function is to introduce some coordination costs within the coalition and to assume that these costs increase with the coalition size.[18] The resulting payoff matrix is shown in Table 5.4.

The incentive structure is summarized by the following three facts:

- *Fact 1*: the profitability condition is satisfied for all c.
- *Fact 2*: the coalition is internally stable for all $c \leq 5$.
- *Fact 3*: the individually optimal coalition size is 4.

As a consequence, under open membership the equilibrium coalition of this game is $\pi^* = \{1,5\}$, whereas under exclusive membership the equilibrium coalition is $\pi° = \{1,1,4\}$ (we are in the case in which $c^* > c°$). Consider indeed any coalition structures in which the coalition is smaller than 5. By Fact 2, no cooperating player wants to leave the coalition. By Fact 3, coalition members prefer to refuse new cooperators once size four is reached. Hence, under the exclusive membership rule the size of the largest internally stable coalition is four. Now consider the structure with a coalition larger than five. By Fact 2, the best-reply of one of the cooperators is to defect. The grand coalition cannot be then a stable coalition structure.

Proposition 6: In a game with Nash conjectures and exclusive membership, in which the profitability function is positive for $c \geq c^m$ and humped-shaped, and free-riding is non-orthogonal, the stable coalition structures are:

- the singleton structure $\pi^S = \{1_n\}$ when $c^\# > n$;
- $\pi^* = \{c^*, 1_{n-c^*}\}$, when $c^m \leq c^\# \leq c^* \leq c^\circ$; and
- $\pi^\circ = \{c^\circ, 1_{n-c^\circ}\}$, when $c^m \leq c^\# \leq c^\circ < c^*$.

Proof: Same as for Proposition 2b. The only difference is that when $c^m \leq c^\# \leq c^\circ < c^*$, the optimal coalition is no longer c^*, but c°.

4.2.2 Rational conjectures

Now consider the case in which players' conjectures are rational, that is, each player correctly anticipates the reaction of the other players to his decision. The definition of stability must be modified to take into account both the introduction of rational conjectures and the adoption of exclusive membership.

Rational conjecture stability with exclusive membership: A coalition is stable if it is internally stable and optimal. It is internally stable if no cooperating player would be better off in the coalition structure induced by his defection. Formally:

$$p(c;\pi) \geq p(1;\pi'), \tag{5.7}$$

for all players in the coalition c, where $\pi = \{c, 1_{(n-c)}\}$, $\pi' = \pi \backslash \{c\} \cup \{c', 1_{(k+1)}\}$ and $c' = c - k - 1$, where k is the number of defections following i's defection ($k+1$ defections including i). It is optimal if no cooperating player has an incentive to accept additional members or to exclude existing members.

Given this definition, the stable coalitions are identified by the following propositions (again, it makes sense to analyse only the case of humped-shaped profitability functions):

Proposition 7: In a game with rational conjectures and exclusive membership in which the profitability function is humped-shaped and free-riding is orthogonal, the stable coalition structures are:

- a sequence of coalitions c^*, c^{**}, c^{***} ... , where $c^{***} > c^{**} > c^*$ and $P(c^{**}) \geq Q(c^*)$, $P(c^{***}) \geq Q(c^{**})$,..., when $1 \leq c^* < c^{**} < c^{***} < \ldots < c^\circ < n$, and c° is sufficiently large; and
- $\pi^\circ = \{c^\circ, 1_{n-c^\circ}\}$, when $c^\circ \leq c^* \leq n$ or $c^* > n$.

Proof: All coalitions c belonging to $[2,n]$ are profitable. If $1<c^*<c^\circ$, all players outside a coalition $c<c^*$ have an incentive to join the coalition. Their rational conjectures are $k=0$ and $k'=c^*-c-1$. Therefore, c^* is stable. When $c^*<c<c^\circ$, all players in c have an incentive to defect. However, if c° is sufficiently large, a coalition $c^{**}<c^\circ$ may exist such that $c^{**}>c^*$ and $P(c^{**})\geq Q(c^*)$. If this is the case, c^{**} is stable (see the proof of Proposition 3). Similarly, a coalition $c^{***}<c^\circ$ may exist such that $c^{***}>c^{**}$ and $P(c^{***})\geq Q(c^{**})$ and so on. Whenever one of the coalitions c^{**}, c^{***} and so on, is larger than c°, the sequence stops. If $c^\circ<c^*<n$, all players outside a coalition c belonging to $[c^\circ, c^*]$ have an incentive to join the coalition. However, c^* does not meet the optimality condition because the optimal coalition is $c^\circ<c^*$. The rational conjectures are $k=0$ and $k'=c^\circ-c-1$. Therefore, c° is stable because players in c° have no incentive to defect (being $c^\circ<c^*$). Finally, when $c^\circ<c^*<n$, all players in a coalition $c>c^*$ have an incentive to defect. There could be a coalition c^{**} such that $P(c^{**})\geq Q(c^*)$, which could be stable under the conjectures $k=c^{**}-c^*-1$ and $k'=0$. However, c^{**} does not meet the optimality condition, and therefore the rational conjectures are $k=c^{**}-c^\circ-1$ and $k'=0$. However, even though $P(c^{**})\geq Q(c^\circ)$, c^{**} is not stable because it is not optimal ($c^{**}>c^\circ$). Therefore, all coalition $c>c^*$ cannot be stable under exclusive membership.

Proposition 8: Consider a game with rational conjectures and exclusive membership in which the profitability function is positive for $c\geq c^m$ and humped-shaped, and free-riding is non-orthogonal. The stable coalition structures are:

- a sequence of coalitions c^m, c^{**}, $c^{***}\ldots$, where $c^m<c^{**}<c^{***}<\ldots<c^\circ$, and $P(c^m)\geq P(0)$, $P(c^{**})\geq Q(c^m)$, $P(c^{***})\geq Q(c^{**})$, ..., when: (i) $c^\#>n$ and c° is sufficiently large, or (ii) $c^m<c^\#\leq n$, $c^m<c^{**}<c^{***}<\ldots<c^\circ<c^\#$ and c° is sufficiently large; or (iii) $c^m<c^\#<c^*\leq c^\circ$, $c^*<c^{**}<c^{***}<\ldots\leq c^\circ$ and c° is sufficiently large; and
- $\pi^\circ=\{c^\circ, 1_{n-c^\circ}\}$, otherwise.

Proof: Same as for Propositions 4b and 7.

4.3 Coalition Unanimity

Let us consider another membership rule often used in the economic theory of coalition stability, namely the so called coalition unanimity. In the *coalition unanimity game* (Yi and Shin, 1994; Chander and Tulkens, 1995; Bloch, 1997) or *game* Γ (Hart and Kurz, 1983), no coalition can form without the unanimous consensus of its members. This implies that players are not free to either join the coalition or to leave it. Therefore, this membership rule introduces restrictions both on entry (as the exclusive membership rule) and on exit behaviours of players. In the decision process, players' messages consist in a list of players as in the previous one. However, if a coalition is formed, it is necessarily composed of all players in the list and as soon as a player defects the coalition breaks up into singletons.

As underlined in Tulkens (1998), the coalition unanimity rule can be considered the opposite of the open membership rule. Under open membership, a player who defects assumes that players in the coalition keep cooperating after his or her defection. Instead, under coalition unanimity, a player knows that his or her decision to free-ride will lead the whole coalition to collapse.

Therefore, the coalition unanimity rule implicitly embodies a conjecture on players' behaviour after a defection takes place. Whereas open membership is characterized by the usual Nash conjecture, coalition unanimity assumes the following conjecture: a member of the coalition who decides to defect assumes that all other members of the coalition will follow his or her decision and will also defect. As said, after a defection the coalition breaks up into singletons. Therefore, a defecting player's payoff is the non-cooperative one.

As a consequence, the definition of stability must be modified as follows:

Coalition unanimous stability (Chander and Tulkens, 1995): A coalition is stable if:

- the payoff of coalition members is larger than the payoff they would achieve in the singleton coalition structure π^S. Formally: $p(c;\pi) > p(1;\pi^S)$ for all players who belong to c, where $\pi = \{c, 1_{n-c}\}$, $\pi^s = \{1_n\}$; and
- the coalition is optimal, that is, no cooperating player has an incentive to accept additional members or to exclude existing members.

This definition of stability is less demanding than the ones previously provided. As a consequence, the equilibrium stable coalition is generally larger, as shown by the following propositions:

Proposition 9: In a game in which the profitability function is monotonic, the stable coalition structure under coalition unanimity is the grand coalition structure $\pi^n = \{n\}$ whatever the type of free-riding.

Proof: As previously seen, when free-riding is orthogonal, all coalitions $c \in [2, n]$ are profitable. Therefore $p(c;\pi) > p(1;\pi^S)$ for all $c \in [2, n]$. When the profitability function is monotonic, the optimal coalition is the grand coalition $c=n$. As a consequence, only the grand coalition satisfies the two conditions defining the coalition unanimous stability. When free-riding is non-orthogonal, all coalitions $c \in [c^m, n]$ are profitable, with $c^m \leq n$. Therefore $p(c; \pi) > p(1; \pi^S)$ for all $c \in [c^m, n]$. Again monotonicity implies the optimality of the grand coalition which thus satisfies the two conditions defining the coalition unanimous stability.

Proposition 10: In a game in which the profitability function is humped-shaped, the stable coalition structure under coalition unanimity is $\pi^\circ = \{c^\circ, 1_{(n-c^\circ)}\}$ whatever the type of free-riding (when free-riding is non-orthogonal, the condition $c^m < c^\circ$ is necessary).

Proof: Again, when free-riding is orthogonal, all coalitions $c \in [2, n]$ are profitable. Therefore $p(c; \pi) > p(1; \pi^S)$ for all $c \in [2, n]$. When free-riding is non-orthogonal, all coalitions $c \in [c^m, n]$ are profitable, with $c^m \leq n$. When the profitability function is humped-shaped, the optimal coalition is c°, the maximand of $P(c)$. When free-riding is orthogonal, obviously $c^\circ \geq 2$. When free-riding is non-orthogonal, we need $c^\circ \geq c^m$. As a consequence, if $c^m \leq c^\circ$, only c° satisfies the two conditions defining the coalition unanimous stability.

5. SEQUENTIAL GAMES

The simultaneity of decisions characterizing the representation of the negotiating process discussed in the previous sections may be replaced by a sequential order of moves, in order to capture the idea of expectations on future reactions which was previously introduced in the case of rational conjectures and coalition unanimity. Therefore, we will focus only on the case of Nash conjectures in a sequential game, thus adopting the concept of subgame perfect Nash equilibrium (stability).

In this context, the stable coalition structures under open membership, exclusive membership and coalition unanimity will be identified, both for linear and circular games.

5.1 Linear Sequential Games

Consider first the case in which players decide one after the other, that is, the order of moves is linear. Without loss of generality, let us assume that player 1 decides first, player 2 decides second and so on. Let us start by analysing the case of open membership. We have:

Proposition 11: If the profitability function is monotonic, and free-riding is orthogonal, under open membership the stable coalition structures are:

- $\pi^* = \{c^*, 1_{(n-c^*)}\}$ when $1 < c^* < n$; and
- the grand coalition structure $\pi^n = \{n\}$ when $c^* \geq n$, that is, $L(c) > 0$, for all $c \in [2,n)$.

Proof: First of all let us recall that, as in Proposition 1, the case $L(c) < 0$ for all $c \in [2,n]$ cannot occur. To identify the subgame perfect Nash equilibrium of the game consider again the definition of stability provided by (5.2a)(5.2b). This definition implies that player i, who decides at stage i, must choose whether or not to join the coalition c eventually formed in the previous stages of the sequential game. Player 1 decides in the first stage when no coalition exists. He or she therefore decides whether or not to be the first member of a coalition. Player i's best reply is as follows: if at least c^* players previously decided to form a coalition, his or her best option is to free-ride. Otherwise, player i decides to cooperate. In addition, by definition of c^*, $Q(c^*) > P(c^*) \approx Q(c^* - 1)$. Hence, all players know that at the equilibrium free-riders achieve a larger payoff than cooperators. Therefore, by anticipating the best reply of the following players, the first $n - c^*$ players decide to free ride, whereas the remaining c^* players decide to cooperate (by definition of c^*). As a consequence, c^* is the stable coalition unless $L(c) > 0$ for all $c \in [2,n)$. In this latter case, the grand coalition forms.

Proposition 12.a: If free-riding is non-orthogonal and the profitability function is positive and monotonic for $c \geq c^m$, under open membership the stable coalition structure of the linear sequential coalition game is the singleton structure $\pi^S = \{1_n\}$.

Proof: In the presence of non-orthogonal free-riding, by definition of c^m, the profitability condition is satisfied for all $c \in [c^m, n]$. As for stability, when $c^\# > n$, then no player has an incentive to join the coalition at any stage of the game. Therefore, the stable coalition structure is $\pi^S = \{1_n\}$. When $c^m \leq c^\# \leq n$, player i chooses to cooperate if at least $c^\#$ players previously decided to join the coalition. If not, he or she prefers to free-ride. Therefore, the first player chooses to free ride and the following ones take the same decision. The stable coalition structure is again $\pi^S = \{1_n\}$.

Proposition 12.b: If free-riding is non-orthogonal and the profitability function is positive for $c \geq c^m$, but humped-shaped, under open membership the stable coalition structures of the linear sequential coalition game are:

- the singleton structure $\pi^S = \{1_n\}$ when $c^{\#} > n$, and
- $\pi^* = \{c^*, 1_{(n-c^*)}\}$ when $c^m \leq c^{\#} \leq c^* \leq n$.

Proof: Again, by definition of c^m, the profitability condition is satisfied for all $c \in [c^m, n]$. Moreover, when $c^{\#} > n$, no player has an incentive to join the coalition at any stage of the game. Therefore, the stable coalition structure is $\pi^S = \{1_n\}$. When $c^m \leq c^{\#} \leq c^* \leq n$, player *i*'s best reply is as follows. Player *i* decides to join the coalition if at least c' players, $c^{\#} \leq c' \leq c^*$, previously joined the coalition. If less than $c^{\#}$ players or more than c^* players previously joined the coalition, player *i* prefers to free-ride. In addition, as already shown, $Q(c^*) > P(c^*) > Q(c^{\#}) > P(c^{\#})$. Therefore, by anticipating the reaction of the other players, the first player chooses to free-ride and the following ones take the same decision, until the last c^* players decide to join the coalition. Therefore, the stable coalition structure is $\pi^* = \{c^*, 1_{(n-c^*)}\}$.

In the case of exclusive membership and monotonic profitability function, the stable coalitions coincide with those obtained in the case of open membership. However, when the profitability function is humped-shaped, we have:

Proposition 13: If the profitability function is humped-shaped and free-riding is orthogonal, under exclusive membership the stable coalition structures of the linear sequential coalition game are:

- $\pi^* = \{c^*, 1_{(n-c^*)}\}$ when $1 < c^* < c^\circ$; and
- $\pi^\circ = \{c^\circ, 1_{(n-c^\circ)}\}$ when $c^* \geq c^\circ$.

Proof: Again, the case $L(c) < 0$ for all $c \in [2,n]$ cannot occur. In the case where $1 < c^* < c^\circ$, the proof of the proposition coincides with the one of Proposition 11. When $c^* \geq c^\circ$, there are three groups of players: the free-riders, the cooperators and those players who would like to cooperate but are excluded from the coalition. Given the definitions of c^* and $c^* \geq c^\circ$, we have $P(c^\circ) > Q(c^\circ)$ and $P(c^\circ) > P(c^*) \approx Q(c^* - 1)$. Therefore, when decisions are taken sequentially, the first c° players decide to cooperate, then $c^* - c^\circ$ players are excluded from the coalition and forced to free-ride, and finally $n - c^*$ players decide to free-ride. As a consequence the stable coalition is c°.

Finally, in the case of coalition unanimity:

Proposition 14: Under coalition unanimity, if the profitability function is positive for $c \geq c^m$ and monotonic, the stable coalition structure of the linear sequential coalition game is the grand coalition structure $\pi^n = \{n\}$

whatever the type of free-riding. If the profitability function is humped-shaped, the stable coalition structure becomes: $\pi^\circ = \{c^\circ, 1_{(n-c^\circ)}\}$.

Proof: Under coalition unanimity, the first player to move knows that if he or she does not choose to join the coalition, no coalition will form. Since all coalitions c are profitable (either for $c \geq 2$ or for $c \geq c^m > 2$), then player 1 prefers to join the coalition. If the profitability function is monotonic, the same decision, and for the same reasons, will be taken by all the subsequent players. If the profitability function is humped-shaped, the first player to move knows that a coalition of size c° will form and that $P(c^\circ) > Q(c^\circ)$. Therefore, it is optimal for the first c° players to form a coalition, whereas the last $n-c^\circ$ players decide to free-ride.

The main conclusion that can be derived from the above propositions is that the stable coalition structures of a linear sequential coalition game coincide, with a few exceptions, with the stable coalition structures of a simultaneous game. The main advantage of the sequential decision structure is that it enables us to identify which players play which role. In simultaneous games, the 'identity' of cooperators is not determined. In sequential games, it is possible to know which players will join the coalition. For example, under open membership and orthogonal free-riding, the first $n-c^*$ players to move are the ones who free-ride, whereas the last c^* movers are those who join the coalition. Under exclusive membership, the first c° players form a coalition, whereas the remaining ones free-ride (either because they are excluded from the coalition or because they are actual free-riders).

The examples provided by Tables 5.2 and 5.3 help to understand our results. Consider Table 5.2 and the rule of open membership. From the decision tree of the game implicit in the payoff matrix, it is easy to see that the best-reply of the last player of the game is to defect if the coalition previously formed is larger than or equal to three. On the other hand, if previous players formed a coalition smaller than 3, the last player's best reply is to join the coalition. The same reasoning can be applied to all players. Hence, the first player decides to form a singleton, similarly the second player, and so on until the last three players form a coalition. The subgame perfect Nash equilibrium of this game is therefore $\pi^* = \{3,1,1,1\}$. In the case of non-orthogonal free-riding (Table 5.3) and open membership, the best-reply of each player at each node of the tree is to defect, whatever the size of the previously formed coalition. Hence the subgame perfect Nash equilibrium structure is the one in which no coalition forms.

5.2 Circular Sequential Games

The last step of our analysis focuses on a further possible assumption on the order of moves of the game. Rather than assuming that players decide one after the other – from the first to the last one – we assume that after the last player has decided, the first player can revise his or her decision. Then the second one can revise his or her decision, and so forth. Therefore, the negotiation goes on sequentially until no player wants to change his or her choice.

The game consists of a sequence of rounds and each round is a linear sequential game. For each player, there is always a next round unless all players stick to the choice made in the previous round. This gets rid of the strategic disadvantage of being the last players in the game. Moreover, either before defecting or before joining the coalition, each player takes into account the reaction of all the other players in the game. Indeed, in a circular sequential game, each player chooses as if he was the first player of a linear sequential game.

Let us focus first on the stable coalition structures of a circular sequential game under open membership. We restrict our analysis to the case of orthogonal free-riding (where the profitability function is positive for all $2 \leq c \leq n$). The extension to the case of non orthogonal free-rider is trivial and is left to the reader.

Proposition 15: In a sequential game in which the order of moves is circular, the profitability function is monotonic, and free-riding is orthogonal, the stable coalition structure of the game under open membership is the grand coalition $\pi^n = \{n\}$, if: (i) $p(n; \pi^n) \geq p(1; \pi^*)$ and $1 < c^* < n$; or (ii) $c^* \geq n$; where $p(n; \pi^n)$ is a player's payoff when the grand coalition forms and $p(1; \pi^*)$ is the payoff as a free-rider in the structure $\pi^* = \{c^*, 1_{(n-c^*)}\}$.

Proof: Assume $1 < c^* < n$ and consider the behaviour of the first player. If he or she chooses to defect, he or she knows that at most the last c^* player will choose to cooperate when $1 < c^* < n$. Therefore, he or she gets a payoff equal at most to $p(1; \pi^*)$. If the player chooses to cooperate and one of the subsequent players free-rides, the first player can always revise his or her decision and choose not to join the coalition, thus obtaining again at most $p(1; \pi^*)$. However, if he or she chooses to cooperate and all subsequent players join the coalition, the player gets the grand coalition payoff $p(n; \pi^n)$. Therefore, if $p(n; \pi^n) \geq p(1; \pi^*)$, the first player can always take the risk of announcing that he or she will join the coalition, because if all other players join the coalition, he or she gets $p(n; \pi^n) \geq p(1; \pi^*)$; otherwise, he or she gets at most $p(1; \pi^*)$. Therefore, in the first round the first player announces that he or she joins the coalition. In a circular game, the second player behaves as if he or she was the first player, and therefore chooses according to the same reasoning. As a consequence, the second player also chooses to join the coalition. Similarly, the third player, the fourth and so on. At the end of the first round, all players have chosen to join the coalition and the grand coalition forms. Therefore, the stable coalition structure is $\pi^n = \{n\}$. In the case $c^* \geq n$, all players have of course an incentive to join the coalition and the grand coalition forms.

The next step to consider is the case in which the membership rule is exclusive. As in the previous sections, this case does not coincide with the one in which the membership rule is open when the per-member partition function is humped-shaped. Then:

Proposition 16: In a sequential game in which the order of moves is circular, the profitability function is humped-shaped, and free-riding is orthogonal, the stable coalition structure of the game under exclusive membership is $\pi^\circ = \{c^\circ, 1_{(n-c^\circ)}\}$ if: (i) $p(c^\circ; \pi^\circ) \geq p(1; \pi^*)$ and $c^* < c^\circ$, or (ii) $c^\circ \leq c^*$.

Proof: Same as for the previous proposition. The only difference is that players find it optimal not to form a coalition larger than c°.

The final case to be considered is the one in which the membership rule is coalition unanimity.

Proposition 17: In a sequential game in which the order of moves is circular, the profitability function is monotonic, and free-riding is orthogonal, the stable coalition structure of the game under coalition unanimity is the grand coalition $\pi^n = \{n\}$. If the profitability function is humped-shaped, the stable coalition structure is $\pi^\circ = \{c^\circ, 1_{(n-c^\circ)}\}$.

Proof: Same as for Proposition 15. The only difference is that when the profitability function is monotonic, each player compares $p(n; \pi^n)$ with $p(1; \pi^S)$ because a defection induces all other players to defect. In the case of orthogonal free-riding, all coalitions $c \in [2, n]$ are profitable and therefore the condition $p(n; \pi^n) \geq p(1; \pi^S)$ is satisfied. As a consequence, the first player announces that he or she joins the coalition in the first stage and all other players follow. In the case of humped-shaped profitability function, the comparison is between $p(c^\circ; \pi^\circ)$ and $p(1; \pi^S)$, where $p(c^\circ; \pi^\circ) \geq p(1; \pi^S)$ because all coalitions $c \in [2, n]$ are profitable.

Again consider the examples of Tables 5.2 and 5.3. In the case of orthogonal free-riding (Table 5.3), the equilibrium structure is the grand coalition. Consider any player in the grand coalition. By Fact 2, he or she has an incentive to defect. If he or she defects, the next player defects as well. Then, a third player deviates and so on. The process stops at $\pi^* = \{1,1,1,3\}$, because in this last structure there is no further incentive to defect. When the second round starts, the first player, in order to decide his or her strategy, compares $p(6; \pi^n) = 12.5$ – his grand coalition payoff – with $p(1; \pi^*) = 6$, – the payoff obtained as a consequence of his or her defection. Therefore, this player has an incentive to revise his or her decision and to choose to join the coalition. But if he or she would be better off by cooperating in the second round, he or she chooses to join the coalition already in the first round. The same reasoning can be applied to all players, thus showing that all players choose to join the coalition.

A similar conclusion can be derived by examining Table 5.3, where free-riding is non-orthogonal. In this case, the cooperative payoff is 1/24, which is larger than 1/49 – the payoff a player would obtain by defecting from the grand coalition after his or her defection is followed by all other players' defection. Therefore, in the first round all players choose to join the coalition.

Summing up, the possibility of revising their choice gives players the possibility to take the risk of joining the coalition in the first round. Ex-post this strategy is rewarded, because all players join the coalition unless they prefer to free-ride on the partial stable coalition c^* that may form at the equilibrium. Therefore, an agreement in which countries can revise their choice is not 'weaker' than an agreement in which signatories are committed to their decision. Indeed, the possibility of revision enhances the incentives for players to sign the agreement (that is, to join the coalition).

6. CONCLUSIONS

The above analyses have identified the stable coalition structures of different games. The common denominator of all games is that in the first stage all players choose whether or not to join a coalition and then in the second stage they set their policy variables. However, the games analysed in the previous sections differ with respect to other important features: the membership rules, the order of moves, the players' conjectures, the shape of the profitability function, the type of free-riding. By changing these features of the game, the stable coalition changes and multiple stable coalitions can emerge.

Table 5.2 and 5.3 below summarize part of our results.[19] Even when assuming Nash conjectures, it is clear that coalitions of different sizes can become stable by slightly modifying the rules and features of the game. Stable coalition structures include the no coalition case, partial coalitions and the grand coalition. Does this lead to the conclusion that coalition theory is of no help in predicting the stable outcomes of a coalition game? The answer is negative. We would rather conclude that coalition theory suggests a set of rules which make it easier to achieve a large and stable coalition. For example, coalition unanimity, if adopted by the negotiating players, is of great help in achieving a large coalition (even the grand coalition). This is true in the case of symmetric players, but it may not be true when players are asymmetric. Most importantly, a coalition unanimity rule may not be adopted by the players, even if it leads to the social efficient outcome, because players may have an incentive to free-ride in the game in which the membership rule is adopted.

This result is shown in Carraro, Marchiori and Oreffice (2001), where the choice of the membership rule is endogenized. The game is therefore formed by three stages. In the first one, players agree on the membership rule, in the second one, they decide whether or not to join the coalition, and in the third one they set their policy variables. Carraro, Marchiori and Oreffice (2001) show that coalition unanimity may not be an equilibrium of the game, even though players generally 'tighten their hands' by choosing a minimum participation constraint at the equilibrium.

Therefore, the conclusion of this paper that coalition unanimity, circular sequential moves and orthogonal free-riding are features of the game that favour the stability of large coalitions is not of great help unless more work is undertaken to establish whether and under what conditions these features of the game can be adopted or implemented by the players of the game. For example, in international environmental negotiations, can players agree ex ante that, whatever the outcome of the negotiations, free-riding agents will not reduce but will also not increase their emissions? Can they agree ex ante to decide sequentially with the possibility of revising their choice ? Are there the incentives to agree on this type of choice (in many actual cases, under unanimity adoption of these ex-ante rules)?

The answer to these questions requires further research on the theory of coalition stability. This new research direction will enhance the applicability of coalition theory to many economic issues and policy relevant problems.

Table 5.5 Stable coalitions with orthogonal free-riding and Nash conjectures

	Open membership (monotonic or humped-shaped payoff)	**Exclusive membership** (humped-shaped payoff)	**Coalition unanimity** (monotonic or humped-shaped payoff)
Simultaneous game	$\pi^* = \{c^*, 1_{n-c^*}\}$, when $1 < c^* < n$ $\pi^n = \{n\}$, when $c^* \geq n$	$\pi^* = \{c^*, 1_{n-c^*}\}$, when $1 < c^* < c^\circ$ $\pi^\circ = \{c^\circ, 1_{n-c^\circ}\}$, when $c^* \geq c^\circ$	*Monotonic payoff:* $\pi^n = \{n\}$ *Humped-shaped payoff:* $\pi^\circ = \{c^\circ, 1_{n-c^\circ}\}$
Linear sequential game	$\pi^* = \{c^*, 1_{n-c^*}\}$, when $1 < c^* < n$ $\pi^n = \{n\}$, when $c^* \geq n$	$\pi^* = \{c^*, 1_{n-c^*}\}$,when $1 < c^* < c^\circ$ $\pi^\circ = \{c^\circ, 1_{n-c^\circ}\}$, when $c^* \geq c^\circ$	*Monotonic payoff:* $\pi^n = \{n\}$ *Humped-shaped payoff:* $\pi^\circ = \{c^\circ, 1_{n-c^\circ}\}$
Circular sequential game	$\pi^n = \{n\}$	$\pi^\circ = \{c^\circ, 1_{n-c^\circ}\}$	*Monotonic payoff:* $\pi^n = \{n\}$ *Humped-shaped payoff:* $\pi^\circ = \{c^\circ, 1_{n-c^\circ}\}$

Table 5.6 Stable coalitions with non-orthogonal free-riding and Nash conjectures

	Open membership (monotonic or humped-shaped payoff)	**Exclusive membership** (humped-shaped payoff)	**Coalition unanimity** (monotonic or humped-shaped payoff)
Simultaneous game	*Monotonic payoff:* $\pi^S = \{1_n\}$, when $c\# > n$ $\pi^n = \{n\}$, when $c^m < c\# \leq n$ *Humped-shaped payoff:* $\pi^S = \{1_n\}$, when $c\# > n$ $\pi^* = \{c^*, 1_{n-c^*}\}, c^m \leq c\# \leq c^* \leq n$	$\pi^S = \{1_n\}$, when $c\# > n$ $\pi^* = \{c^*, 1_{n-c^*}\}, c^m \leq c\# \leq c^* \leq c^\circ$ $\pi^\circ = \{c^\circ, 1_{n-c^\circ}\}, c^m \leq c\# \leq c^\circ \leq c^*$	*Monotonic payoff:* $\pi^n = \{n\}$ *Humped-shaped payoff* $\pi^\circ = \{c^\circ, 1_{n-c^\circ}\}$
Linear sequential game	*Monotonic payoff:* $\pi^S = \{1_n\}$ *Humped-shaped payoff:* $\pi^S = \{1_n\}$, $c\# > n$ $\pi^* = \{c^*, 1_{n-c^*}\}$, $c^m \leq c\# \leq c^* \leq n$	$\pi^S = \{1_n\}$, when $c\# > n$ $\pi^* = \{c^*, 1_{n-c^*}\}, c^m \leq c\# \leq c^* \leq c^\circ$ $\pi^\circ = \{c^\circ, 1_{n-c^\circ}\}, c^m \leq c\# \leq c^\circ \leq c^*$	*Monotonic payoff:* $\pi^n = \{n\}$ *Humped-shaped payoff:* $\pi^\circ = \{c^\circ, 1_{n-c^\circ}\}$
Circular sequential game	$\pi^n = \{n\}$	$\pi^\circ = \{c^\circ, 1_{n-c^\circ}\}$	*Monotonic payoff:* $\pi^n = \{n\}$ *Humped-shaped payoff:* $\pi^\circ = \{c^\circ, 1_{n-c^\circ}\}$

NOTES

A previous version of this chapter, titled 'Endogenous Formation of Environmental Coalitions' and co-authored with F. Moriconi, was presented at the Coalition Theory Network Workshop on 'Coalition Formation: Applications to Economic Issues', Venice, 8–10 January 1998, at the University of Paris X Seminar in 1999 and at the 2000 EAERE-FEEM-VIU Summer School. The authors are grateful to Sergio Currarini, Gilles Rotillon, Tarik Tazdait, the CTN workshop participants and the students of the Summer School for helpful comments and suggestions. Correspondence address: Prof. Carlo Carraro, Department of Economics, University of Venice, S. Giobbe 873, 20121, Venezia, Italy. E-mail: ccarraro@unive.it.

1. It must be acknowledged that the first results on the non-cooperative formation of coalitions in the presence of positive spillovers can be found in the oligopoly literature on stable cartels. See d'Aspremont and Gabszewicz (1986) and Donsimoni, Economides and Polemarchakis (1986).
2. A notable exception is the paper by Barrett (1994), where the coalition is assumed to be the leader of a Stackelberg game.
3. The possibility of equilibria with multiple coalitions is analysed in Carraro (1998, 1999, 2000) and in Finus and Rundhagen (2001). This possibility is also considered in Bloch (1997), Yi (1997) and Ray and Vohra (1999).
4. We consider the equal sharing rule as an assumption, because it is not endogenously determined in the model. However, Ray and Vohra (1999) provides a vindication for this assumption.
5. The open membership game is 'a game in which membership in a coalition is open to all players who are willing to abide by the rules of the coalition' (Yi and Shin, 2000).
6. The exclusive membership game is a 'a game in which the existing members in the coalition are allowed to deny membership to outsider players' (Yi and Shin, 2000).
7. The game Δ is 'a game in which the choice of a strategy by a player means the largest set of players he is willing to be associated with in the same coalition. Each set of all the players who chose the same C then forms a coalition (which may, in general, differ from C)' where C indicates a subset of players (Hart and Kurz, 1983).
8. The coalition unanimity game is a game in which 'a coalition forms if and only if all potential members agree to join it' (Yi and Shin, 1994).
9. The game Γ is a game in which 'each player chooses the coalition to which he wants to belong. A coalition forms if and only if all its members have in fact chosen it; the rest of the players become singletons' (Hart and Kurz, 1983).
10. See Yi (1997) for this distinction.
11. For example, in the case of climate change, both situations are possible. Current estimates of 'carbon leakage' ranges from very small values to quite large ones (Ulph, 1993). Therefore, it is worth analysing both cases and the impact of different degrees of 'carbon leakage' on the outcome of negotiations on climate change control.
12. Botteon and Carraro (1997b) provide some numerical examples of this situation.
13. We assume that if a player is indifferent between joining the coalition or free-riding, then he or she joins the coalition.
14. For this latter case to happen, some positive externalities within the coalition must exist. Otherwise, the likely outcome is a coalition c^* larger than the coalition one would obtain without fixed costs but smaller than the grand coalition (Heal, 1994).
15. If the profitability function is first convex and then concave, there may exist both $c^\#$ and c^*, with $c^* > c^\#$ and $c^* < n$. In this case, the stable coalition would be the coalition c^*, rather than the grand coalition.
16. A minimum participation constraint is a rule which says that a coalition forms only if at least a share α of the n players joins the coalition. A formal analysis of this case is in Carraro, Marchiori and Oreffice (2001), where the share α is endogenized and strategically determined by the n players. An adequate minimum participation constraint is a rule $\alpha^\#$, such that a coalition forms only if at least $c^\#$ players join it.

17. The analysis of the example in which free-riding is non-orthogonal provides a marginal contribution to the comprehension of the result. It is therefore omitted.
18. A less *ad hoc* approach, where positive and negative R&D externalities interact within the coalition, is proposed in Carraro and Siniscalco (1997).
19. Please refer to the Propositions presented in sections 4 and 5 for the exact conditions upon which relies the validity of the results summarized by Tables 5.2 and 5.3.

REFERENCES

Barrett, S. (1994), 'Self-enforcing international environmental agreements', *Oxford Economic Papers*, **46**, 878–94.

Bloch, F. (1996), 'Sequential formation of coalition in games with externalities and fixed payoff division', *Games and Economic Behaviour*, **14**, 90–123.

Bloch, F. (1997), 'Noncooperative models of coalition formation in games with spillovers', in C. Carraro and D. Siniscalco (eds), *New Directions in the Economic Theory of the Environment*, Cambridge: Cambridge University Press.

Botteon, M. and C. Carraro (1997a), 'Burden-sharing and coalition stability in environmental negotiations with asymmetric countries', in C. Carraro (ed.), *International Environmental Negotiations: Strategic Policy Issues*, Cheltenham: Edward Elgar.

Botteon, M. and C. Carraro (1997b), 'Environmental coalitions with heterogeneous countries: burden sharing and carbon leakage', in A. Ulph (ed.), *Environmental Policy, International Agreements and International Trade*, Oxford: Oxford University Press.

Bresnaham, T. (1981), 'Duopoly models with consistent conjectures', *American Economic Review*, **71**, 934–45.

Carraro, C. (1998), 'Beyond Kyoto: a game theoretic perspective', in the Proceedings of the OECD Workshop on 'Climate change and economic modelling. Background analysis for the Kyoto Protocol', Paris, 17–18 September.

Carraro, C. (1999), 'The structure of international agreements on climate change', in C. Carraro (ed.), *International Environmental Agreements on Climate Change*, Dordrecht: Kluwer Academic.

Carraro, C. (2000), 'Roads towards international environmental agreements', in H. Siebert (ed.), *The Economics of International Environmental Problems*, Tübingen: Mohr Siebeck.

Carraro, C. and F. Moriconi (1998), 'International games on climate change control', FEEM Working Paper 56.98, FEEM, Milan.

Carraro, C., Marchiori, C. and S. Oreffice (2001), 'Endogenous minimum participation in international environmental treaties', *mimeo*, FEEM, Venice.

Carraro, C. and D. Siniscalco (1992), 'The international protection of the environment: voluntary agreements among sovereign countries', in P. Dasgupta and K.G. Mäler (eds), *The Economics of Transnational Commons*, Oxford: Clarendom Press.

Carraro, C. and D. Siniscalco (1993), 'Strategies for the international protection of the environment', *Journal of Public Economics*, **52**, 309–328.

Carraro, C. and D. Siniscalco (1997), 'R&D cooperation and the stability of international environmental agreements', in C. Carraro (ed.), *International Environmental Agreements: Strategic Policy Issues*, Cheltenham: Edward Elgar.

Chander, P. and H. Tulkens (1993), 'Strategically stable cost-sharing in an economic-ecological negotiation process', forthcoming in K.G. Mäler, (ed.), *International Environmental Problems: An Economic Perspective*, Dordrecht, Kluwer Academic.

Chander, P. and H. Tulkens (1995), 'A core-theoretical solution for the design of cooperative agreements on trans-frontier pollution', FEEM Working Paper 22.95, FEEM, Milan.

Chander, P. and H. Tulkens (1997), 'The core of an economy with multilateral environmental externalities', *International Journal of Game Theory*, 26, 379–401.

Chwe, M.S.Y. (1994), 'Farsighted coalition stability', *Journal of Economic Theory*, **54**, 299–325.

d'Aspremont, C.A. and J.J. Gabszewicz (1986), 'On the stability of collusion', in G.F. Matthewson and J.E. Stiglitz (eds), *New Developments in the Analysis of Market Structure*, New York, NY: MacMillan Press, pp. 243–64.

d'Aspremont, C.A., A. Jacquemin, J.J. Gabszewicz and J. Weymark (1983), 'On the stability of collusive price leadership', *Canadian Journal of Economics*, **16**, 17–25.

Donsimoni, M.P., N.S. Economides and H.M. Polemarchakis (1986), 'Stable cartels', *International Economic Review*, **27**, 317–27.

Finus, M. and B. Rundshagen (2001), 'Endogenous coalition formation in global pollution control', *mimeo*, University of Hagen.

Hart, S. and M. Kurz (1983), 'Endogenous formation of coalitions', *Econometrica*, **51**, 1047–64.

Heal, G. (1994), 'The formation of environmental coalitions', in C. Carraro (ed.), *Trade, Innovation, Environment*, Dordrecht: Kluwer Academic.

Hoel, M. (1991), 'Global environmental problems: the effects of unilateral actions taken by one country', *Journal of Environmental Economics and Management*, **20**(1), 55–70.

Konishi, H., M. Le Breton and S. Weber (1997), 'Stable coalition structures for the provision of public goods', in C. Carraro and D. Siniscalco (eds), *New Directions in the Economic Theory of the Environment*, Cambridge: Cambridge University Press.

Le Breton, M. and S. Weber (1993), 'Stability of coalition structures and the principle of optimal partitioning', *mimeo*, GREQE, Aix-Marseille.

Mariotti, M. (1997), 'A model of agreements in strategic form games', *Journal of Economic Theory*, **73**, 196–217.

Ray, D. and R. Vohra (1999), 'A theory of endogenous coalition structure', *Games and Economic Behavior*, **26**, 286–336.

Tulkens, H. (1998), 'Cooperation vs. free-riding in international affairs: two approaches', in H. Folmer and N. Hanley (eds), *Game Theory and the Global Environment*, Cheltenham: Edward Elgar.

Ulph, A. (1993), 'Environmental policy, plant location, and government protection', FEEM Working Paper 43–93, FEEM, Milan.

Yi, S. (1997), 'Stable coalition structures with externalities', *Games and Economic Behaviour*, **20**, 201–23.

Yi, S. and H.S. Shin (1994), 'Endogenous formation of coalitions in oligopoly: 1. Theory', Dartmouth College, Working Paper 94–18.

Yi, S. and H.S. Shin (2000), 'Endogenous formation of research coalitions with spillovers', *International Journal of Industrial Organization*, **18**, 229–56.

6. Endogenous coalition formation in global pollution control: a partition function approach

Michael Finus and Bianca Rundshagen

1. INTRODUCTION

1.1 General Remarks

Concern about transboundary and global pollution problems ranks prominently on the agenda of international politics and has led to the signature of several international environmental agreements (IEAs), as for instance the Oslo Protocol on sulfur reduction in Europe in 1994, the Montreal Protocol on the depletion of the ozone layer in 1987, and the Kyoto Protocol on the reduction of greenhouse gases in 1997. This concern is also reflected in numerous recent papers (for example, Barrett (1997a, b); Botteon and Carraro (1997, 1998); Carraro and Moriconi (1998); Germain et al. (1996) and Germain et al. (1998)) on the formation of coalitions in international pollution control since the appearance of Barrett (1991), Bauer (1992) Black et al. (1992), Carraro and Siniscalco (1991), Chander and Tulkens (1992), Hoel (1992) and Tulkens (1979). The *fundamental assumption* of all models is that IEAs must be *self-enforcingly* designed since there is no international agency that can establish binding agreements (Endres, 1997). Consequently, the main problem of cooperation in international pollution control is that of *free-riding*. In reality there are two types of free-riding that negatively affect the success of an IEA (Finus, 2002). The *first type of free-riding* is the incentive of a country to remain a non-signatory or to take on less climate responsibility than other countries, thus benefiting from the higher abatement efforts of neighboring countries. The *second type of free-riding* relates to the incentive of joining an agreement but violating its spirit. Through such a behaviour a country can – at least temporarily – net a free-rider gain.

Though models differ with respect to the specification of the utility function of governments and with respect to the stability concept employed, they can be classified in two groups.[1]

1.2 Repeated Game Models

Repeated game models (RG-models) depict IEAs as an infinitely repeated game where governments agree on some contract in the first stage that has to be enforced in subsequent stages by using credible threats. Credibility is defined in these papers in terms of subgame-perfect or renegotiation-proof equilibria. Some key results of this literature are:

1. Stability of the grand coalition targeting at a globally optimal solution may be jeopardized even in a supergame framework and even if agents discount time little (Barrett, 1994a, b; Mäler, 1994; Stähler, 1996).
2. Even less ambitious abatement targets may be difficult to achieve whenever cooperation would be particularly useful from a global point of view.[2] In particular under these conditions, instability is a problem (Finus and Rundshagen, 1998; Finus and Tjøtta, 2002).
3. There is some evidence that coalitions implementing command and control instead of market-based instruments to achieve their agreed targets may be more successful. In the context of IEAs, command and control instruments imply agreements of higher stability due to a more symmetric welfare distribution that may compensate for their inefficiency (Finus and Rundshagen, 1998).
4. A subcoalition may achieve more than the grand coalition since the free-rider incentive can be controlled more easily within a smaller group of relatively homogenous countries (Barrett, 2000; Finus and Rundshagen, 1998).

RG-models are ideally suited to analyse the second type of free-riding but capture the first type of free-riding only deficiently. The choice of membership is basically reduced to the question: Does a signatory receive more than when it is punished? Moreover, coalition formation has been restricted to a single coalition. Though it is possible to remedy these deficiencies in RG-models, such an undertaking would be very complex and would have to rely on simulations, given the nature of these models. Therefore, our model belongs to the group of reduced stage game models.

1.3 Reduced Stage Game Models

Reduced stage game models (RSG-models) assume a two-stage game where countries decide in the first stage on their membership and in the second stage they choose their emission levels and how they distribute the gains from cooperation. Since payoffs are received at the end of the second stage and since the rules of the game (choice of emission levels and distribution of payoffs) are exogenously fixed, it is possible to reduce the two stages to one stage via backwards induction. This allows defining an equilibrium coalition structure in terms of the membership in the first stage. In the environmental economics literature two approaches have been taken. Scholars of non-cooperative game theory analysed coalition formation using a *partition function*, where the decision of membership depends on individual payoffs of countries, applying the concept of internal&external stability.[3] Scholars of cooperative game theory used the *characteristic function*, where membership is based on the aggregate payoff to a coalition, applying the concept of the core.[4]

Internal&external stability

An equilibrium is defined as a coalition structure where no signatory has an incentive to leave the coalition (internal stability) and no non-signatory has an incentive to join the coalition (external stability). Thus, in the first stage it is assumed that countries only have the choice between acceding to an IEA or remaining a non-signatory where it is assumed that non-signatories play as singletons. In the second stage, it is assumed that signatories jointly maximize their coalition's welfare and that non-signatories maximize their individual welfare. Signatories and non-signatories play non-cooperatively against each other. Either signatories and non-signatories choose simultaneously (Nash-Cournot assumption, for example, Carraro and Siniscalco, 1991, 1993; Bauer, 1992; Hoel, 1992) or sequentially (Stackelberg assumption, for example, Barrett, 1994b). For the distribution of benefits from cooperation, three typical assumptions have been made: i) no transfers (for example, Bauer, 1992; Hoel, 1992), ii) distribution according to the Nash-bargaining solution (Botteon and Carraro, 1997, 1998), and iii) distribution according to the Shapley value (Barrett, 1997b; Botteon and Carraro, 1997, 1998). If countries are assumed to be ex-ante symmetric,[5] all signatories receive the same payoff and the rule of distribution is irrelevant. In the case of asymmetric countries, assumptions (ii) and (iii) are popular allocation rules, though other rules are also conceivable.

Key results of the models are:

1. The number of signatories falls short of the grand coalition and the equilibrium coalition is usually rather small.
2. If signatories behave as Stackelberg leaders the coalition will be more successful since leakage effects of non-signatories can better be accounted for.

3. Similar to RG-models, whenever cooperation would be needed most from a global point of view, the coalition achieves only little (see Note 2).
4. In the case of asymmetric countries, the equilibrium coalition structure depends on the rule of welfare distribution and transfers can help to increase the degree of cooperation.

Core

An equilibrium is defined as a coalition structure where no country or group of countries finds it profitable to form any other coalition structure. In case of a deviation, it is assumed that the remaining players split up into singletons and either (i) minimax the deviating player(s) (α-core), (ii) maximin the deviating player(s) (β-core), or (iii) play a Nash strategy (γ-core) in terms of emissions. The literature has exclusively focused on stability of the grand coalition. Therefore the decision in the first stage is *de facto* a binary choice between no coalition and the coalition comprising all countries. Moreover, in the second stage it is assumed that the grand coalition implements the socially optimal emission vector and that the gains from cooperation are distributed according to a particular transfer scheme, which resembles that of Kaneko's ratio equilibrium (Kaneko, 1977). The key result of these models is that the grand coalition lies in the core.

Remarks and conclusions

RSG-models are ideally suited to analyse the first type of free-riding, that is the choice of membership, but capture the second type of free-riding only deficiently. Once countries have acceded to a coalition they are assumed to comply with abatement and transfer obligations and thus a temporary free-rider gains from signing an agreement, but violating its terms are ruled out by assumption.

Obviously, the two approaches produce quite different results. The models applying the concept of internal&external stability derive a rather pessimistic result with respect to the possibilities of cooperation in international pollution control, whereas the core makes very optimistic predictions. This leads us to three conclusions. First, in order to relate the different results to the implicit assumptions of these concepts, it is important to use one framework. We propose to study coalition formation in the context of the partition function approach, since it seems natural in a non-cooperative environment that players base their decision of membership on individual rather than on aggregate payoffs. Second, we suggest that, whenever this is possible, the rules of coalition formation should be separated from the stability concept used to determine equilibrium coalition structures. The definition of stability is summarized under the definition of an equilibrium concept; the definition of the rules is summarized under the definition of a coalition game. This distinction allows to analyse more clearly how assumptions drive results. Third, since it turns out that internal&external and core stability make extreme assumptions along the spectrum of possible equilibrium concepts and coalition formation games, we also consider various modifications. From the analysis it will be apparent that four fundamental features drive results. The *first feature* relates to whether countries can form only one non-trivial coalition or whether multiple coalitions can co-exist.[6] The *second feature* relates to whether membership is open or exclusive. The *third feature* relates to whether an equilibrium is defined in terms of single or multiple deviations. The *fourth feature* relates to how countries react if a country or group of countries deviates.

In what follows we lay out the model, present definitions and derive some general results in section 2, which form the basis for determining the equilibrium coalition structures under various assumptions in section 3. We will restrict the analysis to simultaneous coalition formation games.[7] In section 4 we compare equilibrium coalition structures, evaluate the different concepts of coalition formation and draw policy conclusions. Section 5 summarizes the main results and hints at possible future research questions.

2. MODEL

2.1 Definitions and Structure of the Coalition Formation

We consider an RSG-model comprising *two stages*. In the *first stage* countries choose their strategy 'membership', in the second stage their emission levels. The choice in the first stage depends on the *rules of the coalition formation game* and the *equilibrium concept* employed. We postpone the details until section 3.

In the *second stage*, it is assumed that countries choose their emissions as to *maximize aggregate payoffs to the coalition to which they belong and play a Nash-Cournot strategy against other coalitions.*[8] Since we assume *ex ante symmetric countries*, this implies that those countries, which belong to the same coalition, choose the same emission level and receive the same payoff. We therefore do not have to consider transfers among coalition members in the second stage. Transfers between coalitions are also ruled out.

Assumption 1: Rules of the Second Stage
Countries are ex ante symmetric, maximize their own coalition's aggregate payoff and play a Nash strategy against outsiders. There are no transfers.

Since the rules of the second stage are ex ante specified, the two stages can be reduced (by backwards induction) to one stage. All relevant information on which the decision in the first stage is based can then compactly be summarized in the per-membership partition function (Bloch, 1997).

Definition 1: Equilibrium Valuation or Per-Membership Partition Function
Let $c=\{c_1, ..., c_M\}$ *denote a coalition structure with M coalitions,* $c \in C$ *where C denotes the set of coalition structures,* $c_j \cap c_k = \emptyset \forall j \neq k$, $\cup c_i = I$, *then an equilibrium valuation is a mapping which associates to each coalition structure* $c \in C$ *a vector of individual payoffs* $\pi(c)=\{\pi_1(c_j, c), ..., \pi_N(c_k, c)\}$ *where* $\pi(c) \in \Pi(C)$ *is the set of payoffs that result from the maximization of players (countries) according to a particular rule, a given sharing rule of the gains from cooperation and a given coalition structure. The first argument in* $\pi_i(c_i, c)$ *refers to the coalition to which country i belongs, the second to the particular coalition structure.*

In section 2.2 we show that for Assumption 1 and for the properties of countries' payoff functions (Assumption 2) there is a unique optimal emission vector for each possible coalition structure. Thus, the set of equilibrium valuations is uniquely defined.

Note that due to the assumption of symmetry, notation simplifies. Suppose all coalition structures comprising two countries are equilibrium coalition structures. Thus, instead of writing $C^*=\{c^{1*}, c^{2*}, c^{3*}\}$ where $c^{1*}=\{\{1, 2\}, \{3\}\}$, $c^{2*}=\{\{1\}, \{2, 3\}\}$, $c^{3*}=\{\{1, 3\}, \{2\}\}$ we may simply write $C^*=\{(2, 1)\}$ or $c^*=(2, 1)$ where the entries indicate the coalition sizes and the asterisks equilibrium coalition structures.[9] For the subsequent notation it will prove helpful to order coalitions according to their size. That is, $c=(c_1, ..., c_M)$ where $c_1 \geq ... \geq c_M$.

An important definition to compare different coalition structures is that of coarsening and concentration (see Yi (1997) and Chapter 3 of this book for a formal definition).

Definition 2: Coarsening and Concentration of a Coalition Structure
A coalition structure c is coarser than a coalition structure c′ if c can be obtained by merging coalitions in c′. A coalition structure c is a concentration of c′ if one can obtain c by moving one member at a time from a coalition in c′ to another coalition of equal or larger size.

For example coalition structure (6, 5) is coarser and more concentrated than coalition structure (5, 5, 1). However, (5, 5) and (6, 4) cannot be compared under coarsening, though (6, 4) is more concentrated than (5, 5). Thus, if a coalition structure c is coarser than c' this implies that c is a concentration of c', though the opposite is not true (see Yi, 1997). Unfortunately, however, neither does concentration allow for a complete ordering of coalition structures. For instance, (4, 3) and (5, 1, 1) cannot be ranked under concentration.

2.2 Properties of the Global Pollution Game

Let the payoff to country *i* in the global emission game be given by:

$$\pi_i = \beta(e_i) - \phi\left(\sum_{j=1}^{N} e_j\right), \tag{6.1}$$

where we assume the following standard properties to hold (see, for example, Folmer and van Mouche, 2000):

Assumption 2: Properties of the Payoff Function
Let payoffs be given by equation 6.1 and assume for $e_i \in [0, e_i^{max})$: $\beta_i' > 0$, $\beta_i'' < 0$, $\phi_i' > 0$, $\phi_i'' \geq 0$ $\forall i$ *and an interior equilibrium emission vector in the second stage.*

That is, benefits from emissions (in the form of consumption and production of goods) increase at a decreasing rate. Damages increase in global emissions at a constant or increasing rate. Assumptions 1 and 2 imply the following:[10]

Proposition 1: Existence and Uniqueness of Nash Equilibrium in the Second Stage
Let payoffs to country i be given by equation 6.1, then there is a unique Nash equilibrium emission vector in the second stage under Assumptions 1 and 2.

Proof: First, note that countries belonging to the same coalition play as a single player. Thus, the choice of emissions constitutes a Nash equilibrium between coalitions in the second stage. Second, note that the first order condition of a country $k \in c_i$, which maximizes aggregate payoff to coalition c_i, is $\beta'(e_k) = c_i \phi'(\Sigma e_j)$ due to symmetry. Total differentiation of the FOC, denoting total emissions of coalition c_i by e^i and total emissions of all other coalitions by e^r, gives the slope of a coalition's reaction function:

$$\frac{de^i}{de^r} = \frac{c_i \phi''(\Sigma e_j)}{(1/c_i)\beta''(e_i) - c_i \phi''(\Sigma e_j)},$$

where *a*) $de^i/de^r = 0$ if $\phi'' = 0$ and *b*) $-1 < de^i/de^r < 0$ if $\phi'' > 0$. Case *a* implies orthogonal reaction functions. Therefore coalitions have a dominant emission strategy which is unique since equation 6.1 implies a strictly concave payoff function of a coalition with respect to emissions. Case *b* implies downward sloping reaction functions that constitute a contraction. Hence, the existence of a unique equilibrium follows from standard theorems (see Friedman, 1986, Theorem 2.5, p. 34 and p. 44) (**Q.E.D.**).

In the following we establish some properties of the global emission game that will be used to derive equilibrium coalition structures in section 3. As preliminary information we analyse emissions of a single country and global emissions.

Proposition 2a: Emissions

(a) *Let emissions of a member of a coalition c_i be denoted by e_i, then for any coalition structure c $e_i > e_j$ if, and only if $c_i < c_j$.*
(b) *Let coalition structure c' be coarser than coalition structure c and denote total emissions by e^T, then $e^T(c') < e^T(c)$.*

Proof:

(a) Consider the first order condition of a member of a coalition c_i, which is given by $\beta'(e_i) = c_i \phi'(e^T)$. By applying Assumption 2, it is obvious that e_i decreases with the size of the coalition c_i.
(b) Assume $e^{T(1)} < e^{T(2)}$ instead of $e^{T(1)} > e^{T(2)}$ would be true where $e^{T(1)}$ are global emissions before and $e^{T(2)}$ after coalitions c_i and c_j have merged. In case there are further coalitions, let c_k be a coalition that is not involved in the merger. Then for members of the coalition:

$$c_k\text{: } \beta'(e_k^{(1)}) = c_k \phi'(e^{T(1)}) < c_k \phi'(e^{T(2)}) = \beta'(e_k^{(2)}) \Rightarrow e_k^{(1)} > e_k^{(2)}$$

$$c_i \text{ (and } c_j\text{): } \beta'(e_i^{(1)}) = c_i \phi'(e^{T(1)}) < (c_i + c_j)\, \phi'(e^{T(1)})$$
$$< (c_i + c_j)\, \phi'(e^{T(2)}) = \beta'(e_i^{(2)}) \Rightarrow e_i^{(1)} > e_i^{(2)}$$

hold, which obviously violate the initial assumption of $e^{T(1)} < e^{T(2)}$ (**Q.E.D.**).

An immediate implication of Proposition 2a is the following corollary:

Corollary 1: Global Emissions
The grand coalition produces the lowest global emissions; the degenerated coalition structure consisting of only singletons produces the highest global emissions.

Proof: Follows from Proposition 2a, part b, and the facts that:

(a) (N) is coarser than c if $c \neq (N)$, and
(b) c is coarser than $(1, 1, ..., 1)$ (if $c \neq (1, 1, ..., 1)$) for each coalition structure c (**Q.E.D.**).

We can now turn to establishing the properties in the global emission game, which, according to Yi (1997), are reminiscent to a *positive externality game*.

Proposition 3: Individual Welfare and Size of a Coalition
Members of smaller coalitions enjoy a higher payoff than members of larger coalitions for any given coalition structure. That is:

$$C_1\colon \pi_j(c_j, c) < \pi_i(c_i, c) \text{ if, and only if, } c_i < c_j.$$

Proof: Since all countries suffer equally from global emissions but members of smaller coalitions choose higher emissions in equilibrium (see Proposition 2a), they have higher benefits and therefore higher payoffs than members of larger coalitions (**Q.E.D.**).

Proposition 4: Individual Welfare and Coarsening
Coalitions, which are not involved in a merger, are better off after the merger. That is:

$$C_{2a}\colon \pi_k(c_k, c) < \pi_k(c_k, c') \textit{ where } c_k \subset c, c' \text{ and } c' \text{ is coarser than } c.$$

Proof: Global emissions decrease through coarsening according to Proposition 2a. Coalitions that are not involved in the merger (outsiders) choose their best reply, which implies constant or higher emissions due to $-1 < de^i/de^r \leq 0$. Consequently, damages are decreasing and benefits of outsiders are non-decreasing through coarsening (**Q.E.D.**).

Conditions C_1 and C_{2a} are sufficient for characterizing equilibria in some coalition games in section 3. However, it turns out that particularly for the more interesting games more properties are needed. Those properties cannot be established for the general payoff function equation 6.1, though it seems that they apply to a large class of functions. In order to make progress, we provide four examples, which reflect typical payoff functions used in the environmental economics literature on coalition formation.[11]

$$\pi_i = b\left(ae_i - \frac{1}{2}e_i^2\right) - d\left(\sum_{j=1}^{N} e_j\right). \tag{6.2}$$

$$\pi_i = b\ln(1+e_i) - d\left(\sum_{j=1}^{N} e_j\right). \tag{6.3}$$

$$\pi_i = b\left(ae_i - \frac{1}{2}e_i^2\right) - \frac{d}{2}\left(\sum_{j=1}^{N} e_j\right)^2. \tag{6.4}$$

$$\pi_i = b\ln(1+e_i) - \frac{d}{2}\left(\sum_{j=1}^{N} e_j\right)^2. \tag{6.5}$$

Whereas payoff functions (6.2) and (6.3) imply orthogonal reaction functions ($de^i/de^r = 0$), payoff functions (6.4) and (6.5) imply downward sloping reaction functions with a slope less than one in absolute terms ($-1 < de^i/de^r < 0$). In the following we use payoff function (6.2) to illustrate our results. In order to establish some further properties in the global emission game, we, again, analyse the effect of coalition formation on emissions.

Proposition 2b: Emissions
Let coalition structure c′ be more concentrated than coalition structure c, then $e^T(c') \le e^T(c)$ holds for payoff functions (6.2) to (6.5).

Proof: Follows from routine computations which show that global emissions for payoff function (6.2) to (6.5) are given by:

$$(6.2)\text{: } e^T = Na - \frac{d}{b}\sum_{i=1}^{M} c_i^2, \quad (6.3)\text{: } e^T = \frac{Mb - Nd}{d},$$

$$(6.4)\text{: } e^T = \frac{Na}{1 + \frac{d}{b}\sum_{i=1}^{M} c_i^2}, \quad (6.5)\text{: } e^T = -\frac{N}{2} + \frac{1}{2}\sqrt{N^2 + 4\frac{Mb}{d}},$$

where $\Sigma_{i=1}^{M} c_i^2$ increases through concentration since, assuming $c_i \le c_j$, $(c_i - 1)^2 + (c_j + 1)^2 + \Sigma_{k \ne i,j} c_k^2 - \Sigma_k c_k^2 = 2(1 + c_j - c_i) > 0$ holds and M decreases or remains constant through concentration (**Q.E.D.**).

Proposition 2b allows stating the following results:

Proposition 5: Individual Welfare and Concentration
Assume payoffs to be given by one of the payoff functions (6.2) to (6.5). Then coalitions that are not involved in a concentration are not worse off after the concentration. That is:

C_{2b}: $\pi_k(c_k, c) \le \pi_k(c_k, c')$ *where* $c_k \subset c$, c' *and* c' *is more concentrated than* c.

If a member of the coalition c_i leaves its coalition to join a larger or equal-sized coalition c_j, then the members of the old coalition are better off. That is:

$$C_3\colon \pi_i(c_i, c) < \pi_i(c_i - 1, c') \text{ where } c' = c \setminus \{c_i, c_j\} \cup \{c_j + 1, c_i - 1\},\ 2 \leq c_i \leq c_j.$$

If a member k of the coalition c_i leaves his coalition to join a larger or equal-sized coalition c_j, then the deviator becomes worse off. That is:

$$C_4\colon \pi_k(c_i, c) > \pi_k(c_j + 1, c') \text{ where } c' = c \setminus \{c_i, c_j\} \cup \{c_j + 1, c_i - 1\},\ 2 \leq c_i \leq c_j.$$

Proof: C_{2b}: Global emissions do not increase through concentration according to Proposition 2b. Coalitions that are not involved in a concentration (outsiders) choose their best reply, which implies constant or higher emissions due to $-1 < de^i/de^r \leq 0$. Consequently, damages are not increasing and benefits of outsiders are not decreasing through concentration. C_3: The first order condition of members of coalition c_i of which a country k joins coalition c_j are $\beta'(e_i) = c_i\phi'(e^{T_1})$ before and $\beta'(e_i) = (c_i - 1)\phi'(e^{T_2})$ after the concentration where $e^{T_1} \geq e^{T_2}$ are global emissions before and after the concentration respectively and where the sign follows from Proposition 2b. Consequently, emissions of the old members of coalition c_i increase through concentration. Hence, damages of old members are not increasing and benefits are increasing. C_4: See Appendix 1. (**Q.E.D.**).

Note that C_4 can also be interpreted in reverse order: joining a coalition that is smaller by at least two members is profitable. Condition C_4 stresses that – once there is some (minimal) amount of concentration – single members have only a marginal effect on reducing global damages by joining larger coalitions but their benefits decrease substantially through increased abatement efforts.

2.3 Stand-alone Stable and Pareto-optimal Coalition Structures

For the characterization and evaluation of equilibria in section 3 we introduce two more definitions: stand-alone stable and Pareto-optimal coalition structures. Whereas the definition of stand-alone stable coalition structures (SAS) is commonly used in the literature (for example, Bloch, 1997; Yi, 1997), the definition of Pareto-optimal coalition structures (PO) seems (to the best of our knowledge) new to the literature, though it turns out to be very useful in characterizing coalition-proof and strong Nash equilibria in coalition games.

Definition 3: Stand-alone Stable Coalition Structures (SAS)
A coalition structure $c = (c_1, \ldots, c_M)$ is stand-alone stable if, and only if, $\pi_i(c_i, c) \geq \pi_i(1, c')$ where $c' = c \setminus c_i \cup \{c_i - 1, 1\}\ \forall i \in I$.

A coalition structure c is *stand-alone stable* if, and only if, no country finds it profitable to leave its coalition and to act as a singleton, holding the rest of the coalition structure constant. From this it follows immediately that *the degenerated coalition structure consisting only of singletons is stand-alone stable by definition*. Stand-alone stability for other coalition structures has to be checked using specific functions. For instance, for payoff function (6.2) it is easily checked that all coalition structures where no coalition comprises more than three coalition members is stand-alone stable.

Definition 4: Pareto-optimal Coalition Structures (PO)
A coalition structure c is Pareto-optimal if there is no other coalition structure c′ where at least one player is better off and no player is worse off, that is, $\forall\, c' \neq c$ *with* $\pi_i(c_i', c') > \pi_i(c_i, c)$ *for some* $i\; \exists j \in I: \pi_j(c_j', c') < \pi_j(c_j, c)$.

Definition 4 implies that there is no other coalition structure c' which weakly Pareto-dominates c. Unfortunately, not very much more beyond Definition 4 can be said about PO at a general level. What can be said is summarized in Proposition 6.

Proposition 6: Pareto-optimal Coalition Structures (PO)

(a) *The grand coalition is a PO.*
(b) *Symmetric coalition structures of the form* $c=(c_1, \ldots, c_1)$ *(including the singleton coalition structure) can never be a PO.*

Proof:

(a) Follows from the fact that the grand coalition generates the highest global welfare.
(b) Since $N \cdot \pi_i(N) > N \cdot \pi_1(c_1, c)$, the coalition structure $c=(c_1, \ldots, c_1)$ is Pareto-dominated by the grand coalition (**Q.E.D.**).

In the case of orthogonal reaction functions an exact characterization of PO is possible.

Proposition 7: Pareto-optimal Coalition Structures for Orthogonal Reaction Functions
For payoff functions implying orthogonal reaction functions, the set of PO, $C^{PO}(N)$*, is given by* $C^{PO}(N) = (N) \cup \{c=(c_1, \ldots, c_M) \mid M \geq 2,\ c_1 \geq \ldots \geq c_M,\ (c_1, \ldots, c_M) \setminus c_j \in C^{PO}(N-c_j)\, \forall j \in \{1, \ldots, M\}, \pi_i(c_M, c) > \pi_i(N, (N))\}$.

Table 6.1 Pareto-optimal coalition structures for payoff function (6.2)

N	Pareto-Optima	N	Pareto-Optima
1	(1)	7	(7), (6, 1), (5, 2)
2	(2)	8	(8), (7, 1), (6, 2)
3	(3)	9	(9), (8, 1), (7, 2)
4	(4), (3, 1)	10	(10), (9, 1), (8, 2), (7, 3)
5	(5), (4, 1)	11	(11), (10, 1), (9, 2), (8, 3)
6	(6), (5, 1)	12	(12), (11, 1), (10, 2), (9, 3), (8, 3, 1)

Proof: Follows from the following facts:

(a) $(N) \in C^{PO}(N)$ by Proposition 6.
(b) $c \in C^{PO}(N) \Rightarrow \tilde{c} \in C^{PO}(\Sigma \tilde{c}_i) \forall \tilde{c} \subset c$.
(c) If $c \in (N) \cup \{c = (c_1, \ldots, c_M) \mid M \geq 2, c_1 \geq \ldots \geq c_M, (c_1, \ldots, c_M) \backslash c_j \in C^{PO}(N - c_j) \forall j \in \{1, \ldots, M\}, \pi_i(c_M, c) > \pi_i(N, (N))\}$, then the smallest coalition has no incentive to form the grand coalition,[12] and no other coalition has an incentive to participate in forming any other coalition structure since each sub-coalition structure is a *PO* itself (**Q.E.D.**).

An implication of Proposition 7 is summarized in the following corollary:

Corollary 2: Non-Pareto-optimal Coalition Structures for Orthogonal Reaction Functions
Assume orthogonal reaction functions. Any coalition structure comprising at least two coalitions of equal size cannot be a PO and is Pareto-dominated by coalition structures where coalitions of equal size merge.

Proof: Since emissions of outsiders not involved in a merge of two coalitions of equal size, $c_i = c_j$, do not change through a merger, $\max \Sigma_{i \in ci \cup cj} \pi_i > \max \Sigma_{i \in ci} \pi_i + \max \Sigma_{j \in cj} \pi_j$ holds by symmetry. Outsiders benefit from a merger by C_{2a} (**Q.E.D.**).

Proposition 7 is illustrated for payoff function (6.2) and $N \in \{1, \ldots, 12\}$ in Table 6.1.

Table 6.1 stresses that Proposition 7 implies that $C^{PO}(N)$ are computed recursively. For instance, for $N=6$, $C^{PO}(N) = \{(6), (5, 1)\}$. (6) is the grand coalition. (5, 1) is a *PO* since $(5, 1)\backslash\{5\} = (1)$ is a *PO* (see $N=1$), $(5, 1)\backslash\{1\} = (5)$ (see $N=5$) is a *PO* and $\pi_i(1, (5, 1)) > \pi_i(6, (6))$. It is also evident that *PO* cannot comprise many small coalitions since such inefficient coalition structures would be Pareto-dominated by coalition structures with larger coalitions. For instance, (..., 3, 2, ...) is Pareto-dominated by (..., 5, ...).

3. EQUILIBRIUM COALITION STRUCTURES

3.1 Preliminaries

In order to avoid knife-edge equilibria and to be consistent with our definition of PO, we make the following assumption that we suppose to hold in the remainder:[13]

Assumption 3: Indifference of Payoffs
If players are indifferent between being a member of a smaller or larger coalition, they join the larger coalition.

In order to determine equilibrium coalition structure(s) from equilibrium valuations, we have to describe the rules of coalition formation and the equilibrium concept. Whereas the rules will be described under each *coalition game*, we introduce the *equilibrium concepts* in this subsection. Since for the α- and β-stability the rules of the coalition formation process are contained in the equilibrium concept, the definition of the equilibrium concept will not be treated separately and is postponed until later (subsection 3.6). For the other coalition games we use the concepts of Nash equilibrium (Nash, 1950), strong Nash equilibrium (Aumann, 1959) and coalition-proof Nash equilibrium (Bernheim, Peleg and Whinston, 1987) to determine equilibrium coalition structures (see, for example, Bloch, 1997). In the context of coalition formation games, we define these equilibrium concepts as follows:

Definition 5: Nash and Strong Nash Equilibrium Coalition Structure (NE and SNE)
Let $G = \{I, \Sigma = \{\Sigma_i\}_{i \in I}, \pi(c(\sigma)) = \pi_i(c_i, c)\}_{i \in I}\}$ *be the first stage of the coalition formation game with countries* $i \in I$*, strategy vectors* $\sigma \in \Sigma$ *(proposals for coalitions), resulting coalition structures c and vectors of payoff functions* π*. Further, let* $\tilde{C}(c^S, \sigma)$ *be the set of coalition structures that a subgroup of countries* c^S *can induce if the remaining countries* $j \in I \backslash c^S$ *play* σ_j*. For a fixed strategy vector* σ *define the reduced game for subgroup* c^S *as* $G_\sigma^s = \{c^S, \{\Sigma_i\}_{i \in c^S}, \{\pi_i(\tilde{c}_i, \tilde{C}(c^S, \sigma)\}_{i \in c^S}\}$*. Then* σ^* *is called a Nash equilibrium (strong Nash equilibrium) with the resulting Nash equilibrium (strong Nash equilibrium) coalition structure (NE and SNE)* c^* *if no singleton* $c^S = \{i\}$ *(no subgroup* c^S*) can increase his (at least one member's) payoff (without reduc-*

ing the payoff of any other member) by inducing another coalition structure. That is:

$$c^*(\sigma^*) \text{ is an NE if } \forall i \in I \text{ and } \forall \tilde{c} \in \tilde{C}(\{i\},\sigma^*)\text{: } \pi_i(c_i, c^*) \geq \pi_i(\tilde{c}_i, \tilde{c}),$$

$c^*(\sigma^*)$ is an SNE if no subcoalition $c^S \subset I$ can induce a coalition structure $\tilde{c} \in \tilde{C}(c^S, \sigma^*)$ with $\pi_i(c_i, c^*) \leq \pi_i(\tilde{c}_i, \tilde{c})$ $\forall i \in c^S$ and $\pi_i(c_i, c^*) < \pi_i(\tilde{c}_i, \tilde{c})$ for at least one $i \in c^S$.[14]

Definition 6: Coalition-Proof Nash Equilibrium Coalition Structure (CPNE)
For $I = \{1\}$ σ_i is a coalition-proof Nash equilibrium if, and only if, it is a Nash equilibrium. Assume that $|I| = n > 1$ and that coalition-proof Nash equilibrium coalition structures have been defined for all $m < n$. Then:

- *σ is self-enforcing if, and only if, for all $c^S \subset I$, $c^S \neq I$, σ_{c^S} is a coalition-proof Nash equilibrium of G^s_{σ}.*
- *σ^* is a coalition-proof Nash equilibrium of G with the coalition-proof coalition structure (CPNE) c^* if, and only if, it is self-enforcing and there does not exist another self-enforcing strategy σ' such that $\pi_i(c_i(\sigma'), c(\sigma')) \geq \pi_i(c_i^*, c^*)$ $\forall i \in I$ and $\pi_i(c_i(\sigma'), c(\sigma')) > \pi_i(c_i^*, c^*)$ for at least one i.*[15]

Whereas an NE requires that a coalition structure is immune to deviations by single countries, an SNE also requires that deviations of any subgroup of countries are not beneficial to the deviators. Thus, the set of SNE is a subset of NE, that is, $C^{SNE} \subset C^{NE}$. Moreover, a *necessary* condition for an SNE is that it is a Pareto-optimal coalition structure, that is, $C^{SNE} \subset C^{PO}$. That is, an NE should not be weakly Pareto-dominated by another NE. However, one has to be aware that, generally, not every weakly Pareto-undominated NE is an SNE, that is, $C^{PO} \not\subset C^{SNE}$.

In contrast to an SNE, an CPNE must only be immune to deviations which are self-enforcing and hence $C^{SNE} \subset C^{CPNE}$. Since coalition-proofness considers self-enforcing deviations of subgroups of countries, the special case of single deviations is also captured and hence $C^{CPNE} \subset C^{NE}$. Thus, we have $C^{SNE} \subset C^{CPNE} \subset C^{NE}$.

The advantage of the NE-concept lies in its simplicity, though in the context of coalition formation it seems natural to consider also multiple deviations. The advantage of the SNE over the CPNE-concept is that it is usually easier to determine equilibrium coalition structures for the former than for the latter concept. However, the SNE-concept does not impose any consistency requirement on deviations. A deviation is deemed feasible even though this deviation may be subject to further deviations. In contrast, coalition-proofness rules out such non-credible deviations. A coalition structure can only be challenged by self-enforcing deviations. Moreover, one may wonder whether requiring a coalition structure to be Pareto-efficient with respect to the entire set of coalition structures is not an unduly restrictive condition. It is this condition which implies that in some coalition games (see sections 3.2 to 3.4), as in many other games of economic interest, no SNE exists.

3.2 Open Membership Single Coalition Game

As mentioned in the Introduction, the concept of internal&external stability has been widely applied in the environmental economics literature. Its roots go back to d'Aspermont et al. (1983) who used this concept to study cartel formation in a Cournot-oligopoly. We study this concept for reference reasons, though it restricts the number of non-trivial coalitions to one. That is, it is exogenously assumed that there is one group of countries (signatories) which form a coalition and that all other countries (non-signatories) play as singletons.

Definition 7: Internal and External Stability
Denote the non-trivial equilibrium coalition of signatories by c_C, $i \in c_C$, *non-signatories by* $j \notin c_C$ *and let the coalition structure be given by* $c = (c_C, 1, \ldots, 1)$.

1. *Internal Stability: There is no incentive for a signatory to leave the coalition. That is,* $\pi_i(c_C, c) - \pi_i(1, c') \geq 0 \; \forall i \in c_C$ *where* $c' = c \backslash c_C \cup \{c_C - 1, 1\}$.
2. *External Stability: There is no incentive for a non-signatory to join the coalition. That is,* $\pi_j(c_C \cup \{j\}, c'') - \pi_j(1, c) < 0 \; \forall j \notin c_C$ *where* $c'' = c \backslash \{c_C, 1\} \cup \{c_C + 1\}$.[16]

From Definition 7 it is evident that internal stability corresponds to the definition of stand-alone stability (Definition 3). The definition of external stability implies *de facto* an open membership rule. That is, non-signatories may accede to the coalition if this is beneficial for them. It is also apparent that only single deviations are considered when determining an equilibrium. That is, an internally and externally stable coalition structure is *de facto* an NE. Thus, internal&external stability may be interpreted as an NE in a single coalition game with an open membership rule. In order to base the subsequent results on a more general footing, we therefore define an open membership single coalition game.

Definition 8: Open Membership Single Coalition Game (OMSCG)
Let the strategy set of country i be given by $\Sigma_i^m = \{c, 1\}$, *a particular strategy of country i be the message* σ_i^m *and* c_i *the coalition to which i finally belongs,* $i = 1, ..., N$, *then:*

$$c_i = \begin{cases} \{i\} \text{ if } \sigma_i^m = 1 \\ \{j / \sigma_j^m = c\} \text{ if } \sigma_i^m = c \end{cases}.$$

Thus, this game is a simple announcement game with only two options. Hence, it is straightforward to state the following result:

Proposition 8: Equilibrium Coalition Structures in the OMSCG
In the open membership single coalition game a coalition structure must be stand-alone stable to be an equilibrium.

Let $c^* = (c_C^*, 1, ..., 1)$ *denote the coarsest coalition structure that is stand-alone stable, then:*

(a) *there exists an NE coalition structure.*
(b) c^* *is the most concentrated NE.*
(c) c^* *and the singleton coalition structure (if* $c_C \neq 1$*) are the only NE if* $c = (c_C, 1, ..., 1)$ *is stand-alone stable for all* $c_C < c_C^*$.
(d) c^* *is the unique CPNE under condition* C_{2a}.
(e) *Suppose* $c_C^* << N$ *so that* c^* *is not a PO, then there is no SNE.*

Proof: The general statement follows from the fact that a country can always leave a coalition by announcing a singleton address. Thus, a necessary condition for a coalition structure to be an equilibrium is stand-alone stability.

(a) If all countries announce the singleton coalition structure, this is a NE and no country can unilaterally form a coalition.
(b) If a member of the coalition changes its message, this country becomes a singleton, which is not profitable by the assumption that c^* is stand-alone stable. If a singleton joins the coalition, stand-alone stability is violated by assumption.
(c) Since all coalition structures $c = (c_C, 1, ..., 1)$, $c_C < c_C^*$, are stand-alone stable by assumption, there is an incentive for a singleton to announce $\sigma_i^m = c$ under Assumption 3 and $c = (c_C, 1, ..., 1)$ cannot be an NE. However, c^* is an NE as shown in (b) above. Moreover, the singleton coalition structure is always an NE as argued under (a) above.
(d) Any deviation of a country or group of countries to form a coarser coalition structure than c^* cannot be a CPNE since stand-alone

stability would be violated by assumption. In any coalition structure c, which is less coarse than c^* singletons have an incentive to announce $\sigma_i^m = c$ instead of $\sigma_i^m = 1$ so that c^* forms since $\pi_i(c_C^*, (c_C^*, 1, ..., 1)) \geq \pi_i(1,(c_C^* - 1, 1, ..., 1)) \geq \pi_i(1,(c_C, 1, ..., 1)) \forall c_C < c_C^*$ holds where the first inequality follows from the stand-alone stability assumption and the second inequality from condition C_{2a}.

(e) If c^* is not a PO, no SNE exists since $C^{SNE} \subset C^{PO}$ (**Q.E.D.**).

According to Proposition 8, the CPNE in the OMSCG is easily derived by computing the largest coalition c_C^* that is stand-alone stable. The check whether coalition structure $c^* = (c_C^*, 1, ..., 1)$ is an SNE too is usually straightforward: comparing the payoffs of the singleton coalitions in c^* with the grand coalition it usually turns out that for N sufficiently large c^* is Pareto-dominated by the grand coalition and therefore no SNE exists. For instance for payoff function (6.2), $c^* = (3, 1, ..., 1)$ is the unique CPNE. As long as $N > 4$, c^* is not a PO and therefore no SNE exists (see Table 6.2 in section 4). Finally, note that there is no exact one-to-one correspondence between an NE in the OMSCG and internal&external stability. As long as $c_C^* > 1$, the singleton coalition structure is not externally stable. However, for practical purposes and the subsequent comparisons, this difference is not important.

3.3 Open Membership Multiple Coalition Game

In the open membership game of Yi and Shin (1995), which we call open membership multiple coalition game (OMMCG) for our purposes, countries can freely form coalitions as long as no outsider is excluded from joining a coalition. Countries choose their membership by simultaneously announcing a message (or in the diction of Yi and Shin they 'announce an address'). Countries that have announced the same message form a coalition. For instance, if $N = 4$ and $\sigma_1^m = \sigma_2^m = \sigma_3^m = 1$ and $\sigma_4^m = 2$, then $c = \{\{1, 2, 3\}, \{4\}\}$ forms. If country 3 changes its message to $\sigma_3^m = 2$, then $c = \{\{1, 2\}, \{3, 4\}\}$ forms.

Definition 9: Open Membership Multiple Coalition Game (OMMCG)
Let the strategy set of country i be given by $\Sigma_i^m = \{1, ..., N\}$, a particular strategy of country i be the message σ_i^m and c_i the coalition to which i finally belongs, $i = 1, ..., N$, then $c_i = \{i\} \cup \{j / \sigma_i^m = \sigma_j^m\}$.

As in the single coalition game, a basic prerequisite for a coalition structure to qualify as an NE is that a coalition structure is stand-alone stable since a country can always leave a coalition by announcing a singleton address.

For instance, this implies for payoff function (6.2) that only coalitions structures $c=(c_1, ..., c_M)$ with $3 \geq c_1 \geq ... \geq c_M$ can be an NE. Suppose $N=4$, then $c^1=(3, 1)$, $c^2=(2, 2)$, $c^3=(2, 1, 1)$ and $c^4=(1, 1, 1, 1)$ are *potential* NE. However, coalition structure c^1 cannot be an NE since a country belonging to the coalition comprising three countries has an incentive to announce the same address as (to join) the singleton country (due to C_4). Though the singleton prefers to remain a singleton (due to C_3), it cannot deny the accession under the open membership rule. Coalition structures c^3 and c^4 cannot be NE since, given the announcements of the other countries, a singleton has an incentive to announce the same address as another singleton (due to stand-alone stability of coarser coalition structures). Coalition structure c^2 is an NE since no country in a coalition comprising two countries has an incentive to become a singleton or to be a member of a coalition comprising three countries due to C_4. Due to $C^{CPNE} \subset C^{NE}$, coalition structure c^2 is the only candidate to qualify as a potential CPNE. It is easily checked that the only coalition structure that could challenge c^2 is the grand coalition, which requires that two or four countries deviate. However, since the grand coalition is subject to further deviations, which are not in the interest of any initial deviator, $C^{CPNE}=c^2=(2, 2)$. Since $c^2 \notin C^{PO}(4)$, there is no SNE.

Due to the simple structure of the game, one can derive quite general results (Yi, 1997; Yi and Shin, 2000).

Proposition 9: Equilibrium Coalition Structures in the OMMCG
In the open membership multiple coalition game a coalition structure must be stand-alone stable to be an equilibrium coalition structure.

Suppose that $c^*=(c_1^*, ..., c_{M_1^*}^*, c_{M_1^*+1}^*, ..., c_{M^*}^*)$ *(or* $c^*=c_1^*, ..., c_{M_1^*}^*)$*) is a stand-alone stable coalition structure with* $(c_1^*=...=c_{M_1^*}^*$ *and* $c_{M_1^*+1}^*=...=c_{M^*}^*=c_1^*-1$*. Further suppose that each coalition structure* $c=(c_1, ..., c_{M_1}, c_{M_1+1}, ..., c_M)$ *with* $M<M^*$, $c_1=...=c_{M_1}$ *and* $c_{M_1+1}=...=c_M=c_1-1$ *is not stand-alone stable, then:*

(a) *There exists an NE coalition structure under condition* C_4.
(b) c^* *is the most concentrated NE coalition structure under condition* C_4.
(c) c^* *is the unique CPNE coalition structure under conditions* C_1 *to* C_4.
(d) *Suppose* $c_1^*=...=c_{M_1^*}^*<<N$ *so that* c^* *is not a PO, then there is no SNE.*

Proof: See Yi (1997) and Yi and Shin (2000) for (a) to (c). (d) See the proof of Proposition 8e (**Q.E.D.**).

The intuition of Proposition 9 is easy to grasp.

(a) Since the singleton coalition structure is stand-alone stable by definition, there will be at least one NE where C_4 ensures that there will be no cyclical deviation patterns.
(b) c^* implies a rather symmetric coalition structure (see Table 6.2, section 4). This is due to two facts. First, a coalition structure must be stand-alone stable. Thus, if the size of the largest stand-alone stable coalition structure is substantially smaller than N, there will be several coalitions. Second, due to condition C_4, $c_1 > c_M + 1$ $(c = (c_1, ..., c_M)$, $c_1 \geq ... \geq c_M)$ can never be an equilibrium since a country of a bigger coalition would have an incentive to join a smaller coalition. By construction, c^* is the most concentrated stand-alone stable coalition structure satisfying $c_1 \leq c_M + 1$. Now consider single deviations:
    (i) A country becomes a singleton, which is not beneficial by the stand-alone property.
    (ii) A member of one of the $c_1^*, ..., c_{M_1^*}^*$ coalitions joins one of the $c_{M_1^*+1}^*, ..., c_{M^*}^*$ coalitions, which by symmetry does not change its payoff.
    (iii) A member of one of the $c_{M_1^*+1}^*, ..., c_{M^*}^*$ coalitions joins one of the $c_1^*, ..., c_{M_1^*}^*$ coalitions, but then $c_1 \leq c_M + 1$ is violated.
(c) This part of Proposition 9 is more difficult to grasp. In the case of deviations, which result in more concentrated coalition structures, it is evident that this is not feasible since the stand-alone stability condition would be violated. In the case of deviations which result in less concentrated coalition structures, it can be shown that this implies a welfare loss to countries involved in the deviation.

Table 6.2 in section 4 illustrates equilibrium coalition structures for payoff function (6.2) and $N \in \{2, ..., 12\}$. It is evident that the CPNE in the OMMCG imply a relatively symmetric coalition structure with small coalitions.

3.4 Exclusive Membership Multiple Coalition Δ-Game

In the Δ-game of Hart and Kurz (1983), which we call exclusive membership multiple coalition Δ-game (EMMCΔG) for our purposes, countries simultaneously announce a list of countries with which they would like to form a coalition. Those countries that mutually list each other will form a coalition. For instance, suppose $N=4$ and $\sigma_1^\ell = \{1, 2, 3\}$, $\sigma_2^\ell = \{1, 2, 3\}$, $\sigma_3^\ell = \{3\}$, and $\sigma_4^\ell = \{3, 4\}$, then $c = \{\{1, 2\}, \{3\}, \{4\}\}$ forms. Countries 1 and 2 have each other on their list and therefore form a coalition. Countries 3 and 4 remain singletons. Though country 4 and also countries 1 and 2 would like to form a coalition with country 3, country 3 can remain a singleton since membership is exclusive. In other words, *a coalition only forms by unanimous agreement*. More formally, we have:

Definition 10: Exclusive Membership Multiple Coalition Δ-Game (EMMCΔG)
Let the strategy set of country i be given by $\Sigma_i^\ell = \{c_i \subset I / i \in c_i\}$*, a particular strategy of country i be a list of countries with which it wants to form a coalition* σ_i^ℓ *and* c_i *the coalition to which i finally belongs,* $i=1, \ldots, N$*, then* $c_i = \{i\} \cup \{j / \sigma_i^\ell = \sigma_j^\ell\}$.

For instance, consider our previous example $N=4$ and payoff function (6.2). In the OMMCG coalition structure, $c^1=(3, 1)$ was not an NE since a member of the bigger coalition likes to join the singleton coalition by C_4, and the singleton cannot deny access. In contrast, in the EMMCΔG, $c^1=(3, 1)$ is an NE since the singleton prefers to stay alone because of $\pi_i(1, (3, 1)) > \pi_i(2, (2, 2))$ due to C_3.

Also in the EMMCΔG a basic prerequisite for a stable coalition structure is stand-alone stability: a country can always announce a list including only itself which is beneficial if a coalition structure is not stand-alone stable. Moreover, by construction, for every SAS c there exists a set of announcements that supports c as an NE. Suppose each country announces a list with only those countries on it that actually form the coalition; then no country can join another coalition by an individual deviation. The only feasible deviation is to form a singleton coalition that is not beneficial if a coalition structure is stand-alone stable. Since the set of SAS is usually large, the equilibrium refinements CPNE and SNE are particularly useful in this coalition game.

For instance, consider our previous example assuming payoff function (6.2) and $N=4$. Then $c^1=(3, 1)$, $c^2=(2, 2)$, $c^3=(2, 1, 1)$ and $c^4=(1, 1, 1, 1)$ are SAS and NE. However, c^3 and c^4 are not a CPNE since singletons have an incentive to merge. c^1 is a CPNE since the singleton has no incentive to join the larger coalition (since the grand coalition is not stand-alone stable) and the members of the coalition comprising three countries can neither enforce the grand coalition nor have they an incentive to form smaller coalitions. Similar arguments establish that c^2 is also a CPNE. Since c^1 is the only stand-alone stable PO and, as shown above, no subgroup of countries has an incentive to jointly deviate, c^1 is the only SNE. More generally, we find (Yi and Shin 2000):

Proposition 10: Equilibrium Coalition Structures in the EMMCΔG
In the exclusive membership multiple coalition Δ-game the set of NE is non-empty and equal to the set of stand-alone stable coalition structures.

Suppose that $c^* = (c_1^*, ..., c_{M^*-1}^*, c_{M^*}^*)$ is a stand-alone stable coalition structure with $c_1^* = ... = c_{M^*-1}^* \geq c_{M^*}^*$. Further suppose that any coalition structure c for which $c_1 > c_1^*$ is not stand-alone stable, then:

(a) *c^* is the most concentrated NE.*
(b) *c^* is the most concentrated CPNE under conditions C_1 to C_3.*
(c) *If there is any other CPNE it comprises exactly M^* coalitions and is less concentrated than c^* under conditions C_1 to C_3.*
(d) *If $c_1^* \leq c_M^* + 1$, then c^* is the unique coalition-proof Nash equilibrium coalition structure under conditions C_1 to C_3.*
(e) *Suppose $c_1^* = ... = c_{M^*-1}^* << N$ so that c^* is not a PO, then there is no SNE.*

Proof: See Yi and Shin (2000) for the general statement and (a) to (d). (e) See the proof of Proposition 8e (**Q.E.D.**).

The intuition behind the proof of Proposition 10 is the following:

(a) First, coalition structure c^* is stand-alone stable by assumption and therefore an NE. Second, by the construction of c^*, this is the most concentrated coalition structure with M^* coalitions and the largest coalition of size c_1^*. Consequently, any other coalition structure will either be less concentrated or will include a coalition of size larger than c_1^*, which by assumption is not stand-alone stable.
(b) c^* is also a CPNE since any deviation that creates a bigger coalition is not stand-alone stable and any coalition that creates less concentrated coalition structures is not profitable by Assumption 3 and conditions C_1 to C_3. Since $C^{\text{CPNE}} \subset C^{\text{NE}}$, c^* is also the most concentrated CPNE.
(c) First, if there was another CPNE coalition structure c, c cannot comprise less than M^* coalitions, since then stand-alone stability would be violated. Second, c cannot comprise more than M^* coalitions because each country could benefit from a joint deviation to c^* if the members of the smallest coalitions in c join the smallest coalition in c^* and so on.
(d) If $c_1^* \leq c_{M^*}^* + 1$, then c^* is the unique coalition structure with M^* coalitions and with the size of the largest coalition equal to c_1^*.

Proposition 10 is illustrated in Table 6.2 in section 4 for payoff function (6.2) and $N \in \{2, ..., 12\}$. It is apparent that the CPNE in the EMMCΔG imply small coalitions and relatively symmetric coalition structures, though they may be more concentrated than the CPNE in the OMMCG.

3.5 Exclusive Membership Multiple Coalition Γ-Game

The exclusive membership multiple coalition Γ-game (EMMCΓG) goes back to von Neumann and Morgenstern (1944) and has been reintroduced by Hart and Kurz (1983) under the name Γ-game. This game is very similar to the previous game. That is, each country simultaneously announces a list of coalition members with which it would like to form a coalition. The only, though important, difference is that a coalition only forms if, and only if, there is unanimous agreement among all prospective members of a coalition to form exactly this coalition. For instance, suppose our previous example $N=4$ and $\sigma_1^\ell=\{1, 2, 3\}$, $\sigma_2^\ell=\{1, 2, 3\}$, $\sigma_3^\ell=\{3\}$ and $\sigma_4^\ell=\{3, 4\}$, then, in contrast to the EMMCΔG, where $c=\{\{1, 2\}, \{3\}, \{4\}\}$ formed, we have now $c=\{\{1\}, \{2\}, \{3\}, \{4\}\}$. This implies that if a subgroup or subgroups of countries jointly deviate, then the coalitions to which they belonged will break apart. Because of this strong assumption, the amount of NE is usually very large and very concentrated coalition structures can be supported as equilibria. More formally, we define:

Definition 11: Exclusive Membership Multiple Coalition Γ-Game (EMMCΓG)
Let the strategy set of country i be given by $\Sigma_i^\ell=\{c_i\subset I / i\in c_i\}$, *a particular strategy of country i be a list of countries with which it wants to form a coalition* σ_i^ℓ *and* c_i *the coalition to which i finally belongs,* $i=1, \ldots, N$, *then* $c_i=\sigma_i^\ell$ *if, and only if,* $\sigma_i^\ell=\sigma_j^\ell\,\forall j\in\sigma_i^\ell$, *otherwise* $c_i=\{i\}$.

For instance, consider our previous example of payoff function (6.2) and $N=4$. All coalition structures $c^1=(3, 1)$, $c^2=(2, 2)$, $c^3=(2, 1, 1)$, $c^4=(1, 1, 1, 1)$ and $c^5=(4)$ are NE. The grand coalition is an NE since $\pi_i(4)>\pi_i(1, (1, 1, 1, 1))$. For the other coalition structures, it is easily checked that no country has an incentive to leave its coalition. The grand coalition is also an SNE since a deviation by a subgroup of countries does not pay. The resulting coalition structure would be less concentrated and the deviators would be members of the largest coalition, which does not pay by C_1. $c^1=(3, 1)$ is also an SNE, since the singleton has neither an incentive to form the grand coalition nor to form a coalition with any other subgroup of countries. For the members of the coalition comprising three countries, the same arguments apply as in the case of the grand coalition. Coalition structures c^2, c^3 and c^4 cannot be SNE since they are not PO. From $C^{SNE}\subset C^{CPNE}$, it follows that c^1 and c^5 are also CPNE. Since c^2, c^3 and c^4

are strictly Pareto-dominated by the grand coalition, which itself is a CPNE, no other coalition structure except c^1 and c^5 can be a CPNE.

Proposition 11: Equilibrium Coalition Structures in the EMMCΓG

(a) *There are at least two NE of which the grand coalition is the most concentrated (coarsest) one.*
(b) *All stand-alone stable coalition structures are NE under condition C_{2a}.*
(c) *All coalition structures are an NE for orthogonal reaction functions.*
(d) *The grand coalition is a CPNE and an SNE under condition C_1.*
(e) *The set of CPNE is equal to the set of SNE coalition structures and comprises the set of Pareto-optimal coalition structures under condition C_1 and orthogonal reaction functions.*

Proof:

(a) In the EMMCΓG a coalition only forms if all coalition members announce the same list of coalition members. If one member announces a different list, this implies *de facto* that the coalition breaks apart. Thus, the singleton coalition structure is a Nash equilibrium by definition and the grand coalition because of $\pi_i(N)>\pi_i(1, (1, ..., 1))$.
(b) Suppose a coalition structure c is stand-alone stable, then $\forall i$ $\pi_i(c_i, c)\geq\pi_i(1, c')\geq\pi_i(1, c'')$ holds where $c'=c\backslash\{c_i\}\cup\{c_i-1, 1\}$ and $c''=c\backslash\{c_i\}\cup\{1, ..., 1\}$. The first inequality sign follows from stand-alone stability, the second from condition C_{2a}. Consequently, $\forall i$ $\pi_i(c_i, c)\geq\pi_i(1, c'')$ holds, which is the condition for an NE.
(c) A Nash equilibrium coalition structure must satisfy $\pi_i(c_i, c)\geq\pi_i(1, c')$ $\forall$ c_i with $c'=c\backslash c_i\cup\{1, ..., 1\}$, which holds for orthogonal reaction functions according to Corollary 2. (c_i is a PO for the members of c_i since emissions of $c\backslash\{c_i\}$ remain constant.)
(d) A deviation by a group of countries, say s, from the grand coalition leads to a coalition structure $c=(c_1, ..., c_M)$ with $c_1\geq...\geq c_M$ and $c_{M-(N-s)+1}=...=c_M=1$ if $s<N$. Since $N\pi_i(N, (N))>c_1\pi_i(c_1, c)+...+c_M\pi_j(c_M, c)$ and $\pi_i(c_1, c)\leq\pi_j(c_j, c)$ $\forall j=2, ..., M$ by C_1, the deviating countries that form c_1 are worse off. Since the grand coalition is a PO by Proposition 6, the grand coalition is a SNE and also a CPNE (due to $C^{\mathrm{SNE}}\subset C^{\mathrm{CPNE}}$).
(e) Suppose that there exists a coalition structure $c\in\mathrm{PO}$ that is not an SNE. Then there exists a set of deviating countries s that can improve the payoff of at least one member without negatively affecting the payoff of other members by deviation to the coalition structure c'.

Coalition structure c and c' may be written as $c=(c^s, \tilde{c})$ and $c'=(c^{s'}, \tilde{c})$ where c^s is the set of coalitions that have at least one deviating member. $c^{s'}$ comprises the coalitions of the deviators and singleton coalitions. Since the deviators receive at least the same payoff in c' as in c, the same must be true for the singletons due to C_1. Hence $c^s \notin PO(\Sigma c_i^s)$, which is a contradiction to the structure of PO for orthogonal reaction functions (see Proposition 7). Thus $PO \subset C^{SNE}$, and since $C^{SNE} \subset PO$ is known, $PO = C^{SNE}$ follows. Moreover, since $C^{SNE} \subset C^{CPNE}$ is known, $PO = C^{SNE} \subset C^{CPNE}$ holds. (Any coalition structure that is not a PO would be subject to a deviation by a group of countries to a PO that were valid, since all PO are CPNE.) **(Q.E.D.)**.

Proposition 12 is illustrated in Table 6.2 in section 4 for payoff function (6.2) and $N \in \{2, ..., 12\}$. It is apparent that SNE and CPNE in the EMMCΓG imply concentrated coalition structures.

3.6 α- and β-Stable Coalition Structures in Single and Multiple Coalition Games

In this subsection, we investigate α- and β-stable coalition structures ($C(\alpha)$ and $C(\beta)$) in the global emission game. These stability concepts constitute a modification of core-stability in the context of the partition function approach (Hart and Kurz, 1983). In order to highlight the similarity between concepts, we briefly recall the definition of the core in the context of the characteristic function. An imputation $\pi^* = (\pi_1^*, ..., \pi_N^*)$ is said to lie in the core if it cannot be blocked by any non-empty coalition. That is, $\Sigma_{i \in I^J} \pi_i^* \geq w(I^J)\ \forall\ I^J \subseteq I$ where $\Sigma_{i \in I^J} \pi_i^*$ follows from max $\Sigma_{i \in I^J} \pi_i$ and I^J is the set of coalition members. Whether an imputation lies in the core depends on the definition of the characteristic function $w(I^J)$. There are three definitions, α-, β- and γ-characteristic functions, which have been used in the context of IEAs. They correspond to the definition of the α-, β- and γ-core. The α-(β)-characteristic function implies that the blocking coalition plays a minimax (maximin) emission strategy. The γ-characteristic function implies that if a country or group of countries deviates, the remaining countries break up into singletons and play best-reply emission strategies in the sense of a Nash equilibrium. In the context of the partition function approach, emission strategies are fixed by assumption (second stage) and are Nash equilibrium strategies. Therefore, the implied behavioural assumption of the definition of α- and β-stability in Definition 12 in the context of the partition function corresponds to that of the γ-core in the context of the characteristic function. However, there remains one difference: in contrast to the definition of core stability in cooperative game theory, the definition of core stability in non-cooperative game theory does not restrict coalition formation to the grand coalition.

Definition 12: α- and β-stable Coalition Structures ($C(\alpha)$ and $C(\beta)$)[17]
A coalition structure c is α-stable if there does not exist a group of countries s and a partition c^s $(\Sigma c_i^s = s)$ *such that for all partitions* c^{N-s} *formed by external players* $\pi_i(c_i^s(c^s, c^{N-s}) \geq \pi_i(c_i, c)$ $\forall i \in s$ *and* $\exists j \in s: \pi_j(c_j^s(c^s, c^{N-s}) > \pi_j(c_j, c)$.

A coalition structure c is β-stable if there does not exist a group of countries s such that for all partitions c^{N-s} *of external countries there exists a partition* c^s *of s such that* $\pi_i(c_i^s(c^s, c^{N-s}) \geq \pi_i(c_i, c)$ $\forall i \in s$ *and* $\exists j \in s: \pi_j(c_j^s(c^s, c^{N-s}) > \pi_j(c_j, c)$.

α-stability implies a minimax strategy and β-stability a maximin strategy (in terms of membership!) of which the latter is known to be at least as strong as the former. Hence, generally, $C(\beta) \subset C(\alpha)$ holds (Kurz, 1988). However, in the context of the global emission game an even stronger result holds.

Proposition 12: Equivalence of $C(\alpha)$ and $C(\beta)$ in the Global Emission Game
A coalition structure c is α-stable if, and only if, it is β-stable under condition C_{2a}.

Proof: Country $i \in s$ receives the lowest payoff for $c^{N-s} = \{1, ..., 1\}$ (**Q.E.D.**).
Thus, we can redefine α- and β-stability in the context of a global emission game.

Proposition 13: Definition of α- and β-stable Coalition Structures in the Global Emission Game
A coalition structure c is α- and β-stable if, and only if, there does not exist a group of countries and a partition c^s $(\Sigma c_i^s = s)$ *such that* $\pi_i(c_i^s(c^s, 1, ..., 1)) \geq \pi_i(c_i, c)$ $\forall i \in s$ *and* $\exists j \in s: \pi_j(c_j^s(c^s, 1, ..., 1)) > \pi_j(c_j, c)$ *under condition* C_{2a}.

Proof: See the proof of Proposition 12 (**Q.E.D.**).
Before characterizing the α- and β-stable coalition structures in the global emission game, three remarks are in order.

1. A deviation from a coalition structure triggers the break-up of not only the coalition to which the deviators belonged, but of all coalitions.

Thus, punishment after a deviation is stronger than in the case of the EMMCΓG. This should lead to concentrated equilibrium coalition structures.

2. α-β-stability considers all kinds of deviations without imposing any consistency requirement on deviations. Thus, α-β-stability resembles an SNE in other coalition games.
3. Like internal&external stability, α-β-stability does not distinguish between the rules of coalition formation and the equilibrium concept. However, different from internal&external stability, it is not that straightforward to figure out the rules of coalition formation of α-β-stability. The only rule that is obvious is that multiple coalitions can form. Therefore, we interpret α-β-stability in the following as the equilibrium concept and call the game (without rules) itself just a multiple coalition game.

Proposition 14: α- and β-stable Coalition Structures in the Multiple Coalition Game

(a) *The grand coalition is* α-β-*stable under condition* C_1.
(b) *Suppose a coalition structure c is* α-β-*stable, then c is a PO.*
(c) *Suppose a coalition structure is a PO, then it is* α-β-*stable under condition* C_1 *and orthogonal reaction functions.*

Proof:

(a) The grand coalition generates the highest global welfare and $\pi_i(c_i^s, (c^s, 1, ..., 1)) \leq \pi_j(1, (c^s, 1, ..., 1))$ holds by C_1.
(b) Assume $c \notin \text{PO}$. Then there exists a coalition structure c' which Pareto-dominates c. Hence, there exists a subgroup of countries s, namely $s = N$ such that $\pi_i(c'_i, c') \geq \pi_i(c_i, c)$ $\forall i \in s$ and $\exists j \in s : \pi_j(c'_j, c')) > \pi_j(c_j, c)$. Hence, c is not α-β-stable.
(c) Suppose that there exists a coalition structure $c \notin \text{PO}$ that is not α-β-stable. Then there exists a set of deviating countries s that can improve the payoff of at least one member without negatively affecting the payoff of other members by deviation to the coalition structure c''. Coalition structure c and c'' may be written as $c = (c^s, \tilde{c})$ and $c'' = (c^{s'}, 1, ..., 1)$ where c^s is the set of coalitions that has at least one deviating member. $c^{s'}$ comprises the coalitions of the deviators and singleton coalitions. Further consider coalition structure $c' = (c^{s'}, \tilde{c})$ where only those countries which have deviating members in their former coalition split up into singletons. Since the deviators receive at least the same payoff in c'' as in c, the same must be true for the singletons,

which stem from c^s due to C_1. Also in c', all countries receive at least the payoff as in c. Hence, $c^s \notin \mathrm{PO}(\Sigma c_i^s)$, which is a contradiction to the structure of *PO* for orthogonal reaction functions (see Proposition 7) (**Q.E.D.**).

In order to allow for a robust comparison of the traditional concepts internal&external and core-stability used in the analysis of stability of IEAs, we also determine α- and β-stable coalition structures in a single coalition game. In order to save space (and since a definition is straightforward), we refrain from providing a formal definition and turn directly to the results, which we summarize such that they allow for a direct comparison with equilibrium coalition structures in the OMSCG in section 4.

Proposition 15: $C(\alpha, \beta)$ in the Single Coalition Game
Suppose that only coalition structures of the form $c=(c_1, c')$ where $c'=c \backslash c_1 \cup \{1, ..., 1\}$ or $c'=\varnothing$ are feasible. Further denote an α-β-stable coalition structure by $c^*=(c_1^*, 1, ..., 1)$ and the largest stand-alone stable coalition structure by $c=(c_C, 1, ..., 1)$, then:

(a) *The grand coalition is α-β-stable under condition C_1.*
(b) *If there are other α-β-stable coalition structures apart from the grand coalition, then $c_1^* \geq c_C$ under conditions C_1 and C_{2a}.*

Proof:

(a) The assumption of a single coalition structure poses no restriction in the case of the grand coalition and the proof of Proposition 14a applies.
(b) i) Suppose $c=(c_C, 1, ..., 1)$ is Pareto-dominated by the grand coalition. Then any finer coalition structure will also be Pareto-dominated by the grand coalition by C_1 and C_{2a}. Hence c and any other finer coalition structure than c cannot be α-β-stable by Proposition 15a.
  ii) Suppose $c=(c_C, 1, ..., 1)$ is not Pareto-dominated by the grand coalition. Then c can be α-β-stable but Pareto-dominates any coalition structure which is finer than c and is not Pareto-dominated by any coarser coalition structure than c.

The first statement follows from $\pi_i(c_C, (c_C, 1, ..., 1)) \geq \pi_i(1, (c_C-1, 1, ..., 1)) \geq \pi_i(1, (c_1, 1, ..., 1)) \geq \pi_i(c_1, (c_1, 1, ..., 1)) \forall c_1 < c_C$ where the first inequality sign follows from stand-alone stability, the second from C_{2a}, and the third from C_1. For $c_1 > 1$ at least the third inequality is strict and for $c_1 = 1 < c_C - 1$ the second inequality is strict. For $c_1 = 1 = c_C - 1$, members of c_C are indifferent or better off by stand-alone stability and singletons are strictly better off if c_C instead of c_1 forms by C_{2a}. The second statement follows from $\pi_i(1, (c_C, 1, ..., 1)) > \pi_i(N, (N)) \geq \pi_i(c', (c', 1, ..., 1)) \forall c_C < c' < N$ where the first inequality follows by assumption and the second by C_1 and C_{2a} (**Q.E.D.**).

Propositions 14 and 15 are illustrated in Table 6.2 in section 4 for payoff function (6.2) and $N \in \{2, ..., 12\}$ from which it is evident that equilibrium coalition structures in the single and multiple coalition game are very concentrated.

4. COMPARISON AND EVALUATION OF EQUILIBRIUM COALITIONS

4.1 Introduction

In this section we compare and evaluate the equilibria under the different coalition games. An obvious criterion for a comparison is coarsening and concentration. From an ecological and welfare perspective it is also interesting to analyse how differences in equilibrium coalition structures translate into differences in global emissions and global welfare.

Proposition 16: The Effect of Coarsening and Concentration on Global Welfare and Global Emissions

Let coalition structure c′ be coarser than coalition structure c, then:

a) $\Sigma e_i(c') < \Sigma e_i(c)$*, and*

b) $\Sigma \pi_i(c') \geq \Sigma \pi_i(c)$ *for payoff functions implying orthogonal reaction functions.*

Let coalition structure c′ be more concentrated than coalition structure c, then:

c) $\Sigma e_i(c') \leq \Sigma e_i(c)$ *for payoff functions (6.2) to (6.5), and*

d) $\Sigma \pi_i(c') > \Sigma \pi_i(c)$ *for payoff function (6.2).*

Proof:

(a) See the proof of Proposition 2*a*.

(b) Countries that are not involved in a merger do not change their emissions. Thus, $\max \Sigma_{i \in c_i \cup c_j} \pi_i \geq \max \Sigma_{i \in c_i} \pi_i + \max \Sigma_{j \in c_j} \pi_j$.

(c) See the proof of Proposition 2*b*.
(d) See Appendix (**Q.E.D.**).

From Proposition 16 it is evident that a comparison of equilibrium coalition structures allows for rather general conclusions with respect to the ecological implications, those with respect to the welfare implications are more specific. Thus, despite the assumption of ex ante symmetric countries, if coalition structures can only be compared with respect to concentration, general conclusions are only possible for payoff function (6.2). For other payoff functions it might well be the case that a coalition structure c' is more concentrated than a coalition structure c and global welfare is higher under c than under c'. In fact, it is easily confirmed for payoff function (6.3) that if c' is only more concentrated but not coarser than c, then global welfare will always be higher under c than under c'. For payoff functions (6.4) and (6.5) a comparison depends on the specific coalition structures.

In order to illustrate the subsequent discussion, equilibrium coalition structures under the different coalition games are displayed in Table 6.2 for payoff function (6.2) and $N \in \{2, ..., 12\}$.

4.2 Single versus Multiple Coalitions

A vast amount of the literature analysing coalition formation of IEAs applied the concept of internal&external stability. In subsection 3.2 we argued that internal&external stability has two weaknesses, namely it considers only single deviations and exogenously restricts the number of non-trivial coalitions to one. We showed that the first weakness could be remedied by applying the concept of a coalition-proof Nash equilibrium (CPNE), and the second weakness by considering an open membership multiple coalition game (OMMCG). In this subsection we want to analyse how the second weakness affects coalition formation.

Proposition 17: Single versus Multiple Coalitions in Open Membership Games

Suppose that there is a stand-alone stable coalition structure (SAS) where $c_1 = c_C$, $c = (c_1, ..., c_M)$, and that any coalition structure where $c_1 > c_C$ is not stand-alone stable. Further suppose that N is large enough ($N > (c_C - 1)^2$)[18] *and that the most concentrated coalition structure consisting of coalitions c_C and 1 in the OMSCG and c_C and $c_C - 1$ in the OMMCG is stand-alone stable, then under the open-membership rule the unique CPNE in the OMMCG is coarser than the unique CPNE in the OMSCG under conditions C_1 to C_4.*

Table 6.2. Equilibrium coalition structures for payoff function (6.2)

N	OMSCG	OMMCG	EMMCΔG	EMMCΓG	C(α,β)-*SCG*	C(α,β)-*MCG*
2	*(2)*	*(2)*	*(2)*	*(2)*	*(2)*	*(2)*
3	*(3)*	*(3)*	*(3)*	*(3)*	*(3)*	*(3)*
4	*(3,1)*	(2,2)	*(3,1)*, (2,2)	*(4)*, *(3,1)*	*(4)*, *(3,1)*	*(4)*, *(3,1)*
5	(3,1,1)	(3,2)	(3,2)	*(5)*, *(4,1)*	*(5)*, *(4,1)*	*(5)*, *(4,1)*
6	(3,1,1,1)	(3,3)	(3,3)	*(6)*, *(5,1)*	*(6)*, *(5,1)*	*(6)*, *(5,1)*
7	(3,1,1,1,1)	(3,2,2)	(3,3,1), (3,2,2)	*(7)*, *(6,1)*, *(5,2)*	*(7)*, *(6,1)*, (5,1,1)	*(7)*, *(6,1)*, *(5,2)*
8	(3,1,1,1,1,1)	(3,3,2)	(3,3,2)	*(8)*, *(7,1)*, *(6,2)*	*(8)*, *(7,1)*, (6,1,1)	*(8)*, *(7,1)*, *(6,2)*
9	(3,1,1,1,1,1,1)	(3,3,3)	(3,3,3)	*(9)*, *(8,1)*, *(7,2)*	*(9)*, *(8,1)*, (7,1,1)	*(9)*, *(8,1)*, *(7,2)*
10	(3,1,1,1,1,1,1,1)	(3,3,2,2)	(3,3,3,1), (3,3,2,2)	*(10)*, *(9,1)*, *(8,2)*, *(7,3)*	*(10)*, *(9,1)*, (8,1,1), (7,1,1,1)	*(10)*, *(9,1)*, *(8,2)*, *(7,3)*
11	(3,1,1,1,1,1,1,1,1)	(3,3,3,2)	(3,3,3,2)	*(11)*, *(10,1)*, *(9,2)* *(8,3)*	*(11)*, *(10,1)*, *(9,1, 1)*, (8,1,1,1)	*(11)*, *(10,1)*, *(9,2)* *(8,3)*
12	(3,1,1,1,1,1,1,1,1,1)	(3,3,3,3)	(3,3,3,3)	*(12)*, *(11,1)*, *(10,2)*, *(9,3)*, *(8,3,1)*	*(12)*, *(11,1)*, (10,1,1), (9,1,1,1)	*(12)*, *(11,1)*, *(10,2)*, *(9,3)*, *(8,3,1)*

Note: *Notation as in the text. In the OMSCG, OMMCG, EMMCΔG and EMMCΓG, CPNE are displayed. Equilibria which are a PO are displayed italic. They are SNE in the first four games.

Proof: Follows immediately from Propositions 8 and 9 (**Q.E.D.**).

Proposition 17 suggests that the predictions of the models based on internal&external stability have been too pessimistic. If coalition formation is not restricted to one non-trivial coalition, several coalitions will emerge in equilibrium, which imply lower global emission and higher global welfare than if countries can only form one coalition. How robust is this conclusion? First, the comparison between coalition structures in the two games can be established on the basis of the criterion of coarsening for which general conclusions have been derived in Proposition 16. Second, also in the two exclusive membership games multiple coalitions emerge in equilibrium that are also superior in terms of global emissions and welfare compared to those in the OMSCG.[19] Third, Bauer (1992) showed for asymmetric payoff functions that multiple coalitions emerge if internal&external stability is not restricted to single coalitions. Though she does not compare single versus multiple coalition structures, a straightforward computation would show that multiple coalitions are superior to a single coalition for her example.

Considering that all IEAs constitute single agreements, two controversial conjectures come to mind. First, if existing IEAs are the result of an unrestricted coalition formation process, then the predictions of our model are wrong. However, as argued above, it seems that this result is very robust, though it has been derived from stylized models. Second, if coalition formation has been restricted for institutional and/or political reasons in the past, this suggests altering the rules in the future. For instance, under the Kyoto Protocol the US insisted that they would only ratify the treaty if developing countries also would accede to this agreement. Thus, it may be the case that more could have been achieved if separate agreements were designed for industrialized countries, developing countries and countries in transition. This last remark points at the possibility to reconcile both conjectures. Taking a broader perspective, some modern IEAs, as for instance the Montreal Protocol, may be interpreted as separate agreements under the umbrella of one treaty since they impose differentiated abatement obligations on participants.

4.3 Open versus Exclusive Membership

In order to study the effect of the membership rule on equilibrium coalition structures, we compare CPNE in the open membership multiple coalition game (OMMCG) and the exclusive membership multiple coalition Δ-game (EMMCΔG). This selection is motivated as follows:

1. In both games the remaining countries do not revise their membership if a country or a group of countries deviates.
2. For sufficiently large N no strong Nash equilibrium exists in both games (see Propositions 9 and 10).

Proposition 18: Open versus Exclusive Membership in Multiple Coalition Games

Any CPNE in the EMMCΓG is more weakly concentrated than the unique CPNE in the OMMCΔG under conditions C_1 to C_4.

Proof: Follows directly from Propositions 9 and 10 (**Q.E.D.**).

Proposition 18 suggests that an exclusive membership rule leads to equilibrium coalitions implying lower global emissions (payoff function (6.2) to (6.5)) and higher global welfare (payoff function (6.2)) than the open membership rule. Considering that the protocols of all major past IEAs allow for unrestricted accessions of new members, this suggests that it might be worthwhile to consider changing this rule in the future. Such a change might be interpreted as implying that the public good agreement IEA turns into a club good agreement with respect to the membership. Under exclusivity, only if all countries agree that outsiders join their club, accession is possible. This interpretation also highlights another dimension. Whereas in the context of other economic problems it is usually a disadvantage if participants have to agree by unanimity rule, this may turn out to be conducive to the overall success of coalition formation in a positive externality game.

How robust is this result? First, this conclusion can be confirmed when comparing equilibrium coalition structures in the OMMCG with those in the EMMCΓG, though we do not provide a formal proof here (see Finus and Rundshagen, 2002a). Second, under very general conditions (general payoff functions allowing for asymmetric payoffs) it can be shown that any NE, CPNE and SNE in the OMMCG is also an equilibrium in the EMMCΔG, but there may be additional equilibria in the EMMCΔG (Finus and Rundshagen, 2002a; see also Proposition 19 below). Of course, in the general case, those additional equilibria may not always be superior to those in the OMMCG. Thus, if we assume that countries always agree on efficient coalition structures among the set of equilibria, then the above conclusion holds. However, if we doubt this, then the conclusion has to be qualified. Nevertheless, we may conclude that open membership should not always be taken for granted when designing an IEA and that in many cases exclusive membership may lead to better outcomes.

4.4 Severity of Punishment

Different from repeated game models, there is no explicit threat strategy of punishment in reduced stage game models in case of deviations. Nevertheless, there is an implicit punishment in some coalition games. In order to analyse the effect of this implicit punishment we compare equilibrium coalition structures under the exclusive membership multiple coalition Δ- and Γ-game (EMMCΔG and EMMCΓG) and α-β-stable coalition structures ($C(\alpha, \beta)$ in the multiple coalition game (MCG). For a comparison it is helpful to recall two facts: i) α-β-stability is similar to an SNE, and ii) in the EMMCΔG an SNE may fail to exist for large N (see Proposition 10).

Proposition 19: Equilibrium Coalition Structures in the Exclusive Membership Multiple Δ- and Γ-Game and α-β-stable Coalition Structures in the Multiple Coalition Game

(a) *Let the set of SNE in the EMMCΔG and EMMCΓG and the set of α-β-stable coalition structures in the MCG be denoted by $C^{SNE}(\Delta)$, $C^{SNE}(\Gamma)$ and $C(\alpha, \beta)$ respectively, then $C^{SNE}(\Delta) \subset C^{SNE}(\Gamma) \subset C(\alpha, \beta)$ under condition C_{2a}.*

(b) *Let the set of CPNE in the EMMCΓG be denoted by $C^{CPNE}(\Gamma)$, then $C^{SNE}(\Gamma) = C^{CPNE}(\Gamma) = C(\alpha, \beta)$ for payoff functions implying orthogonal reaction functions and under condition C_1.*

(c) *Let the set of NE in the EMMCΔG and EMMCΓG be denoted by $C^{NE}(\Delta)$ and $C^{NE}(\Gamma)$, then $C^{NE}(\Delta) \subset C^{NE}(\Gamma)$ under condition C_{2a}.*

(d) *Suppose the most concentrated CPNE in the EMMCΔG is Pareto-dominated by the grand coalition, then there is no α-β-stable coalition structure in the MCG and no CPNE in the EMMCΓG, which is less concentrated than the most concentrated CPNE in the EMMCΔG under conditions C_1 to C_3.*

Proof:

(a) Let $c^{\Delta}(c^s, c^*)$, $c^{\Gamma}(c^s, c^*)$ and $c^{\alpha,\beta}(c^s, c^*)$ be the resulting coalition structure if a country or group of countries s deviates from c^* and forms c^s. Then from Definitions 10, 11, and 12 $c^{\Delta}(c^s, c^*) \geq c^{\Gamma}(c^s, c^*) \geq c^{\alpha,\beta}(c^s, c^*)$ where '$\geq$' implies 'at least as coarse as'. Consequently, $\pi_i(c_i, c^{\Delta}) \geq \pi_i(c_i, c^{\Gamma}) \geq \pi_i(c_i, c^{\alpha,\beta})$ by C_{2a}. Thus if a deviation is not profitable in the EMMCΔG, it will also not be profitable in the EMMCΓG and MCG. If a deviation is not profitable in the EMMCΓG it will also not be profitable in the MCG.

(b) Follows immediately from Propositions 11 and 14.
(c) Follows from Propositions 10 and 11.
(d) Denote the most concentrated stand-alone stable CPNE in the EMMCΔG by c^*. If c^* is Pareto-dominated by the grand coalition, then any other coalition structure that is less concentrated than c^* will also be Pareto-dominated by the grand coalition by C_1 and C_{2b}. (The smallest coalition in c^* receives the highest payoff by C_1 and will lose in any other coalition structure which is less concentrated than c^* by C_{2b}.). Because the grand coalition is α-β-stable in the MCG and a CPNE in the EMMCΓG by C_1 and C_{2a} (see Propositions 11 and 14), and since a $C(\alpha, \beta)$ (CPNE) cannot be Pareto-dominated by another $C(\alpha, \beta)$ (CPNE), any $C(\alpha, \beta)$ in the MCG and any CPNE in the EMMCΓG cannot be less concentrated than c^* (**Q.E.D.**).

Parts a) and c) of Proposition 19 highlight the fact that the harsher the (implicit) punishment by the remaining countries in case a country or a group of countries deviates, the easier it is to sustain a coalition structure as an equilibrium. Whereas the remaining countries stick to their membership decision in the EMMCΔG, the remaining countries of those coalitions to which the deviators belonged will break up into singletons after a deviation in the EMMCΓG. In a $C(\alpha, \beta)$ in the MCG the threat of punishment is even harsher: any deviation triggers the break-up of all remaining countries into singletons irrespective to which coalition they belong. Part d) stresses that harsher punishments will usually result in more concentrated coalition structures, which is evident from Table 6.2. Part b) qualifies the previous statements in the case of orthogonal reaction functions. In this case the different degrees of punishment do not lead to different equilibria in the EMMCΓG (CPNE and SNE) and MCG ($C(\alpha, \beta)$).[20]

From an applied point of view one may argue that the implicit punishment implied by α-β-stability is very harsh and unrealistic. This is also true for the exclusive membership multiple Γ-game, though the assumption that the coalition of the deviators break apart may be defended as a strong form of an exclusive membership rule: only if states find exactly their ideas of an IEA reflected in the draft of a protocol will they be prepared to sign it. In contrast, the assumption in the exclusive membership multiple Δ-game that countries do not react after deviations may seem a very optimistic prediction of potential deviators. However, one may also argue that this assumption captures quite well the limited punishment options in reality. From a theoretical point, one may criticize all three assumptions since in neither game the reactions by players not involved in a deviation are defined in the sense of a best-reply. An obvious remedy and extension could therefore be the application of some notion of farsighted equilibrium instead of NE,

SNE and CPNE as analysed in Chapters 4 and 5 of this book. However, it seems that this research strategy can only work in the case of open membership and exclusive membership of the Δ-type. In the case of the exclusive membership of the Γ-type, the break-up of the coalition after a deviation follows from the rule of the game and therefore the application of a farsighted equilibrium seems less straightforward.

4.5 Comparison of the State of the Art

In this section we compare the two state of the art concepts internal&external and core-stability for the analysis of IEAs within the partition function approach, using the 'modern' description of these concepts as developed in sections 3.2, 3.3 and 3.6. In order to draw robust conclusions we compare equilibrium coalition structures for the assumption of single and multiple coalitions. Since in open membership games usually no SNE exist, we have to compare CPNE in these games with α-β-stable coalition structures, despite the fact that α-β-stability resembles more an SNE than a CPNE.

Proposition 20: Coalition-proof Nash Equilibrium Coalition Structures in Open Membership Games and α-β-stable Coalition Structures in Coalition Games

(a) *Any C(α, β) in the SCG is weakly coarser than the unique CPNE in the OMSCG under conditions C_1 and C_{2a}.*
(b) *Suppose the unique CPNE in OMMCG is Pareto-dominated by the grand coalition, then there is no C(α, β) in the MCG, which is less concentrated than the CPNE in the OMMCG under conditions C_1 to C_4.*

Proof:

(a) Follows from Propositions 8 and 15.
(b) Follows from Propositions 18 and 19d (**Q.E.D.**).

On the one hand, α-β-stability poses no restrictions on deviations and therefore a coalition structure is subject to more challenges than a CPNE in the open membership games. On the other hand, any deviation in an α-β-stable coalition structure is accompanied by a substantially harsher punishment than a CPNE in the open membership games. Obviously the latter effect dominates the former effect: α-β-stable coalition structures are more concentrated than CPNE in the open membership games regardless of whether it is assumed that only a single coalition or also multiple coalitions can form. Thus, the crucial assumption responsible for the different results obtained in the literature on IEAs is that core-stability implies a substantially harsher punishment in case of deviations compared to internal&external stability.

4.6 Evaluation of the Results

The previous results demonstrated that the success of forming coalitions to combat global pollution very much depends on the rules of the coalition game and the equilibrium concept applied to determine equilibrium coalitions. However, irrespective of differences, the results indicate that we should expect some cooperation in global pollution control. In the OMSCG, OMMCG and the EMMCΔG, coalitions will be rather small and usually the grand coalition is not stable (as long as N is sufficiently large). The grand coalition is among the CPNE and SNE in the EMMCΓG and the $C(\alpha, \beta)$ in the single and multiple coalition game, though also other (suboptimal) coalition structures are among equilibria. This may be seen as an encouraging result and is summarized in the following proposition.

Proposition 21: Global Emissions and Welfare of Equilibrium Coalition Structures
Any non-trivial equilibrium coalition structure (if one exists) in the coalition games of section 3 implies lower global emissions and Pareto-dominates the singleton coalition structure under condition C_{2a}.

Proof: In the two open membership games and the EMMCΔG an equilibrium coalition structure must be stand-alone stable. Thus, $\forall i: \pi_i(c_i, c) \geq \pi_i(1, c') \geq \pi_i(1, c'')$ holds where $c' = c \backslash c_i \cup \{i\} \cup (c_i \backslash \{i\})$ and $c'' = c \backslash c_i \cup \{1, \ldots, 1\}$ and where the first inequality follows from stand-alone stability and the second from C_{2a}. For any country j that is a member of a coalition $c_j \neq c_i$, $\pi_j(c_j, c) > \pi_i(1, c'')$ holds by C_{2a}. Any equilibrium in the EMMCΓG and any $C(\alpha, \beta)$ in the SCG and MCG must also satisfy $\forall i: \pi_i(c_i, c) \geq \pi_i(1, c') \geq \pi_i(1, c'')$ with the same notation as above and where the first inequality sign follows from the equilibrium condition and the second from C_{2a}. Accordingly, any country j that is not a member of coalition c_i must be strictly better off than in the singleton coalition structure by C_{2a}. The statement with respect to global emissions follows from Corollary 1. (**Q.E.D.**).

However, we have to be aware that in the case of the EMMCΓG and the α-β-stable coalition structures in the SCG and MCG, this optimism hinges on a harsh punishment in the case of a deviation. Moreover, we have to recall that reduced stage games do not capture the second type of free-riding, namely joining an agreement but violating its obligations. This is evident by considering the following result:

Proposition 22: Equilibrium Coalition Structure in the Two-Country Case
For $N=2$ the grand coalition is the unique CPNE, SNE and $C(\alpha, \beta)$ in the coalition formation games analysed in section 3.

Proof: Follows from $\pi_i(2, (2)) \geq \pi_i(1, (1, 1))$ by Proposition 6. Therefore (2) is stand-alone stable and the most concentrated coalition structure. **(Q.E.D.)**.

That is, in the two-country case the coalition game is *de facto* a prisoners' dilemma game, but in all coalition games full cooperation is the unique equilibrium outcome since the first type of free-riding vanishes. In contrast, in a repeated game full cooperation would only be an equilibrium outcome if the second type of free-rider incentive can be neutralized by appropriate threats of punishment in case of a deviation and if countries discount time sufficiently low.

5. CONCLUDING REMARKS

At a most general level our results may be summarized as follows:

1. The possibility of forming multiple coalitions increases the overall success of combating global emissions.
2. An exclusive membership leads to a more concentrated coalition structure than an open membership rule that may be conducive to the overall success of IEAs.
3. The more stability of coalitions increases and the more concentrated coalition structures can be supported, the harsher the implicit punishment if members leave their agreement.
4. The definition of Pareto-optimal coalition structures is a convenient tool to analyse equilibrium coalition structures.
5. The partition function approach allows for a more complete characterization of core-stable coalition structures. Moreover, this approach allows for a better comparison of non-cooperative and cooperative game theoretical concepts when studying coalition formation.

For future research we would like to suggest four directions. First, it would be interesting to endogenize the choice of rules in order to explain why particular rules have emerged in the past (Carraro et al., 2001). Second, it would be worthwhile to analyse which role international institutions can play in shaping these rules (Ecchia and Mariotti, 1998). Third, though in the context of symmetric countries the assumption of no transfers and that countries maximize the joint welfare of their coalition seems 'natural', this assumption is less obvious in the context of heterogeneous countries. On the one hand, this implies a search for optimal transfer and abatement allocation schemes that lead to the highest overall success of IEAs. On the other hand, this implies modelling the decision about these issues as an endogenous agreement process between countries (Ray and Vohra, 1999). Fourth, it would be interesting to construct a coalition game where α- and β-stability is a strong Nash equilibrium. This would allow separating the rules of coalition formation and the equilibrium concept as in other coalition games, and therefore more sound policy conclusions could be derived with respect to optimal design of IEAs (Finus and Rundshagen, 2002a).

NOTES

The first author would like to acknowledge support by the Volkswagen-Foundation, Germany, under grant number II 69 982, and by WIMEK (University of Wageningen) under grant number 213800/059748. Both authors have greatly benefited from helpful comments by participants of seminars and lectures at the University of Wageningen, The Netherlands, a seminar at the University Hagen, Germany and a workshop on 'Coalition Theory' at the CORE, Louvain-la-Neuve, Belgium. In particular the authors would like to thank Carlo Carraro, Alfred Endres, Jörn Martiensen, Henry Tulkens, Ekko van Ierland, Pierre van Mouche and Hans Peter Weikart for fruitful discussions. Moreover, research assistance by Frank Brockmeier has been very helpful for the completion of this article. Contact details for both authors: University of Hagen, Institute of Economic Theory, Profilstr. 8, 58084 Hagen, Germany. E-mail: Michael.Finus@fernuni-hagen.de and Bianca.Rundshagen@fernuni-hagen.de.

1. See Finus (2001) and Finus and Rundshagen (2002b) for an overview of the literature.
2. That is, in equilibrium, global welfare generated by the coalition is close to that in the Nash equilibrium and the gap between the coalition equilibrium and the social optimum is large.
3. Examples include Barrett (1994b, 1997a, b), Bauer (1992), Botteon and Carraro (1997, 1998), Carraro and Siniscalco (1991, 1993, 1997), Hoel (1992), Hoel and Schneider (1997), Jeppesen and Andersen (1998) and Petrakis and Xepapadeas (1996).
4. Examples include Chander and Tulkens (1992, 1995, 1997), Eyckmans and Tulkens (1999), Germain, Toint and Tulkens (1996, 1998), Germain, Toint, Tulkens and de Zeeuw (1998) and Kaitala et al. (1995).
5. Ex ante symmetric refers to the assumption that all countries have the same payoff function though they may receive different payoffs depending on whether they become a signatory or remain a non-signatory (or in the general context which coalition they join).
6. A non-trivial coalition means a coalition of at least two countries.
7. In the context of IEAs, sequential move coalition games are treated in Finus (2001), Ch. 15 and Finus and Rundshagen (2001a, b).
8. This assumptions resembles Chander and Tulkens' (1995, 1997) 'partial agreement Nash equilibrium' (PANE) in the context of the γ-core.
9. Thus c_1 denotes a coalition within a coalition structure and c^1 a particular coalition structure.

10. Though the assumption of interior solutions is not necessary for most of the subsequent propositions, it simplifies proofs.
11. See, for instance, Barrett (1994b, 1997a), Bauer (1992), Botteon and Carraro (1997), Carraro and Siniscalco (1991), Finus and Rundshagen (1998), Hoel (1992) and Stähler (1996).
12. Recall that the members of the smallest coalition derive the highest payoff in any given coalition structure due to C_1.
13. We take this assumption, which does not affect the generality of the subsequent results, from Ray and Vohra (1999).
14. Originally, a SNE is defined as an equilibrium where no subcoalition can deviate such that the welfare of each member increases. We use a stronger version here to be consistent with Assumption 3.
15. The previous footnote (with appropriate changes) applies to CPNE as well.
16. We use '$<$' instead of '$\leq$' to be consistent with Assumption 3.
17. The definition has been adjusted to reflect Assumption 3.
18. This condition ensures that there is a partition of N with $c_1 = c_c$ and $c_i \in \{c_C, c_1\}$ $\forall$ $i \in \{2, ..., N\}$.
19. A general proof seems straightforward.
20. In the case of non-orthogonal reaction functions it is easily confirmed that a coalition structure may be α- and β-stable in the MCG but not an SNE in the EMMCΓG. For instance, consider payoff function (6.4) and assume $N=5$ and $b=5d$. Then, $c=(3, 2)$ is a PO and α- and β-stable in the MCG but not an SNE in the EMMCΓG.

REFERENCES

Aumann, R. (1959), 'Acceptable points in general cooperative n-person games', in A.N. Tucker and R.D. Luce (eds), *Contributions to the Theory of Games*, IV, (Annals of Mathematics Studies 40), Princeton: Princeton University Press, pp. 287–324.

Barrett, S. (1991), 'The paradox of international environmental agreements', *mimeo*, London: London Business School.

Barrett, S. (1994a), 'The biodiversity supergame', *Environmental and Resource Economics*, **4**, 111–22.

Barrett, S. (1994b), 'Self-enforcing international environmental agreements', *Oxford Economic Papers*, **46**, 804–78.

Barrett, S. (1997a), 'Toward a theory of international environmental cooperation', in: C. Carraro and D. Siniscalco (eds), *New Directions in the Economic Theory of the Environment*. Cambridge: Cambridge University Press. Ch. 8, pp. 239–80.

Barrett, S. (1997b), 'Heterogeneous international agreements', in C. Carraro (ed.), *International Environmental Negotiations: Strategic Policy Issues*. Cheltenham: Edward Elgar, pp. 9–25.

Barrett, S. (2000), 'Consensus treaties'. Preliminary Draft, Washington, DC: John Hopkins University.

Bauer, A. (1992), 'International cooperation over greenhouse gas abatement', *mimeo*, Seminar für empirische Wirtschaftsforschung, Munich: University of Munich.

Bernheim, D., B. Peleg and M.D. Whinston (1987), 'Coalition-proof Nash equilibria. I. concepts', *Journal of Economic Theory*, **42**, 1–12.

Black, J., M.D. Levi and D. de Meza (1992), 'Creating a good atmosphere: minimum participation for tackling the "greenhouse effect"', *Economica*, **60**, 281–93.

Bloch, F. (1997), 'Non-cooperative models of coalition formation in games with spillovers', In C. Carraro and D. Siniscalco (eds), *New Directions in the Economic Theory of the Environment*, Cambridge: Cambridge University Press. Ch. 10, pp. 311–52.

Botteon, M. and C. Carraro (1997), 'Burden-sharing and coalition stability in environmental negotiations with asymmetric countries', in: C. Carraro (ed.), *International Environmental Negotiations: Strategic Policy Issues*, Cheltenham: Edward Elgar. Ch. 3, pp. 26–55.

Botteon, M. and C. Carraro (1998), 'Strategies for environmental negotiations: issue linkage with heterogenous countries', in N. Hanley and H. Folmer (eds), *Game Theory and the Global Environment*, Cheltenham: Edward Elgar. Ch. 9, pp. 180–200.

Carraro, C., C. Marchiori and S. Oreffice (2001) 'Endogenous minimum participation in international environmental treaties', *mimeo*, Milan: Fondazione Eni Enrico Mattei.

Carraro C. and F. Moriconi (1998), 'International games on climate change control', Milan: Fondazione Eni Enrico Mattei Working Paper 56.98.

Carraro, C. and D. Siniscalco (1991), 'Strategies for the international protection of the environment', Working Paper, March 1991, Milan: Fondazione Eni Enrico Mattei.

Carraro, C. and D. Siniscalco (1993), 'Strategies for the international protection of the environment,' *Journal of Public Economics*, **52**, 309–28.

Carraro, C. and D. Siniscalco (1997), 'R&D cooperation and the stability of international environmental agreements', in C. Carraro (ed.), *International Environmental Negotiations: Strategic Policy Issues*, Cheltenham: Edward Elgar, pp. 71–96.

Chander, P. and H. Tulkens (1992), 'Theoretical foundations of negotiations and cost sharing in transfrontier pollution problems', *European Economic Review*, **36**, 388–98.

Chander, P. and H. Tulkens (1995), 'A core-theoretic solution for the design of cooperative agreements on transfrontier pollution', *International Tax and Public Finance*, **2**, 279–93.

Chander, P. and H. Tulkens (1997), 'The core of an economy with multilateral environmental externalities', *International Journal of Game Theory*, **26**, 379–401.

d'Aspermont, C., A. Jacquemin, J.J. Gabszeweiz and J.A. Weymark (1983), 'On the stability of collusive price leadership', *Canadian Journal of Economics*, **16**, 17–25.

Ecchia, G. and M. Mariotti (1998), 'Coalition formation in international environmental agreements and the role of institutions', *European Economic Review*, **42**, 573–82.

Endres, A. (1997), 'Negotiating a climate convention – the role of prices and quantities', *International Review of Law and Economics*, **17**, 201–24.

Eyckmans, J. and H. Tulkens (1999), 'Simulating with RICE coalitionally stable burden sharing agreements for the climate change problem', CES ifo Working Papers Series, No. 228, Munich.

Finus, M. (2001), *Game theory and international environmental cooperation*. Cheltenham: Edward Elgar.

Finus, M. (2002), 'Game Theory and International Environmental Cooperation: any practical application?' in C. Böhringer, M. Finus and C. Vogt (eds), *Controlling Global Warming: Perspectives from Economics, Game Theory and Public Choice*, Cheltenham: Edward Elgar. Ch. 2.

Finus, M. and B. Rundshagen (1998), 'Toward a positive theory of coalition formation and endogenous instrumental choice in global pollution control', *Public Choice*, **96**, 145–86.
Finus, M. and B. Rundshagen (2001a), 'Endogenous coalition formation in global pollution control', Milan: Fondazione Eni Enrico Mattei, Working Paper No. 43.2001.
Finus, M. and B. Rundshagen (2001b), 'Sequential move unanimity equilibria in a public good model', Working Paper No. 308, Hagen: University of Hagen.
Finus, M. and B. Rundshagen (2002a), 'How the rules of coalition formation affect the outcome in positive externality games', preliminary draft, Hagen: University of Hagen.
Finus, M. and B. Rundshagen (2002b), 'The formation of coalitions in international pollution control', Working Paper No. 320, Hagen: University of Hagen.
Finus, M. and S. Tjøtta (2002), 'The Oslo Protocol on Sulfur Reduction: the great leap forward?', *Journal of Public Economics*, forthcoming.
Folmer, H., and P. van Mouche (2000), 'The acid rain game. A mathematically rigorous analysis', in P. Dasgupta, B. Kristroem and K.-G. Loefgren (eds), *Festschrift in Honor of Karl Göran Mäler*, Cheltenham, UK and Brookfield, US: Edward Elgar.
Friedman, J.W. (1986), *Game Theory with Applications to Economics*. Oxford: Oxford University Press.
Germain, M., P.L. Toint and H. Tulkens (1996), 'Calcul économique itératif et stratégique pour les négociations internationales sur les pluies acides entre la Finlande, la Russie et l'Estonie', *Annales d'Economie et Statistique*, **43**, 101–27.
Germain, M., P.L. Toint and H. Tulkens (1998), 'Financial transfers to sustain cooperative international optimality in stock pollutant abatement', in S. Faucheux, J. Gowdy and I. Nicolai (eds), *Sustainability and Firms: Technological Change and the Changing Regulatory Environment*, Cheltenham: Edward Elgar. Ch. 11, pp. 205–19.
Germain, M., P.L. Toint, H. Tulkens and A. de Zeeuw (1998), 'Transfers to sustain core-theoretic cooperation in international stock pollutant control', CORE Discussion Paper No. 9832, Center for Operations Research and Econometrics, Louvain: Université Catholique de Louvain.
Hart, S. and M. Kurz (1983), 'Endogenous formation of coalitions', *Econometrica*, **51**, 1047–64.
Hoel, M. (1992), 'International environment conventions: the case of uniform reductions of emissions', *Environmental and Resource Economics*, **2**, 141–59.
Hoel, M. and K. Schneider (1997), 'Incentives to participate in an international environmental agreement', *Environmental and Resource Economics*, **9**, 153–70.
Jeppesen, T. and P. Andersen (1998), 'Commitment and fairness in environmental games', in N. Hanley and H. Folmer (eds), *Game Theory and the Environment*, Cheltenham: Edward Elgar. Ch. 4, pp. 65–83.
Kaitala, V., K.-G. Mäler and H. Tulkens (1995), 'The acid rain game as a resource allocation process with an application to the international cooperation among Finland, Russia and Estonia', *Scandinavian Journal of Economics*, **97**, 325–43.
Kaneko, M. (1977), 'The ratio equilibrium and a voting game in a public goods economy', *Journal of Economic Theory*, **16**, 123–36.
Kurz, M. (1988), 'Coalition value', in Roth, A. (ed.), *The Shapley Value: Essays in Honor of Lloyd Shapley*. Cambridge: Cambridge University Press, pp. 155–73.

Mäler, K.-G. (1994), 'Acid rain in Europe: a dynamic perspective on the use of economic incentives', in E.C. van Ierland (ed.), *International Environmental Economics. Developments in Environmental Economics 4*. Amsterdam: Elsevier pp. 351–72.
Nash, J. (1950), 'Equilibrium points in n-person games', *Proceedings of the National Academy of Sciences*, **36**, 48–9.
Petrakis, E. and A. Xepapadeas (1996), 'Environmental consciousness and moral hazard in international agreements to protect the environment', *Journal of Public Economics*, **60**, 95–110.
Ray, D. and R. Vohra (1999), 'A theory of endogenous coalition structures', *Games and Economic Behavior*, **26**, 286–336.
Stähler, F. (1996), 'Reflections on multilateral environmental agreements', in A. Xepapadeas (ed.), *Economic Policy for the Environment and Natural Resources: Techniques for the Management and Control of Pollution*, Cheltenham UK and Brookfield USA: Edward Elgar. Ch. 8, pp. 174–96.
Tulkens, H. (1979), 'An economic model of international negotiations relating to transfrontier pollution', in K. Krippendorff (ed.), *Communication and Control in Society*, New York: Gordon and Breach, pp. 199–212.
von Neumann, J. and O. Morgenstern (1944), *The Theory of Games and Economic Behavior*, New York: Wiley.
Yi, S.-S. (1997), 'Stable coalition structures with externalities', *Games and Economic Behavior*, **20**, 201–37.
Yi, S.-S. and H. Shin (1995), 'Endogenous formation of coalitions in oligopoly', *mimeo*, Department of Economics, Dartmouth College.
Yi, S.-S. and H. Shin (2000), 'Endogenous formation of research coalitions with spillovers', *International Journal of Industrial Organization*, **18**, 229–56.

APPENDIX

Proof of Condition C_4 in Proposition 5

Payoff function (6.2):

1. Equilibrium emissions of a member of coalition c_k are given by:

$$e_k(c_k) = \frac{ba - c_k \cdot d}{b}. \tag{6A.1}$$

2. Equilibrium emissions of countries which are not involved in the concentration remain the same due to orthogonal reaction functions.
3. Computing payoffs of country k which left coalition i before and after the accession to coalition j delivers:

$$\pi_k(c_i, c) - \pi_k(c_j + 1, c') = \frac{c^2(c_i + c_j - 3)(c_j - c_i + 1)}{2b} > 0 \text{ if } 2 \leq c_i \leq c_j. \tag{6A.2}$$

Payoff function (6.3) and (6.5):

From the proof of Proposition 4 it is known that global emissions remain constant through concentration (which is not a coarsening), that is, $e^{T_1} = e^{T_2}$ where e^{T_1} denotes global emissions before and e^{T_2} after the concentration. Consequently, emissions of countries which belong to coalitions not involved in a concentration do not change through concentration. From the first order condition of coalition members belonging to coalition c_i of which a member leaves to join coalition c_j, it is evident that those members expand emissions after the concentration ($\beta'(e_i) = c_i\phi'(e^{T_1}) \Rightarrow \beta'(e_i) = (c_i - 1)\phi'(e^{T_1})$). Accordingly, the payoff of country k belonging to coalition c_i and joining coalition c_j ($2 \leq c_i \leq c_j$) decreases through concentration since benefits decrease due to lower emissions and damages remain constant.

Payoff Function (6.4):

If a member of a coalition c_i k joins a coalition c_j equilibrium emissions are given by:

$$e^{T(1)} = \frac{Nd}{1 + {}^{d}/_{b}\,(c_i^2 + c_j^2 + CR)},\; e_k^{(1)}(c_i) = \frac{a(b + (c_i^2 + c_j^2 + CR)\cdot d - c_i dN)}{b + (c_i^2 + c_j^2 + CR)\cdot d}, \tag{6A.3}$$

and

$$e^{T(2)} = \frac{Nd}{1 + {}^{d}/_{b}\left((c_i - 1)^2 + (c_j + 1)^2 + CR\right)},$$

$$e_k^{(2)}(c_j + 1) = \frac{a(b + ((c_i - 1)^2 + (c_j + 1)^2 + CR)\cdot d - d(c_j + 1)N)}{b + ((c_i - 1)^2 + (c_j + 1)^2 + CR)\cdot d}, \tag{6A.4}$$

where the superscript 1 indicates the initial situation and 2 the situation when a member of coalition c_i joins coalition c_j, T stands for total emissions, and $CR = \Sigma_{k \neq i,j} c_k^2$. Inserting those emissions in payoff function (6.4) and computing $\pi_k^{(1)} - \pi_k^{(2)}$ delivers a rather big term which, however, can be shown to be negative using $2 \leq c_i \leq c_j$ (**Q.E.D.**).

Proof of Proposition 16d

A concentration may involve either: a) a merger of coalition c_i and c_j, or b) a country k of coalition c_i leaves coalition $c_i > 1$ and joins coalition c_j, $c_i \leq c_j$. Any concentration follows from a sequence of these actions. Since non-active players receive at least the same payoff from concentration by C_{2b}, it suffices to look at the effect on the 'active' players if this is unambiguously positive.

In case a) we find for payoff function (6.2):

$$c_i \cdot (\pi_i(c_i + c_j, c') - \pi_i(c_i, c)) + c_j \cdot (\pi_j(c_i + c_j, c') - \pi_j(c_j, c)) = \frac{c_i c_j d^2 (c_i + c_j)}{2b} > 0, \tag{6A.5}$$

and in case b):

$$\pi_k(c_j + 1, c') - \pi_k(c_i, c) + c_j \cdot (\pi_j(c_j + 1, c') - \pi_j(c_j, c)) + (c_i - 1) \cdot (\pi_i(c_i - 1, c') - \pi_i(c_i, c) = \frac{d^2(c_i + c_j)(c_j - c_i + 1)}{2b} > 0, \tag{6A.6}$$

which obviously can be signed unambiguously (**Q.E.D.**).

Index